Directions
by Indirections

Directions
by Indirections

John Barton of the Royal Shakespeare Company

Michael L. Greenwald

Newark
University of Delaware Press
London and Toronto: Associated University Presses

Associated University Presses
440 Forsgate Drive
Cranbury, NJ 08512

Associated University Presses
25 Sicilian Avenue
London WC1A 2QH, England

Associated University Presses
2133 Royal Windsor Drive
Unit 1
Mississauga, Ontario
Canada L5J 1K5

The paper used in this publication meets the minimum requirements of the American National Standard for Permanence of Paper for Printed Library Materials Z39.48-1984.

Library of Congress Cataloging in Publication Data

Greenwald, Michael L., 1945–
    Directions by indirections.

    Bibliography: p.
    Includes index.
    1. Barton, John, 1928–   —Biography.
    2. Theatrical producers and directors—English—
    Biography.   3. Dramatists, English—20th century—
    Biography.   4. Royal Shakespeare Company.
    5. Shakespeare, William, 1564–1616—Stage history—
    1950–   .   6. Shakespeare, William, 1564–1616—
    Stage history—England.   I. Title.
    PN2598.B434G74   1985   792'.0233'0924 [B]   83-40605
    ISBN 0-87413-264-9 (alk. paper)

Printed in the United States of America

Contents

Appendixes

Foreword

There is a book to be written one day, about why it is that so many Cambridge graduates are currently so successful in the theater. Oxbridge has traditionally supplied the British establishment with its leaders but the theater people I am thinking of all studied at Cambridge (where there is still no drama faculty) within a very short period during the 1950s. This period produced leading actors aplenty, a few playwrights, and, perhaps most pertinently, some national newspaper drama critics who share their rave reviews. But the most important names to note, amongst a long list of ex-Cambridge directors, are Peter Hall and Trevor Nunn, the director-managers of the National Theatre of Great Britain and of the Royal Shakespeare Company.

Chance had these two men born within ten years of each other in the same county of East Anglia. Intelligence and diligence (their distinguishing marks to this day) won them both scholarships to their local ancient university. There, at Cambridge, chance was personified in John Barton, a direct contemporary with Peter Hall. They acted and directed together at the Amateur Dramatic Club and then, in concert, nursed the fledgling RSC at Stratford. "Oh yes," the caretaker of the ADC told me when he heard of the partnership raising a Shakespearean storm, "Mr. Barton always used to help young Mr. Hall when he got into difficulties!" Not perhaps the most reliable witness, but you never know! Trevor Nunn, too young to have met either of them at Cambridge, was recruited to Stratford. When Hall left, Barton remained to serve the succeeding Nunn regime. That future book about the Cambridge Influence must have its central chapter on John Barton: *Directions by Indirections* could be excellent source-material.

For actors like me, who knew him as an amateur director at Cambridge and as a professional at Stratford, John Barton is a master of many sorts. First I recall him as a task-master, when he chastised frisky undergrads to take our acting seriously; to be, for example, on time for his long, action-packed rehearsals; to watch each other's work critically; to learn how to improve even as we were enjoying ourselves—to behave, he used to say, like professionals do. This is all at odds with the false reputation of Barton the Academic. Of course, even twenty-five years ago, he had an unrivaled grasp of the history of stage production and, with his knack of chewing razor blades even as he chain-smoked his

cheroots, he was the image of eccentricity. The hair and beard were unkempt—
as they still are—the long green cardigan flopping almost to his knees, but there
was nothing academically dry or impractical about his help, particularly to this
tyro actor.

I was rehearsing as the ancient Justice Shallow in his 1959 version of both
parts of Shakespeare's *Henry 4th*, (perhaps a tryout for his triumphant *Wars of
the Roses* at the RSC). I was to lead my old friend Falstaff, visiting my estate in
rural Gloucestershire, onto the stage with: "Nay you shall see my orchard,
where, in an arbour, we will eat a last year's pippin of my own grafting. . . ." A
simple line, but note the nouns "orchard," "arbour," "pippin," instructed
Barton: "fill them with the love you feel for them, make them warm as the
afternoon's summer sunshine. They are actual places and objects but they
won't exist in the audience's imagination until you invest them with the old
man's personality." He encouraged my voice to extend deep into my boots and
then flute upwards—an octogenarian whose control wavered. I listened to his
own fruity speaking of the line (he had played a famous undergraduate Shallow), his mouth brimming with saliva, his thin lips chewing the words and as
the long face aged, so the shoulders hunched in sympathy and even his hands
fluttered frailly. Again and again he made me do that entrance, as I tried to
imitate him. He would not give in until I began to learn. My first taste of
Barton the master, with me his grateful pupil.

Next we did *Three Sisters*. The first three acts were indoors, played within
tapestried screens. The last, in the open air, was a bare stage scattered with
autumnal leaves. Barton was so alive to the varied moods, so perceptive to the
unspoken thoughts of the characters' lives, that his production remains for me
an examplar for what Chekhov can be—hilarious, sentimental, and tragic by
turns. Despite his lifetime with the Elizabethans, it is with Chekhov that
Barton is most intimately at home. His private view of life is wry: he smiles a
lot and thinks a lot. He looks lonely. He is apolitical: he never judges others.
Time and again he invokes a Chekhovian feel in his Shakespeare, counterpois-
ing the rhetoric with a gentler poetry of everyday realism. But it is never
imposed as an alien personal statement—it grows from his masterly appreciation of Shakespeare's range of style and interest.

He has been accused, because of his frequent rewriting of the classics, of
wanting to distort the playwright's intention by substituting one of his own
devising. But on the whole, he has restricted his adaptations to those parts of
old plays that are unworkable for modern audiences. How to express the ebb
and flow of ancient myth in *The Greeks*. How to avoid misplaced laughs in
Ibsen's crude plotting in *Pillars of the Community*. How to paint the majestic
sweep of *The Wars of the Roses*. Barton's eye and ear are always attending to
how a play will look and sound. He wants the audience to appreciate and relish
every aspect of theatricality. He will direct the actor to speak a long speech
quickly and deftly and then is not afraid to cut it down to size. And then, if it

still seems too long, he will play some evocative music under the words. In his search for the essence of a speech or a play he is no academic purist. Rather he is a master of staging. Cambridge University found him but the theater claimed him for its own.

Ian McKellen

Acknowledgments

Though I could not have known it at the time, this book began in the summer of 1973 when my wife, Demetra, and I first visited Stratford. There, quite by chance, we saw Barton's staging of *Richard II,* images of which still come easily to my mind. My next visit to Stratford in July 1976 brought another chance encounter with a Barton production, the wonderfully entertaining and thoughtful *Much Ado About Nothing.*

As I considered a dissertation topic at the University of California, Santa Barbara (where I attended graduate school specifically because it has for a long time hosted the RSC "actors-in-residence" program), I soon realized that there were virtually no major studies of Barton's lengthy career, this despite the fact that Barton had dared to rewrite Shakespeare, that he had staged the classics with all the audacity and frequently with more clarity than Peter Brook, that he had as much to do with the successful evolution of the RSC as Peter Hall and Trevor Nunn. With typical graduate-student arrogance, I resolved to right this wrong.

In one sense this is, I hope, an objective study of Barton's career: as a "foreigner" I was obliged to sift through the many volumes of RSC press clippings, journalistic interviews and feature stories, and other evidence to learn exactly where Barton stands in the eyes of his critics, his defenders, and his colleagues. I have tried to offer a balanced assessment based on the varied, and frequently contradictory, material at my disposal. I must acknowledge my enormous debt to the many British theater critics who have recreated and judged Barton's work. They are indeed the abstract and brief chronicles of our theater. In another sense, however, this is admittedly a subjective work. I admire Barton, both as man and artist, and getting to know him, his work, and his theater practice has been as rewarding as it has been instructive.

This work could not have become reality without the cooperation and support of many people. To them, I—like Sebastian in *Twelfth Night*—"can no other answer make but thanks / And thanks, and ever thanks; and oft good turns / Are shuffled off with such uncurrent pay." These include: John Barton, who patiently endured two interviews and a careful, page-by-page reworking of the original manuscript; the many RSC artists with whom I spoke, particularly Tony Church, whose accounts of the Cambridge years have been invaluable; Ian McKellen for the personable Foreward; Judith Cheston of the RSC Press Office for setting up the interviews; Irving Wardle of the *Times* for sharing his perceptions with me; the Regents of the University of California, whose fellowship funded my research; my mentors at UCSB whose insights and encouragement kept me both honest and enthused: Bert O. States, William R. Reardon, Robert A. Potter, Homer Swander, and in particular Robert Egan, who promoted my work and patiently helped shape the initial drafts with me; the Augustinian Fathers of Saint Augustine's Priory in Hammersmith and Saint Mary's Priory in Birmingham for providing lodging and moral support to this gypsy scholar; Professor David Male of Homerton College, Cambridge University, for his hospitality and memories of Barton's work; the staff at the Shakespeare Centre Library in Stratford for lugging up all those massive scrapbooks for a month; Professor Jay Halio of the University of Delaware, who urged publication of this book and who provided friendship and sage counsel as it moved toward the press; Professor Marvin Rosenberg of UC-Berkeley for his perceptive comments as external evaluator; the anonymous evaluator for Cambridge University Press who, though rejecting the manuscript, yet offered sound advice and corrected a couple of glaring errors; Mrs. Betty Sherman for typing huge sections of the manuscript; and Elizabeth Reynolds, associate editor of the University of Delaware Press, who diligently helped prepare the manuscript for publication. And, of course, a very special thank-you to Demetra, who stood beside me at the back of the stalls in Stratford in 1973, and who has continued to stand beside me since then.

"A Prologue Armed"

> I always wanted to be a writer; I didn't want to be a
> director. . . . I look at my career as a continual—not exactly
> "war"—but as being a director who wants to be a writer. The
> most important fact about me is that I *had* to rework these
> texts that I came upon. They have something to do with some
> mythical depths in me. I don't understand it. I don't know
> why. . . .[1]
>
> John Barton
June 1983

In his over-twenty-year career with the prestigious Royal Shakespeare Company, John Barton has established himself as one of the foremost stage directors
of classical dramas in the twentieth century. Specifically, he is noted for his
"scholarly" approaches to difficult texts, particularly of Shakespeare's later
plays. It is a reputation founded largely on his Cambridge tenure as student and
don. Barton scoffs at the notion that he is a scholar[2] in the traditional sense of
the word—"It is a travesty to call me a scholar, which implies careful, painstak-
ing precision which is not my area at all. . . . I'm a theater beast"—and
emphasizes that he accepted a fellowship at Cambridge for six years solely
because he believed it would give him the security to pursue his primary
"passion": playwriting. As we shall see, the Cambridge experience in some
ways impeded his creative intentions and drove him into the professional theater as a director, textual adapter, acting teacher, and ultimately—but only very
lately—a writer of his own accord:

> I've only seen this in the last two to three years that what drives one to do the
> work [i.e., directing] is a seeking to find something that one's lost, or seeking
> something that one's never found. And there are hints in the different pieces
> of material that one picks up. Sometimes one rewrites the material to pursue
> the search even further. Sometimes one's lucky and there's a piece that haunt-
> ingly brings out resonances and parts of one's own myth, and it's all there
> and you don't have to change a word of it.

For Barton, then, his long and accomplished directorial career has been a continued quest, albeit unknowingly, for an order, a meaning, in a modern world that too frequently lacks order and defies meaning. As he says, "It's because one doesn't see solutions that one directs a play. You have to agree to doing a particular play, open on a given date, agree to define. I direct because that's a context in which I can define order whereas in my internal searchings I am still looking." Not unexpectedly, Launcelot—Malory's Flawed Knight, the Healing Knight of the Quest who "dreams, tries to be moral, and channels his violence"—is the mythical figure that most appeals to Barton.

And Shakespeare, the creator of similar "Flawed Knights" (such as Hamlet, Hal, Coriolanus, and Hector), is the writer who most excites Barton's imagination: "What's so wonderful about Shakespeare is that he has it all there: the poetry, the characters, the story, the myth, and the politics. Those are the five most important things." By working through much of the Shakespearean canon as director and textual adapter, Barton—and the RSC that he has guided to maturity—has given fresh insight into the plays and the means by which they are brought to reality on stage.

Such an accomplishment should satisfy most men. But Barton yet seeks something more personal, something created from within: "I believe that it's only in a work of art that you find order. That's why I am now writing a myth—it's to do with looking for order that you don't see outside. Some people become socially active; some go inside, which is what I suppose I've done."

In recent years the conflation of several events have dissipated the creative writing block that has plagued Barton for almost a quarter century. He now writes daily, creating a personal myth—"an original story fed by the Greek, Arthurian, and Norse myths." Ironically, Barton does not intend his creation for the theater; it is being written strictly as a narrative. Fatefully, notes Barton, three of his most recent theatrical enterprises have led him to his eclectic creation: in 1980, he adapted and staged a ten-hour telling of the Trojan War, *The Greeks* (produced by the RSC at the Aldwych Theatre; see chapter 10); in 1982 he acted the role of Sir Thomas Malory in a British television special conceived and directed by Gillian Lynne (of *Cats* fame; Lynne was inspired by watching Barton read excerpts from Malory—"the greatest prose in the English language"—as they prepared a Shakespearean production). In the spring of 1983 Barton was invited to adapt and stage Ibsen's prentice work, *The Vikings of Helgeland*, at *Den Nationaler Scene* in Bergen, Norway. The play, which Barton calls simply *The Vikings*, is rooted in ancient Norse myth. One of its central characters constantly asks the question, "What is the meaning of all this?"—a question that has driven Barton to undertake his own "myth" and, throughout his directorial career, to explore with particular fervor those plays that deal with "doomed romanticism" and the chaos that follows (e.g., the chronicle plays, *Troilus and Cressida, The Greeks*) and the inevitable healing that must restore order (e.g., *Twelfth Night, The Winter's Tale*). Shakespeare, as well as the medieval playwrights who preceded him and the Elizabethan and Jacobean theater atists who worked with him, has figured as centrally in the evolution of "Barton-the-Mythmaker" as have the Greeks, Malory, and the Norse.

While considering Barton's varied and productive career and the Cambridge beginnings that shaped it, one must remember that his work—whatever salutary effects it has had on the understanding of Shakespeare and his theatrical viability in this century—has been but a means to an end for one who has always insisted that the production of a stage play is "a journey of discovery." His most important discovery to date?

> I suspect that what one's been doing in production, without knowing it, is in some way finding that myth because so many elements from the past go into it. I begin to see a hope, a purpose, a shape, a meaning. But it is to do with the need to write this missing thing. . . . I know I can't do it without doing the practical work. Why does one direct? There's a very simple reason: if you lock yourself into the study, you're stuck with yourself and you dry up.

Notes

1. Interview with John Barton, London, June 17, 1983. All Barton comments in the Prologue are from this interview.

2. The original title of this work was to have been *The Scholar's Eye.* Barton asked that I reconsider the title because, he believed, it put a false emphasis on his career: "It's putting the wrong thing at the center. What's at the center is this dialectic process between the writer and the director." In light of his arguments against the "scholar" label, and particularly in light of his remarks about the evolution of his writing career, I believe the present title is more accurate in its summary of Barton's career.

Directions by Indirections

1
Ambition's Ladder: From Cambridge to Stratford

What does one do when Eton, despite its prestige and tradition, has no school play to accommodate would-be actors? What does one do when one is too ill to play football, yet needs an outlet from the rigors of an English prep school education? If you are John Adie Bernard Barton, you approach the headmaster and outline a plan to bring Shakespeare to the venerable campus in his original medium: live theater. Having gained Eton's permission to turn producer in 1947, the young Barton staged the first part of *Henry IV* while acting the flamboyant role of Hotspur himself. Inspired by his modest success, Barton found that Shakespearean stage production would remain "a passion" with him ever after.[1] The passion would grow into a career, the career into a reputation as one of this century's significant stage directors, textual adapters, and acting teachers. Also, as he has discovered only recently, the passion would lead him towards fulfilling a personal quest towards an understanding of life's complexities, which he is currently trying to set down in a multi-source myth he simply labels "My Story." His evolving story aside, to trace his personal growth from the Cambridge dramatic societies through his over-twenty-year career with the Royal Shakespeare Company is to chart a corresponding growth of postwar British stage practice.

In many ways Barton is the exemplar of the contemporary British director: he is well educated and served his apprenticeship within university dramatic societies before joining the ranks of commercial theater; he couples a scholarly interest in ferreting out solutions to textual problems with a resourceful use of strong theatrical instincts; and he is inclined to make specific, often provocative, interpretive statements that, however controversial, promote new insight into complex works.

Barton's interest in the theater developed later in life than that of his RSC colleague Peter Brook, who mounted a three-and-a-half-hour production of *Hamlet* in a toy theater at age five.[2] Barton had given little thought to the theater until the Eton experience. At Eton he wrote diligently and prolifically, preparing himself for what he surmised would be a career as a writer, by editing the Eton *Chronicle*. Among the youthful priorities of the son of a prominent London accountant, Sir Harold Montague Barton, the theater was then "very, very low down. . . . I suppose I liked the theatre. I'd been to the theatre. I liked Shakespeare. But the urge came when I was 18 or 19."

When Barton entered Cambridge in the fall of 1948, he found two channels to guide his "urge" to be a theater artist, specifically a playwright: a distinguished faculty challenged his mind and provided insights transferable to stage practice; and, more important, the energetic Cambridge dramatic societies became laboratories in which Barton and his colleagues could test the theories of the lecture hall. Soon Barton dominated these societies as "the big whiz kid director . . . the most positive force there."[3] Barton's Cambridge prestige is the more remarkable when one considers that he was vying with individuals who would emerge as some of the leading talents in contemporary British theater: directors Peter Hall, Toby Robertson, Peter Wood, David Jones, and later, Trevor Nunn and Jonathan Miller; actors Tony Church, Ian McKellen, Clive Swift, and Derek Jacobi; designer Timothy O'Brien; composer Leslie Bricusse; and dramaturg Ronald Bryden. These artists, and their Oxford counterparts, would assume the leadership of the English theater in the 1960s.

At midcentury the "Oxbridge" minds that would within a decade revitalize the theater amalgamated the insights of diverse critical and practical theory to devise a production style that in its subsequent maturity would be the foundation of the Royal Shakespeare Company, the National Theatre, the Prospect Theatre Company and others. Ironically, in 1951 Kenneth Muir concluded a fifty-year survey of Shakespearean studies with the suggestion that "perhaps the most useful direction Shakespearean criticism could take during the next generation is towards a synthesis of existing methods. This is a consummation devoutly to be wished, but unlikely to be achieved."[4] Muir's pessimism was premature: even as he wrote, his aspirations were being fulfilled by the "the next generation" of theater practitioners who were then absorbing the critical approaches of Bradley, Spurgeon, Knight, and Wilson; the production theory of Artaud, Stanislavski, Brecht, Meyerhold, Copeau, and Laban; and the philosophical, psychological, and anthropological insights of Nietzsche, Jung, and Frazer. Barton and his contemporaries thus inherited a rich legacy from the theorists who preceded them. Perhaps their ultimate legacy is an intelligent eclecticism that extracts the most fruitful aspects of modern dramatic thought and shapes it into viable practice.

Of the various Cambridge instructors that influenced Barton, the most important was George "Dadie" Rylands, an academic who also enjoyed a lengthy and influential career in the professional theater. While a student at Cambridge himself, Rylands wrote a dissertation on Shakespeare's poetry, focusing on the evocative power of the words and sound, a topic in which Barton has shown pronounced interest. Published as *Words and Poetry* in 1928, Rylands' study traces the evolution of Shakespeare's poetic abilities, but it is not strictly a literary analysis: it always promotes the practical values of translating Shakespeare's words on the page to a life on the stage. The young Rylands counseled that Shakespeare's words are "isolated, arranged in a metrical pattern, where not only the value or values of each word must be considered, but also the close interdependence of one upon the other: for every word is quick to take colour from its companion, and will gain or lose emphasis according to its position in the line."[5] Thirty years later, Rylands, then an established producer, lamented that "our producers and players today—and our audiences—care overmuch for the eye and all too little for the ear."[6] His Cambridge pupils, particularly Barton, have done much to rectify the problem.

When Barton arrived, Rylands was a popular and respected figure at King's College, renowned "not as a scholar nor a critic," but as "a distinguished producer whose viewpoint is therefore valuable and salutary."[7] Barton acknowledges that Rylands was indeed "the big theatre influence at Cambridge":

> I knew him very well because I was in his college and he supervised me . . . I think his presence and his insistence on verse speaking made me very aware of it. He enormously stimulated me, and I owe a lot to him because he pushed me forward. But I think that how I teach it, how I pass it on, is entirely my own.

Barton's method of "passing it on" was recorded for our benefit in a special nine-part television series on British television telecast in July 1984. Entitled "Playing Shakespeare," the Barton-written and narrated script employed twenty-two of the RSC's finest actors who, under Barton's guidance, explored various Shakespearean texts—not surprisingly, mostly those with which Barton has had pronounced success—to illustrate that both the Elizabethan verse and prose are a kind of "stage direction in short hand. In it Shakespeare himself is offering directorial help and stimulus to the actors."[8] The particulars of Barton's methodology as illustrated in "Playing Shakespeare" are considered in the last chapter's analysis of "the Barton style." Here it is enough to note that the seeds of Barton's style were sown at Cambridge under the tutelage of Rylands, about whom Peter Hall has said: "It was George Rylands who taught me the structure of a line of Shakespeare."[9] Tony Church, another Rylands disciple, detects considerable influence of Rylands on Barton's directing methods:

> [Rylands] had fantastic control of rhythm and pace. He was also a fanatic about "getting on with it." I think that's affected the way John directs, too. Rylands couldn't bear unnecessary pauses in Shakespeare because he always said that Shakespeare had written those where he wanted them . . . The cues have to be taken up and the thing served forward all the time. This is the way you hear John directing and always has been.

Other Cambridge scholars played a role in Barton's development, though less directly. Muriel C. Bradbrook was the resident expert on Shakespearean stage conditions, a subject on which Barton wrote one of two theses. Though Barton claims no direct influence, her book, *Elizabethan Stage Conditions: A Study of Their Place in the Interpretation of Shakespeare's Plays* (1931), insisted that the young scholar-directors know the conditions and conventions of playing before tackling the content of Shakespeare's dramas. Ian Richardson, an actor in a number of Barton's RSC productions, calls Bradbrook "the little mother of all the geniuses of the Hall-Barton time . . . there are constant references to her scholarship in the preparation of the text at the RSC."[10] Bradbrook's influence on Barton's thinking can be traced largely through the work of his wife, Anne Barton, who completed her doctoral work under Bradbrook in 1961 (see chapter 8).

One could not study literature at Cambridge at midcentury without also considering the views of "the best thing on the English faculty": F. R. Leavis, patriarch of the *Scrutiny* School of Criticism.[11] Hall remembers Leavis's teaching as being "concrete, unsentimental, and unfailingly perceptive. Although he clearly hated the theatre, his lectures taught me the meaning of poetry, and a great deal about the social responsibility of the arts."[12] Barton, however, was not a Leavis disciple. He recalls attending perhaps one Leavis lecture, but otherwise having little contact with him. Nonetheless, like other Cambridge students, he developed the Leavis faculty of scrupulously combing the text to consider every possible meaning. Barton's debt to Leavis also comes through a close associate, Trevor Nunn:

> Trevor was in Leavis' college [Downing] and was supervised by him and got a great deal out of Leavis which has stood him in good stead . . . I think inevitably if you've been colleagues you rub off on one another.

A. P. Rossiter, whose book *Angel with Horns* Barton has called "the most perceptive and helpful piece of critical writing made yet" about Shakespearean problem plays,[13] was also at Cambridge during Barton's time. Barton attended some Rossiter lectures but "didn't deal with him precisely." Even in private conversation Barton seems reticent to admit scholarly influences, partly because he dislikes the academic label that has followed him since his arrival at the RSC in 1960. "It was an inevitable label, but I always thought I was much less well read, or literary, or intellectual than a number of my colleagues and I still do think that." His longtime secretary, Penny Gold, however, has said that Barton "does a good deal of critical background reading, although that's not something he advertises in the rehearsal room"[14] Barton amends Gold's commentary by noting that in the years since she has left his employ, he has done less and less background reading.

Predictably, Barton prefers bibliographic criticism more than literary criticism: "I was always interested in that [because] it would bear on the texts of the plays." His fondness for, and reliance on, bibliographical criticism can be traced to the "acting editions" that he develops for his productions. Here, though, one sees more of the would-be playwright than the fervent scholar at work.

At Cambridge Barton wrote two theses that have proven useful in his directorial work: one dealt with the translation of Anglo-Saxon poetry, which accounts for Barton's affinity for language and his expertise in editing and interpreting difficult texts; the other, a study of Elizabethan stage practice, has likely influenced the customarily sparse settings of RSC productions (though the legacy of William Poel, Harley Granville-Barker, Bradbrook, and others cannot be ignored). Barton was quick to apply the knowledge gained in the preparation of both theses: in 1952 he directed a production of *Julius Caesar* as a reconstructed Elizabethan performance.

Barton's most significant development at Cambridge was achieved in the student-run dramatic societies. During his student and research fellow days, Barton acted in over forty productions, directed numerous others, influenced many more, and wrote three Fry-like dramas of his own. One may wonder how he reconciled the demands of forty roles with those of a fulltime scholar: "I didn't," he says. "That's the truth on't."[15]

Barton attributes his growth as an artist to the opportunities to work, fail, improve, and succeed offered by the dramatic societies:

> Oxford and Cambridge have no drama departments, no theatre studies. It's all done by the undergraduates and therefore, if you've got intelligent people they get going, they do their own thing in the Oxbridge context, and they gain a great deal of experience and that sort of professionalism which doesn't really exist in the drama school context where people are under supervision and are being told what to do.

The combined dramatic societies were, in effect, a repertory company in which promising students could act, direct, and write for as many as ten productions during an academic year. To these activities Barton added another: theater administration. Using his accountant-father as a resource, he restructured the Amateur Dramatic Club (ADC), established a bookkeeping system, and turned the student-financed organization into a profitable enterprise.

At Cambridge Barton found no less than seven major societies through which he could apply his maturing talents: the ADC, the Cambridge Marlowe Society, the Mummers, the Cambridge Theatre Group, Footlights, the University Actors, and the Comedy Theatre Group. Naturally, there was uneven talent spread among these groups, and the quality of performance varied greatly. In February 1952, speaking as the dominant figure among the student societies, Barton wrote a lengthy editorial for *Varsity* in which he counseled his peers to produce less work so that "more might be taught and learnt."[16]

Of the named societies, the first two were of particular importance to Barton. He rose through the administrative ranks of the ADC to become its president and the most respected theater figure on campus. The Cambridge paper, *Varsity*, featured a "Profile" on Barton (see appendix A), focusing on a policy he and Hall would take to the RSC a decade later:

> As President he tries to encourage a high standard of performance in the ADC Theatre. He refuses to air his criticisms to the press, as he feels himself far too much involved in Cambridge Drama to sit in public judgment on his colleagues. But he usually makes private criticisms after unsatisfactory productions, and it is to his credit that he makes no enemies by his candour. He has found that adverse criticism is of more practical help than congratulation. . . . He is a strong advocate of mutual criticism within the theatrical circle. . . .[17]

Barton's developmental work was done under the ADC banner, but it was the Cambridge Marlowe Society that was the showcase for the university's best talent. The society was formed in 1908—the war poet Rupert Brooke was among its founders—with the aim of reviving Elizabethan and Jacobean masterpieces neglected by the commercial theater; it freely experimented with the techniques fostered by William Poel. The Marlovians traditionally do not publish cast lists for their performances, thus it is difficult to ascertain exactly what Barton contributed to the society. Much of his work was so well known that his roles and direction became commonplace despite the society's best intentions.

Since 1930 the Marlowe Society had been administered by Rylands. In the late 1940s, Rylands relinquished his duties to others, and students such as Peter Wood, succeeded by Barton and then by Hall, continued the legacy. Rylands returned occasionally to do work in which he had a particular interest.

One of the Marlowe Society's monumental undertakings began in the summer of 1957, when Barton was a research fellow at King's College. Argo Records planned to produce complete recordings of the entire Shakespeare canon by a permanent company to ensure continuity for the project. The Marlowe Society accepted the challenge and began recording the thirty-seven plays at the rate of five or six a year, a task completed in 1963, totaling 139 records. During the initial sessions, Barton read several roles, including Nestor in *Troilus and Cressida*, Aufidius in *Coriolanus*, and Brutus in *Julius Caesar.* The Marlovian cast was bolstered by some noted professionals, including John Gielgud, Peggy Ashcroft, Irene Worth, and Michael Hordern. The project was successful: *Records and Recordings* awarded the group its highest acclamation for "the remarkable achievement in verse speaking and the clarity and illumination they brought to Shakespeare's texts,"[18] accolades frequently assigned to Barton productions.

Barton served his theater apprenticeship first as an actor with the ADC and then followed the traditional path from minor roles to his first major part: Sir Toby Belch in *Twelfth Night* in 1950. He specialized in character roles, particularly old men. At one point he played ten successive old men—"distinguished for certain mannerisms of voice and movement, which practically every member of the ADC could imitate to some degree."[19] His best work included Justice Shallow ("the old man I loved most"); Ulysses in Giradoux's *There Shall Be No War in Troy;* and Tiresias in Sophocles' *Oedipus* (the combination of which first exposed Barton to "Greek" plays, a relationship that culminated in 1980 with his epic staging of *The Greeks*). His most famous role at Cambridge was Mercutio in *Romeo and Juliet,* which he codirected with Rylands. The production, which also featured Peter Hall as Tybalt, was successful enough to warrant a run at London's Phoenix Theatre in 1952. Barton's last performance at Cambridge occurred in 1959 when he played Mortimer to Derek Jacobi's Edward II in Toby Robertson's production of the Marlowe play, which was invited to Stratford-upon-Avon, where it played in an outdoor setting.

Professionally, Barton acted briefly with the Oxford-Cambridge Players (though he was primarily their director), later known as the Elizabethan Theatre Company. In 1962–63 (and sporadically since then), Barton toured with the RSC as a reader of his script, *The Hollow Crown,* which brought him to New York in January 1963. He was praised by Broadway critics while working in a small cast that included Dorothy Tutin and Max Adrian. His stint in *Hollow Crown* showed him that he was not temperamentally suited for a career as a professional actor: "I hated it . . . I couldn't stand doing it night after night, but I admire actors who can." As stated in the Prologue, Barton has recently returned to acting: he narrated Gillian Lynne's televised version of Malory's Arthurian tales while actors performed a dumb show version of the epic. (In 1959 Barton himself had devised and directed a recording of Malory's work for Argo Records; it featured Harry Andrews.)

Barton is best remembered at Cambridge as a director of imagination, insight, and some daring. He began his directing career for the ADC in October 1949 with an ambitious double bill, *The Critic* and *Macbeth,* which received mixed notices from Cambridge critics. Double bills were not uncommon on that campus, a fact which prompted Trevor Nunn recently (September 1982) to ask Barton to stage a double bill of *Titus Andronicus* and *Two Gentlemen of Verona* at Stratford. In 1950 Barton and Toby Robertson staged Jonson's *The Alchemist,* in which Barton also played Face. The directors were censured for encumbering the production "with every clever irrelevance they could contrive to confuse and infuriate—top hats and tail coats, a doll's house that opens and shuts,[20] sandwich boards, stuffed swans, showers of feathers—and by this dramatic alchemy they have inverted Jonson's gold to dross."[21]

Throughout the remainder of his student days, and during his subsequent residence as a research fellow, Barton directed numerous plays, a sampling of which illustrates his range and ambition: *Two Gentlemen of Verona* (as part of a twin bill with a Rylands-directed *Dr. Faustus* at the Cambridge Festival, 1951); Marlowe's *Edward II* (December 1951—still considered one of the most extraordinary productions ever seen at Cambridge[22]); *Lady May* (an original musical composed by Julian Slade); *Titus Adronicus; Romeo and Juliet; Henry IV,* Parts I and II (with Clive Swift as Falstaff, Ian McKellen as Justice Shallow, and

Derek Jacobi as Hal); *Volpone;* Greene's *Friar Bacon and Friar Bungay;* and Jean Anouilh's *Antigone* (which further enhanced his partiality for Greek myth and for political plays couched in classic myths; Barton himself played Creon when his leading actor left the show). Perhaps Barton's most-remembered production as a Cambridge director was Chekhov's *Three Sisters* (featuring Ian McKellen). Despite his Shakespearean reputation, Barton is a Chekhovian at heart. Many of his productions have a Chekhovian quality, particularly in the wistfulness of their endings. Remembering his success with *The Three Sisters*— which he admits was itself influenced by the Moscow Art Theatre's production that he saw in London in the mid–1950's—Barton declares: "I am passionate to do Chekhov . . . and I quite often have Chekhovian elements in what I do, quite commonly." (See chapter 4 for examples of his Chekhovian handling of *Twelfth Night* and *Love's Labour's Lost;* also his recent *La Ronde* was judged decidedly more Chekhovian than Schnitzler.)

Was Barton influenced by any of the leading directors working in England in the early 1950s as he developed his own skills at Cambridge? Apparently not. "I think one was pretty critical of most of the productions one saw, except for Peter Brook and Tyrone Guthrie. I don't think one thought especially highly of anyone else," said Barton, who did admit to a "marginal influence" by Guthrie. He qualified his remark by adding, "I don't think one saw enough of his works to be hugely influenced by him." Barton believes Guthrie to be "a man of immense theatrical imagination, a giver of great delight," but one whose talents were limited because he never really tried to explore the content of a play.[23] During a 1957 radio broadcast, Barton praised Brook as England's "acknowledged master" from whom one expected only the very best work. Generally, it is safe to assume that none of England's practicing directors had a significant influence on Barton's growth, other than to inspire him to upgrade the quality of Shakespearean stage direction, which he judges "dreadful" prior to the RSC.

The young play-going Barton did see three works that profoundly affected his philosophy of the theater and the manner in which he brings plays— Shakespearean and others—to the stage. The previously mentioned visit to London by the Moscow Art Theatre and its productions of *Uncle Vanya* and, in particular, *The Three Sisters* infused in Barton a life long passion for Chekhov's simplicity and sparseness. Barton's evenings with the MAT in the mid-1950s shaped his subsequent work. In 1956 Brecht's Berliner Ensemble spent a summer in London, an event, coupled by the almost coincidental stagings of Osborne's *Look Back in Anger* at the Royal Court Theatre and Joan Littlewood's production of Behan's *The Quare Fellow* at Stratford East, that infused the British theater with a new social consciousness. Barton saw the Berliner Ensemble's production of Brecht's *The Days of the Commune*, which he terms "the greatest theatrical experience I've ever had without a doubt. . . . It's one influence that I totally acknowledge, and it's haunted me. It goes into my work." From the Brechtians Barton learned the power of diversity and ambiguity in the theater ("Though it was a palpably didactic, left-wing play, they gave to it the love and ambiguity that they give a greater play"), the overwhelming virtue of silence on stage (describing a pivotal moment in the play, in which a group of revolutionists vote whether or not to use terror in their campaign, Barton remembers that the company's use of silence "made the moral point without being didactic"), and the theatrical viability of diverse styles ("They drastically switched styles to get a different mood . . . which I now deeply believe in doing, which I suppose fed into *The Greeks*"). Furthermore, the Berliner Ensemble experience showed Barton that "you can get great theater out of poor material. They hadn't rewritten the material, but they'd *'rewritten'* it in terms of the direction and acting so that they transformed it into a major work." And in terms of the evolution of the Royal Shakespeare Company, which, largely under Barton's guidance, has established itself as a peer to such companies as the Moscow Art Theatre and the Berliner Ensemble, Barton emphasizes that his visit to *The Days of the Commune* in 1956 taught him "the staggering impact of a great company."

One other theater experience in the mid-1950s—which, for Barton, was otherwise a "deadly" time in the British theater—has had a lasting effect on his career. In London he saw Ugo Betti's *The Queen and the Rebels* ("a very bad play with a wonderful idea"), which starred Irene Worth in "the greatest performance" Barton has ever seen an actress give. As with *The Days of the Commune*, Barton left the theater with "the idea that fine theater can come out of indifferent material." His subsequent work as a director has been noted for finding the theatrical viability of works previously thought poor theater; specifically, *Troilus and Cressida* and *All's Well That Ends Well* stand as examples of Barton's mastery over "unplayable" scripts.

While directing at Cambridge, Barton also developed—of necessity—a skill that has served the RSC well during his professional career:

> I found myself in my acting days doing stage fights and continually getting minor injuries. So I evolved a technique of making everything *look* as dangerous as possible, while at the same time ensuring the maximum of safety. I've never had a fencing lesson in my life, and know nothing at all about proper fencing. I worked out a form of fighting which can (I hope) be more theatrical and exciting than the real thing. The latter can be dull to watch because the movements are often minor and not theatrically valid.[24]

Barton's fight sequences have gained a reputation for vividness: the battles in *The Wars of the Roses* and Hector's death at the hands of Achilles' Myrmidons in *Troilus and Cressida* are frequently cited as examples of Barton's excellence with stage combat.

The production for which Barton will be most remembered at Cambridge, and one that epitomizes the young scholar-director's work, was the aforementioned *Julius Caesar*, staged for the Marlowe Society in March 1952. Using a

1599 diary by a Swiss traveler who saw that play acted "in a straw-thatched theatre across the water," Barton, then twenty-three, and the Marlovians attempted to reconstruct on the Cam that Elizabethan performance on the Thames. Their theater was converted to a facsimile of the Globe by adding a thrust stage strewn with straw, a quasi-tiring house, and side boxes to house bearded dandies. The actors wore Elizabethan costumes, carried Roman swords with their rapiers and selected pieces of antique clothing to suggest Caesar's Rome. The play was followed by a bucolic romp called "Thumpkin and His Crying Mum," which contained ghostly goings-on, deceits, clownage and tumbling. Barton's boldest decision was to employ what is surmised to have been the Elizabethan dialect. He enlisted a Cambridge philologist to coach his players to speak the 350-year-old language authentically. Barton admits that he "cheated" a bit on the language to challenge his actors:

> . . . whenever there was a dispute when a sound changed, I went for the tougher, rougher alternative. I did certain things that had probably gone out by Shakespeare's time, like pronouncing the 'k' in words with 'kn.' I thickened it to the full sound, and I found it gave an extraordinary extra texture to the language.[25]

Most of the vowels received new values. For example, the long "i" became a long "ay." Caesar said, "Ay met a lay-on against the Capitol."[26] "War" became "wharre," "fight" became "fate." The overall effect was to give the language a roughness, an immediacy lost in the intervening years. There were advantages to the deployment of the older language: Barton remembers that "one found the in-built sneer in 'Breutus is an hounerable mun' [sic] lends itself to that repetition by Antony in a way which modern English doesn't."[27] There were liabilities as well: "I will seek Pindarus the while" became "Ay will seek Pindarus the whale." *Varsity* cheekily reported that Pindarus the Whale was a duly recognized member of the cast.[28] On balance, those who heard the production, either as spectators or performers,[29] favored the antiquated language. Church, who played several roles, says he has "never forgotten the wonderful sound of Cassius in the storm scene: 'Ay bare my boozim to the thoonder stoe-erm.'" The commercial press praised the bold experiment. *The Guardian* (Manchester) found "so much out of the ordinary that it ought to be repeated elsewhere . . . the play seems more plausible than usual."[30] *The Observer*'s reviewer was glad the experiment was made, but also found himself "glad to hear no more of the Ades of March."[31]

Barton recalls the production fondly and would like to restage his Cambridge *Caesar*, but laments that "nobody wants me to. They think it would not be commercial. It's been a play I've wanted to do for years, but neither Peter Hall nor Trevor Nunn thought it would be a good idea." Ironically, the production was a success at Cambridge: the 600-seat Arts Theatre was sold out during its week-long run,[32] a testimony to its producer's imagination, as much as to the curiosity of its concept. Barton again believes the time has come for another Elizabethan-language Shakespeare and will likely do one at Stratford in the near future, though not necessarily the *Caesar.*

Throughout his Cambridge days Barton was a man of uncommon vision. Peter Hall was then much more concerned with modern drama than the Elizabethan Barton, and he remembers that "even in those days Barton dreamed of a definitive production of the *Henry VI* plays. . . . I was fascinated and intrigued by his dreams, but I never thought it would concern me as a director."[33]

Not all of Barton's Cambridge dreams were of definitive Shakespearean productions. He was yet driven by his "passion to be a playwright," a quest that thirty years later still beckons him. While an undergradute, he wrote three plays (which he now remembers as being "dreadful"), each indicative of his theater and social interests. Looking back upon those plays now, he recognizes that even then there were forces at work within him that today are compelling him to write his "modern myth." *That's All One,* written and staged by Barton in 1951, was described, in Polonius-fashion, as a "comical-historical-musical-pastoral." It was given a vaguely medieval setting, festooned with anachronisms "so gaily outrageous and so fundamentally English-Beer-Bawdy-Cricket that his audience was almost discerned [*sic*]."[34] Among other things, the play dealt with the tragic death of a cricketeer in medieval England. Though panned for its uncertainty of mood, the play is a useful catalogue of its author's passions: things English, cricket, medieval sensibilities (typified in the works of Malory), the juxtaposition of opposite moods, the mythic tales. Later that term Barton submitted another play, *Brown Ptarmigan,* to a Cambridge playwriting competition and won second prize.

Barton's most successful undergraduate play was *Winterlude* (1953). Peter Hall directed its premiere, while Barton played the "ambiguous villain." Described by its author as a "Ruritanian political drama,"[35] the play dealt with a princess escaping an unsuccessful rebellion, a heroic officer, and a disillusioned commander of the Black Guard (Barton's role). It resembles, in some ways, *The Queen and the Rebels,* but Barton wrote it before he saw Betti's drama. Barton's script was praised for its exploration of conflicts of permanent human interest—"the conflict between the romantic and realistic soldier, loyalty to ideas out of self-interest, the comforts of war and the ravages of peace,"[36] themes that Barton has explored in his best directorial and adaptive work, particularly *Troilus and Cressida* and *The Greeks.* Barton is drawn to the plays that explore "doomed romanticism" ("I find that very moving"), and the theme inspires his best directorial instincts. *Winterlude* is an early attempt to articulate his views on the matter. "It was also a crucial element of my mind in *The Greeks,*" says Barton, and—one can surmise—it will play a central role in his current work on his mythic saga.

Winterlude is a seminal chapter in Barton's development because it is conspicuously a political play. Just as the label *scholar* has haunted Barton throughout his directorial career with the RSC, so too has the label *nonpolitical* been affixed to his work. True, he is the least overtly political of the RSC directors, but he is imbued with a love of political theater that can be traced back to his Cambridge days. He cites both acting roles (for example, the Inquisitor in *Saint Joan* and Ulysses in *There Shall Be No War in Troy*) and directorial choices (specifically Anouilh's *Antigone:* "I loved that play") as cornerstones of his political bent. The Berliner Ensemble further fueled his affinity for political plays, but, he stresses, he is not a political activist:

> I'm not political in the sense that at bottom I do not sardonically believe that politics can solve things, that politics is to do with finding solutions. . . . That's why I would never be a political activist. What I think of politics can be summed up in a sentence which I wrote in *The Peloponnesian Wars* [staged as a Studio project at the Aldwych Theatre in 1965]. It goes: 'In theory, politics is concerned with disposing events. But events happen first, and politics is the art of trying to undo harm already done.'

For Barton, then, the best "political" plays are those that try to sort out events on the human level rather than those that provide solutions. "That's why *Troilus and Cressida* is my favorite play," says Barton. "They're seeking order." *Winterlude* presaged this predilection some thirty years ago on the Cam.

With an eye on a possible future in the professional theater, Barton helped found the Oxford-Cambridge Players in 1952. The original company was established at Oxford a year earlier by Colin George, Barton's counterpart at the Oxford Dramatic Society (OUDS), and Paul Almond, an aspiring Oxford playwright, in order to: (a) provide a quasi-professional outlet for university actors who expected to enter the commercial theater; (b) "establish a school of classical acting which would provide . . . actors for the Old Vic and Stratford"; (c) take classic works to areas other than "the large theatres of accepted cities"; and (d) present Shakespeare in the Elizabethan manner.[37] In July 1952 young performers from the two distinguished universities toured England with productions of *The Taming of the Shrew* and a Barton-directed *Henry V*. Theirs was an existence with which Shakespeare's vagabond actors would identify, since they slept and performed in a variety of unconventional accommodations. The company motto—"Into a thousand parts divide one man"—best describes the production style employed by these neo-Elizabethans, thirteen men and three women, each of whom played multiple roles on a single portable set consisting of an inner stage and balcony, and, where possible, a flexible forestage. In November the company played at Cambridge, where Barton's direction was lauded for its "distinctive impress of speed and fluidity on almost every scene (which) proves that Elizabethan staging techniques derive freedom and spaciousness from its very paucity of materials."[38]

Encouraged by its success, the Oxbridge company regrouped the following summer, rechristened as the Elizabethan Theatre Company. They were soon joined by Michael MacOwan, a director perhaps best known for his modern-dress staging of *Troilus and Cressida* in 1938. MacOwan was attracted to the company by its commitment to the power of Elizabethan verse speaking: "They have learned to make Shakespeare's language their own by an understanding of the whole climate of thought and the feeling which it produced."[39] MacOwan cited Rylands and Oxford's Neville Coghill for their donnish influence on the young actors' proficiency.

Henry V was televised by the BBC in May 1953, and was among the first telecasts of a Shakespearean play. The *Radio Times* review of Barton's production (directed for television by MacOwan) credited the university backgrounds of the performers as the impetus for the company's success: "Never have the performances come so close to the spirit of the original. This has been made possible through the collaboration of scholars and men of the theatre; the remarriage has proven fruitful."

Toby Robertson, who would later head the acclaimed Prospect Theatre Company, played the Chorus and four other roles by merely changing an article of costume, applying a dab of makeup, or donning a wig in full view of the audience. *Stage* magazine applauded the Barton-Robertson "chameleon-like tactics," noting that they had the virtue of "reviving for the modern theatre-goer an aspect of Elizabethan staging of which we are seldom reminded."[40]

The company spent the summer of 1953 touring Barton's *Henry V,* played nearly uncut, and a MacOwan-directed *Julius Caesar* that was remarkably similar to the *Caesar* staged at Cambridge a year earlier, though it did not employ the reconstructed language. The company traveled throughout England, from London's Westminster to Buckland Abbey's Tithe Barn. Generally well received were the intelligence of its verse speaking, the ingenuity of its staging, and the young performers' fidelity to Shakespeare's intentions. Some critics thought reproducing Shakespeare's "limitations" (multiple casting, lack of scenic variety, incongruous costuming) was overdoing the idea of loyalty.

Though the effort was truly ensemble in intent and practice, Barton emerged as the company's luminary: on the whole his directorial notices were more favorable than those of the veteran MacOwan's. The *Times* found his work "swift, businesslike, and yet imaginative,"[41] and the *Yorkshire Post* called it a revelation.[42]

Just as important, Barton was developing into an excellent acting teacher, a skill that would advance him to Stratford and for which he is yet highly regarded in the English professional theater. "John Barton obviously understands how to get the best out of young actors," proclaimed the *Daily Telegraph;*[43] . . . Barton has learnt among his contemporaries the secret of making [the company] act," echoed *The Times.*[44]

Barton left England in the fall of 1953 to accept a lectureship in the drama department at the University of California, Berkeley. In addition to lecturing on English Renaissance drama, he directed *Coriolanus* and *Measure for Mea-*

sure, productions he dismisses as being "of no great note." His year at Berkeley was not a happy experience. Among other things, he developed a dislike for university drama schools—"they are a bit between the two stools of an English department and a drama school." Furthermore, he feels there is also a problem about the standard of teaching: "You tend to get people running drama departments who are not good enough to be making it in the theatre."

Barton returned to Cambridge for the fall term, 1954, accepting a fellowship to do research on modern drama, a choice he now terms "a great mistake":

> I thought, quite wrongly, when I took a fellowship I'd get security and I would write. But then, having been quite fluent with a pen in my early 20s, I got a horrible writing block for years. I was very unhappy at Cambridge because I was supposed to be writing a critical book which I couldn't do. I had no capacity for that whatsoever. . . . I felt more and more unhappy in that milieu. I made a wrong decision: I should have become a director eight years before.

Barton admits that he does not respond as creatively to twentieth-century playwriting as he does to classical texts, which likely accounts for his inability to complete the study of modern drama: "I don't myself feel the same challenges with modern drama; its problems and opportunities seem more limited to me. The precision of Pinter, say, I admire and enjoy immensely, but it doesn't attract me creatively."[45] Furthermore, Barton cites modern drama's general lack of plotting ("A director's first job in the theatre is to entertain, to tell a good story") and its "reductive" characterization as reasons for his lack of enthusiasm for contemporary works: "They look for the worst in everybody in society. I believe that the Shakespearean thing is to find a touch of humanity at the unexpected moment." This is purely conjecture, but Barton's failure to produce the critical study may explain his self-professed inability to discuss works critically outside the rehearsal process. "I have little talent for critical exposition," he insists, but the give-and-take of the rehearsal hall arouses his instincts: "If I have rows and rows of faces listening to my views, I can't do it; but if I'm challenged and questioned, I can tick because I'm in the usual situation for a director in rehearsals."[46]

Barton's mental block concerning interpretation was secondary to his writing block, which only now, he feels, is beginning to free itself. "It was torture to write anything," he recalls, "I have a cupboard full of notebooks, forty to fifty unfinished plays."[47] Several of Barton's unfinished works include a Napoleonic triology and a triology about the rise of the Plantagenets—which, significantly, was the genesis of his controversial *King John* adaptation. The realization of *The Greeks* in 1980 and *The Vikings* in 1983 has convinced Barton that he may finally be free of the writing block. He excitedly talks about "My Story" as yet another sign that his longtime goal to be a writer is finally emerging as a reality: "I realize I've stumbled onto something I've been looking for for thirty years. I've tried lots in theater; I'm hoping I've found it." Subsequent discussions of Barton's theatrical adaptations must always be colored by this last statement.

The later Cambridge years were not unproductive despite their frustrations. Barton advanced in the ranks of academe; he was appointed Lay Dean of King's College in 1956 and continued his work with the Marlowe Society. The 1956–57 academic year was particularly productive for Barton. He was able to flee from the modern drama book to the familiarity of medieval and pre-Elizabethan drama when the BBC commissioned Barton to develop a thirteen-part radio show, *The First Stage,* which would trace the development of early English drama. Barton selected representative scripts from the medieval mystery play "The Creation" to Kyd's *Spanish Tragedy* to "present the best of them in adaptations and extracts, and to trace our dramatic history up to the blossoming of the Elizabethan public theatres in the 1580s."[48] (See appendix B for a complete list of programs and plays.)

Barton introduced the series and concluded them with a lecture entitled "The Rise and Fall of English Didactic Drama." Some of Barton's critical commentary reveals attitudes that have informed his production philosophy. He has long justified his reworking of Shakespeare's texts by invoking a theory of "continuous copy"—that is, the Elizabethan practice of altering and revising texts to fit particular needs and circumstances. He traces this practice to a medieval custom assimilated by subsequent generations of English dramatists: ". . . there is some precedent for such drastic treatment [of *The First Stage* scripts] as the authors of one cycle were not above borrowing liberally from one another. This is in effect an exhibition of what went on with most plays in the course of their history" (13–14). Barton's finished product is a prodigious piece of scholarship that synthesizes the best of early English drama.[49] The editorial skills Barton acquired proved useful six years later when he tackled the *Henry VI* cycle in preparation for *The Wars of the Roses.*

During the summer of 1957 Barton and Rylands evaluated the season's productions at the Shakespeare Memorial Theatre in Stratford for BBC audiences.[50] Barton, the youthful don, was not timid about discussing the work of England's prestigious directors. Douglas Seale's *King John* was judged by Rylands and Barton to be "restless"; Barton doubted whether Seale "really got hold of the play's intentions."[51] Even Peter Brook, whom Barton admired, received grudging praise: "My disappointment [with *The Tempest*] such as it is, is simply because it was a Brook production and one expects the very, very best from him. It is only fair to say that I have in fact never seen the play better or more dramatically done."[52] Some of Barton's criticisms, like Caesar's ghost to Brutus, would return to haunt him when he directed at Stratford. For instance, Barton questioned Peter Hall's cutting of *Cymbeline* (but called his Cambridge colleague's work "a producer's triumph");[53] seventeen years later he would perform major surgery on the same text—*and* insert a major section of his own devising (see chapter 7). Of Brook Barton would ask, "Why does a toad stool on which Ariel is standing suddenly rise? One wonders, what is added or suggested thereby?" Similar questions were asked of Barton's *Richard II*, which included a hydraulic bridge that raised and lowered the monarch. Barton's scholarly idealism would eventually give way to a director's desire to create exciting visual images.

As both an antidote to the writing block and the need to be a playwright, Barton began work on *The Hollow Crown* in 1959. An anthology of writings about England's royalty,[54] it has consistently been among the most popular works in the RSC repertory since its initial reading in 1960. Written for three men and a woman, backed by a small musical consort, *The Hollow Crown* explores the falls and foibles of kings and queens as seen through the eyes of historians, playwrights, novelists, diarists, the monarchs themselves—and a precocious Jane Austen who, at age fifteen, decided to write a history of English royalty. Barton was drawn to the subject of kingship because he has an irresistible attraction to royalty that he feels is shared by many:

> I think it [the attraction] is simply because they *are* kings and queens. People want to know what goes on behind the official face: they like the faults and quirks behind great people. When I cast around . . . for something that would make a good anthology, this came to mind because, like sex, it is a subject in which all people are perenially interested.[55]

Barton admits that work on *The Hollow Crown* has helped him when directing plays about monarchs. His reasearch into the lives of royal characters enabled him to see "the reality behind Shakespeare's inventions." Barton's productions have been criticized by their general lack of emphasis on the political elements. Michael Bogdanov, a former Barton assistant and now a respected director with the National Theatre, claims Barton's productions do not reflect a social conscience.[56] Barton, as we have seen, claims a strong, though not activist, political bias in his work. He aligns himself with the humanist movement (though he avoids the "humanist" label): "It's the human content that I'm interested in. I'm very interested in political plays; I love them, but I think for what goes on in Shakespeare's political plays, I don't think there is an 'ism.' "

Despite these diversions, Barton remained discontented: "I realized gradually that I was a fish out of water and cut off from directing." Salvation came in January 1960 when Peter Hall, who had just convinced the board of governors at the Shakespeare Memorial Theatre that he could best revitalize Shakespearean production at Stratford, summoned his Cambridge mate to teach the actors of his new company to speak the verse as they had learned it from Rylands. Barton was "delighted" to leave Cambridge and take up Hall's challenge, though he emphasizes that he was not dissatisfied with academic life per se: "It was simply that I gradually realized I was a director. Also, I couldn't concentrate on my main interest: Elizabethan stage history."

At Stratford, Hall gathered his novice company to deliver a manifesto in which he delineated RSC policy towards verse speaking:

There is no mystique about Shakespeare's verse. It is a craft that you can learn very quickly and it should not be labored in rehearsal. It is in our new Studio that we want to tell you about line-structure, alliteration, rhyme, and counter-rhyme, and the meaning of imagery. . . . An intelligent understanding of the form and expression of your text is as much the raw material of your creation as knowing the name of the character you are playing.[57]

Barton's primary task in the early days of the company was to make Hall's policy a reality. Word of the Cambridge verse work seeped to the public through newspapers and magazines. The April 1960 issue of *Shire and Spire* contained an oracular sentence: "An expert in voice production is working with Mr. Hall and his assistant director—bearded Cambridge don, John Barton— and ultimately we should see an acting style which will be Stratford's own."[58] The resultant acting style was anatomized in 1965 by John Russell Brown:

The company has been taught to scrutinize every word in a play so that they know, always, what they are saying. . . . Generalizing and debilitating resonance and overblown fulness of phrase have been rinsed away, and most individual quirks and flourishes of elocution. There is no compensating pursuit of pure diction—everyone sharing the same vowel sounds and treating the consonants with equal respect—but the words are alive, as far as the actors understand them.[59]

Initially, this quality was not easily achieved. Church remembers an early company meeting at which Barton outlined his proposals: "John caused an absolute furor amongst the members of this company, most of whom didn't know anything about it, by giving a lecture on Shakespearean verse speaking." In addition to working on specific scripts from the plays in production to master the verse, Barton inaugurated sonnet classes that yet remain the backbone of the RSC actor-training procedure. Mike Gwilym, a graduate of a Barton sonnet class, describes the rationale employed by the RSC's premiere verse teacher:

John treats the sonnets as if they are soliloquies. And the exercise is to see how much meaning you can convey by the reading of a sonnet which is very, very condensed. He tries to show you how the structure of the verse, the caesura, the upward inflection can make the meaning clear. He does that— not as a teacher—to encourage you to do that with your speeches in the play.[60]

"Playing Shakespeare," the nine-hour telecast of 1984, shows Barton's techniques with sonnets and Elizabethan scripts.

The RSC hierarchy realized that actor training would have to extend beyond the revolution in verse speaking, which Hall feels is "the best thing I've done in my life."[61] In 1962 Michel Saint-Denis began the RSC Actors' Studio with Barton as his assistant. Saint-Denis was a propitious choice for the directorship of the studio: he had done much to improve English acting technique since his arrival from France in the 1930s, when he began teaching concepts developed by his uncle, Jacques Copeau, who was among the most significant director-teachers of this century.

Work at the studio began in late 1962, funded in part by a Gulbenkian Foundation Grant. In addition to Saint-Denis and Barton, teaching duties were shared by Peggy Ashcroft and Donald Sinden; Litz Pisk taught movement briefly for the young company. Later, Cicely Barry was employed as its voice teacher, a position she still holds. Courses included verse speaking, speech and vocal problems, singing, movement, period and modern fencing. The RSC actors applied these skills to works from Greek tragedy to music hall: English miracle plays, Elizabethan and Jacobean drama other than Shakespeare's, works by Molière, Chekhov, Brecht, as well as Wesker, Pinter, and other new wave British dramatists were also used. There were innovative experiments with nontheatrical works such as diaries, sermons, legal speeches, and poems. *Flourish*, the RSC newsletter, described the purpose of the studio to patrons: "To train and develop each individual actor's potential to its utmost and to explore continuously all forms of staging and dramatic presentations."[62] Some of the explorations led to production: the anthologies (for example, *The Peloponnesian Wars* and *Respice Finem*, a humorous look at death) were an outgrowth of workshop exercises. Though *The Greeks* did not reach fruition until 1980, its germination began in the studio in the mid-1960s (See chapter 10).

In 1964 Saint-Denis became ill and studio work withered, though Barton continued to do sonnet work and other exercises. Though Barton's reputation with the RSC rests primarily on his directing and writing skills, it should not be forgotten that his contributions to actor-training, and the corresponding growth of the RSC "style," are among his most important gifts to contemporary stage practice.

Barton was not merely the RSC's resident dramaturge and acting teacher during the company's initial year. Remembering his directing accomplishments at Cambridge and with the Elizabethan Theatre Company, Hall assigned *The Taming the the Shrew* to Barton. The comedy joined *Two Gentlemen of Verona*, *The Merchant of Venice*, *The Winter's Tale*, and *Troilus and Cressida* (which Barton codirected with Hall: see chapter 3) in the company's first repertory.

In terms of Barton's personal growth, *Shrew* was memorable for two reasons: it was an indication of events to come since Barton wrote an alternative acting edition for his players. Less fortunately, a cast "mutiny" nearly cost Barton his career at Stratford. The *Shrew* cast was headed by Dame Peggy Ashcroft, who was playing Kate for the first time in her career at age fifty-four, and by the ascendant Peter O'Toole as Petruchio. Several weeks before the opening, Ashcroft and others approached Hall with grievances concerning Barton's directorial methods. Church, the production's Hortensio, explains the near-disaster:

[Barton had] worked out his conception in too much detail before coming on the floor. The back-and-forth and rough-and-tumble of the rehearsal process with experienced professionals who were not expecting just to fit in was something of which he had no experience whatsoever . . . the veterans felt that John did not trust the actors, that he was hanging all his ideas *on* us, that the ideas had to work by themselves, but not *through* us.[63]

Hall, pressured because of his longtime relationship with Barton, apparently asked Barton to leave, but he refused: "I doggedly stuck it out and hung on . . . because I felt all would sort itself out."[64] Barton survived the ordeal and today numbers Ashcroft among his most ardent supporters.

The Taming of the Shrew, whatever its backstage problems, was one of the successes of the RSC's first season and was retained in the repertory for two more seasons (though restaged by Maurice Daniels). Much of the production's appeal can be attributed to Barton, who combined Shakespeare's text with another version of the comedy called *A Pleasant Conceited Historie called The Taming of a Shrew,* printed by Peter Short in 1594. This version makes greater use of the Christopher Sly convention, and Barton used extracts from it to emphasize that "the play within the play was acted by strolling players for the entertainment of the drunken tinker."[65]

After opening his production with the initial exchange from *"A Shrew,"* in which Sly is ejected from an inn by an angry tapster, Barton added Shakespeare's induction with the huntsmen. But at its conclusion Sly did not "disappear" as in Shakespeare's text (at the end of 1.1), but remained to be entertained by the traveling actors. Throughout, Barton inserted fragments from the alternate play and occasionally lines of his own devising. In 5.1. Barton added a provocative sequence. During the Gremio-Baptista argument about jailing the old man, Barton inserted the following exchange:

Sly: I say they shall not go to prison.
Actor: No more shall they not, my lord, they will run away.
Sly: Will they run away, sir? That's well; then give some more drink, and let tham play again.

Sly drinks contentedly and settles down to watch a happy play without jailings. The exchange was modified by Barton from 4.2. 45–52 of *The Taming of a Shrew* and reminds the audience of both the play-within-the-play that Shakespeare "forgets" and of the darker side of Shakespeare's farce—of a world in which people go to jail and in which love is not always bliss. Finally, Barton incorporated the epilogue from *"A Shrew,"* an interesting sequence in which Sly is reminded that he must go home to face *his* wife. The drunken tinker does not dread the ordeal because

I now know how to tame a shrew!
. . . .

I'll go to my wife presently
And tame her, too, and if she anger me.

Barton's interpolations of the Sly plot from the alternate source offended some. Bernard Levin surmised that the director "apparently imagines that without help from him Shakespeare could never live through the last act. But the result is that he not only kills Shakespeare stone dead but shovels the earth over him and stamps it down."[66] Barton's revision, however, did provide a solution to an age-old dilemma that has plagued scholars such as Sir Arthur Quiller Couch, who has addressed the problem of Sly's disappearance: "We *do* want to know what becomes of him at the end."[67] Barton's scholarship and theatrical imagination satisfied this wish and kept intact the sense of the play-within-the-play. Some confusion, however, was created by the device: "Sly had to move constantly from interior to exterior . . . in order to keep tabs on the story of Petruchio and Kate."[68] The longterm benefits—a more consistent and unified structure—seemed a worthy price to pay. Kenneth Tynan noted that the device "works splendidly, framing the play as its author never did."[69]

In the larger context of his work with the RSC, Barton's invention was interesting because it represents what has become a favorite theme: the overlap between art and life. In 1960 he never allowed his audience to forget that the piece of life they were watching was a play: a prompter sat on the fringe of the playing area and occasionally became embroiled in the action, while, through portals of the inn, the audience could see the actors rehearsing their parts prior to an entrance. The final exit of the Players, missed by Sly who had passed out from the drink, is described by Cheryl Brahms: "Having made a magic they extinguished it in as brilliant and heartbreaking a *coup de theatre* as any I've seen. A black cape swirls—out go the candles of the wedding feast. A purse is thrown to the Epilogue and he and all the Mummers are on their way to Chipping Camden."[70]

Despite the success of the production and its incorporation into the company's repertory for several seasons thereafter, Barton was not to direct *solus* at Stratford for five years, perhaps a result of the internal problems that arose during *Shrew*. He did direct an opera, *Carmen*, at Sadler's Wells in November 1961, a production that began a long association between Barton and designer Ralph Koltai. After *Shrew*, though, Barton devoted his RSC energies to teaching acting classes, devising anthologies, and providing Hall with behind-the-scenes advice. Barton-the-director was still warring privately with Barton-the-would-be-playwright. He and Hall began fleshing out ideas for the *Henry VI* cycle they had dreamed of at Cambridge. In general, however, Barton maintained an unassuming posture. While appearing in *The Hollow Crown* on Broadway in 1962, Barton received a call from Hall asking him to return to England to complete work on the *Henry VI* texts. Again Barton accepted Hall's invitation and returned to London to immerse himself in a project that would lead him—and the RSC—to a place of eminence in world theater. Barton-the-playwright flew home to script *The Wars of the Roses*.

2

"Feats of Broils and Arms":
The Wars of the Roses (1963) and *The Henriad* (1964)

As the Royal Shakespeare Company prepared for its fourth season in the winter of 1963, press releases from the Royal Shakespeare Theatre prompted more than a little curiosity among the news media. Peter Hall announced that he and Barton were restructuring the *Henry VI* cycle into two plays that would join *Richard III* in a "new" trilogy called *The Wars of the Roses*. The January 25, 1963, issue of *Stratford-upon-Avon Herald* dutifully reported Hall's bold plan and added that "an academic of no mean brilliance" would be the RSC's "consulting surgeon on the plays."[1] The anticipation of seeing the chronicle unfold again was clouded by reservations about an "adaptation."

Barton and Hall had first discussed a definitive production of the *Henry VI* plays during their undergraduate days at Cambridge. Barton, Hall remembers, "spoke from the first of a perceptive analysis of power and the inevitable corruption of politicians."[2] When Hall assumed the artistic directorship at Stratford, the two renewed plans for a staging of the trilogy. Hall first asked Peter Brook to direct them, but Brook refused—"not because he disliked the material, but because he thought it needed three years of detailed work" (ix). Two years later, Hall again asked Brook to head the project; Brook again refused and suggested that Hall himself chair the production.[3]

Confronted with the dual problems of establishing a new theater and those of a director challenged by three of Shakespeare's least-known works, Hall sought help from his Cambridge colleague. Each was assigned tasks as the project began, but soon lines of responsibility became blurred: "In general John Barton provided a formidable literary technique and an astonishing ability to write pastiche early Shakespearean verse, and I provided the interpretation, the *raison d'être*. But our collaboration was so close that in detail it would be impossible for either of us to remember who thought of what" (ix).

If the four plays were to be presented as a cohesive unit, then drastic textual work had to precede production. Hall and Barton, realizing the enormity of

their undertaking—which Hall calls "the ultimate literary heresy" (vii)—
placated their misgivings by offering four rationales for their boldness:

1. *the quality of the originals* . . ."[4] Hall, who had seen the originals performed twice,[5] believed that the plays would not work in unadapted form; he
remembered them being "a mass of angry and undifferentiated barons, thrash-
ing about in a mass of diffuse narrative" (vii). Barton cited the "dreadfully
uneven quality" of the trilogy, noting their mass of "dramatic deadwood,
cliches, and inconsistencies."[6] He emphasized, however, that such notions
should not serve as "the chief justification for our adaptation."

2. *"the extent to which the plays are Shakespeare's* . . ."* (Barton, xxii).
Barton provided a scholarly analysis of theories that Shakespeare may not have
been the sole author of the *Henry VI* trilogy. The evidence as argued by, among
others, J. Dover Wilson *(The New Cambridge Shakespeare)* and A. S.
Cairncross *(The New Arden Shakespeare)* left Baron "increasingly doubtful
whether the *Henry VIs* are wholly Shakespeare" (xxiii). Barton believed that
the original texts were playing versions hastily put together by Shakespeare,
perhaps to link them with *Richard III:*

> I believe that Shakespeare's revision was fitful, pragmatic, and hasty, and that
> the result is not something of which he would have claimed "this cycle is
> more or less as I want it," but rather "it will serve." Consequently, I regard
> our adaptation not as an improvement of absolute Shakespeare but as a
> further revision of only partly revised originals (xxiv).

The argument is a variation on the "continuous copy" theory that Barton
frequently cites as justification for his alterations, maintaining that an
Elizabethan or Jacobean play was not necessarily a set thing, but "a changeable
commodity which often had a complex stage history" (xxiii). A given text—and
the three parts of *Henry VI* are prime examples—could be altered according to
various theatrical, literary, or political pressures. Barton recounts an incident
from the RSC experience with *The Wars of the Roses* as a practical example of
the phenomenon of continuous copy: when publishing the text of their working script, Barton and Hall came across lines that Shakespeare had not written
and neither—they thought—had Barton. Barton suspects the lines evolved
from a rehearsal in which an actor needed a few lines, which were made up on
the spot.[7]

3. *The desire to stage the Henry VIs and Richard III as a cycle.* Hall believes
that the four plays were "almost certainly conceived as a cycle. It is likely that
the success of the first part compelled sequels . . ." (xii). Hall based his assumption on the construction of *Richard III,* whose focus on a single character
indicates a different attitude towards playwriting than the *Henry* plays, which
lack a central focus.[8]

4. *"response to theatrical pressure* . . ."* (Barton, xv). If the cycle was to be
presented in repertory, Hall and Barton agreed that the three Henry plays must

be condensed into two evenings' work: "We wanted people to see the whole *Wars of the Roses* cycle, which would have been difficult if we had not compressed the four plays into three." The producers soon found that cutting did not adequately solve the dramatic problems, which led Barton "to knock the text about" much more than he had first envisioned.[9]

Barton and Hall were governed by more than artistic pressures: like most producers, they were confronted by economic demands that precluded the young company from presenting three of the lesser-known plays in a season. Necessarily, the four plays had to be condensed because "to have performed the three *Henry VI* plays as they stand was out of the question" (xv–xvi). J. C. Trewin dismisses such notions from the RSC directors: "Four sessions are by no means too long. Some of us have met the three parts of *Henry VI* staged at full length . . . without feeling we have lost any shred of meaning, political or human."[10]

Hall and Barton may have had other reasons for altering the texts. Thematically, the two directors read the plays as "an intricate pattern of retribution, of paying for sins, misjudgments, and misgovernments."[11] These are themes that stir Barton and have stimulated his most recent work, particularly his "myth." Barton recalls that it was intended that *The Wars of the Roses* should be "more politically oriented than the original plays." To that end, Barton invented a number of lines to heighten these political themes. For instance, late in *Richard III* Barton added a speech, spoken by Rivers to Ratcliffe, that precisely addresses the themes defined by Hall:

> Thou are no more than fortune's instrument;
> And though thou seest thyself disposing death,
> Thy own disposing shall be like to mine.
> Yet take we both the self-same comfort now
> That howsoe'er a curse may breed and breed,
> Yet at the last it needs must spend itself.
> When all the roses in this ravag'd land
> Are plucked out, and every proud man slain,
> Then at the last this dreadful storm may cease
> And, fury spent, this England may have peace.[12]

Hall and Barton were cognizant of the magnitude of their undertaking. Hall stresses their culpability in his introduction to the published text of *The Wars of the Roses*: "If this adaptation has made a fool of anybody, it is not Shakespeare, but Barton and Hall. We have consciously joined the despised ranks of the men who knew better than Shakespeare" (vii). Seventeen years after his work on this adaptation, Hall recanted his actions:

> I wouldn't do it now. I believe we cut Shakespeare in quite a horrifying way. We don't know how to do it. You don't cut Wagner, Mozart, but you fill in Shakespeare and say "He didn't know what he was doing. . . ."[13]

Asked if he shared Hall's regret about the "horrifying" treatment of the *Henry VI* cycle, Barton replied, "No, I think much more one can knock about and adapt things than Peter does . . . I would certainly stand by my version."[14]

Barton began his "version" in the fall of 1962. His first draft, which consisted primarily of trimmed versions of Shakespeare's material, led him to write quasi-Shakespearean sections: "I soon found that normal linear cutting not only left the plays still too long, but presented us with new problems. Inconsistencies in plot became more noticeable, and the agglomeration of battle scenes worried us more and more" (xvi). By January the "rewrite" was held up when Barton accompanied *The Hollow Crown* to New York. Originally, he intended to complete a second draft between shows, but bronchitis and the demands of performance deterred his progress. Hall called Barton home to London, where he worked twelve hours a day slashing and rewriting. Each evening the two met to review Barton's daily work in anticipation of approaching rehearsals for the production: "Peter and I talked things over and then I went off and wrote some stuff and took it along like a dog with a bone and got Peter's reactions. Most of the solutions were mine, but Peter would make comments about what was needed or not needed."[15]

Barton found the reshaping more challenging than the rewriting. He did not consciously attempt to "ape Shakespeare's style, but to fill out what we took to be his thematic thinking . . . it is not really a piece of Shakespearean pastiche. Its wording provides, I hope, a reasonable simulation of what might be found in an Elizabethan play in the early 1590s—something which is not particularly difficult to achieve" (xxv). In 1975 Barton, discussing his controversial revision of *King John* on the BBC, clarified what he meant by a "reasonable simulation" of early Elizabethan style:

> Early in his career, Shakespeare was simply writing in an idiom that a lot of Elizabethan playwrights might have used, which is why a lot of scholars have thought that, in *Henry VI*, maybe, the hand of other playwrights like Peele and Kyd might be found. Shakespeare hadn't, in those early plays, in all the bits that I reworked, come out with an individual authentic voice. It is not all that difficult to do a pastiche of that sort of dramatic language that Elizabethan playwrights in general might have used around the early 1590s. What would be totally impossible would be to capture the style of Shakespeare once he actually got going.[16]

Though Barton's rewrites were remarkably disciplined, he occasionally wrote elaborate passages typical of the early Elizabethans; Hall kept a rein on Barton's literary enthusiasm.[17] Barton nonetheless enjoyed the heady experience of juxtaposing his words with Shakespeare's: "I enjoyed doing it in such a way that nobody would know where the joints were."[18] Hall, by the way, once objected to a passage of "pure Barton," and Barton defended himself, wondering whether he had indeed composed the passage in question. Hall told him not to be silly. To be sure, they looked up the disputed passage: Barton had in fact *not* written the lines; Shakespeare had.[19]

A Shakespeare-*cum*-Barton acting edition was finally delivered to the assembled RSC cast. Though it would change in rehearsals, it represented "one of the most drastic revisions of Shakespeare since the time of the Restoration."[20] Four plays had been reduced to three; some sixty characters had been cut or absorbed into others; of Shakespeare's original 12,350 lines in the four plays, only 6,006 remained, supplemented by 1,440 of Barton's devising—a total of 7,450 lines for the acting edition.[21]

Though there have been academic attempts to analyze Barton's revised edition,[21] the most effective analysis remains Barton's own summary of the "specific considerations" he and Hall sought to accomplish during that winter of 1963:

1. *"Our wish to make each play as much of a whole as possible . . ."* (Barton: xxi). Condensing three plays into two required reshaping the action into dramatic units, each with its own character, themes, and narrative builds. Barton restructured the narrative elements of the three *Henry VIs*—the war with the French and Talbot's heroism, Gloucester's protectorship, Henry's ineffectual reign, the rise of Queen Margaret, the rift between the houses of York and Lancaster, Henry's fall, Edward's rise, and the emergence of Richard of Gloucester—into two plays. The first he titled *Henry VI* and used materials from *1 Henry VI* through 3.3 of *2 Henry VI*—the death of Winchester. Thus the play was less about Talbot and the French wars and more about the plot against Humphrey and the nobles' ploy to weaken Henry's monarchy. One critic subtitled the play "team picking,"[23] an apt description since Barton emphasized the alliance of the English barons who seek power in the wake of Henry V's death. Furthermore, the Cardinal's deathbed accusation to Henry (sc. 25) indicates that England is doomed to chaos. Barton was originally concerned that the scene of the Cardinal's death lacked "organic importance" to sustain the theme he envisioned for the first play of the new trilogy: ". . . self-seeking and wickedness breed guilt in the doer and rejection by other people" (xiii). The Cardinal's accusation, injected by Barton, provided a clearly defined moment of recognition; Henry's response—"I thought for all the best"—pointed the action toward the second play, which dealt with the young king's guilt and fall.

The great irony of the trilogy's action is that Henry's "saintliness" precipitates the evil of England's tragic civil wars. Barton felt that Henry's role was poorly defined, and he outlined the problem in a memo to Hall:

His saintliness is only a label, and his weakness an uninteresting fact, not explored dramatically in the way that, say, Richard II's weakness is explored. He is not complex, merely wet. He would become more interesting if we gave him a definite line of development throughout the play (xviii).

The adaptation focused on Henry's growth from a naive, unconfident monarch who relies too heavily on the counsel of self-serving lords to one who courageously banishes Suffolk. Henry's growth is charted in a series of Barton-constructed lines that define his naiveté, increasing awareness, and maturity:

(To Gloucester:)
But I have read in many holy books
Self-will is sin and much displeaseth heaven.

(Sc. 6)

(To Gloucester:)
Young though I am, my lord, the time is come
That I must choose and act for mine own self.
If I am King, then I must act the King.

(Sc. 17)

(To Margaret:)
Henceforth I will be deaf to any pleading.
My loving Gloucester bade me be a King,
Which I, too weak and foolish, did avoid:
Now, by my oath and by my hallow'd crown,
I will uphold my conscience and my will.

(Sc. 23)

The second part of the Barton trilogy—*Edward IV*—was more diffuse than the first since it illustrated the carnage resulting from Henry's malfeasance. It depicted the intimate battles in Henry's household; thus Margaret's role was enlarged to show her contempt for marriage to a weak husband. The Cade rebellion (transposed by Barton to align it more logically with the civil wars and to keep it from distracting from the climax of Winchester's deathbed scene) and the bloody wars of the York and Lancaster factions enabled *Edward IV* to illustrate the curse on the House of Lancaster invoked by the Bishop of Carlisle at the end of *Richard II:*

O, if you rear this house against this house,
It will the woefullest division prove
That ever fell upon this cursed earth.

(4.1.145–47)

The curse reaches its culmination with the ascendence of Richard, duke of Gloucester. The emphasis on slaughter in the second play made Richard's emergence as the evil consequence of the misdeeds of Richard II, Bolingbroke, and Henry VI seem more natural.

Of the two plays, *Henry VI* was more favorably received by critics:

Politically the first play is of greater interest than the second, where the complexities of court factions give way to a series of bloody campaigns. In *Edward IV* one also loses sight of Henry, a far more absorbing figure than the beef-witted sensualist Edward.[24]

Kenneth Tynan concurred, noting that the first play was "a subtler diversion," while the second was mainly "carnage and cutlery."[25]

Barton did little more than trim *Richard III* to permit its excessive length to fit more compatibly with the design of the trilogy. He added passages that referred to events in the *Henry VI cycle* and created the role of Princess Elizabeth, whose marriage to Richmond helped unify the warring families.

To compress the action of *Henry VI* Barton deleted a number of scenes, including:

—Joan's seduction of Burgundy away from the English cause (1, 3.3). Barton did, however, write lines to account for his defection; these are found in scenes 8 and 9.
—The subsequent apparition of fiends appearing to Joan.
—Talbot's encounter with the countess of Auvergne (1, 2.3).
—Suffolk's bargaining for Margaret's hand (1, 5.3).
—The court scene in which Gloucester's wife has her ears boxed by the Queen (2, 2.3).
—The rustic banter between the Armorer and Peter Thump (2, 2.3).

Other than repositioning the Cade rebellion, the most significant alteration Barton made from the design of the original was Suffolk's death. Shakespeare has him killed at sea by Walter Whitman; Barton dispatches Margaret's lover in a street brawl at the hands of a trio of citizens. Barton explained his choice: ". . . the original scene was too long to be included in a compressed version of the plays. It would have delayed and weakened the theatrical climax of the concluding scene in Winchester's bedchamber."[26]

2. ". . . *scenes of baronial brawling are set in the context of meetings at the council-board. . .*" (xxi).

Barton, "at the risk of historical anachronism," deleted references to Parliament to focus on encounters between the nobles: "I have made Gloucester set up a machinery of government which is ultimately used against him because of the King's weakness." The sixth scene of the Hall-Barton script—108 of the scene's 168 lines are Barton's—initiates this revision. Gloucester explains his revolutionary democratic idea to the assembled lords:

> When we are met upon with some troubled question,
> Let us resolve it by our general voice:
> And when the matter hath been given vent
> Let the opinion of the greater part

> Be straight upheld, and those that are outvoic'd
> Yield their intents unto the general.
>
> (Sc. 6)

Warwick responds: "In faith, it is a pleasing policy." Scholars and critics did not find it as "pleasing"—or at least a Shakespearean policy. Kenneth Muir argued that "it seems quite wrong to introduce the unhistorical principle of a majority vote on the King's council,"[27] and an anonymous critic for *The Times* objected to Barton's revision of medieval history: ". . . to substitute semi-Brechtian machinery amounts to plain literary fraud."[28] Barton adamantly denies any Brechtian ideological intent in his or the production's work: ". . . it would have appalled Brecht. In our moral, historical, or philosophical interpretation of the action we did not take a Brechtian view. He would have violently repudiated Shakespeare's historical vision."[29]

3. *"We inserted a number of cross-references . . . and linking passages. . ."* (xxi).

Barton identifies his major cross-reference as "the use of the council-table throughout the trilogy. This was the key production point, more obvious in the theatre than in the text itself" (xix). Though there is no printed record of where Barton and Hall received their inspiration for the table as the symbolic linchpin for their production, it is possible that the idea came from Jan Kott's discussion of power politics in the first chapter of *Shakespeare Our Contemporary*. Entitled "The Kings," the chapter analyzes the history plays in terms of a "Grand Mechanism": the hate, lust and violence of political man that "transforms the executioner into a victim, and the victim into an executioner."[30] Kott theorizes that Shakespeare did not deal with the Grand Mechanism as something abstract:

> . . . in Shakespeare's plays the struggle for power is always stripped of all mythology, shown in its "pure state." It is a struggle for the crown between people who have a name, a title, and power . . . for Shakespeare power has names, eyes, mouth and hands. It is a *relentless struggle of living people who sit together at one table* (8; italics added).

If the Hall-Barton concept for the council table was not a direct outgrowth of Kott's idea, it nonetheless emerged as its powerful realization in theatrical terms. Barton acknowledges that the council table was intended to heighten the political themes of the play that fascinated him and Hall.

Kott influenced the production in other ways. Hall, who qualfies his enthusiasm for *Shakespeare Our Contemporary* by noting that it "has the disadvantage of sometimes moving very far away from the text," read a proof copy of the book while en route to Stratford for the first rehearsal of *The Wars of the Roses*:

His analysis of the staircase of power in the histories was a great support to our production. His political thinking, which is essentially continental . . . expressed something current in Shakespearean appreciation (xi).

Barton claims not to have read Kott before his work on the production, and further notes that as codirector, "I didn't think about it at all."[31] Trevor Nunn, the RSC's artistic director, has since acknowledged the company's debt to Kott's ideas as they were manifest in *The Wars of the Roses.*[32]

Barton also found himself obliged to provide expository material to link the plays. *Edward IV* begins with two scenes (26 and 28) that effectively link the action of the first and second plays. These sequences represent "the most concentrated amount of new material in the whole version" (xvii).

It was also necessary for Barton to devise linking passages at the beginning of *Richard II:* the first two plays were organized to segue naturally into the Crookback's drama. Some critics felt *Richard III* was thus reduced, despite Barton's careful planning to link the action of the plays. Gareth Lloyd Evans, for one, felt "the flaw of the adaptation" became apparent when *Richard III* was spliced to the *Henry VI*'s, however cunning the revision:

> The cubbish Gloucester . . . fails utterly to become the witty, hypnotic, elemental danger of Shakespeare's play. . . . The wooing of Anne, the deceiving of Clarence, the deception of the citizens of London—in short all the incredible victories of Richard—become more credible.[33]

Further clarifying passages were needed for deleted characters, shifts in time and locale, and clarification of character titles, alternames, and relationships of characters unfamiliar to audiences unversed in English history. Hodgdon's *Jahrbuch* study of Barton's revisions summarizes the links found in *The Wars of the Roses:* the use of kingship epithets, clarifying pronoun references, changing verb tenses to the present, and devising transitional introductions.[34]

4. "*. . . to remove as many minor characters as possible . . . to carry over important characters from play to play . . .*" (xxi).

To modern audiences the plethora of nobles named after English counties can be confusing under the best of circumstances. Hence, Barton excised lesser nobles, clerics, minor politicos, and commoners, while combining others (e.g., John Hume, John Southwell, Sir Robert Brakenbury and the Keeper of the Tower simply became the Lieutenant of the Tower). By focusing on the prominent characters who move the action, Barton's edition has greater clarity and cohesion, though there is a liability to such revisions: when the "little people" are deleted, one loses the sense that the powerful are supported by lesser beings whose complicity makes a significant contribution to "the Grand Mechanism." Though purists may question Barton's emendations, Stratford audiences, in the main, were thankful for the clarifications.

5. *"We stressed the political and economic heritage left by Henry V..."* (xxi).

The opening sequence of Barton's *Henry VI* found a number of lords gathered around the casket of the dead monarch, talking in conspiratorial tones in the flickering light of the bier's candles. The play's first words were not Shakespeare's, nor were they Barton's. Over the theater's loudspeaker came the voice of Henry V, reading from his will, a document found in Hall's *Chronicles*:

> ...since I now shall be taken from you, I charge you all to render your allegiance unto my son, King Henry the Sixth. (Sc. 1)

The will defines the Protectorate of Humphrey and the roles assigned to Bedford and the duke of Burgundy. When *The Wars of the Roses* was added to the *Henriad* in 1964, the addition of the will reading from Hall's *Chronicles* became an effective link between the two tetralogies. Barton and Hall also stressed the Henry V legacy "so that the French scenes in our *Henry V* should relate more firmly to one of the main themes in the whole cycle, the Curse on the House of Lancaster" (xxi). Barton's fifth scene best illustrates this choice: Bedford expresses his qualms about the ambition of certain English lords and then speaks Barton's lines to foreshadow events to come:

> Such mutiny and division is to come,
> That England's grass will smother up our graves
> And lime will long consume our rotten bones
> Ere these divisions be resolv'd and spent.

Bedford's prophecy echoes the Bishop of Carlisle's speech, and was doubtless inspired by images from Carlisle's "curse" in *Richard II* (4.1.136ff).

6. I *"tried here and there to bring the idea [i.e., misused sanction words] more in the open"* (xxi).

Hall remembers that in the years since he and Barton first talked about the contemporary implications of the history plays, he became "more and more fascinated by the contortions of politicians, and by the corrupting seductions experienced by anybody who wields power" (x). Hall collected sanctions— words, phrases, platitudes that governmental leaders used in the media to camouflage party politics or unwieldy ambitions: "not in the public interest"; "the taxpayer's money"; "the country is not ready for it"; and "let me say quite frankly...–" Shakespeare's political leaders were not strangers to such phrase-making: "God's will"; "Fortune"; "by Saint George"; and "The common Weal" abounded. Hall found in his discovery a key to unlocking the relevance of the *Henry VI* cycle:

> What had seemed like conventional rhetoric was really, when spoken by Warwick or Richard III, an ironic revelation of the time-honoured practices

of politicians. I realized that the mechanism of power had not changed in centuries (xi).

Barton, too, was struck by the dramatic potential of sanctions. Although he liked their irony, he felt they read "much of the time as crude bombast" (xxi) and fashioned simpler versions of his own. A key example concludes scene 18; it is spoken by Hume, who justifies his betrayal of Eleanor:

> Methinks these naughty times
> Do breed a kind of honesty in knaves:
> I that betray her grace betray a traitor;
> And yet I yield her to a pair of traitors
> Whose gold's more treacherous than the other's gilt.
> And yet again these lofty traitors tell me
> They do their treasons on the King's behalf:
> They swear 'tis so; should I suspect their oaths?
> I dare not do't. What, that serve the crown,
> and am well serv'd with crowns for my good service?
> Then let this business go what way it will.

8. ". . .*the plotting between York and Warwick which prepared the way for The Wars of the Roses should be carefully placed* (xxi).

Shakespeare does not, of course, provide an intimate encounter between York and Warwick. In act 2, scene 2, of *2 Henry VI* there is a meeting among Salisbury, Warwick, and York that ends with Warwick telling York:

> My heart assures me that the Earl of Warwick
> Shall one day make the Duke of York a King.
>
> (2.2.78–79)

From this brief encounter Barton devised a fully developed scene (sc. 16, at the interval of the play) comprised of extracts from five different Shakespearean scenes; it is among the most inventive and effective of Barton's revisions, particularly because it creates an impressive climax to the first movement of the trilogy. It invests York with a potency that is immediately comprehensible to the audience. More important, it strengthens and clarifies the role of Warwick.

Throughout the first two plays Barton composed passages to enhance Warwick's role as king-maker; the most telling is found in scene 26 (which, significantly, opens *Edward IV*). Alone on stage after a council scene, Warwick watches Henry VI depart. The speech, with four lines appropriated from the lieutenant in Suffolk's death scene (*2 Henry VI*, 4.1.95–98) is Barton's:

> Heaven preserve thee in thine innocence!
> And yet methinks it will be shook anon.
> For if Jack Cade, whom I myself did raise,

> Thrive not in this, I'll rouse Plantagenet.
>   For [*Shakespeare's lines:*]
>   Now the house of York, thrust from the crown
>   By lofty proud encroaching tyranny,
>   Burns with revenging fire, whose hopeful colours
>   Advance his half-fac'd sun, striving to shine:
>   [*resume Barton:*]
>   Twas I that made thy spring, and now thy summer
>   Shall flourish by my means and my direction.
>   Then since I may no longer sway the Council,
>   'Tis swords must now uphold my policies.
>   Then, York, be King and proper as you may
>   Whate'er befalls, 'tis I shall bear the sway.

Later (sc. 45), Clarence greets Warwick: "Thanks, mighty lord, that makes and unmakes kings." Warwick's clearly defined position gives the plays a firmer ground on which to rest their diverse strands of action.

9. "*. . . to stress and clarify the importance of young Princess Elizabeth in Richard III*" (xxii).

Though Shakespeare did not include Princess Elizabeth in his version, Hall and Barton agreed that their telling of the bloody epic needed her presence "to bring out the historical and thematic point that her marriage with Richmond defined the reconciliation of York and Lancaster . . ." (Barton, xxii). Barton bolstered the Princess's significance by adding a speech by the Bishop of Ely in scene 66 (cf. *Richard III*, 4.1); he speaks to the Earl of Darby:

>   . . . go sound Elizabeth
>   Tell her, the fearful cause of all our sorrows
>   Is the unnatural and bloody strife
>   'Twixt York and Lancaster and haughty Woodville:
>   Which foul division may not be resolv'd
>   But by regrafture of these houses' blood
>   Through marriage betwixt Richmond and her daughter.

As a general rule (Hall's), Barton did not try to match Shakespeare's excellence as a composer: his alterations and additions were factual rather than evocative. He merely enlarged upon Shakespearean images, the most notable example of which occurs in scene 25, the conclusion of *Henry VI.* Margaret, using Barton's words, laments Suffolk's death:

>   . . . His beauty fang'd, his body torn assunder,
>   As if a pack of wolves had savag'd him.

King Henry responds, again in Barton's words:

>   My wolves, my wolves: for I did make them so.

Shakespeare had earlier used the image of wolves (2, 3.1.191–92: "Thus is the shepherd beaten from thy side / And wolves are gnarling who shall gnaw thee first." Barton was consistent with Shakespeare's design *and* one of Hall's thematic preoccupations:

> The new men—the Yorks, the Warwicks, the Buckinghams, the Somersets, and the Suffolks—are ruthless and hypocritical. . . . These new men team up in packs in order to fight, just as wolves unite to hunt. The instinct of the pack is only assuaged by the *destruction* of the rival pack; if you don't destroy it, it will destroy you.[35]

Elsewhere Barton borrowed images from other of Shakespeare's histories. The gardener's speech from *Richard II* (3.4.54ff) was echoed by Cade in scene 27:

> . . . I rather mean to weed you. Why think you we bear the bills and hooks and hoes? We are a sort of gardeners to the commonweal, and mean greater harm than weeding.

Hodgdon has charted Barton's images and found that of the twenty-six he devised, most paralleled Shakespeare's by repeating and varying figures of speech common to the basic texts. These images include: fortune's wheel, the phoenix, traps, hawking, cruelty, the summer sun, shipwreck, falling, gold, and biblical treason.

Actually, the heavy cutting of the script was accomplished largely through the deletion of poetic excesses by the young Shakespeare. Hence, Barton himself used imagery and poetic flights sparingly. Peggy Ashcroft remembers one passage in which Barton-the-would-be-playwright got the better of Barton-the-judicious-adapter. Originally, the passage was to have been spoken by the dying Bishop of Winchester as a climax to *Henry VI.* Hall cut the passage because it was too flamboyant, yet Ashcroft refers to Barton's invention as *"magnificent!"*[35] Ironically, the deleted line is likely the most quoted of Barton's inventions:

> A man's a dog, and dogs do crave a master (xi).

Whatever their reservations about revising Shakespearean texts, the critics were generally impressed with the quality of Barton's literary efforts. Felix Barker suggested that—on the whole—Barton's revision stands as "a case of improving Shakespeare without disturbing the essentials or tampering with the finest passages."[37]

Predictably, not everyone shared Barker's enthusiasm. In November 1964 the Manchester *Guardian* hosted a debate, moderated by Gareth Lloyd Evans, between Barton and Kenneth Muir, who represented the scholarly world. The question for resolution was "How far can we cut Shakespeare?" Muir summarized the major academic objections to the adaptation:

I don't object to cuts of passages which a modern audience would not understand. . . . I don't even object on principle to *adapting* the plays. . . . But when we look at the adaptations of previous centuries, it is obvious that they have so far been inferior to the originals; and it is rather improbable that where Dryden failed a modern producer will succeed. . . . I suppose there is some excuse for adapting *Henry VI*, since here, if anywhere, we might hope to improve on Shakespeare's prentice work. But the adaptations, though skillfully done, seemed to me less effective on the stage than the straight production of the three plays at Birmingham.

Barton countered with variations of the aforementioned rationales.

Though the adaptation prompted much debate and controversy, there was nearly unanimous praise for its mounted production. The editorial page of *The Times* (London), as well as its arts pages, heralded the RSC's accomplishments: "This enterprise, neither a pious gesture nor a theatrical stunt, ranks as the current Stratford regime's greatest service to Shakespeare so far."[38] That paper's Sunday critic, Harold Hobson (with whom Barton would have less favorable encounters in the ensuing years), declared, "I doubt if anything as valuable has ever been done for Shakespeare in the whole previous history of the world's stage."[39] Allowing for journalistic hyperbole, Hobson's enthusiasm was typical of the praise to the stagings of *The Wars* cycle.

Hall and Barton were assisted by Frank Evans. The size of the project precluded the possibility of one man handling the demands of staging three plays—seven the following year (when Clifford Williams and Peter Wood, another Cambridge alumnus, joined the directorial consortium). Actually, Barton was not intended to be among the directors at the outset, but Hall, exhausted from the rigors of running the RSC's Stratford and London theaters, collapsed and was bedridden for several weeks. With some pride, Barton remembers that the actors asked him to fill Hall's role[40]—thus liberating him from the onus of *l'affaire shrew*. Barton identifies some of the tasks for which he had primary responsibility: "I did the Bosworth scene in *Richard III* and the council scenes. I did all the French scenes in *Henry VI*, and I was always allocated all the battle scenes."[41] Barton's proficiency at staging fights made him the obvious choice for fight choreographer. His battle scenes were singled out in many reviews for their excellence: "All the battle scenes, of which there are a great number . . . are brilliantly handled. Fight after fight seems different from the one before, with perhaps the crown going to a magnificent two-handed sword duel between York and the elder Clifford."[42]

According to Williams, who worked on the 1964 revival of *The Wars* and the new productions of the *Henriad*, Barton played another central role: "John Barton had been very instrumental in formulating the concepts and ideas, but acted very often as a—how can I put it?—a 'contrary spirit.'"[43] Barton scrutinized the "undertext" of the plays to explore all their shades of meaning and cajole his directing partners into seeing the myriad possibilities. Hall then gave Barton's subtexts "breath" with "simple explanations to the actors couched in modern phrases, urging them to find the truth in their *own* reactions."⁴⁴

The directorial team was determined to countermand the romantic design and playing style associated with Shakespeare's histories. Kott's postwar view that "the action takes place on earth, the cruellest of planets, and among men, who are more cruel than beasts" precluded the possibility of the lush, banner-waving patriotism of Olivier's midwar *Henry V.* The RSC turned to Brecht's theater for a model on which they could make strong political statements in the context of an antiromantic, antiillusionistic style. Barton, though admittedly influenced by Brecht's Berliner Ensemble (see chapter 1 and the discussion of *The Days of the Commune*), denies a Brechtian ideology in the production. The RSC's playing style was indeed influenced by the German, who, like the young English company, reacted to a romantic, rhetorical mode of acting.⁴⁵ The Brechtian technique was not embraced by all observers, particularly Lloyd Evans: "I . . . object to any attempt to show that Shakespeare is like Brecht or Beckett. I thought all the plays suffered from an infusion of Brecht."⁴⁵

The directors and designer John Bury sought a sparse, physical image for the production. They found it, according to Hall, in Bury's rendering of a "cruel, harsh world of decorated steel, cold and dangerous. The armory of Warwick Castle was our inspiration" (xi). Bury, who had worked at Joan Littlewood's Theatre Workshop (where Brechtian methods were used liberally), explains the use of steel images for the production: "It was a period of armour and a period of the sword: they were plays about warfare, about power, about danger . . . And this was the image of the plays. We wanted an image rather than naturalistic surroundings . . . we were trying to make a world: a dangerous world, a terrible world, in which all these happenings fit."⁴⁷

The finished set was covered with steel plates; on either side of the stage were *periaktoi* that could be turned to suggest different locales and to modify the playing area. A large-scale map of France filled the background when the action shifted across the channel. A huge metallic wall, with descending grills, dominated the upstage area; in its center were oversize double doors that "slice into or grip the action like the cruel jaws of a vice."⁴⁸ The entire set could be swung offstage for battle scenes, which were then played against the blackness of the proscenium opening. J. C. Trewin noted the multisensory effectiveness of Bury's sparse design: "All is stern, metallic and ringing. The stage is wide and bare, a sounding board for fierce words and fierce deeds."⁴⁹

Two props dominated the set: the council table, of which much has been said, and an oversized throne on a dias that was run on and off the stage by a system of tracks. One critic noted the throne was "oddly contemporary yet not without the dignity of history. It would have graced Coventry Cathedral or the Shell Building."⁵⁰ During the battlefield scenes, there was a large hand-pulled cart, gray and cold-looking, reminiscent of Mother Courage's traveling canteen.

John Bury also designed the costumes and carried the metallic images into the

clothing of these pawns of history. He sought a "timelessness" to deromanticize the period, but judged his efforts a failure. His description of the eventual
solution also reflects key Barton attitudes about costuming:

> What we try to do now is to remain true to the period silhouette, but by use
> of tailoring techniques, choice of materials, modern parallels, to reduce the
> historical identity down to essentials and to create a costume which is truly
> functional in telling us as much as possible about the wearer. . . . The image
> must be precise and organic.[51]

The costumes were muted, blue and bronze in color. They became rusted,
ripped, more disheveled and blood-spattered as the cycle progressed. York's
rise to power was suggested by a blazing gold costume. Richard and his henchmen were dressed in black leather with metallic studs befitting their sinister
presence. The nobles carried oversized swords—constant visual reminders of
the awesome power they wielded. If the RSC directors wanted the visual
elements to eradicate memories of "pretty" Shakespeare, Bury's designs accomplished the task efficiently; furthermore, they established a trend in RSC
productions that has lasted until the 1980s.

It is likely the production's performance accomplishments would not have
been as successful without the longterm training begun at the RSC Actors'
Studio in the winter of 1960. The acting style reflected the design elements:
sparse, highly selective, antiromantic, yet robust and lifelike. Robert Speaight,
a prominent Shakespearean actor turned theater critic, noted that the
framework established by the directors allowed the actors to move with ease:
"The right balance was struck between baronial brawling and intelligible
speech. These were tough customers and they talked toughly."[52]

The company invented business illustrating—too explicitly, some would
say—that the age about which Shakespeare wrote was not one of fluttering
banners, shining armor, or sanctimonious chivalry. It was chaos that the production highlighted: Clifford's corpse was mercilessly stabbed by York's sons,
decapitated on stage, and the head tossed like a football before being impaled
on a pike; murderers were strapped to a medieval torture wheel, and severed
heads decorated Richard's wall.[53] Clarence was drowned in the malmsey-butt
on stage, rather than off, as the words of Shakespeare's text suggest. Perhaps
the most graphic scene was Margaret's taunting of captured York: she dipped a
paper in the blood of York's son, fashioned the bloody napkin into a crown,
and placed it on his head. As she said "Was it you would be England's King?"
she drove a sword through his chest. Speaight called the moment "a masterpiece of theatrical invention."

The production's ultimate strength was the company's ability to humanize
the participants in history's drama. From king to soldier, the RSC actors etched
characterizations that showed individual and collective ambition, as well as the

grief that plagued England's cursed country. Lloyd Evans wrote that "the concentration on personages rather on historial ambience" gave the plays a "sharp immediacy . . . and heightened interest in characters who are all too often lost in the limbo of historicality."[54]

Though Dame Peggy Ashcroft was perhaps the RSC's only *bona fide* "star" as production rehearsals commenced, several actors emerged as important figures on the English stage. David Warner achieved international prominence while playing the delicate and monkish Henry VI. Casting a relative unknown in this pivotal role represented a major interpretative decision by the directors. Warner, a lanky, craggy-faced actor, was ideally suited to the role of the awkward monarch. He and his directors fashioned one of Shakespeare's least interesting kings into a near tragic figure whose inability to rule wisely leads England to chaos. This was best illustrated at Henry's death: as Richard of Gloucester stabbed Henry, he planted an ironic kiss on the monarch's bare head. Henry returned the kiss to the future king—a loving embrace of forgiveness. It was also a "kiss of death" and reinforced Hall's program essay, "Blood Will Have Blood." No moment in the trilogy better captured the directors' vision.

The production's other inspired casting was Ian Holm as Richard III. Small of stature, Holm's physique naturally scaled down the crookback's size and gargantuan propensity for evil. He seemed still the little boy seeking the paper crown in the Barton-written scene (34) in *Edward IV;* this child of violence saw murder as just another game. Holm's interpretation made Richard seem "not the splendid machiavellian entertainer of stage tradition . . . but embodying in his own anarchic self a judgment on the country he rules."[55]

The one role to appear throughout the Barton-revised trilogy is Margaret. One of the great services of the RSC project was that it enabled audiences to trace Margaret's development from a shy French maid to an adulterous and ambitious wife to a battlefield gorgon to an embittered old woman—"the embodiment of the curse which is one of the themes of the plays."[56] The role demanded a protean actress of great skill, and Ashcroft's Margaret was the most universally admired performance by production commentators.

On August 22 and 31, September 5 and 14, and October 5, 1963 (as well as five occasions in London in 1964), the trilogy was played in succession (with lunch and dinner intervals), a marathon of nine hours and fifty-five minutes. The enterprise was apparently the result of a "half-joking suggestion to Peter Hall . . . which was seized upon by him with delight."[57] While most critics, audiences, and actors were enthusiastic about the experience, there were reservations that define a liability of the Hall-Barton design: " . . . the effect is cumulatively deadening to the senses. *Richard III*, coming in the last three hours, does not lift up the heart: it sickens it, leads to a cynical shrugging. For a masterpiece of this length one seems to need an ending with catharsis."[58] The directors, however, might counter such criticism by noting that Shakespeare may not have intended catharsis as much as a warning that we must be ever-vigilant of men whose misgovernment would destroy our institutions. Hall's program note specifies the RSC's attitude towards an "uplifting" ending:

> All that Shakespeare finally gives us as a lesson of human experience is that at the end of any life, of any cycle of misery, selfishness, and destruction you can only hope to be left with a regenerative principle. A baby, for example; or Richmond founding a new dynasty; or the hope of young love marrying. The problems are not over, but life as a principle goes on.

Bouyed by the successes of 1963, the RSC forged plans to stage the *Richard II, Henry IV,* and *Henry V* tetralogy with *The Wars of the Roses* the following season as the RSC's contribution to the Shakespeare quadricentennial. Audiences could then see precisely how the murder of Richard II causally necessitated the bloody wars leading to the succession of Richard III a century later. Hobson's essay on the importance of the RSC project provides a context in which the *Henriad* fits logically into the design of *The Wars:* "[It] takes on a more cataclysmic significance. The deposition of Richard is seen . . . quite simply and unforgiveably, as a crime against God. . . . The dazzling feature of the Stratford season is the discovery and demonstration that Shakespeare believed as fervently as Claudel or Newman in a religion which . . . by the passion with which it is held, and the verbal glory which expresses it, is sustained upon the stage in an outrageous magnificence."[59]

Barton prepared texts for the *Henriad,* but, given the acknowledged quality of these scripts, found little reason for drastic alterations. He cut a number of lines but was strikingly conservative compared to his *Henry VI* excisions: *Richard II,* 327 lines (11 percent); *1 Henry IV,* 181 lines (6 percent); *2 Henry IV,* 603 lines (18 percent); and *Henry V,* 754 lines (23 percent).[60] Barton did little rewriting-composing and only slight restructuring of scenes (for example, in *Henry V,* the first 22½ lines of the Chorus' act 4 speech were placed before 3.7 to accommodate an interval after 3.6). To minimize the surfeit of lords, Barton permitted the Lord Cambridge to bear the entire conspiracy with the French against Henry; elsewhere Exeter absorbed the role of Warwick in *Henry V.* By and large, Barton and Hall stuck by the pledge they made when working on the *Henry VI* cycle not to tamper with mature Shakespeare.

John Bury's versatile sets, with the ubiquitous council table and iron-grated walls, were used for the four added plays. Because *Richard II* is of a texture different from any of the other works in the cycle, it was more embellished. Too, *Richard II* represents England before "the fall," and the artistic choice to bathe the production in sumptuous golds and whites proved an effective contrast to the darker hues of the ensuing dramas. The RSC program for *Richard II* contained extracts from conversations among the three directors that summarize the interpretation governing the design and thematic elements of the play:

Richard II is strongly medieval in character, an extended ritual. . . . Its nostalgic vision refers back through a strange, perpetual haze of legend and myth to a time of peace and plenty. . . . The profusion of images drawn from light, jewelry, astronomy and the bright colors of nature, the interplay of metaphor and rhyme, the flowing counterpoint of idea and form, reveal a beauty so poignant and acute that its dissolution is not only expected but welcomed.[61]

By beginning with a clearly defined "golden world," the triumvirate gave the seven plays a focus and direction. From *Richard II*'s white and gold finery to *Richard III*'s black leather, iron-studded livery, the septology effectively charted England's decline.

Of the four added plays to *The Wars* cycle, *Henry V* seems—on its surface—the least compatible. The RSC was confronted with not only its formidable stage history of chauvinistic pageantry, but also with the memory of Olivier's stirring film version made expressly to bolster English spirits during World War II. Shakespeare's jingoistic Chorus challenged the directors to find a proper niche within their schema without contorting the original. Hall's program note for the *Henry V* production offers their solution: " . . . the play is quite as much a criticism of the Chorus' view of the story. . . ."[62] Hall's essay was supplemented by a page of quotations entitled "Tudor Opinions on War," which emphasized the horrors of warfare that the RSC illustrated throughout the larger cycle. Trevor Nunn, Barton's assistant on the 1966 revival of the *Henriad*, looks back on the 1964 production to clarify the Hall-Barton-Williams thinking:

> I think our production pointed to a disparity between the role of the Chorus and the events actually contained within the play itself. It showed us the Chorus as an Elizabethan/High Renaissance figure speaking eloquently, confirming exciting myths and fictions for an audience: the events which were then revealed in the play were very different, more real, harder, cooler, more ambiguous.[63]

The costuming and setting established in *The Wars* cycle showed that Henry's soldiers were not the healthy, spirited troops of previous productions. The directors took quite literally Henry's description of his minions before the Battle of Agincourt: "Warriors for the working day" (4.3.109). Several critics commented on the Breughellike quality of the RSC soldiers. The Barton-staged battles emphasized the smoke, grime, the horrible sounds of war: swishing arrows, exploding cannons, the cries of the wounded, the confused shouts of frightened men were piped over the RST's sound system while men with pikes and banners moved across the darkened cavern upstage. Milton Shulman praised Barton's ingenuity: "The intelligent use of electronic sound effects and thunder-flashes did more to convey the battles of Harfleur and Agincourt than the orthodox mélée of sword play so often used on these histories."[64]

The plays are about more than armies, and again the combined productions' strength was founded on meticulously delineated characters. David Warner played Richard II, provocative casting given the strong similarities—as well as marked differences—between Richard II and Henry VI. Both are martyrs to others' ambition, and the death of each precipitates violent civil war. Somewhat untraditionally, Warner's was an introspective, philosophic, even self-destructive king. The directors' collective notes define Richard's tragedy as a self-knowledge that becomes increasingly perceptive and devastating: "The sick man cannot cure himself, but he knows his sickness." Nonetheless, critics were generally unsympathetic to this interpretation, calling it a modernistic, rather than medieval, approach: "It is hard to believe that such a King could endanger his country by his extravagant and foolish pride. Mr. Warner gives him too much sensibility and not enough eccentricity."[65]

Whatever Warner's shortcomings, he and his directors invested the drama with telling business to provide a context for the following plays. As Richard handed his crown to Bolingbroke—"On this side my hand, and on that side thine" (4.1.183)—he suddenly turned it upside down to connect it with the well and buckets of the following speech.[66] The ritual of passing the crown— here within a relatively civilized context—formed the through-line of the re-maining six plays, the last of which showed the barbaric appropriation of the crown.

The two parts of *Henry IV* are less about appropriating crowns than the passage from ignorance to knowledge by present and future kings. Thus the RSC emphasized the guilt of Henry IV, which is "fostered by the disturbance which plague the first years of his reign. . . . He emerges as a cold, lost man, devitalized, ill in mind and body, his own worst betrayer."[67] Among the distur-bances that plague the King is madcap Hal, played by Holm as a Hamletlike stranger to the court who, despite the surface gaiety of the tavern scenes, recognized that the time was out of joint, that he must set it right. Hotspur, whose superficial chivalry is rejected by Hal, was cogently, if unconvention-ally, analyzed by Barton in the *Guardian* debate:

> Our treatment of Hotspur can be paralleled with Redgrave's in 1951. This was a reaction against the romantic view of Hotspur. Many of the parts of *Henry IV* are examinations of figures of vanity in the medieval sense set against the true chivalry and on the side of Hal. . . . The old romantic view makes Hotspur a chivalric hero. It is true that he has enormous charm and panache, but he is an anarchic, glory-seeking mercenary. This is very much in the text, as is the sexual coarseness in both his scenes with his wife. (*Guardian*, November 26, 1964)

Barton here alludes to the sexually graphic leave-taking devised for Lord and Lady Percy—an action Muir found unbelievable: "The aristocratic Hotspur would not nearly copulate with his wife in the castle courtyard in the presence of servants." This was not the only Hotspur business to be questioned. He was killed in a farmyard fight by Hal; an ignominious death that ended quite literally in a pig trough, which, Barton explained, was intended "to stress the reality of war against the romantic fantasy which Hotspur had about it."

Hugh Griffith, in what several critics called a definitive performance,[68] played Falstaff, not as a romantic but as a reminder of what the good life at Eastcheap implies: "deceit, murder, swindling, chaos, vanity, viciousness—an attack on the basic and precious laws which bind men together."[69] The production only furthered what Shakespeare intended by his popular portrait of "this reverend vice": that greed and serving self-interest were as much a part of the world of Eastcheap and its oaken tables as they were at the palace with its great metallic council-table. Despite Falstaff's depravity, the RSC directors invested him with sympathetic qualities as well: his dalliance with Doll Tearsheet was played with subdued, nearly Chekhovian humor. Such Chekhovian resonances in the Falstaff and Justice Shallow scenes, along with the autumnal setting for Eastcheap, are trademarks of Hall and Barton productions. Both favor the "dying time" of year and its inherent melancholy (see chapter 4). A particularly poignant moment is recreated in Speaight's account of the second tavern scene. After a riotous beginning, recorders began to play to register a change of mood:

Falstaff has Doll on his knee; the shadows close in; and inexorable truth of mortality pierces the masquerade. From now on—we feel it in our bones— nothing will ever be the same. Falstaff is allowed his full meed of pathos. . . . Something almost recognizable as love goes out to meet him from the trollop on his lap—and this is another moment of truth.[70]

The moment was right for a play about a country in the midst of its own autumnal decline: it was a reminder of what could be if Vice, Greed, and Vanity were banished from all the world.

If *2 Henry IV* is an autumnal prelude to the wintry days of *The Wars of the Roses*, then *Henry V* is an Indian summer (Hall's program note calls it "a red and gold land of hope and glory at Agincourt"). The directors could not allow the cycle to bask in the glow of Henry's brilliance since he is not the redeemer sent to save the Lancastrian line: he is still his father's son, and his country— despite the "sanctions" of God, England, and St. George—still faces years of suffering. The deromanticization of Henry the Fifth was again accomplished by a casting coup. Ian Holm's small stature automatically brought the King back to a realistic size that befitted the concept of the seven productions. Not only did Holm's physique effect "a smaller Henry than Shakespeare created," but the RSC's choice to "consistently abjure the traditional flourishes" abetted the untraditional and revelatory approach to the King.[71] Among the "flourishes" moderated by Holm and his directors were the ringing prebattle speeches. Rather than delivering them—Olivierlike—as grandiloquent, patriotic rallying cries, King Harry pulled individual soldiers aside to speak short sections to each; when a general exhortation was needed, Holm mounted a scaling ladder—"as Monty (Field Marshall Bernard Montgomery) used to climb on a jeep to talk to his troops"[71]—to address his men. Holm's Henry retained Hal's self-doubts: "Again and again, he turns away from his battered and weary soldiers to commune with his conscience. He is never certain God is a warrior, let alone an English jingo. And victory when it comes . . . is a miracle which is both unexpected and undeserved."[73]

Partly because of financial necessity,[74] largely because of the popular success of the histories, *Henry V* and the two *Henry IV*s were kept in the RSC repertory for two additional years. Barton, again an independent director in the company (*Love's Labour's Lost*, 1965: see chapter 4), oversaw a directorial team that would "rethink" the histories. In 1965 Barton restaged *Henry V*, a production that was "immeasurably improved" over the 1964 version for moderating some of the more overtly Brechtian elements.[75]

In 1966 Barton, assisted by Williams and the RSC's newest director, Trevor Nunn, restaged the three plays dealing with Hal's maturation; each took particular responsibilities: Barton, the chair, oversaw the Falstaff scenes, verse-speaking, and fights; Williams, the Henry IV scenes and movement, while Nunn, staged the Hotspur and Shallow scenes, and established the characterization. The triumvirate examined the lessons of the company's earlier experiences with the histories. Barton believed *The Wars* led him to a greater acceptance that it is a director's job not to improve Shakespeare, but to creatively permit the playwright to manipulate the director's imagination.[75]

Barton's cadre rendered subtle changes, though the antiwar spirit of the previous productions was maintained, even heightened. For *Henry V* there as an intriguing program note: "Shakespeare himself might have had inklings that his play was about more than the lovely war at Agincourt, might have indeed written a secret play for the benefit of an intellectual elite, and that the modern producer is entitled to hint at the subtleties contained therein." The note ended, however, with the caveat: "He cannot do more because the language will not let him."

Because the trilogy was no longer played within the epic sweep of seven plays, two values changed: first, there was a deemphasis on elements that suggested "a sense of occasion." The production now exploited the plays' realism.[77]

Some interpretative changes resulted from significant cast changes. Tony Church, now Henry IV, emphasized the physical decay of the dying king rather than the anguished guilt for usurping Richard II.[78] Norman Rodway, as Hotspur, transformed the fiery rebel from a Scotsman (as he was played in 1964) to an Irishman; he returned more nobility and wit to the role than was displayed earlier.[79]

Falstaff underwent the most drastic revision, significant because Barton was specifically responsible for shaping Paul Rogers's playing of that role. A number of critics cited the intellectual clarity with which the role was invested. The

Barton-Rogers Falstaff was less the gluttonous buffoon than "an aristocratic knight whose intelligence is blunted by his consistent refusal to face unpleasant facts. He is caught in a changing world . . . a conservative, admiring the squirarchy and the values disintegrating with the decline of Henry IV's reign."[80] And, in a motif that Barton would find useful for other Shakespearean heroes (for example, Richard II, 1973; King John, 1975; and particularly Hamlet, 1980), this Falstaff was a lover of theater—"his parodies of plays and players, his juggling with platitudes, are both scholarly and funny."[81]

In one other casting change of note, Ian Richardson assumed the role of the Chorus. Richardson had just spent a season playing Marat in Peter Brook's acclaimed staging of Peter Weiss's play, and Barton invited him—as an antidote to a year spent in "that bathtub"—to play "something rather extravagant."[82] Barton directed Richardson to play the Chorus as an Elizabethan actor-manager, thus evoking memories of Toby Robertson's theatrical Chorus in Barton's *Henry V* for the Oxford-Cambridge Players in 1953.

After the 1966 season the Hall-Barton histories were honorably retired from the RSC repertory. Fortunately, the Barton-adapted *Wars of the Roses* has been preserved by the BBC, which televised the trilogy in 1965. Barton supervised the telecast to ensure the integrity of the original work. The RST was converted into a television studio so that the essence of the staged version would remain intact in the new medium.

In addition to establishing the theatrical viability of some of Shakespeare's least-appreciated plays and illustrating an interpretative relationship among the sequence of history plays, the Hall-Barton enterprise brought to the Royal Shakespeare Company other dividends. The intensely communal effort defined the maturing company's purpose and potential. In a retrospect of the RSC's first decade, Peter Roberts assessed the importance of *The Wars of the Roses:*

> Asked, therefore, to define the RSC's emerging house style, it would be to *The Wars of the Roses* that I would point. It was . . . nothing to do with the application of the tenets of some authority on the theory of the drama. Neither was it the copy of some existing house style like the elegantly mannered delivery of the Comedie Française, or the elaborate naturalism of the Moscow Art Theatre. It was something that resulted from the need for a raw young troupe to find its identity with sufficient certainty to celebrate adequately its resident dramatist's 400th birthday.[83]

A September 1964 letter to the editor of *The Times*, signed by nine prominent British drama critics, praised the Royal Shakespeare Company as one of the national treasures of the Commonwealth. Leading the list of "remarkable achievements" by the company was the "monumental mounting of the cycle of Shakespeare's histories."[84] Despite the RSC's many accompanishments since the histories, nothing yet has matched that enterprise for its size, importance, and daring, though Nunn's *Nicholas Nickleby* marathon—and perhaps Barton's *The Greeks* (see Chapter 10)—are worthy successors. As a prime mover behind *The Wars* project, Barton merits importance in discussions of both the RSC's accomplished history and contemporary stage practice.

A review of *The Wars* in the *Bristol Evening Post* defines the dilemma that yet confronted Barton: "The inescapable truth is they—the director on the one hand and the scholar on the other—have emerged from their task with a marathon of savage grandeur."[85] Barton's contributions to the histories extended far beyond scholarship, though undeniably it was a catalyst for the enterprise. His theatrical contributions to *The Wars* and the *Henriad* should not be minimized. Unfortunately they were, and he worked in Hall's shadow. When Hall left the company in 1967 to head the National Theatre, Trevor Nunn assumed the RSC's directorship. To be sure, Barton preferred not to be a theater administrator, primarily because it would detract from his ambition to be a writer ("I put all my spare time into that"), secondarily because he feels he is not temperamentally suited for the pressures of running a theater: "I've run seasons, but anybody who knows me would know that I would be the last person in the world to run a theatre." Thus Nunn became the RSC's most visible figure. It was not until 1968 and *Troilus and Cressida* that Barton finally was recognized as one of the most gifted directors in England.

3
Wars and Lechery:
Troilus and Cressida (1960, 1968, 1976), *Coriolanus* (1967), and *Julius Caesar* (1968)

A. P. Rossiter has questioned the theatrical efficacy of *Troilus and Cressida,* which is among the least-produced plays in Shakespeare's canon: "How can you expect to interest a theatre-going audience in what even its admirers admit is a bad stage play: a play whose twenty-four scenes . . . include at most *four* that can be called 'dramatic'?"[1] The play's diffuseness, inconstant characters, and elusive tone have troubled critics for centuries. Whatever his other accomplishments, chief among the legacies of John Barton may be his affirmation of the theatrical and dramatic viability of *Troilus and Cressida.* Few theater artists in this century have been so intimately involved with this difficult play. He has faced *Troilus's* myriad challenges four times in the past quarter century:

1956: Staged battle scenes and assisted with some text work for the Cambridge Marlowe Society;
1960: Assisted Peter Hall in the RSC's initial season at Stratford; the production was revived in 1962 for the Cambridge Festival and at the Aldwych.
1968: Directed for the RSC at Stratford; the production was revived the following year at the Aldwych, and toured Europe, Japan, and New York;
1976: Codirected with Barry Kyle for the RSC at Stratford.

To place Barton's work with the play in perspective, there is no verifiable record of a production of *Troilus and Cressida,* including Shakespeare's era, until 1898 in Munich;[2] in this century there have been but a half dozen productions of import,[3] excluding minor revivals at various Shakespeare festivals.

As the century's leading investigator of *Troilus's* myriad challenges, Barton is particularly qualified to discuss the play's complexities. He believes it is one of Shakespeare's greatest plays, but refuses to tie it down to a label: "It continu-

63

ally invites a varying response . . . *Troilus and Cressida* is unique and brilliant and resists labelling; one confines it terribly and minimizes its richness if one tries to categorize it."[4]

The increased interest in *Troilus and Cressida* is also attributed to events of the twentieth century: global war, the threat of nuclear annihilation, collapsing economic systems, and a philosophic shift to existential relativism.[5] Contemporary audiences, accustomed to the multigenre works of Pirandello, Genet, Beckett, Albee, and Pinter have less difficulty accommodating the varied tones of Shakespeare's work. Furthermore, audiences familiar with Brechtian theater practice are no longer jarred by the intellectual detachment provoked by Shakespeare's script. Una Ellis-Fermor argues that, given discord as the central theme of *Troilus*, "it is hard to imagine how else it should be formally reflected but in a deliberately intended discord of form also."[6] Such remarks about Shakespeare's "alienation effect" were echoed by Barton in rehearsal notes to his cast in 1968:

> What kind of play is *Troilus and Cressida?* What is its general tone? Should this tone seem to an audience cynical, romantic, poetic, obscene, intellectual or absurd? The play contains all these contradictory elements in order to show life as a series of discords. Shakespeare doesn't impose a uniform tone; he offers a jarring mixture on all levels: characterisation, text, plot and action. This structure is a deliberate and organic orchestration of dissonances and each actor is part of the orchestra—more, I think, than in any other of his plays.[7]

Hall included *Troilus and Cressida* in the RSC's first season as part of a five-play exploration of the range of Shakespeare's comedy. The inclusion of *Troilus* in the season was a heady choice by young directors responsible for building both an audience and a reputation for the new company. The success of the play at Cambridge no doubt encouraged the decision, and—also in 1956—Tyrone Guthrie's mock-operetta *Troilus and Cressida* showed Old Vic audiences that there was theatrical life in the little-known play. Though Guthrie's version was comic, nearly farcical, Hall and Barton would not compromise the darker elements of the text. Hall appraised patrons of the direction that *Troilus* would take in the RSC's first "comic" repertory:

> . . . the fun is almost always spoiled by a dark side that arises from Shakespeare's sense of how men really are. . . . This same humanity takes the sardonic *History of Troilus* and *Cressida* to tragedy. Written in the disillusionment of Shakespeare's middle age, its comic tone is ironic and the dark side is uppermost; it satirizes heroes and heroism, and shows the fate of romantic love in a world of cynics and egoists.[8]

"Dark," "sardonic," "disillusionment," "ironic," and "cynical" were more than rhetoric for Hall's program note: they became the cornerstones on which he and Barton based the 1960 production, as well as Barton's later versions.

To explore the play's innate darkness, Hall and Barton had to deromanticize the myths of the Trojan War. A performance space was needed that would not evoke the romantic past of antiquity, but the harsher realities of a primitive Mediterranean culture in the midst of a prolonged war. Barton recalls Hall's preproduction vision of the play's design: "He wished to make the design more austere and more selective—to give the fullest possible focus on the actor."[9]

Leslie Hurry's design consisted of two elements: in the background, a large backcloth with an abstract design in black and red—"the hue of dried blood."[10] In the foreground was the set piece for which the production became known: a low octagonal enclosure filled with white sand. Thus the production was labeled "The Sandpit *Troilus*." Barton recalls that "there was a great deal of talk about what the floor texture should be . . . [and] the sandpit gave the right 'Mediterranean heat-epic' quality and everyone responded to it."[11] The critics responded, generally favorably, by assigning it a metaphorical significance: ". . . a comment on obliterating time that grates all to 'dusty nothing' ";[12] ". . . a wasteland . . . the playground of overgrown schoolboys;"[13] and ". . . the whiteness of the sand answered the redness of the backcloth, as the satire of the play answers its violence."[14] Tony Church, a member of the 1960 company, believes the sandpit unified the play's varied concerns:

> Cressida ran the sand through her fingers when talking about time . . . and played in it with her feet. When people lay about on rugs it suggested an extraordinarily steamy and erotic mood. Ajax, sulking, made sand piles, and it then became a child's sand-box. . . . When Hector was killed and dragged off covered with blood, one had a bullring image—with Hector a bloody piece of meat. . . . It was the most powerful design image I've ever seen.[15]

Furthermore, because it was a proper environment for whoever occupied it, the set accommodated the diffuse action of the script. Metaphysically, the concept had an added advantage: ". . . correspondences between camps and characters could be visually pointed and the action could be seen as less the result of particular social pressures and more the result of universal forces in man."[16]

Hall and Barton did not select anachronistic or abstract costuming for the production: their Greeks and Trojans dressed in the Homeric style—an innovation in itself as other major productions this century opted for non-Greco costumes: Elizabethan, modern, Ruritanian. Though intent on showing the parallels between the decline of the ancient Homeric civilization and ours, the directors avoided modern costuming and employed a naturalistic acting style to link the two ages. Paradoxically, had they resorted to modern military clothing (as Barton did in parts of *The Greeks*), the play might have lost some of its immediacy as audiences became distracted by a directorial gimmick. The directors trusted the inherent relevance of the text without imposing external devices, thus disproving Rossiter's claim that *Troilus* never was a play about ancient Greeks and therefore should not look like one.[17]

Their austere approach agreed upon, Hall and Barton began work with their actors. Barton worked mostly on the battle sequences and the text (which he sparingly cut: only 533 of the original 3,326 lines[18]): "Peter took main responsibility for the production."[19] No doubt the two discussed the play at such length, however, that they were of a single mind and, in the final analysis, it matters little who is credited with the production.

Their collaboration rendered a unified vision of the play that ameliorated its troublesome structure. In particular, they found in Hector and Achilles, rather than the titular lovers, the linchpin that held the plot together. By focusing on these two emblems of misplaced nobility and self-serving pragmatism, the story—climaxed by Achilles' savage killing of Hector—achieved a cohesiveness that no longer made the act 5 battle scenes seem anticlimactic: as *The Times* reported, "The essential soundness of the production lies in its gradual isolation of Hector and Achilles, symbols of the conflict between chivalry and brutal opportunism to which the ruin of Troilus by faithless Cressida is secondary."[20] Cressida's infidelity and Troilus's hard-earned disillusionment are, in this context, seen as by-products of a larger world picture, a playing-out of Barton's notion that the play is at one and the same time both "the most romantic and most antiromantic play in Shakespeare's canon."

In 1968 Barton would give Hector and Achilles even more prominence—for the latter, some would say too much prominence. In 1960 each was more fully integrated into the design of the whole. Hector was played with dignity and manliness; few of his lines were cut (only thirteen in total, ten in the Trojan Council scene). Unfortunately, none of the reviews of the 1960 production— nor its 1962 revival—indicate how Hector's troublesome *volte-face* was staged. But there are many accounts of his death, staged by Barton, which became one of the most remembered aspects of this and the two subsequent productions. Sebastian Shaw, who played Ulysses in 1968, recalls that Barton specifically wanted Hector's death to symbolize the central theme of the play: all things come to nothing.[21] Hence, it was staged as a ritual of sinister brutality. Amidst a smokey battlefield, Hector stood without armour and clad in a white tunic; he was then slowly surrounded by the Myrmidons, dressed in black and carrying large, black, beetlelike shields. The Myrmidons raised their spears slowly and with concentrated thrusts wounded Hector, then stepped backward to allow Achilles to finish the bloody task. Achilles struck Hector, who fell at his feet; Achilles slowly turned over the dead body with his foot. Later, Hector was dragged from the arena, leaving blood stains on the white sand.

The spokesmen for the production's darkly satirical tone were Pandarus and Thersites, whom Barton and Hall used to chart the play's thematic development, much as Hector and Achilles were guides for its narrative line.[22] Pandarus was played by Max Adrian as a lean, macabre, and dangerous force— "a scamp without for a moment being ridiculous. As a result he provides the one focus of the aroused, indulgent and corrupt impotence of the whole play."[23] His Grecian counterpart, Thersites (Peter O'Toole) was similarly dark, "a performance that comes as close to a naturalistic interpretation as the part would allow, avoiding the overtly comic and sharply cynical without any loss of power."[24] British audiences no doubt recognized Thersites as a Jacobean "angry young man," not unlike its age's Jimmy Porter.

The other Greek and Trojan warriors were generally played satirically: Ajax was a moronic, even punch-drunk bully with a "mentally retarded laugh,"[25] Nestor, whom Barton would render more nobly in 1968, was "a parody old man, to end all parody old men, a Polonius so far gone in his dotage as to seem merely stupid,"[26] perhaps the most ill-conceived characterization in the production. There were, on the other hand, voices of reason in either camp. Priam was a respected king, patriarch to a decaying civilization. Ulysses was "a soldier with a brain in his head,"[27] whose linguistically difficult "degree speech" (1.3.75–137) was virtually uncut; proportionately fewer of Ulysses' lines were cut, thus giving his role greater emphasis. When Cressida passed among the sportive generals, Ulysses refused to kiss her, which retained his moral integrity. His "Daughter of the Game" speech, as read by Eric Porter, seemed an indictment of the cause of the prolonged war as much as a condemnation of Cressida.[28]

Barton's act 5 battle scenes were generously praised for their integrity and excitement. Hall and Barton recognized that the dissonant combats, punctuated by Thersites' cynical railings, formed the emotional climax to the play.[29] Consequently, the emphasis on the war plot did not diminish the love plot: if anything, the tale of naive Troilus and the more worldly wise Cressida gained clarity because her faithlessness seemed less wanton, more the result of a society in which truth and honor were relative values at best.

Despite its unpleasant subject matter, *Troilus and Cressida* was a popular and critical success in that season of comedies, a testimony both to the acumen of the directors and their company and to the mood of the times. Nothing would happen in the ensuing eight years to diminish its grim impact.

Barton prepared for his solo work on *Troilus and Cressida* in 1968 by staging two Shakespearean tragedies set in antiquity: *Coriolanus* in 1967, and *Julius Caesar*, which opened in April 1968—four months before *Troilus* premiered. There are thematic and theatrical elements in each production that were apparently shaped by the 1960 *Troilus* and, more important, influenced Barton when he was working on his version of the drama.

Coriolanus is best remembered for Ian Richardson's portrait of the Roman aristocrat. Barton's casting was daring because Richardson's slight build is contrary to the muscular warrior image associated with the role, a bias of which Richardson was cognizant: "We decided to play him more as an athlete than a weight-lifter or a wrestler. . . . John Barton said to me, 'What you lack physically, you can make up for vocally.' Nobody questioned the fact that I was smaller than the Coriolanuses they were used to, either in stature or muscle."[30] Production reviews vindicated Barton's choice, citing Richardson's innately "epicene stage personality" as a strength of the portrait: "And why Ian Richardson is such a triumph of casting . . . is [because] there is something womanish, in this case, mother-bound, elusively there."[31] The Roman leader was interpreted as an immature youth who saw battlefields as extensions of the gymnasium, "a place where young men may flex their muscles and indulge in a ritualistic game . . . athletes peacocking their way through opposing lines of shields and swords,"[32] which was a concept Barton explored a year later in *Troilus* to greater effect.

There were other elements in *Coriolanus* that Barton reemployed for *Troilus:* the set was "overgloomy . . . barbaric looking,"[33] dominated by primitive totems towering above the palisade,[34] not unlike the animal heads that hovered over Barton's *Troilus* set the following year (and in 1976). The warriors dressed in black leather (as were Achilles' Myrmidons) and they crushed Coriolanus with huge, black, beetlelike shields.

1968, the year that brought permanent fame to John Barton, *the director,* began inauspiciously with a poorly received production of *Julius Caesar* (". . . it never rose above the pedestrian . . . it never came close to the play's potential grandeur, its tragedy never ignited our interest or our concern"[35]). Like *Coriolanus* and *Troilus,* Barton's *Caesar* emphasized the decline of civilization and the innate brutality of man. The RSC program contained pictures and references to Hitler, Napolean, and other tyrants, and the production emphasized that *Caesar* was about political tyranny in the twentieth century. The costumes were a curious amalgam of Roman, Elizabethan, and modern dress—black leather jerkins, dark togas, and jackboots that evoked memories of modern Fascism. The conspirators greeted one another with "Heil Hitler" salutes.[36] Rarely has Barton so self-consciously explored modern parallels. To be sure, political brutality dominated people's minds in 1968: the Viet Nam War was raging, people in Europe and America were protesting war and nuclear arms, the day after *Caesar* opened in Stratford Dr. Martin Luther King was assassinated, and race riots were commonplace ("The Praetorian Guards . . . holding their staves ready to whack the Roman crowds as if they were riotous Negroes in Detroit"[37]).

Just as *Troilus* demythologizes Greek heroes, Barton sought to deromanticize Brutus in the production's boldest interpretation. Under Barton's direction, which rendered Rome "in unrelieved gloom,"[38] and Barry Ingham's acting, Brutus emerged as "a pretty nasty piece of work: quarrelsome, vain, loudmouthed with a nasty jeer in his voice. He even laughs at the murder of Caesar."[39] With a deflated Brutus, Barton explored more thoroughly the relationship between Casca and Caesar suggested by Plutarch. Gareth Lloyd Evans wondered whether Barton's academic knowledge of the text and its source had not dominated completely his theatrical instincts.[40] A preproduction press release defined Barton's thinking on these characters: "It is a much more ambitious play than is sometimes imagined. The characters are apt to be misread. The danger is to push the characters into something more four-square than they really are until you reach the stodgy Roman interpretation."[41]

The production's most daring moments involved Caesar himself, whom

Barton saw as the central character of the play. At the moment of his death, Caesar (Brewster Mason) grasped Brutus's dagger and inflicted the final thrust himself. This unorthodox staging may have had its roots in *Coriolanus,* whose titular character was also a party to his own death in Barton's production. Richardson, the Cassius of Barton's *Caesar,* recalls his and Barton's thinking about Coriolanus's death:

> . . . even that final sacrifice [his death] he turns into a glorious thing for himself. This is why I didn't allow them to kill me. I threw myself at them. This is his final statement—I am the only one capable of killing me.[42]

Shakespeare brings back Caesar's Ghost once after his death; Barton added two appearances—twice on the plains of Phillipi: at the parting of Brutus and Cassius, and then at the moment of Brutus's suicide.

Two elements of the production were harshly criticized, which is surprising because each is normally considered a Barton strength. The battles were called "laughable in their tameness,"[43] a criticism that Barton counters by affirming that they were done "deliberately the way they were because they are not battle scenes. The way the text goes is that they keep coming from the battle but nothing happens on the battlefield. I set it up as a casualty station where the dead and wounded were being tended (personal interview, June 1983)." The crowd scenes, so impressive in the Elizabethan *Caesar* at Cambridge, were chastised as being "feeble."[44]

The shortcomings of *Julius Caesar* were soon forgotten when *Troilus and Cressida* opened in August to critical acclaim. When it was revived at the Aldwych in 1969, *The Daily Telegraph* greeted it as "one of the peak achievements of contemporary British theatre."[45] The thread that binds the laudatory notices is found in Frank Cox's *Plays and Players* essay: "Its strength is not to be realized in some external fashion . . . but rather in an ability to dig deep into the intellectual content of the lines and present with clarity what it discovers."[46]

Essentially Barton discovered that Thersites' pronouncement in 5.2— "Lechery, lechery! Still wars and lechery! Nothing else holds fashion" (194–95)—was the pivotal line of the play. While discussing the divergent philosophies of the play, he noted that by act 5 Thersites' philosophy "achieves a monstrous domination."[47] Added testimony to the director's purpose comes from John Nettles, the 1976 Thersites, who says the latter production emphasized discoveries Barton made in 1968: "one of the discoveries he made was that the voice of truth was Thersites."[48]

In 1960 Hall and Barton emphasized the slaying of Hector by Achilles as the climax of a great story in which the lovers were victims of a war that destroys personal values. In 1968 the unpopularity of the Viet Nam War prompted societies on both sides of the Atlantic to reassess their political, moral, and sexual values; thus Barton exploited the topicality of *Troilus and Cressida* by equating war and sex: "Mr. Barton has interpreted the tragicomedy as a war between Mars and Venus, showing that all kinds of psychological motivations, including sex, are at work in the subconscious when war is being waged. The lust to kill is a form of lechery . . . a Freudian view of the play that anticipated Freud."[49] Antithetically, Benedict Nightingale's *New Statesman* review argued that the director may have forced the interpretation: "It is a striking and daring aperçu, more suited . . . to Genet than Shakespeare, but the text does not seem to sustain it."[50] To the contrary, there are indeed lines that support Barton's reading, the most notable of which do not come from Thersites, but from the "romantic" lovers:

> Cressida: In that I'll war with you.
> Troilus: O virtuous fight . . .

(3.2.170–71)

In 1970 Barton, looking back on his work with the play, declared that "*Troilus and Cressida* is more a director's play in the accepted sense of the term. It is a very difficult play to do . . . calling for the development of visual resources on a grand scale as well as the orchestration of very long speeches full of argument and subtle thought."[51] Timothy O'Brien's design, as in 1960, retained the Homeric setting, but with significant changes: the sandpit was discarded (to avoid comparisons with the earlier version?) and was replaced by massive raked beams supported by square blocks that surrounded the essentially bare acting area. Perhaps O'Brien was inspired by the Prologue's suggestion of "massy staples, and corresponsive and fulfilling bolts" that "sperr up the sons of Troy against the invaders" (17–19).[52] A black cyclorama (Barton's customary preference) backed the action; coconut matting covered the floor and a haze of smoke permeated the atmosphere.[53] The open and abstracted set—still vaguely suggestive of antiquity—allowed for the fluidity of action. And, as this is a play about people watching other people, the raked beams surrounding the open space provided perches from which the characters could view others: Pandarus and Cressida atop the walls of Troy watching the returning Trojan army in 1.2; Thersites, perched vulturelike, watching Ulysses watching Troilus watching Diomedes and Cressida in 5.2.

Of more importance were Barton's costume choices; these were as sparse and primitive as the set. The director underscored the sensuality (i.e., "lechery") of war by clothing his warriors in the skimpiest of costumes, particularly in the battle scenes. Ronald Bryden suggested that Barton and O'Brien derived the costumes from Attic pottery to create "friezes of bare-torsoed warriors in tiny kilts and huge, bird-like helmets, bearing tall spears and totems of flying sphinx and bull." The critic further admired Barton's picture of a Mediterranean tribal world where "wealth consists of bracelets, herds and lives taken . . . a proper background to a play which explores the fundamentals of human value and society."[54] The birdlike helmets, it should be noted, are part of an image pattern Barton prefers: in 1973 he dressed Northumberland as a giant bird of prey in *Richard II* (see chapter 5) and in 1974 Cloten was bedecked in feathers to suggest his predatory nature (see chapter 7). Furthermore, the costuming (or lack of it) reflected the theater's growing tolerance for nudity in the late 1960s; such an approach would have been unthinkable in 1960, but an outgrowth of the anti war activism was an enlargement of sexual freedom. The so-called Free Love movement paralleled the antiwar movement. The battle cry of the streets—"Make love, not war"—was amended by Barton's actors to read: "Making war *is* making love." Thus his battle sequences in act 5 became homosexual dances that joined the forces of Venus and Mars.[55] The pervasive image one took away from the production was that of glistening bodies of virile men locked in combat. "The production," wrote Irving Wardle of *The Times*, "reawakens in you the real savagery of erotic art."[56] Sebastian Shaw, who played Ulysses, said that Barton enrolled his actors in a health club to lift weights in preparation for the show.[57] The sight of nearly naked masses prompted one critic to dub the production "Torso and Cressida,"[58] while another opted for "Troilus and Calcutta," a reference to the nude musical, *Oh! Calcutta!*[59] A more caustic critic felt Barton's concept encouraged characters to divide "more easily into straights and queers than Greeks and Trojans."[60]

The emphasis on sexuality was not limited to costume choices. Troilus (Michael Williams) reclined sensually, stroking a sword dreamily as he compared Cressida's bed to the India Alexander conquered;[61] during the Hector-Achilles exchange in 4.5—"Tell me you heavens, in which part of his body / Shall I destroy him?" (241–42)—the combatants chose where they wished to plant their swords in "a scene of brilliant decadence."[62]

Not surprisingly, there was considerable objection to the explicitness of the production: "In his determination to emphasize the stench of lechery and corruption that surrounds these decadent characters, John Barton has underlined every gesture and every speech that could be remotely interpreted as indicating some form of sexual excess."[63] Such comments from journalists and offended RSC patrons were answered by former Stratford director David Jones, who no doubt discussed the controversial choice at length with Barton: "Shakespeare's bitter, tormented picture of a world where honor in war turns to butchery and the idealism of love is at the mercy of sexual appetite is certainly not for weak and sensitive souls. But Barton's production—brilliant and nerve-jangling, compassionate—seems to me one of the finest and strongest things to have been done at Stratford in recent years."[64]

Barton and O'Brien incorporated key animal images into the dark setting. A huge medallion of a bull, emblematic of both the bestial natures of the combatants and the cuckoldry of Menelaus (and Troilus?), dominated the background. Thersites, a grotesque image of decaying man himself, wore an obscene red phallus. At the conclusion of the play, it remained on stage, lying next to a discarded sword, beneath the bull medallion. The director's interpretative concerns were best captured in this final, frozen picture.

Echoes of the Viet Nam experience reverberated throughout *Troilus and Cressida*. In his directorial notes, Barton compared the two wars: "The basic situation . . . is ludicrous, but also an insoluble impasse where both sides are inexorably committed." In *Shakespeare Survey*, Lloyd Evans judged Barton's juxtaposition of the Viet Nam War with Troy as "forced, meaningless, and irritating."[65] Barton denies that Viet Nam was the impetus for his production, noting that the modern war was merely a useful parallel to Shakespeare's play. Nettles, the 1976 Thersites, said that Viet Nam was discussed frequently in rehearsals (though Barton says that it was primarily Kyle who led such discussions):

> (We discussed it) all the time, all the time. Because that's what the Prologue says, "Beginning in the middle. . . ." We're talking about a long, long war. Barton had this lovely idea—about seven years into the war, Helen must have been a bit over the top. And there you have the reason for the war had actually gone wrong. And the blast of mortality had actually shaken her beauty a little. And it was even more pointless; their youth were dying.

Barton's deflation of Helen would become a central issue in *The Greeks* in 1980.

The parallels with Viet Nam were only a way into the script. The common ground for the Trojan and Vietnamese wars was a world rapidly degenerating into moral anarchy, which inevitably leads to a generalizing of one's attitudes to minimize the bankruptcy of one's spirit. Again Barton's notes to his cast defined such issues:[66] his remarks recall Peter Hall's discourse on "sanction words" in *The Wars of the Roses*.

More than a few reviewers thought they also detected the influence of Polish existentialist Jan Kott, whose thesis that "the world in which war exists is absurd . . . but the world goes on, and one has to give it a purpose in order to preserve the sense of the world's existence and a scale of value"[67] does indeed parallel Barton's attitude in his work with *Troilus*. To be sure, Barton's rehearsal notes assert that he does not consider the play totally pessimistic—"It does not necessarily say that the whole of life is chaos"—and emphasize that positive values are indeed celebrated. He cites Aeneas's and Nestor's chivalry, Hector's generosity, and Cressida's love before she leaves Troilus as "good things to have around." Tony Church, who played Pandarus for the European tour in 1969, says Barton searched for the "good" in *Troilus and Cressida* and found it in "the heroic ideals the play smashes."[68]

The diffuse plot and convoluted language are not the play's greatest challenges; both can be deciphered with diligent labor. The characters, on whom the action focuses and who embody its themes, are perhaps the most enigmatic Shakespeare created. Barton offers a solution to those who attempt to bring them to life in the theater:

> All the characters in the play are made up of inconsistencies, opposites, and extremes. Each of these jarring elements should be played for what it is, and

not smoothed out: The Trojans turn Helen into an ideal—"a theme for honour and renown." The Greek Diomed sees her as a whore. She herself, in her brief appearance, is neither. Shakespeare doesn't label her, but gives us a glimpse of a human woman.

Collectively the Greeks and Trojans represent contrasting views of life around which the play is structured. Barton's notes tell us "the Greeks are basically in touch with reality, and destructive, while the Trojans are self-destructive, romantic and blind." His sympathies leaned toward the Trojan camp, which represent a dying order, but one whose passing is to be lamented. To illustrate this, Barton devised business to show that the Trojans were more respectful of traditions and authority than their Greek rivals: during the duel scene (4.5) Nestor's speech recalling his bout with Hector's grandfather (182–99) was rendered warmly and suggested a respect for the chivalry of bygone days. Hector then good-naturedly engaged the old man in an arm-wrestling match, gallantly allowing Nestor to beat him. Hector's famous about-face in 2.2 was also motivated by respect for old age. The prompt copy contains the stage direction "Priam rises" immediately before Hector's line "Hector's opinion / Is this in way of truth" (187–88), an implication that Hector defers to his father's wishes. This physical action, coupled with Barton's rehearsal note that characters like Hector are "more effective at analysis than at upholding any positive course of action," solved one of the most problematic moments of the script.

Barton saved his most satiric thrusts for the Greeks, whose "arid intellectualism" he expressed "in nihilistic satire and undisciplined self-indulgence."[69] If the Trojans are the focal point of the satire—as they were in Guthrie's Ruritanian version—the weight of the play tends to fall toward comedy. Their defeat seems the outcome of an ordered world, an affirmation of Ulysses' speech on the degrees of the cosmos. If the Greeks are more loutish—as in the Barton production—and the Trojans more humane, though not less erroneous, there is a more cynical, darker vision offered by the play's resolution. Misapplied intelligence triumphs and we are left with the bitter aftertaste suggested by W. W. Lawrence's 1931 observation that "the ending of the tale is in accord with the facts of human experience; life often settles nothing, it leaves the innocent to suffer and the guilty to prevail."[70]

Barton's Ulysses was a cunning, even treacherous general, vain about his own intellect, cynical about that of his comrades—particularly Agamemnon. Shaw, highly praised for his portrait, described his character as a man "in love with his own mind."[71] Conversely, Nestor was played sympathetically, a well-intentioned old warrior, a marked contrast to the old fool of the 1960 production.

No element of the production was as widely discussed as Alan Howard's portrayal of Achilles. Shaved of all body hair, dressed in assorted "camp" outfits, Achilles was the quintessential symbol of Greek decadence. In *Shakespeare and the Idea of the Play*, Anne Barton concludes that Achilles and

Patroclus "stand at the center of the evil which afflicts the Greeks . . . (and) contrives to cheapen everything it touches."[72] Barton and Howard devised business to illustrate Achilles' licentiousness. At Hector's arrival in 4.5, he appeared "on a little sedan in full drag and blonde hairpiece to dance with the man he is to kill,"[73] hissing snakelike at his victim (later, on the battlefield Barton dressed Achilles in gold, with serpentine black lines over his body). Barton insists that Achilles was not "in full drag" for this controversial sequence: "I *did not* put Achilles in full drag. . . . He put on a piece of cloth and a hair piece. He did it totally masculine. The idea was that he was mocking Helen, not that he was camping it up." Specifically, Achilles was trying to trick the cuckolded Menelaus into thinking that he was Helen. Earlier, Achilles and Patroclus acted out a travesty of the Menelaus-Helen wedding for which the war was fought; the prompt copy describes the moment at 2.3.69— "Myrmidons pull away and form wedding arch as Patroclus and Achilles rise . . . and exit camping."

Barton's vision of Achilles prompted considerable outrage, partly because of its indelicacy, mostly because there seemed little textual support for the lengths to which Barton and Howard allowed the character to evolve. W. A. Darlington admitted that "the thing could hardly have been done better," but challenged the concept because he believed Barton had substituted "one of the Bard's characters [for] another of his own invention."[74] To his credit, Darlington did not fire his critical salvoes and retreat; he challenged Barton to his own game and researched the scholarship on Achilles to conclude that "Shakespeare nowhere shows any sign of intending to make homosexuals of the two characters. This idea has been read into the play by modern theatrical directors and has been hardened into a stage tradition. . . . What is keeping Achilles out of the war is not love for Patroclus, but for Polyxena, Princess of Troy. He will not fight against his lady's country."[75] Barton was bemused by the criticism:

> We were attacked for presenting Achilles as an effeminate homosexual, which was something that had never entered our minds. We saw him as bisexual, a view which is surely embodied in Shakespeare's play and is also the view which the Elizabethan audience would have taken. What we did do was show him *playing* at effeminancy and homosexuality in order to mock and outrage the Greek generals. The real man we saw is embodied in the aggressiveness and destruction which surges from him when he confronts Hector and when he finally appears on the battlefield. We hoped we had made that plain enough, especially as Alan played most of the part with great vocal virility and power.[76]

Though Barton saw Thersites as the dominant voice of the play, Rylands had taught him that there are two choruses for *Troilus and Cressida*, Thersites and Pandarus. Both Kott and Rossiter have suggested that these two "clowns" are but two sides of the same coin, which may explain Barton's innovative linking of the two vile characters in the Epilogue. Pandarus was accompanied by

Thersites' drum-playing and dancing to a chantlike rhythm that underscored the old pimp's speech: "The two old parasites huddled together chanting their litany of despair."[77] Barton's Pandarus was more cynical than the more broadly comic rendering by Max Adrian in 1960. Several critics noted that David Waller, Barton's Pandarus in 1968 and 1976, patterned Cressida's uncle after Frankie Howerd, whose leering performances in British sex farces rely heavily on sexual innuendo—"He bawls out the word 'bed' as others might shout 'fire.' "[78] Where Max Adrian was a lean, macabre, dangerous Pandarus, Waller was more effete, vulgar, portly, and lethargic, "an altogether sadder pimp who knows exactly what he is doing and can't bring any vicarious pleasure to the job."[79]

Despite the play's title, the lovers under Barton's direction were "incidental to the plot, developed by the machinations of opposing forces, the war and obscenity which overwhelmed their destines."[80] They did, however, bolster the director's "war equals lechery" interpretation, particularly in an erotically charged scene in which Cressida lured Troilus back to her bed the morning after their first tryst (4.2). The scene was climaxed when Cressida dropped both her covering and her coyness and ran offstage with Troilus in pursuit.[81] This battle of the sexes, playful and erotic, paralleled the military gamesmanship on which the production focused: bedroom or battlefield, relationships were means of self-gratification.

Cressida's motivations are as troublesome as Hector's, for she, too, makes a seemingly inexplicable about-face: once in the Greek camp she violates her vow of eternal love for Troilus. Barton's notes attribute Cressida's enigmatic nature to her innate honesty: "She is almost always open about how she feels at a given moment. . . . Basically, she reacts according to how she is treated. She becomes Troilus's Cressida, and then Diomedes' in response to the image each has of her." In act 1, an awkward, adolescent Cressida (Helen Mirren) fell to the ground on her back and opened her legs satirically, an inept attempt to be sexually sophisticated and witty with Pandarus.[82] The farewell scene was played honestly, her words the declaration of a sincere but shallow woman who was true to the moment. She was equally "true" to her new Greek masters by increasingly displaying her pleasure to the attention lavished upon her. In becoming Diomedes' Cressida, she also responded truly, "overwhelmed by her new found excitement to the point of slithering down the length of his body to the floor."[83] Darlington cited this "original reading" as one of the production's strengths.[84] Mirren originally minimized Cressida's sensuality and, in the process, learned much about the character: "I fought against the sensualist, the open, free, sexy, ordinary, slightly silly girl. I wanted to make her intelligent and sharp and sexy, but neurotically sexy, something she absolutely isn't."[85]

If Cressida is anything less than a victim of the times, then Troilus is an unsympathetic fool. Under Barton's direction, Michael Williams's Troilus evolved from a high-spirited youth to an angry, more knowledgeable young man. His eulogy for the slain Hector was delivered defiantly, an outburst to an unyielding cosmos. Some critics thought he was perhaps too angry—"he is outraged but not destroyed."[86] Barton describes Troilus as the extreme example of a number of characters who define life according to their needs: "He looks at life most subjectively and is hence the one hurt most when confronted with reality. He can't resolve the two opposites discovered by his senses and brutalises himself in order to survive." Barton's analysis suggests that Troilus is indeed the modern existential hero described by Rossiter: "M. Sartre would tell Troilus that his anguish was the index of awareness of existence come alive for the first time; and simultaneously, a demonstration of his 'responsibility' for the Trojan War . . . the result is rational insanity: alienation."[87] During the betrayal scene Barton's Troilus collapsed into Ulysses' lap, Ulysses' laughed cynically, and the young Trojan learned the absolute meaning of pain and brutality. Barton's perverse *Pieta* seemed an apt symbol for a production calculated to teach us about the pain of being human. This moment, however, bordered on tragic recognition. But Troilus does not grow beyond this moment, and the last glimpse of him on Barton's battlefield was as a bitter youth, unable to rationalize the harsh blows with which the world rebuffed him.[88]

As in the 1960 production, Barton's battles were staged to educate the audience to the horrors of war. They were highly stylized in slow motion, "the figures moving on clouds of steam like prehistoric monsters,"[89] to the thunderous accompaniment of the amplified, echo-chamber sound of swords crashing on metallic shields.[90] Again, the death of Hector was the narrative, emotional, and theatrical climax of the production as it emphasized the sacrificial slaughter of a chivalric ideal. Shaw remembers the moment as among the most extraordinary scenes he has witnessed in his fifty-year stage career. Alone and unarmed, Hector was surrounded by Achilles' forces, who, in dancelike movements, advanced on the Trojan warrior. A journalist for the *Leamington Spa Courier* best describes the death scene:

> In one supreme moment the dark arena of shields and spears emerges from the clouds of mist to the sound of heavenly murmurings, and with mechanical resolution the unarmed Trojan is gored to death. Hector rises once, staggers towards Achilles like a wounded bull, and is brought bleeding to the ground as the Greek's sword point falls upon his neck like a matador's final thrust.[91]

A production as conceptually bold as Barton's *Troilus* is bound to elicit polar responses. The majority of commentaries praised Barton's work in tones similar to Frank Cox, who admired the production's combination of scholarship and theatricality.[92] Others felt Barton was self-indulgent. Gareth Lloyd Evans, while analyzing "dissociated action" in RSC productions of the late 1960s, called Barton's *Troilus and Cressida* "only an extreme example of what seems a general condition" in which directors feel they bore audiences if they give them too much of Shakespeare's poetry.[93] More succinctly, *The Scotsman*'s critic objected to the production because "the director speaks louder than the playwright."[94]

Apparently, however, audiences wanted to listen to the director as much as the playwright. When the production transferred to the Aldwych in the summer of 1969 in a tighter, more disciplined performance,[95] it was a popular success. Shaw recalls that it was the most sought-after ticket during the 1969–70 London season. Predictably, Trevor Nunn again asked Barton to restage the play as part of the 1976 Stratford season.

Barton initially refused Nunn, suggesting that Nunn himself direct the project, but the latter refused. Michael Tubbs, who rewrote Guy Woolfenden's original score of the 1968 *Troilus* and served as music director in 1976, said the production was "thrust" upon Barton, who reluctantly accepted because "John has always been somebody who would step in and do something for the company when there was a need for it being done."[96] Unfortunately the production was deemed a poor imitation of the earlier version: ". . . an undermining of the bold certainties of his earlier version . . . [which was] one of the most memorable achievements of the RSC."[97] Actors in the 1976 company agree that their director was preoccupied by memories of the earlier work. Church (now cast as Ulysses) called the production "a great mistake . . . because he wasn't far enough away from the original. He partly rethought it and partly didn't; it was all at bag ends." Mike Gwilym, whose Troilus was praised, felt the production was a "mish-mash" because Barton incorporated considerable business from the 1968 production that the actors "didn't like doing."[98] Barton himself regards the latter *Troilus* "a great mistake": "I shouldn't have done that at any rate. My heart wasn't in it, but it was a necessary part of the season."[99] In 1976 he also staged his highly regarded *Much Ado About Nothing* (see chapter 6) and *The Winter's Tale* (with Trevor Nunn; see chapter 7), and he assisted Nunn with *King Lear* at the RSC's Other Place. Understandably, Barton was exhausted and the opening of Troilus in August was delayed two weeks. He was assisted by Barry Kyle, who was assigned the Trojan scenes, while Barton took the Greek because, says Gwilym, "that was what he was most interested in."

Barton retained many elements used in 1968: the emphasis on sensuality and lechery, typified by nearly naked warriors in combat ("Barricades of buttocks"[100]); the outrageous behavior of Achilles (though the more overtly decadent actions between Patroclus and Achilles were toned down); the prominence of Thersites' point of view; the sultry, steamy battle scenes and the ritualized slaughter of Hector. Other ideas, according to some critics, "merely vulgarized what [Barton] did before without apparently adding new insights."[101] For example, as she turned to leave the stage in the betrayal scene, Cressida lowered a head veil to reveal a gaudy courtesan's mask on the back of her head.[102] A number of life-sized dolls representing Helen and Cressida were used to show that women were chattel in this world.[103] Diomedes carried a doll replica of Cressida before the betrayal, the Greek generals had used the same doll for their amusement as a prelude to the kissing scene (4.5), and Thersites toyed with such a doll during the epilogue.[104] One wonders if perhaps Barton was also borrowing from another of his productions: the 1974 *Dr. Faustus* liberally used puppets and dolls (see chapter 9).

Purely theatrical devices now heightened the narrative and thematic values of the script. This impetus was found in the prologue, which Barton now assigned to the character he knew to be the play's spokesman: Thersites. John Nettles, who spoke the prologue as an archaeologist sifting through the ruins of Troy, spat out the line ". . . what may be digested in a *play*" (29). David Zane Mairowitz felt Barton and his company were seizing the theater metaphor—a Barton favorite—as an excuse to impose "gimmicks and grotesqueries" on the play.[105]

Whatever his intentions, Barton's 1976 *Troilus and Cressida* was pointedly theatrical: Pandarus, in the Helen-Paris scene (3.1) sang "Love, love, nothing but love" as a bawdy music hall ballad, punctuating the already obscene lyrics by illustrating its lubricities with a giant bolster;[106] and, in one of the most striking innovations, the Trojan Council scene was preceded by a formal ritual in which Priam's sons donned huge mythic animal masks and worshipped before a large chalice.[107]

Thematically, Barton seemed more content to explore the ambiguities of the play.[108] Lloyd Evans suggests that the Barton-Kyle interpretation presented "what may be modishly expressed as an 'Absurdist' view of it. What they seem to be saying is: 'This is how it is—stupid, pitiable and unpleasing—basically pointless.' "[109] If Lloyd Evans's perception is correct, this would represent a major thematic shift from the earlier production, which ascribed the carnage of war to uncontrolled passions. The latter production seemed to say that man is hopelessly irrational, that he can no longer blame his humanity on passionate excesses.

Thus the 1976 production was more savage in its satiric portrayal of the Greeks and Trojans. The former especially were treated harshly: Barton found every opportunity to deflate the Greek generals, "whose actions are as theatrical as their thoughts."[110] Agamemnon played the camp cook, carrying a pan of "chops" about, ignored by Ulysses and his colleagues;[111] the Greek debate in 1.3 was begun by Nestor noisily banging on a gong, Ajax conducting music with his sword, and Ulysses upstaging Agamemnon's speech. The Greeks, older, gray-bearded, paunchy, wore floppy straw shepherd's hats and tiptoed about the camp to avoid long-winded Agamemnon. Ulysses' intellectual prowess was further undercut during his speech about the corroding power of time in 3.3 (145ff): Ulysses entered reading a large book, which Achilles appropriated to use as a stool. As the speech concluded, the book collapsed under Achilles, who fell down laughing, a suggestion that Ulysses' wisdom is a shakey prop on which to rest. Mairowitz aptly summarizes Barton's vision of the Greek retinue: ". . . a collection of idiots and misfits who have forgotten the original intent of the war."[112] Nettles questioned the efficacy of the director's caricatures of the generals: "The cluttering up, the underlining was what was wrong with *Troilus and Cressida*. If the Greek generals are going to be fools, that shouldn't be shown the minute they appear, otherwise they have no place to go."

The Trojans seemed more attractive, Oriental, solemn; they were lean, young, athletic, and sensual: "dashing delinquents, working at a war that has long ceased to have more than a casual interest in Paris and Helen."[113] Kyle, who staged most of their scenes, arranged them in formal symmetry to suggest their superficial concern for order and, as the masked ritual suggests, the traditions of the past. Michael Pennington's Hector emerged as a more contradictory, less likable character than in the RSC's previous productions. He suggests the reason for this less-heroic Hector:

> Hector in *Troilus* . . . is such a perplexing character because, seeming to be the voice of reason and the voice of authority and the voice of morality and humanity, nevertheless more than anybody [in the play] does the most atrocious things. . . . Hector is the nicest man in the world, but then he is capable of deciding to go back into battle and slaughter 80 unarmed Greeks on a whim. That ambiguity is something that interests Barton.[114]

The troublesome "about-face" speech to the Trojan Council was delivered directly to the audience (intended as a purely theatrical speech? see the discussion of Hamlet's soliloquies—also delivered by Pennington—in chapter 8), after which he "feebly climbed down and joined the jolly young blimps he had just accused of being unfit to hear moral philosophy. Why? Because that is the kind of thing people do."[115] Later, Hector slew Patroclus on stage in a spear fight at 5.5 (Barton substituted the fight for Agamemnon's speech at line 6), even though the script calls for Patroclus's death offstage. To add greater ignominy to Hector's death, Achilles "scalped" Hector's helmet of its plummage and threw it to the battlefield, where it was later kicked by Ulysses.

Though the war plot was played more satirically—even farcically—Barton's handling of the lovers was more realistic. In 1972 he told *Shakespeare Survey* that "what happens, by the end, to Troilus and Cressida . . . is not black comedy. . . . I feel a great compassion for what becomes of Troilus and Cressida."[116] Roger Warren found that in 1976 the lovers "for the first time in [his] experience held the center of the play."[117] Cressida (Francesca Annis) was more aggressive in her pursuit of Troilus, and throughout she was more reflective, more aware of her own complexity. For *Guardian* critic Michael Billington "she captures better than anyone Barton's delight in human contradictoriness. Even in her first passionate declaration of love for Troilus, she breaks off in a sudden fit of physical self-hatred."[118] Her bawdier nature was played down: Barton trimmed some of the banter between Pandarus and Cressida to make her less lascivious, and the bawdy gesture of the 1968 production (Cressida reclines, legs spread) was deleted.[119] Gwilym's Troilus was impulsive and tempestuous, but not without humor, which gradually gave way to cynicism after Cressida's betrayal and Hector's death. Several critics questioned the smile that

Gwilym employed during Troilus's speech about Hector's death. The actor says that Barton instructed him to find occasion to smile, to inject humor, albeit cynical, into a speech to minimize the emotional heaviness and self-pity. In the 1984 television series, "Playing Shakespeare," Barton repeated his instructions concerning the speech for the viewers' benefit:

> Try it as if you've decided that, because everything is so grievous, you can only survive by shutting off your grief. Try *enjoying* discomforting the other Trojans who don't realize the horror of things as you do. When you get to the "who shall tell Priam so" show that you have changed. You are not the emotional young man of the rest of the play, but you have grown up and are grimly self-controlled. Make it an *objective* prophecy.

To undercut Troilus's self-pity in 1976, Barton had Ulysses applaud the young Trojan's outburst at the conclusion of the betrayal scene, a gesture that merged the theatrical and cynical elements of that production.

The scene in which Troilus and Cressida pledge their love (3.1) was stylized and best captured in visual terms Barton's various interpretations of the play. During the "virtuous fight" sequence (170ff), the director had the lovers assume a formalized position, described by Richard David in *Shakespeare in the Theatre:*

> . . . the lovers crouch and join hands as if actually wrestling; an odd pose, but one that I found effective, and that enabled the wrestlers, circling in their ring, each to make their declaration frontally to the audience, with Cressida prone, appealing to heaven, for her "If I be false . . ." At this point there could be no doubt that she meant as truly as Troilus.[121]

The ritualized formality gave the exchange of oaths a solemnity that was eventually undercut by ensuing events.

Whether one likes or finds fault with Barton's several approaches to *Troilus and Cressida,* one must acknowledge that the experiences offered by Barton—and Hall and Kyle, with whom he worked—did no little service to the play. His inventiveness, even in its excess, seemed appropriate to the spirit of experimentation that inspired Shakespeare in the early seventeenth century.

4

"The Owl and the Cuckoo":
Love's Labour's Lost (1965, 1978), *Twelfth Night* (1969), *All's Well That Ends Well* (1967), *Measure for Measure* (1970), and *The Merchant of Venice* (1979, 1981)

Though Barton is best known for textual revisions and such boldly conceived productions as *Troilus and Cressida,* his most successful work in terms of critical response has been the staging of Shakespeare's comedies. When *Twelfth Night* opened in 1969, J. W. Lambert's enthusiastic review for *The Sunday Times* concluded by noting the director's maturation at Stratford: "I look forward to more from, I am convinced, a director standing on the threshold of mature greatness."[1]

With the comedies Barton has relied little on those practices that have gained him a reputation as a studious and imaginative—if not a little eccentric—director. With the exception of *Love's Labour's Lost,* whose esoteric Renaissance humor needs cutting, Barton did little to alter the original texts. Instead, he focused his insights clearly on the texts as written and allowed his actors—rather than theatrical embellishments—to communicate Shakespeare's intentions. Gareth Lloyd Evans, whom Barton had irritated with *Troilus and Cressida,* refers to *Twelfth Night* as "a superb demonstration of the difference between imposed and acquired interpretation. The truth is that, in this case, because the director himself has 'experienced' the text rather than forced it to experience him, we in the audience 'share' the production."[2] Paradoxically, when Barton strayed from the discipline of the comedies to the outlandishness of *King John* (see chapter 5), critics used the former, particularly those staged from 1965 to 1970, to remind him of his potential.

For Barton the Director, 1965 was a pivotal year. His success as editor and codirector on *The Wars of the Roses* mitigated the problems attending *The Taming of the Shrew* in 1960, and Hall encouraged Barton to direct again. He directed *Love's Labour's Lost*, opening new territory for both himself and the RSC. Given its academic milieu, its complex language, and the structural problems of a prentice work, the infrequently performed comedy was a natural choice for Barton: "It has always been one of my favorites, not because it contains great philosophical insights or remarkable verse . . . but it takes a highly conventional piece of Elizabethan artifice and shows nature breaking through all the rules."[3]

An ironist, Barton consciously seeks polar values in his work, an approach he learned well from the Berliner Ensemble in 1956. In the television series "Playing Shakespeare," Barton instructed his audience that "perhaps the actor's most difficult problem is how to handle irony. . . . It comes up in Shakespeare so often and there's so much more of it than people realize." His treatment of the comedies as a whole, and *Love's Labour's Lost* in particular, is memorable for the ironies he and his casts discovered in these plays. His 1965 program note for *Love's Labour's Lost* reflects his fascination with Shakespearean irony:

> On every level the play is built on apposition and paradox. Everything derives from Shakespeare's favourite juxtaposition of ceremony and Nature. . . . Every character and situation is turned topsy-turvy. The play ends with the moral dialogue of the learned men: When the meadows are full of delight, look out for the cuckoo; and when blood is nipped and ways be foul—be merry, like the note of the owl.[4]

The remarks establish a formula favored by Barton when staging plays in general, the comedies in particular. He, too, looks for the cuckoo and the owl: his work with serious drama invariably seeks the comic strain; his comedies, the melancholic.

Barton notes that *Love's Labour's Lost* is unique among Shakespeare's comedies in that it does not offer a happy ending: "It grows sadder and more profound as it closes."[5] Accordingly, he explored the play's darker side. John Russell Brown assessed this approach: ". . . individual performances and stage setting alike announce that a solemn recognition of death's inevitable demands is the final purpose of the performance: everything must give way to this."[6]

The stage setting incorporated both the melancholia of his concept and some Barton research into the play's origins, which suggest that it was written for a performance in the garden of an Elizabethan country house. Sally Jacobs' setting suggested "the sun-drenched lawn of a formal garden,"[7] but the trees surrounding it were bare, no doubt anticipating the bitter-sweet ending in which the lovers are separated by the news of the French king's death. W. A. Darlington questioned the design—"Why set the play, which must be supposed to happen in high summer, in the glade of utterly bare trees?"[8] R. B. Marriott answered that the concept gave the play an unusual unity and purpose: "Near the end, as the lovers prepare to face their year of sacrifice away from each other, the melancholy deepens. This unifying atmosphere is the major achievement of the production."⁹ Thus the visual elements countered audience expectations about comedy's customary brightness. Just as Barton and Hall sought to "de-prettify" the English history plays, there is a corresponding deromanticization of the comedies.

The visual choices should not imply that Barton deprived the play of its comic values. He was fully aware of its comedic conventions, typical of plays written in the 1580s, and suggests that Shakespeare was also discovering "in fits and starts" the comedy of mood and character. Because the play is composed from various comic strands, it presents problems to performers insensitive to these varied styles; Barton's program note defines them:

> The variety of styles demands a wide variety of style in playing, sometimes artificial, sometimes naturalistic. The change from one to the other is often sudden and arbitrary. Each element has to be accepted for what it is, and yet a harmony must be found between them.

Barton's company found such harmonies, as the lighter moments threw the darker into greater relief, and vice versa.

Barton explored several themes in addition to that of nature exerting its will on men's actions: for example, he considered maturation and the "roles" the lovers play: "The men are as much in love with being in love as with the thing itself . . . the girls, too, are not what they seem. By themselves they are more deb than courtier." Perhaps the most distinctive theme Barton extracted from the text was the importance of oaths:

> The Spanish Court's oath of Mortification at the beginning is ridiculous and impracticable. But it is an oath all the same, and a serious one. So when the King and the rest break it at the first sight of a woman's eyes, the girls are justified in questioning their oaths of love.

Michael Pennington, who played Dumane in 1965 and Berowne in 1978, further clarifies his director's attitudes about the comedy's ethical substance: "People *do* take oaths and people *do* break oaths and they *do* play around with other people's emotions . . . the task that is set at the end of the play is a serious task which the women instinctively know they have to impose in order to find out where their men's hearts really are. As in all Shakespeare's comedies there is a serious moral concern."¹⁰ To heighten the "oath theme," Barton altered the text slightly. The encounter between the King of Navarre and the French Princess (5.2.343–57)—"Nor God nor I delights in perjured men"—was relocated after 426 (427–84 were cut); the line signaling Costard's entrance, "Thou part'st a fair fray," pointed up that the fair fray was over broken oaths rather than some aimless banter between Berowne and Boyet. Barton justified his textual liberties by noting that the play "contains parallel passages which clearly represent Shakespeare's own revision alongside earlier sections they were intended to replace."[11] Barton took two other significant liberties: the play's final line, Armado's, was reassigned to Boyet, probably because Barton intended him to have additional prominence throughout the production.[12] The final song about the owl and the cuckoo was *recited*, not sung, by the village rustics, "in front of great wicker models of a cuckoo and an owl with practical eyes and beaks."[13]

Two characters in particular were presented from uncustomary perspectives, and these represent Barton's major contributions to a renewed understanding of the play. Boyet was given a well-defined social context, which made his presence necessary. As played by Brewster Mason, he became "a point or reference for the young men and girls alike in their move toward maturation."[14] Alexander Leggatt cites Barton's inventive and intelligent humanizing of Boyet as an example of how a perceptive director can develop a whole social ambience that extends beyond what the dialogue suggests.[15] For Barton, Boyet was an experienced senior advisor to a princess on her first diplomatic mission. He carried the state staff of office; at the news of the king's death, he slowly crossed to his "new" queen, knelt, and solemnly delivered the staff to her. The moment, says Leggatt, established "a helpful context for the new dignity and seriousness of the Princess in the moments that followed, and suggested the more serious world from which the world of courtship was just a holiday." Boyet's sobriety throughout set the tenor of the production, and thus it was fitting that he should have the play's final word.

More surprising, Don Armado, the blustering Spanish captain, though still humorous, was played as a weary Don Quixote. His graver nature apparently set a pattern from which Barton would cut the figure of Sir Toby Belch four years later.

Thirteen years later Barton returned to the play. Pennington, the only carry-over from the 1965 production, remembers that the first version "was not a happy production," but finds it "warming" that his director returned to the play and did "very much better with it."[16] Barton himself dismisses his first attempt at the play as "not very good." He had, of course, matured as a director and John Peter noted in *The Times* that his work on *Twelfth Night* apparently strengthened his later work on *Love's Labour's Lost*.[17] Thus the whirligig of time runs away: the 1965 *Love's Labour's Lost* no doubt had helped Barton shape his approach to *Twelfth Night*.

In 1978 Barton again sought the underlying melancholia of Navarre, and Ralph Koltai's design immediately appraised RSC patrons that the play occurs in the dying time of year. Instead of the bleak, bare trees of 1965, Koltai gave his director "real" trees whose gold and russet leaves fluttered to the stage as the audience assembled. Customarily the play is set in pastoral greenness, but Wardle found this setting "a better solution for a comedy showing the triumph of nature over artifice . . . the whole emphasis of the show is to unite the setting and the down-to-earth characters in demolishing every form of artificiality from affectations of language, to the denial of physical desire."[18] To emphasize the changing seasons, Barton devised a silent prologue, recorded in the prompt copy:

> Costard, Jaquenetta, Dull, and a Forester enter with brooms and, directed by Dull, sweep the stage clear of leaves. On clearance, the lords enter and rustics exit, watching lords as they leave.

The rustics were obviously aware of the lesson they would teach the lords: the springtime of youth must give way to the harsher realities of the world's will. The prologue was an effective "bookend" to its counterpart, the song of the owl and the cuckoo. Again the "song" was recited (by Nathaniel and Holofernes, supported by the other rustics), and Anne Barton's program note suggests a rationale for this verbalization:

> The final song presents a wholeness of outlook in which fact and fancy, youth and age, life and death are held in equilibrium. The unifying effect of the music must not be underestimated, but still *this harmony is essentially verbal.*[19] [italics mine]

Barton's staging of the finale was a particularly well-conceived moment, an indicator of a particular Barton talent:

> . . . the stage became filled with harmonious echoes of country sounds— exquisitely capped by the hooting of a *real* owl above their heads, magically reinforcing Shakespeare's own final emphasis upon the ordinary real ties of country life. Such an extraordinarily complex scene, which takes the breath away with its combination of gaiety and sadness, its blending of affairs of state, of the heart, of the countryside, is Mr. Barton's special territory as a director.[20]

Again Barton explored the themes of maturation, the life cycle, and the battle of the sexes, but with even more clarity. He used the well-intentioned but poorly executed pageant of the Nine Worthies to underscore the immaturity of Berowne and his academic colleagues who mercilessly mocked the locals—a cruel contrast to the earnestness of the amateur performers. Their mockery was judged "one of the most sobering and touching moments" in the play, "partly because the pageant is so marvelously funny."[21] The pageant, replete with a float and a five-piece band, included Nathaniel as Alexander on an oversized hobby horse whose front was too heavy to keep the would-be warrior upright; he carried an overlong lance that further hindered his conquest of the world (though a gracious French Princess obligingly propped up Alexander's sagging lance). Armado was also equipped with a huge red lance and walked about on cothurni. The fun was cut short by Pennington's scathing delivery of "Take away the conqueror, take away Alisander." There was nothing charming or indulgent about Berowne's tone: "It is cruel and contemptuous. And just as his cruelty denies him Rosaline, so it precipitates the abrupt interruption of death upon the merriment. . . . After this, the entrance of Marcade as a messenger of death seems inevitable."[22]

Throughout, Pennington played Berowne as a practicing skeptic, coupled with an "intense, almost erotic lyricism for the great defense of Love."[23] Under Barton's guidance, he built his interpretation around the "lover's eye" speech (4.1.284–360), which Barton heightened by placing an interval at the conclusion of this scene and by transposing a couplet from lines 213–14 of that scene to replace Shakespeare's last three lines of the original speech:

> We cannot cross the cause why we were born;
> Therefore on all hands must we be foresworn.[24]

The transposition offered a respectable rationale for Berowne's intellectual sleight-of-hand and enhanced the primary thrust of Barton's interpretation: the idea of intellectual arrogance and posturing romanticism being brought down to earth.[25]

To bring "posturing romanticism" down to earth, Barton shifted the love interest from Berowne and Rosaline to the King and French Princess who were played, very uncharacteristically, as physically plain beings who possessed an interior beauty and integrity that contrasted with the interior uncomeliness of handsome Berowne. As the King, Barton cast portly Richard Griffiths, "a chubby, untidy, bespectacled figure . . . perhaps trying to make up in learning what he lacks in dignity."[26] Opposite him was the French Princess (Carmen du Sautoy)—"a ringletted hoyden in grannie glasses, who takes it for granted that her girls should get down and polish her shoes, but never pulls rank until, as mortality darkens the scene, she undergoes transformation into a queen."[27] The evolution of these "ugly ducklings" into responsible rulers enhanced the maturation theme. Having exposed the humanity of these royal figures, Barton's company prepared for a more effective ending in which the surface gaiety of Navarre gave way to serious concerns. Roger Warren believed that the production's strength lay in Barton's ability to probe "the implications of imagery and characterization . . . fleshing out his discoveries in terms of concrete theatrical effects and sustained, detailed characterization which have the supreme advantage of increasing admiration for the text." The production's love of humanity and inventive theatricality transcended the limitations of the artificial Renaissance humor that frequently cause directors and audiences to approach *Love's Labour's Lost* warily.

As Barton approached *Twelfth Night* in the summer of 1969, he was faced with a problem quite the opposite of that presented by the relatively little-known *Love's Labour's Lost. Twelfth Night* is perhaps the best known of Shakespeare's comedies, and the director was acutely aware of the challenges presented by its popularity:

The text is so familiar, I think, to everyone that there's a danger of staleness. I suppose I started with the idea that the play should as far as possible emerge uncluttered: free from previous conceptions, clichés, traditional interpretations of specific characters or scenes. . . . I tried to avoid imposing an ostentatious directional hand: it's very much an actor's play. The text contains an enormous range of emotions and moods, and most productions seem to select one—farce or bitterness or romance—and emphasize it throughout. I wanted to sound all the notes that are there.[28]

Barton's production goals serve as a useful checklist to measure his finished product, which was enthusiastically received by critics and audiences. Coupled with the previous year's *Troilus and Cressida, Twelfth Night,* proclaimed *The Observer,* elevated Barton to the status of "the best Shakespearean director in [England] at this moment."[29] The production was kept in the RSC's repertory through the 1972 season, and it ultimately played a total of 202 performances at Stratford, London, Australia, and Japan,[30] a testimony to its appeal. Most important, it received highest praise from Barton's sternest critic, John Barton: of the many productions he has done in his twenty-five years with the RSC, he believes that *Twelfth Night* is one that, more than any other, he "got right" (his customary benediction for a scene or piece of business).[31]

Though Barton may have approached *Twelfth Night* "free from previous conceptions," in actual practice there seem to be influences that steered him toward his melancholic interpretation. His work with *Love's Labour's Lost* in 1965 suggested the viability of a more somber approach to Shakespearean comedy. Several critics believed they detected a discernable influence of Peter Hall's 1958 staging of *Twelfth Night* at Stratford.[32] That production, revived for the RSC's first season in 1960, offered a mood that was "instead of Maytime gaiety . . . a bit gloomy and fusty-dusty. Comedy became subdued in the dull amber hues."[33] Trevor Nunn, while a student at Cambridge, saw Hall's production and remembers that its "autumnal setting and its melancholia seemed definitively right. He had touched a Chekhovlike centre of the play; it was unarguable."[34] Nunn believed Barton's 1969 production carried Peter Hall's perception further.

Yet another influence may have shaped Barton's thinking: Anne Righter Barton, whom the director had married the previous summer, wrote a program note for the production that, according to Stanley Wells, "undoubtedly he approved, and that may be taken as reflecting some of his views on the play."[35] Her ideas were expanded into a 1972 essay, *"As You Like It* and *Twelfth Night:* Shakespeare's Sense of an Ending," which cogently argues, by comparing the resolutions of the two comedies, that the latter breaks away from the classicism of its predecessor because "the final act of *Twelfth Night,* a world of revelry, of comic festivity, fights a kind of desperate rearguard action against the cold light of day."[36] Whether Mr. Barton's ideas grew from Mrs. Barton's emerging criticism or vice-versa cannot be accurately determined. Christine Avern-Carr, who has examined several Stratford productions of the play, notes the interdependence of Barton's "staged essay" and his wife's literary essay: "There is no doubt [her] ideas were illustrated by Barton's production, although one cannot say whether the ideas came before the production or whether they emerged from it; it is remarkable that any theatrical realization should be so closely connected to a piece of serious literary criticism, evolving in parallel to each other."[37]

Judi Dench, who played Viola to exceptional acclaim, suggests that Barton entered rehearsals with a notion about the play's melancholy notes: "John Barton was the one who said it's such a bittersweet play, that if you do that [i.e., play it purely for comedy], it tips over. . . . There's so much bitter-sweetness tinging all those characters, that you cannot play too much on the comic side and in that totally optimistic way, though Viola *is* an optimist and the catalyst of the play."[38] As with *Love's Labour's Lost* four years earlier, the choice to play *Twelfth Night* bittersweetly enhanced, not diminished, the inherent comedy. Several critics believed "the comedy is more satisfying because of the winter chill in the air of a production that never lets us forget that *Twelfth Night* is the last rite of the festive season"[39]—an idea echoed in Anne Barton's program note:

> By its very nature, holiday is not eternal. It is only an interval in the everyday, destined to yield in the end to the sober order it has momentarily overthrown.

Tony Church called the "wistful, melancholy" strain a revelation, but emphasized that "it was also the funniest *Twelfth Night* I've ever seen . . . the actual boisterous scenes, the duel and the knockabout stuff has rarely ever been funnier. John will push that sort of thing to its limits and it won't crack."[40]

As Barton discovered that Thersites was the spokesman for *Troilus and Cressida,* so he found that Feste set the tone for *Twelfth Night.* Again, he may have derived a notion from Hall's production, which prompted a writer for the *Evening Telegraph* (Coventry) to note that Feste (then played by Max Adrian) "suggests that unknown heartbreak which is at the centre of perhaps the most enigmatic character Shakespeare ever drew."[41] Feste's somber closing song about "the wind and the rain" and his wistful observation that "youth's a stuff will not endure" (2.3.50) provided Barton with textual clues for the tone of the production.

Most observers found Barton's interpretation instructive. Sheila Bannock wrote that Barton enabled Stratford audiences to see the complex pattern of "all those apparently somber paradoxes of the play which always seemed to have been glossed over."[42] John Barber, who predicted (rightly) that the work would go on record as the RSC's "best production for many seasons," judged Barton's work to be true to the festive spirit, but enhanced with a concern for "people who misuse time, sadly deceiving themselves and deceived in each other."[43] Barton's colleagues, typified by Nunn, proclaimed the production a watershed moment in modern Shakespeare interpretation:

. . . in showing us that Belch, Aguecheek, Malvolio, Feste, *and* Maria and Orsino were all of an age who would bitterly understand "Youth's a stuff will not endure," [Barton] unlocked the dark and melancholic half of the play, in contrast to which, while "golden time consents," Viola and Olivia and Sebastian play their games of disguise and romance.[44]

Barton also examined the theme of "madness" in theatrical terms, a notion Anne Barton defined in the RSC program:

For Elizabethans, the very title of this comedy would have stirred associations with an annual period of revelry: a feast at which the world is turned upside down . . . and ordinary rules of conduct were reversed. The sea-captain who first tells Viola about Ilyria might justly have said to her what the Cheshire Cat tells Alice: "They're all mad here." . . . Malvolio alone tries to check this prevailing atmosphere of abandon, this abdication from common sense.

During Feste's interrogation of Malvolio as Sir Topas, the Clown asked the imprisoned Puritan, "Are you not mad indeed or do *you* but counterfeit?" (4.2.110)—an emphasis that signaled Barton's controlling purpose: "I decided that John Barton was digging me in the ribs and remarking that this was a play in which everyone was a madman or a pretender or both, and in which sanity and frenzy, reality and illusion, were so intermixed that only a jester could hope to distinguish them."[45] Certainly the play's language supports Barton's perception: in 4.3 Sebastian soliloquizes that his reason persuades him that he is mad—"or else the lady's mad." Barton heightened the moment by including the muted, offstage cries of Malvolio to punctuate Sebastian's analysis of Illyria's madness, an invention Alexander Leggatt cites as a worthy case of the director's ability to juxtapose the various strands of a Shakespearean text.[46]

References to madness and dreams may have also inspired Barton's setting, rendered by Christopher Morley, which consisted of a long, bare gallery of lattice-work in which sunlight only half penetrated. Sheila Bannock declared that the set reminded her "of a dream tunnel, a journeying place of the mind," and when the upstage doors opened, in the murky distance, characters entered, "like familiar images in a dream, [and] moved forward in our consciousness before they assumed active roles."[47] Viola's first entrance (1.2) suggested she was entering a dream world: she emerged "in a flourish of the RSC's favorite smoke,"[48] accompanied by the sea captain and three undefined characters "who look as if they lived under the sea rather than on it."[49] The smoke effect was used again during the Sebastian-Viola reunion in act 5.

To enforce the melancholic tone, the actors were dressed in subdued tones. One critic felt the austere design and the somber costumes suggested an Illyria in total eclipse.[50] Actually, there was selected use of brighter colors in the set, primarily in the white wicker furniture, which defined locale, and in the selective use of sunlight, which filtered through the lattice-work. Because the director carefully chose when he used sunlight, its presence was the more effective, particularly when brother and sister were reunited.

One of the elements that constitutes a "Barton style" is a discriminate use of sound and music to heighten a moment or define a theme. He maintains that the best way to generate emotion is through music, which, in his productions, includes an orchestrated use of sound effects: "I care passionately about music and take a terrific interest in it (personal interview, June 1983)." *Twelfth Night* is frequently cited as the exemplar play of his aural technique. Melancholy and the relentless surge of time were magnified by the sounds of the sea: rolling waves and sea birds. Richard David interpreted Barton's sea sounds to be a reminder "of that sense of the changes and chances of life that is surely intrinsic to the mood of the play as in its basic situations."[51] A careful reading of the text—and perhaps of Dover Wilson's analysis of the play's sea imagery— suggested to Barton that the sea is important to the psychic life of these characters. Thus he underscored key moments by a calculated use of sea sounds. For example, during the Duke's opening speech, the phrase "dying fall" was accompanied by the sound of waves crashing against the shore; moments later, Valentine's report about Olivia's "answer" was echoed by sea gulls; in 2.4, Viola's line about women and roses—"To die, even when they to perfection grow" (40)—was backed again by the plaintive cry of curlews. And, most significant, as Viola and Sebastian moved toward one another in silence, the sound of the relentless sea announced their reunion. Tony Church, who joined the cast for later performances, describes the moment:

> Viola turns around and they catch each other's faces on the half angle. There is an absolute silence and then suddenly, about three times louder than it had been before, *woooosh!*, it comes again, the sound of the sea. The tears poured down one's face. Absolutely astonishing.[52]

Michael Tubbs was commissioned by Barton to devise a musical score, based on traditional melodies, to supplement the action and mood. Tubbs recalls Barton's brief to him regarding music for *Twelfth Night:* ". . . the music will not be something that draws attention to itself. . . . It's something that people will latch onto very quickly, something that feels familiar, even if it isn't."[53] Tubbs was able to find traditional music associated with the play, added a few pieces (notably some Christmas rounds to the "party scene" of act 2), and wrote some music that evoked the mood of the period. "Come, Come Away Death," described as "old and plain" by the Duke, was actually written for the production—an "instant traditional song," as Tubbs describes it—by Guy Woolfenden, one of Barton's favored composers.[54] Prior to the show, a young guitarist played softly on stage. He was joined by Orsino about fifteen minutes before "curtain," and as the house lights dimmed, the guitarist segued into "the dying song," supplemented by the faint sounds of the sea in the distance. Tubbs recalls that "you could hear a whisp of guitar and a whisp of the sea; it was very discreet . . . but the atmosphere it produced was extraordinary." Though some critics found the aural effects obtrusive,[55] the majority agreed that the sound and music were "an acceptable and unobtrusive complement to the verbal imagery, a poetic way of directing a poetic play."[56]

Technical embellishments notwithstanding, Barton's most memorable effects were achieved by his actors, whom he cautioned at the outset of rehearsals: "I issued a caveat to the cast at the start of rehearsals against 'business'—*Twelfth Night* seems to have a tendency to accrue business at many points."[57] The company spent its rehearsal time exploring the human element of characters perhaps too familiar to Shakespeare's audiences, an effort that won highest praise. Speaight believed he had never seen "these familiar parts better played, and rarely played as well."[58] Bryden observed that "everyone is connected to everyone else, with a sympathy which never confuses sentiment with sentimentality that is the subject of this comedy."[59]

Although Orsino was not caricatured as a Renaissance romantic lover *in extremis,* Barton implanted business in the first scene—distracted by thoughts of Olivia, he neglected to sign documents offered by servants—to suggest that Illyria's leader was inattendant to serious responsibilities by his passion.[60] During "Come Away Death," Feste, ever the cynic, mocked the Duke's excesses as he circled the pining regent "with a curious dragging walk, pressing his hand to his brow, excessively underlining the melancholy. . . . Orsino, of course, is too wrapped up in self-pity to notice, but Judi Dench's Viola is sharp enough to see what he's about."[61] In the actual playing of the Duke, however, Barton and Charles Thomas (Richard Pasco in 1971) seemed to follow the advice of M. M. Mahood, whose character analyses were quoted generously in the RSC program: "[Orsino is] not a moony Duke . . . this absurdity must never submerge what is genuinely romantic in the role."[62]

Olivia owed her characterization, in part, to Hall's 1958 production in which he cast a much younger actress than was customary for the mourning sister: ". . . many of us are meeting Olivia for the first time . . . in some ways an outrageous portrait, a pouting doll, a giggling coquette."[63] Barton cast Lisa Harrow, then one of the RSC's youngest actresses, and maintained Olivia's girlishness that Hall discovered, yet toned down some of the silliness of the earlier characterization. The RSC program suggested further bases for the director's thinking about Olivia: Mahood pointed out that Shakespeare "deliberately turned the widow he found in his chief source to a young girl . . . then, when the fair young man appears, we watch the awakening of the Sleeping Beauty," and John Russell Brown wrote in 1961 that "another Olivia may be suggested: a very young girl, at first afraid of meeting the world and therefore living in a fantasy of seven years mourning." Olivia's maturation was marked by the finale: after Malvolio thrust his chain of office into her hands at his angered exit, she compassionately followed him with "a troubled glance."[64] Even in the moment of her happiness, she showed concern for her troubled steward.

The most enthusiastic commentaries were given to Judi Dench's Viola, a role ideal for her talent and looks: "She can seem genuinely boyish without for a moment ceasing to be womanly. The whole colour of this production derived, under the director's hand, from her radiant performance."[65] In addition to superb comic playing, Viola embodies the melancholia of the production. In her "riddle" to the Duke in 2.4, Dench inserted a "catch in the voice" on the word "brother":

> I am all the daughters of my father's house
> And all the *brothers* too . . .
>
> (119–20)

The moment bridged the fictional world of comedy and the real world of human sorrow that Barton showed the play to contain in equal measure.[66] From her first entrance, Barton framed Viola with an aura of spirituality transcending the merely comic world. In the short scene in which she and Feste bicker about his tabor (3.1), they "seem to discover in each other the same bewildered hard-pressed love of life."[67] To establish a bond between the two, Barton invented business at that scene's conclusion that is recorded in the prompt copy. As Feste says, "Who you are and what you would are out of my welkin" (60), the prompt says Feste crosses to Viola "as if [he] realized who [she] is." If there was a problem with the Barton-Dench Viola, suggests Simon Gray, a critic-turned-playwright, it was that she was too nice:

> Viola . . . is far too delightful to take advantage of Olivia or in any way embarrass the audience. . . . Shakespeare's Viola, in fact, is a much more knowing girl than Mr. Barton's, much more complex, and consequently the comedy in her relationship with Olivia is both more intensely erotic and altogether more dangerous.[68]

Gray felt Barton invested the characters with too great a moral consciousness, and that the play would have indeed been darker had a more malevolent side of the characters been allowed to emerge.

The lovers are bound to approach melancholia, however a director chooses to interpet *Twelfth Night;* Feste's ballad suggests that Renaissance lovers since Petrarch are a melancholic lot. Thus, it was in his rendering of the clowns that Barton found the darkest strains of the play. Certainly the relationship between Toby Belch and Maria was as clearly defined as one could imagine. Bill Fraser, a British television star with little classical experience, played the old knight as "the black sheep of a noble family, aware of his precarious situation and, indeed, of his alcoholic fecklessness."[69] The portrait seems to have borrowed its coloration from Barton's handling of Paul Rodgers's Falstaff in 1965. He was less boistrous than we normally perceive Sir Toby. It was, however, his carefully defined relationship with Maria for which the production will be remembered. Olivia's handmaiden was decidedly older, a spinster who sees in Toby a last chance to marry. Barton cheated the text a bit to effect this characterization: he trimmed Toby's descriptive line—"Look, where the youngest wren of nine comes" (3.2.65)—to negate the youthfulness of the role; it was one of the few instances where Barton countered the script to achieve his ends.[70] Though critics quibbled with the liberty,[71] the effects Barton and his actresses (first Brenda Bruce, then Elizabeth Spriggs) achieved seems a small price to pay for so human a characterization: saucy serving wenches are no short commodity in Renaissance comedy.

Several pieces of silent business heightened Maria's relationship with the aging knight: she lurked in a shadow to look back anxiously at the old profligate draining one more tankard; she threw a scathing look to Malvolio, a glare of "sly vindictiveness of a woman who resents his stifling of the few moments of fun" in her and Toby's life; she uttered a false "good night" in hope of luring Toby to bed and Toby's reply—"Tis too late to go to bed now"—was addressed to her, a rejection of her favors (2.3.175). Andrew sympathetically kissed her hand as she exited, holding back tears, and Feste sang softly, "Youth's a stuff will not endure." Most tellingly, after the scene in which the clowns bait Malvolio, Toby pulled Maria aside to deliver "Come by and by to my chamber" (4.3.70), a line usually directed to Feste. Harold Hobson describes the attendant business that made the scene memorable:

> [Toby] slips a ring on her finger and then immediately removes her glasses [Maria wore "granny" glasses throughout the play]; she puts them back on again, but not before a faint smile of timid happiness, on the verge of tears, passes across her face. . . .[72]

Again Feste supplemented the moment with the refrain, "Youth's a stuff will not endure."

Of the clowns Aguecheek most naturally attracts sympathy from the audience. "I was adored *once*, too" (2.3.166), he wistfully tells his companions. Taking this line as a cue, Barton and Barry Ingham devised an Aguecheek who was "no nincompoop"—as he is perhaps too often played—"but one of nature's put upons."[73] This Aguecheek was a forerunner of Chaplin's tramp, an eternal loser who forever trudged after Olivia with a pathetic bunch of flowers, but, given his luck, they were yellow flowers: "When he hears that Olivia cannot abide anything yellow, he quietly and sadly conceals the little bunch of primroses with which he had been hoping to woo her, and thereafter carries only pink flowers."[74] The most striking innovation was making Sir Andrew a Scotsman. Fittingly, he carried bagpipes—believed to be the set Barton gave to

O'Toole when he played Petruchio in 1960[75]—which enhanced the merrimak-
ing in act 2. Unfortunately, Toby invariably sat on them and, in a fitting
conclusion to his ill fortune, the bagpipes fell apart on the hapless Aguecheek.
The play's darkest side was manifested in Toby's unkind dismissal of Andrew
in act 5, a moment Anne Barton emphasized in her 1972 essay on the play's
troubled ending:

> [Toby] turns savagely on Sir Andrew's well-meant offer of assistance and
> companionship in misery. "Will you help—an asshead and a coxcomb and a
> knave, a thin-fac'd knave, a gull?" (5.1.196–99). Only a moment before, Sir
> Andrew had wished "for forty pound" that he was safely at home again. It
> was the genuine accent of the reveller for whom the party has suddenly
> become poisonous . . . the man for whom day breaks after a night of
> abandon . . . Sir Andrew does not reply to Sir Toby's abuse. He simply
> vanishes, never to appear again. (Barton, "*As You Like It* and *Twelfth Night*,"
> p. 174.)

Malvolio is, of course, *the* actor's role in the play and Barton cast Donald
Sinden, perhaps the RSC actor with the greatest comic range, as the steward.
Costumed as "a Victorian cartoon Humpty Dumpty, all bald, ruffled and
painfully etched sneer lines, with spindly legs disappearing into baggy, emas-
culated-looking breeches,"[76] Sinden allowed the intense seriousness of the Puritan to provide the comedy. Ray Seaton saw in Malvolio "the spiritual tiredness
of an old man who, having failed to find his true self in life, has settled on a
pose.'"[77] Speaight admired the portrait: "[Sinden's] Malvolio towered above his
persecutors—a bigger man than they, for all his grotesque infatuation. This was
a superb performance in the vein of high comedy, leaving the right bitterness in
the mouth when the play's flight from realism might have seemed too precipi-
tate."[78] Again, Anne Barton's program note provides a clue to the director's
choice of a more dignified Malvolio: he "alone tries to check this prevailing
atmosphere of abandon, this abdication from common sense. As soon as he
does so, he becomes the enemy: the churl, the sober-sides at the carnival who
refuses to yield himself to the extraordinary." Milton Shulman, however, believed that such emphasis may have been contrary to the spirit of the play: "It
may be in attempting to force Malvolio into this pose of symbolic rationality
that the role has lost a good deal of cruel humor normally associated with it."[79]

There were, of course, exceptional comic moments in Sinden's performance,
but even these stemmed from the choice to ground Malvolio in a dignity:
having put Olivia's ring on his finger for safe-keeping while pursuing Caesario,
Malvolio found he could not get it off and struggled to maintain his dignity
while removing it during the speech at 2.2.5–10. When he was dressed in the
ridiculous costume the tricksters had devised for him, the cross-garters fit so
tightly that he could not straighten his knees.[80]

After his ignominious behavior before Olivia, Malvolio was sent to a "dark
room," for Barton a trap door from which Malvolio's head protruded—"a
talking head, desperately rolling its eyes,"[81] an appropriate image for a produc-

tion exploring the madness of Illyria. Their gag accomplished, the clowns were sobered, overcome "not by remorse, but by the knowledge that their pranks are childish indulgences."[82] Simon Gray argued that the production weakened its purpose, which was to find *Twelfth Night's* dark side, by showing the clowns shamed and aghast at their actions ("Feste takes off his beard with weary disgust"), thus returning the play to its customarily morally safe grounds.[83] Stanley Wells counters Gray by arguing that Shakespeare builds into the final scene "a kind of moral pointer" that guides our attitudes about Malvolio's cruel treatment. He cites Fabian's speech (5.1.365–68), which claims that "the device" against the steward was revenge—mitigated by laughter—for the insults perpetrated against them. The lines were emphasized by Fabian's kneeling to Olivia as he spoke them. Finally, adds Wells, the other characters had drawn "enough of our sympathy to keep the balance in their favor."[84] Yet Malvolio's final exit—"shattered but dignified"—clearly illustrated that all was not harmonious in Illyria despite the marriages, a point well-argued in Anne Barton's 1972 essay.

The production's darkest strains were produced by Feste—Gray's commentary notwithstanding. Through his wit, he created the spirit of revel important to the play. His wisdom prompted the production's penetrating melancholy: "all pleasure for him is gone, but not the sympathy of true knowledge of the human spirit. This gives the whole production a strong and impressive unity of development in action and feeling."[85] Barton used Feste (Emrys James) as a musical commentator; not only did he punctuate specific moments with appropriate melodies, he frequently bridged scenes to provide a phrase of music to introduce or sustain a moment. J. Middleton Murry, also quoted in the RSC program, says of Feste's music, "It is an art—aloof, abstract, akin to himself. At the last, he is left alone on stage." Barton also made much of the fact that Feste was alone on stage at play's end. Wells, who frequently saw the production during its several-years' run, best describes the effect of its final moment:

> The song with which he ends the play was acted out with elaborate mime; he lolled in the fourth stanza, for instance, to imitate the tosspots with drunken heads. He stood for the last verse and left by the side of the stage as the lights faded. He, too, belonged to the world of reality, not of illusion.[86]

Again Anne Barton provides an understanding of the director's intent for this final image: audiences leaving *Twelfth Night's* experience face "a jolt of reality" as they, too, recognize that "all holidays come to an end." The trip back to reality has Feste as its guide, and the world to which he consigns us is one in which "the rain it raineth every day." In its insistence that there is such a world beyond the laughter for which *Twelfth Night* is readily known, Barton's production extended the play's truth.

Barton's interpretation of the so-called problem comedies—*All's Well That Ends Well* and *Measure for Measure*, as well as *Troilus*—has done much to enhance his reputation as one of the foremost illuminators of difficult texts in the twentieth century. The general acclaim bestowed on *All's Well* is likely surpassed only by that of *Twelfth Night.* Barton came to this play as openly and as devoid of preconceived notions as any play he has directed. Ian Richardson, who played Bertram, remembers that Barton "hadn't had time to do his homework . . . he came to the text purely."[87] Like most directors who are confronted with this perplexing play's reputation for being theatrically unviable, Barton entered the project with some concern:

> At first I was afraid of directing the play. . . . I remember saying to the cast at the outset, "Let's try and trust this play, explore it and find out how it works, and stage it simply without gimmicks." We then found after a couple of frightened, doubtful weeks, that the play does work without jazzing it up, though I wasn't sure it did when I embarked on it. I ended up thinking the play much finer and more cohesive than I, or, indeed, most people had ever suspected.[88]

Generally, critics believed that Barton, had assuredly gone "a long way to suggest that Shakespeare, the man of the theatre, was rather less confused than the studious critics who have blamed him for not writing a reasonable romance."[89]

As he had done on several occasions, Barton found himself competing with memories of a Guthrie production. In 1959 Guthrie had staged *All's Well,* relocating it in the early twentieth century. In this context Helena's pursuit of Bertram was played as a Shavian female quest à la Anne Whitefield's pursuit of Jack Tanner. Speaight judged Barton's more conventional approach more satisfying that Guthrie's gimmickry, though it "demythologized the play."[90] Not only did Barton find it necessary to delineate the tragic and comic strains in the play—Guthrie had settled squarely on the latter—but he found himself confronted by other disparate elements that Rossiter defines as "the discord produced by playing off a harsh, disturbing human reality against conventional story-book sentimental expectations."[91] Barton encouraged the contrary tones to surface in equal measure: the fantastic elements were played as "givens," and the company created psychologically real portraits of people who happened to find themselves in extraordinary circumstances. An anonymous writer for the *Glasgow Citizen* clarifies Barton's focus:

> . . . [Barton] has mined a wealth of humanity, sometimes warm, sometimes harsh, but always real and breathing, out of what can be seen as simply a very unpleasant play. . . . Shakespeare's concept is very immediate, at a very human level, using it now warmly, now cruelly, to thrust his insight. John Barton complements this with an oddly efficient impression of languor. . . .[92]

"Melancholy" and "languor" suggest a favored Barton approach to this and other comedies.

An unsigned note in the RSC program suggests Barton's thematic concerns;

There is something irretrievably modern about *All's Well.* Everywhere, the same dialogue is in progress: between the old and the young.

No one knows better than the old people. The King shows that when he quotes Bertram's father to him—"Let me not live. . . ."

The entire speech better defines Barton's tone for the production:

> King: "Let me not live"—
> This his good *melancholy* oft began,
> On the catastrophe and heel of pastime,
> When it was out—"Let me not live," quoth he,
> "After my flame lacks oil, to be the snuff
> Of younger spirits, whose apprehensive senses
> All but new things disdain; whose judgments are
> Mere fathers of their garments; whose constancies
> Expire before their fashions."
>
> (1.2.55–63; italics mine)

Melancholy became the play's dominant key; the generation gap its theme. A "Youth Movement" was in progress in 1967 and the RSC program dutifully printed pictures of representatives of the era, most notably the Beatles. Production observers took the program's cue and understood Barton's interpretative approach. Desmond Pratt judged that Barton helped audiences appreciate the play's modernity as he "contrasted the final frustration of age with the first frustration of youth,"[93] while Peter Ansorge felt that the probe of the generation gap theme was revelatory and consistent with the RSC's announced intention to do Shakespeare's plays "because the play makes some demand on our attention."[94] Contrarily, Herbert Kretzmer proclaimed that the company's determination to be "with it," was "singularly half-witted in this case," arguing that the play is about snobbery, not age differences.[95]

In actuality, Barton's production left all options open. He avoided contemporary dress and music to stress its modern parallels. The production was as austere and unadorned as perhaps any he has brought to the RSC. Timothy O'Brien's set consisted of a small stage on the larger stage backed by a "severely formal archway" on which lights were played to change colors to reflect the play's elaborate patterns.[96] The hues were somber: russet and browns for the countess's house, deep blue, backed by flickering candles, for the king's palace. Most color was provided by the marching Italian soldiers, played with "comic opera" efficiency,[97] who swirled massive red banners that matched their red tunics. The actors were costumed in roughly Carolinean clothing, dark and elegant, which gave the whole production "a flowing and consistent style of sophistication and rich baroque grace."[98] In effect, the Barton and O'Brien design reflected the play's content.

Though the production design and interpretation were judged models of "restraint and dignity,"[99] Barton was less restrained in his editing of the text. He cut approximately 509 lines from the script's original 2,760 (18 percent); more significantly, he transposed a number of speeches, phrases, and lines to effect greater clarity. For example, the expository passage between Helena and the Gentlemen in 5.1 was incorporated into the Helena-Diana scene of 4.4. Large sections of the last five scenes were trimmed to speed the narrative to its conclusion. There was no critical dissension occasioned by Barton's textual liberties; on the contrary, he was praised for improving the play's "theatrical fluency."[100]

The production's ultimate success was its ability to make real several of Shakespeare's most enigmatic characters. Bertram and Helena may well be Shakespeare's least attractive "comic" protagonists. Bertram's aloofness, his callous treatment of Helena, his libertine behavior with Diana, and Helena's calculating shrewdness, her "selfishness," her obstinacy, provide special challenges to the performers assigned these roles. Barton cast Richardson as Bertram (Barton: "One of the best things he ever did; he was perfect casting for it") and Estelle Kohler as Helena; the success of his interpretations was realized, in part, by this propitious casting.

Barton and Richardson did much to correct a critical wrong: under their scrutiny, Bertram emerged as "a harmless rather than a willful, amiable rather than cruel, weak rather than venal" young courtier.[101] The majority of critics were impressed by the amount of humor Barton found in the role;[102] this was in marked contrast to Guthrie's "sulky lieutenant" eight years earlier. Considering Barton's approach to directing—such as finding the irony, seeking the opposite tone—one appreciates this seemingly revolutionary, certainly revelatory, interpretation. Additionally, Richardson's youthful demeanor enhanced the role. Like Coriolanus, whom the actor also played in 1967, Bertram seemed "a boy to be pampered and caressed by women," a concept that explains how his boorish behavior could still be appealing to Helena.[103] Two program notes also explained Richardson's rendering of the role:

> Bertram's conduct has recently been viewed with less repulsion. It is realized that his attitude to a match with a poor girl would have seemed normal and not snobbery in Shakespeare's time. . . .

This statement was accompanied by a quotation from Muriel C. Bradbrook: "For the Elizabethans marrying out of one's degree was a debasing of the blood which blemished successive generations. The question of blood and descent versus native worth was an ancient subject of debate on the stage."[104] Armed with these attitudes, Richardson could then play Bertram more lightly, more wittily than the more customary petulant aristocrat. He was more victim than victimizer, and used wit to deflect the slings and arrows tossed at him by the grateful King and Helena. The wedding scene provided a memorable picture of

Bertram in his moment of defeat: he aimlessly picked confetti off his broad-brimmed hat while Helena beamed.[105]

Estelle Kohler's Helena was neither saint nor witch but an "ordinary inconsistent person . . . a girl determined to get her own way . . . but a nice girl just the same."[106] Instead of attaining her desires through a cold calculation and penetrating intelligence—like a Shavian heroine—the Barton-Kohler Helena was more the innocent confronted with the injustice of the world:

> . . . a wide-eyed, troubled creature, with a nervous cough, who lifts her head in dignity once she has dared to confess her love. [She has] the air of a darling child. Such an interpretation brings more humanity into the play at the cost of its cerebral depth.[107]

Richardson's witty performance and Kohler's childlike innocence did not mitigate the seriousness of their relationship. Wit and charm will not sustain a marriage, and Barton encouraged his actors to explore the darker areas of their relationship that were, in fact, made more painful for their wit and charm:

> A painfulness in the relationship between Bertram and Helena has a significant effect in adding depth to the characters, reality to their final union. As Bertram's dislike of Helena turns to love, so the pain vanishes, yet one senses that there will always exist between the pair a different sort of pain, a poignancy which could well mean that all will, in fact, end well and that Bertram will be even more loving and faithful than if he had adored Helena at first sight.[108]

Such a conclusion, however, may not exactly be what Barton and his actors had in mind. When asked what Bertram has learned from his experience, Barton replied:

> I don't think Bertram's learned very much; he's grown up a bit, he's learnt to value Helena more than he valued her at first, he's seen through Parolles, but he's still a pretty selfish and stupid man. I think that "cynical" isn't quite the right word for the ending: the tone is more one of a worldly tolerance of people. There's no certainty that Bertram and Helena live happily ever after. Bertram ends with a couple of lines which don't tell us much: "If she, my lord, can make me know this clearly, / I'll love her dearly ever, ever dearly." Their surface meaning is clear enough, but in the context of the whole scene, they also contain shame, awe of the King, and a resolve, at that moment, to make the best of things. Whether Bertram did in fact love her dearly ever is something which is surely made questionable by all we know of him from the play as a whole. And the situation is well summed up in the text itself when the King says, "And *if* it end so meet / The bitter past, more welcome is the sweet."[109]

Barton successfully suggested the possibilities of both the optimistic and pessimistic portents of the marriage. The play is not a "happy-ever-after" fairy tale nor an acrid negation of the forces of regeneration. Barton's finale maintained the ambiguities of the text as it showed Bertram whispering his platitudes to the King, smiling enigmatically at his mother, then leading the young "aimlessly" off stage, "while the old courtiers remained behind frightened but smiling at death."[110] Barton proudly believes that maintaining the ambiguity of the ending was "the most important thing we did with the production." He would consciously enjoy a similar ambiguity three years later with *Measure for Measure*'s ending.

Detailed portraits of the lesser characters also brought new insights. The King (Sebastian Shaw) relished his *deus ex machina* role with a gentle authority that did not apologize for the machinations of the playwright's ending: "He never means to be plausible, only applauded."[111] An interesting detail was that as he spoke the epilogue at play's end, "The king's a beggar, now the play is done," Shaw stood alone, facing the audience, puffing a lengthy pipe; it was exactly the same pose he would employ to begin *Measure for Measure* as the Duke three years after—though Barton notes that the pose was not intentionally staged to recall *All's Well.* Two other oldsters emerged as characters typical of the Barton style. The Countess of Rousillon (played by Catherine Lacey, who had acted the role at Stratford in 1935) was portrayed as "a raucous, kindly mock-turtle . . . [who] does not snarl at the behavior of the young; she spends her days upon a bench, drenched in Chekhovian melancholy and chatting aimlessly to a bitter, world-hating clown."[112] Ian Hogg played the Clown sardonically, something of a cross between Feste and Thersites. Perhaps Barton took his cue from Lafeu's description of the Clown—"a shrewd knave and unhappy." John Peter argued that this was a misinterpretation because "unhappyp means mischievous" rather than "malcontent."[113] Elizabreth Spriggs gave the widow, Diana's mother, a lusty earthiness that made the bed trick seem more probable and less contrived than it reads.[114]

Much of the evening's visual humor was provided by the Florentine guard marching in precision—with some notable lapses—to the harumphing of a rotund sergeant-major. One critic believed this "red-cloaked idiocy" was so broad that the audience might have been inclined "to lose the sense of the heartlessness in which the bitterness of the comedy lies."[115] Parolles (Clive Swift) was less a braggart—in the *commedia*'s Capitano tradition—than a congenital liar. In a scene that may have prepared Barton for his treatment of Malvolio, the unmasking of Parolles was treated as black comedy to emphasize the cruelty rather than the fun of the moment. The *Financial Times* said Barton's treatment of the scene revealed the "unwontedly realistic quality" of *All's Well That Ends Well:* "It is not about puppets or humours; it is about people."[116]

Stanley Wells's 1976 essay for *Shakespeare Jahrbuch* considers the strengths and weaknesses of the current generation of Shakespeare directors in England. Wells, who has seen virtually every production at Stratford since 1960, appraises the RSC's best work:

I can think of . . . Shakespearean productions in which I have felt that, in general, the director has subdued himself to the medium in which he was working, creating an unpretentious production which caused the play to work in the theatre in a way which seemed like a realization of the implications of the text. At Stratford I think of John Barton's *All's Well That Ends Well*. . . .[117]

In 1970 the principals who had enjoyed the success of *All's Well*—Barton, Shaw, Richardson, and Kohler—regrouped to accept the challenges of *Measure for Measure*. Shaw recalls that Barton approached him with an offer to act the part of the Duke. Initially Shaw declined, saying that he did not understand the role, to which Barton answered, "Neither do I. Let's make this a journey of discovery."[118] Barton does not remember the conversation and suspects that it may have been a ploy to get Shaw to attempt one of Shakespeare's most enigmatic characters.[119] Nonetheless, the anecdote indicates the reluctance with which directors and actors approach one of the most problematic of the problem plays.

Like the 1967 production of *All's Well*, Barton staged *Measure* austerely and in a manner that tolerated the ambiguities of the script and its complex characters. As opposed to his work on the former, Barton came to *Measure for Measure* well prepared. He had researched the scholarship on the play, having read, among others, Wilson Knight, R. W. Chambers, Muriel Bradbrook, and their varied opinions about the religious nature of the play. Asked if his production was a reaction against the "religious" interpretations, Barton replied:

Not primarily. I read the critics, but basically what I try to bring out in a play is what I myself find out in it. I think that, without doubt, one has to take religion into account in that the religious background is strong in the play, but—maybe this is just a matter of personal taste—I don't like taking a symbolical or allegorical or philosophical or metaphysical view of the play, mainly because I'm a director working with actors. In practice, I did not find any particular critic especially helpful about the play.[120]

Actually, there may have been one critic who shaped Barton's thinking. The RSC program quoted J. M. Nosworthy, who in 1969 wrote about the varied critical responses to *Measure for Measure* and concluded: "The ambiguities of the play are almost countless and increased familiarity only serves to emphasize that one concept is inseparable from another."[121] Nosworthy's observation serves as a beacon light for the production. Barton passed on his discoveries to his cast:

I find the division of opinion more significant about the play than any one particular view of it. I in fact made an abstract for the actors of the views of some ten critics, and suggested that the truth might lie somewhere in between. I urged that if they depended on one view only, e.g. Wilson Knight's, they would be taking too narrow a view.[122]

Accordingly, Barton consciously emphasized the play's ambiguities. Jane Williamson's essay on significant twentieth-century productions of *Measure for Measure* concluded that Barton's version, "in contrast to many earlier presentations, has sought . . . to emphasize rather than minimize the complexities and ambiguities of character and action."[123] If there was a consistent criticism of his work, it was that he did not clearly take a stand to clarify the play's enigmas. Milton Shulman surmised that Barton may have been "as uncertain as the Bard obviously was about whether the theme is to be treated seriously or flippantly,"[124] and Benedict Nightingale thought perhaps the production was Barton's "idea of a straight, impersonal reading," and dismissed the piece as "a markedly less imaginative and energetic production than his *Troilus and Cressida*."[125] Neither was Barton himself satisfied with the production in its entirety: "It wasn't very good and it's another I want to do again."

If there was a dominant theme in Barton's interpretation, it perhaps lay in Isabella's admonition to Angelo:

> Man, proud man,
> Drest in a little brief authority,
> Most ignorant of what he's most assured,
> His glassy essence, like an angry ape
> Plays such fantastic tricks before high Heaven
> As make the angels weep.
>
> (2.2.145–50)

That Angelo, the Duke, and Lucio are variations on the "proud man" theme is evident, and Barton's production supported what one knows about these men. The production was revelatory in its depiction of a "proud woman" to parallel the proud man. Speaight suggests that the "Isabella problem" is *not* her refusal to sleep with Angelo to save Claudio ("A girl of her milieu and in her circumstances could have contemplated no such thing; I do not believe that Shakespeare . . . would have expected her to"), but is more the question of why, having declined to pay the price that Angelo is asking, she then informs Claudio that, if she *had* been prepared to pay it, he might still have been reprieved. Speaight feels that Barton and Estelle Kohler succeeded in explaining Isabella's attitude:

The answer, of course, lies in a single line before which most actresses jib, like a horse before a five-barred gate. "More than our brother is our chastity." Here, in a flash of defiant self-revelation, Miss Kohler let us see that her chastity—like the chastity of Angelo himself—is corrupted by pride. The pride that betrayed *him* to lust has betrayed *her* to cruelty. Each will have to be punished by humiliation—he by public exposure, and she by pleading forgiveness for the man she had accused.[126]

The production's most-discussed moment came at the end of the play. The Duke offered his hand to Isabella in marriage, but as the company exited ceremoniously, Isabella did not join the Duke nor her brother, but remained alone, downstage, staring into the auditorium. It was surely Barton's most conscious attempt to make a statement, but it was ambiguous. It could be interpreted as a proud woman's rejection of a Duke whose hubristic attempt to "play God" nearly led to disastrous consequences. Sebastian Shaw suggested this possibility in a Manchester *Guardian* interview:

[The Duke] is getting his comeuppance. He thinks she'd make a nice queen. He's had women but he's never actually fallen for anyone. It's different for an old man to court a girl, and he's so stupid he thinks this one up; he knows what he'll do. He'll produce the brother in the end and she'll be grateful and she'll fall in his arms. But he learns the biggest lesson of all, that you can't do what you want just because you're Duke. And it takes the whole play to learn it.[127]

D. A. N. Jones's *Listener* review suggested that Barton's production was "feminist" in its depiction of a "passionate, independent girl preserving her own integrity" and that the ending was an exclamation of another type of pride: Isabella is frustrated and the silent rage written on her face is a haughty realization that "she is to be a chattel after all—and all has not ended well."[128] Thus, Barton's Isabella, having tasted independence in her proud denial of Angelo, is a woman who would not go gentle unto a good night in the Duke's palace. The Bartons themselves entered into the debate on the significance of Isabella's action—or nonaction—at play's end. Anne Barton offered her opinion in the RSC program:

We do not know how Isabella reacts to her sovereign's extraordinarily abrupt offer of marriage in the final moment of the play, because she says nothing in reply. It is at least possible that this silence is one of dismay.

Gareth Lloyd Evans asked Barton to explain his thinking about the business; Barton's answer provides insight into the play, his rehearsal methods, and the business itself. Evans's question raises the most common critical opinions for Isabella's silence:

Gareth Lloyd Evans: . . . did she in fact not agree to marry the Duke because the Duke was older than usual (as indeed he certainly looked), or because she couldn't forgive him for pretending that Claudio was dead and was, as it were, indulging in a kind of feminine umbrage; or was it because Isabella found sex repugnant?

> John Barton: Well, all those thoughts occurred to us in rehearsal, but that's not quite the way we tackled it. Again, what we did was to ask the question, "What would Isabella have done when the Duke made his proposal?" . . . This is a situation which comes up again and again in rehearsal: Shakespeare doesn't provide a certain answer and one has to find one. One tends to do so by trying to deduce what a character's response would be from everything that we know about that character elsewhere in the play. What I actually intended was that Isabella's response should be open-ended. I suggested to Estelle Kohler . . . that she was in no state at that moment to accept the proposal, and I asked her to reject it and yet think about it. The last thing that I presented on the stage, when everybody had gone off at the end of the play was Isabella wondering, puzzling about what she should do.[129]

Not unexpectedly, the unconventional ending prompted a range of critical response. Speaight called it "a brilliant inspiration,"[130] While, at the other end of the spectrum, Trewin argued that Shakespeare was merely coiling up the ropes of his comedy and "to suggest anything different is to take things too far."[131] Barton's business was clearly a rejection of the conventions of comedy and nudged the play a step closer to tragedy.

Barton narrowed the play's social context to concentrate on the psychological interplay of the central characters. Thus the action was played in an empty room of paneled walls and parquet floors, which made the play "a chamber production";[132] it had "a clinical (puritanical?) cleanliness, a distortion of the geometrical form it adumbrated, and a realisation almost of Angelo's mentality."[133] By enclosing the action, almost claustrophobically, Barton minimized the social implications that throw the actions of the Duke, Angelo, and Isabella into relief.

Other than its general ambiguity, the production was most often criticized for not suggesting the underbelly of Vienna. Peter Brook, who successfully staged the play in the early 1950s, once said that "the disgusting, stinking world of medieval Vienna is absolutely necessary to the meaning of the play."[134] According to Ronald Bryden, Barton's failure to adhere to Brook's dictum was the production's shortcoming:

> What's missing is any theatrical representation of the fact that Angelo falls from virtue and he joins the huge sinful majority; any vivid sense of the scurrilous, teeming Vienna whose stews and dungeons educate the Duke in the realities of fallen man.[135]

Michael Bogdanov, then Barton's assistant, concurs that the weakness of the production lay in its inability to place the psychological study into a social perspective: "There was no real social content to the production. (Barton) didn't really understand what the fundamental 'rot' of Vienna was—which has to be analyzed before you can do the piece."[136] Bogdanov staged the prison scenes, which were largely extraneous to the main action because Barton and his assistant "didn't talk out the social condition of the play and why its prisoners were in prison." Bogdanov said he therefore devised a Brechtian musical interlude "which didn't have anything to do with that play." Barnardine, the accused murderer, was perhaps the one gesture towards social statements in the production. His contrariness was stressed through an obscene blasphemy: he grabbed the Duke's cross—the Duke visits him in friar's garb— and immersed it in a chamber pot.[137]

If Barton's handling of *Twelfth Night* bordered on the Chekhovian, his treatment of *Measure for Measure* was Strindbergian in its analysis of complex characters torn by conflicting sexual demands. John Barber praised Barton for offering "a bleak appraisal of the evil in men's minds . . . remarkable for its refusal to cuddle up to the nice characters or to pretend that the nasty ones are bad all through."[138]

Barton directed Ian Richardson to ground Angelo in the austerity of his own childhood:

> When John Barton approached me about Angelo, he said, "Use your Scottish Presbyterian background. Use that fanatical John Knox thing that you should know about". . . . I can remember the polished pews and the bareness of the kirk and the bible-punching minister. I can remember that my poor cousin who became pregnant had to emigrate to Canada. She was literally banished to avoid chatter, and suddenly I find myself with a character who says to a pregnant lady, "Dispose of her to some fitter place."[139]

The casting of the slight, youthful Richardson as Angelo was an interpretative statement itself, particularly when coupled with the casting of Shaw as the Duke. Thus the Duke was played as an older, feebler man; Angelo was young, handsome, and virile. The tendency would be to reverse the roles because, stereotypically, Angelo is thought of as a stern Puritan. Richardson and Barton did not allow Angelo to become a lecherous monster, but constructed instead a Bradleylike subtext to minimize his villainy:

> He's never fallen in love before. He can't help it if he's highly sexed, no more than Isabella. There's an undeniable attraction between the two, which is why they both resort to such violent means to avoid it. When Angelo realizes that she's not going to take the initiative, he has to take the plunge, and because he's inexperienced, the plunge is a clumsy one. But she doesn't stand on her saintly honor and say, "How dare you?" Oh, no, she says if you don't sign a pardon for my brother, I will proclaim you for what you are. Whereupon, Angelo resorts to basics and says, "Who'll believe you?" You will save your brother by yielding up your body to me or you will die." They are both blackmailing each other which is a curious thing for two saintly people to do.[140]

In 2.4, Richardson illustrated Angelo's "clumsy" attempt at seduction by impetuously seizing Isabella's hair, pulling her down on his desk—the production's "judgment table"—and stroking her from breast to groin.[141] Though the description reads as vulgar, it was a gesture of a man incompetent in the ways of love (or lust). The *Cambridge Daily News* called the attack on Isabella "a quick, intuitive and virtually innocent attempt at seduction" and argued that Angelo "is to be pitied for he knows that he is wrong . . . yet he is also to be despised for he remorselessly perverts justice."[142] When Angelo assumed the office in the Duke's stead, he eased himself into the Duke's chair "like a nervous child . . . not at all sure that he is ready for high office."[143] The desk behind which he sat, by the way, was used to define character differences between its rightful owner, the Duke, and the would-be ruler, Angelo. In the opening scene, when the Duke is the seat of power, the desk was cluttered with books and the paraphenalia of office; after the Duke relinquished his desk to Angelo, it was swept clean of books and wiped free of dust—a visual metaphor of Angelo's superficially ordered mind.[144] When Angelo hears that the Duke is to return, while seated at the spot on which he attempted to seduce Isabella, "his head crashed on the desk in disappointment, frustration and uncertainty exclaiming between sobs, "Alack, when once our grace we have forgot, nothing goes right" (4.4.32).[145] It was the production's most powerful attempt to invest Angelo with pathos.

Isabella, like Angelo, was proud, "a commanding, self-assured novice,"[146] more attuned to twentieth-century sensibilities than Jacobean. As Richardson suggested, she was not averse to her own sexuality, although Anne Barton's program note suggested otherwise: "Isabella's purity conceals an hysterical fear of sex which scarcely allows her to speak of her brother's fault, and leads directly to her unlovely attack on him in prison." A writer for the *Leicester Mercury*, however, perceived a more human Isabella, one aware of her sexuality:

> Begging for her brother's life, she extended her arms as if to embrace Angelo, only to adopt a praying posture—a neat trick. And with her passionate, but near fascinated, disgust at the suggestion she should forfeit her virginity, Isabella was much more than a stereotype of virtue.[147]

To show her superiority over Angelo, Barton devised business in the confrontation scene in 2.4: as Angelo, overcome by his lust, moved toward Isabella, he stepped from behind his desk and she, in escaping, replaced him. She thus became his judge and was in the best possible position to deliver the line, "Men their creation mar / In profitting by them" (127–28).[148]

If Angelo was treated more sympathetically and Isabella more sensually than customary, Barton's depiction of the Duke was no less innovative. Of the Duke Barton has said:

There are . . . two ways in which one can look at the Duke; one can take him as a symbolic figure, but it is very difficult for an actor to bring a symbolic figure to life. If one is rehearsing *Measure for Measure*, rather than just studying it, one has to answer questions about what the Duke is really like, and what's going on inside him, and that leads to finding out about a human being rather than defining an allegory.[149]

The emphasis throughout Barton's *Measure for Measure* was on the Duke's humanity, particularly those attributes that make him human rather than god-like: his shortcomings. Speaking to the Shakespeare Conference at Stratford, Barton described the Duke as "a complex, inconsistent man," adding that "the *point* of the part is its inconsistencies."[150] Sebastian Shaw clarifies Barton's perception of the Viennese Duke:

A stupid man is the Duke. Not a symbol of power divine, but *thinks* of himself as power divine. One thing you discover is, the Duke is completely inconsistent. Quite a lot of people are, though they're not allowed to be so in plays.[151]

The casting of Shaw in the role of the Duke represented a critical statement by Barton. Shaw's advanced age worked against the image of the Duke as a virile leader: here he became something of an eccentric old man whose curiosity about the younger generation causes him to step back from the city he rules and examine it as "a benign eccentric schoolmaster that had gotten slightly out of hand."[152]

A 1968 Anne Barton comment was included among a series of program notes entitled "The Duke: Misguided . . . The Duke as Providence." The Bartons perceived the former as appearing

. . . less in the guise of Providence—a divine power temporarily made Flesh, guiding the action of the plot with a sure and restless hand—than as an image of the comic dramatist himself, trying to impose the patterns of art upon a reality which resists such schematization. As such he is continually frustrated and surprised by the unpredictability (not to mention the insubordination) of his elected cast of characters.

Critics were divided in their appraisal of the unconventional Barton-Shaw Duke. Wardle believed that he "captures all the possible aspects of the character except its awful authority,"[153] while Bryden judged him the most human he had seen, "a creature of genuine doubts and complexity."[154] Peter Thomson of *Shakespeare Survey* thought the various eccentricities that Barton devised for the Duke—the pipe-smoking scholar in his study, the administrator to a group of giggling counselors, the "quizzical fondness for Lucio"—"wasn't always distinguishable from simple-mindedness," a factor that may have "exposed more triteness than sagacity in his pronouncements."[155] John Barber was less accepting of the old Duke's eccentricities: "The Duke is not a pathetic old man."[156] Barton would not dispute Barber's opinion: when asked what "discoveries" he had made while journeying through *Measure for Measure*, Barton replied, "If I did the play again, I wouldn't have an 'old' Duke. I wanted him to be older, but I think it should be a man in his 50s."[157]

There was a moment, however, when the age and eccentricity enhanced the production. After his silent rejection by Isabella, the Duke momentarily dropped "into near senility, afraid of himself, his powers and how he must appear to others."[158] Shaw, with shaking hands and downcast head, simply replaced his spectacles on his nose and turned slowly to exit. There was a genuine melancholia in the moment, and it reminded us that "this Duke, at any rate, had still a thing or two to learn about human nature."[159]

When Barton began work on *Measure for Measure* he was aware of critical commentary that questions the play's shift from a realistic basis in the first half to a contrived, fairy-tale quality after Isabella's interview with Claudio in prison. His solution to the problem defines a formula for success when staging Shakespeare's complex comedies:

> The actors, if they have brought their characters to life in exploring the first half, can carry through that life into the play's more superficial resolution. I felt, in fact, that what seemed a problem in the study largely melted away in the theatre, when those characters were embodied by living actors.[160]

Barton verifies Harley Granville Barker's turn-of-the-century notion that "it is unwise to decide upon a disputed passage without canvassing all its dramatic possibilities."[161] Barton and the RSC have made this command the cornerstone of their work.

Measure for Measure completed a five-year sequence in which Barton concentrated primarily on Shakespeare's comedies. Though he occasionally returned to them—in contexts that will be discussed later—it was not until the later 1970s that he again gave them his full attention. In 1976 he created a Victorian world for *Much Ado About Nothing* (see chapter 6), and in 1978 devised a visually stunning *Midsummer Night's Dream* (see chapter 7), as well as a restaging of his popular *Love's Labour's Lost*. It is not surprising, then, that Barton would add yet another of the comedies to his repertory. In May 1978 he produced *The Merchant of Venice* at the RSC's The Other Place (TOP), and the following year the play was transferred to the Gulbenkian Studio in Newcastle prior to its London run at the RSC's former in-town studio, The Warehouse.[162]

The Other Place, a converted warehouse a block from the Royal Shakespeare Theatre in Stratford, was founded in 1975 as an alternative space to the massive main house. Here experimental works and scaled-down versions of the classics are performed to encourage the company's talent to extend its range by playing in an intimate space with little external embellishment. The small, arena theater enhances audience-actor contact and encourages a subtler playing style. It also challenges actors and directors to communicate efficiently and economically to TOP's patrons. Barton first worked there in 1975 (*Perkin Warbeck:* see chapter 9); *The Merchant of Venice* represents his first staging of a Shakespeare play in TOP's demanding quarters.

The Merchant of Venice is also a problem play for modern audiences: after the holocaust of World War II it is difficult to accept a play that offers "Jewbaiting" as its central premise. Barton's choice to place the racial harangues quite literally in the laps of his audience was bold indeed. The proximity of actor and audience necessarily meant that the production would "concentrate maximum attention on crucial events taking place dead centre, expecially Bassanio's choice, the trial, and the finale."[163] But bigotry is only one aspect of the play, and Barton found ways to mitigate its unpleasantries without compromising its message. The claustrophobic setting enabled audiences to hear anew the play's contrary notes.

There was virtually no scenery on stage, but Barton and Christopher Morley suggested a nearly modern society in which bigotry and narrow-mindedness were as prevalent as they were in Elizabethan England. The costuming and set pieces were vaguely Edwardian, to represent Europe on the verge of the twentieth century, but a few short years from the holocaust. Shylock appeared in the uniform of the central European ghetto, and, as we might expect from Barton, Portia and Nerissa suggested a rather Chekhovian manner, "especially in the *Three Sisters*-like severe black dresses . . . with buttoned up necks and muttonchop sleeves."[164] The young Venetians wore velvet suits and fur-collared overcoats; they shared after-diner brandy and cigars, suggesting a male-dominated and very closed society.[165] But Barton's *Merchant* differs from his work on *Othello* and *Much Ado* (see Chapter 6) because he did not meticulously recreate a world, but rather suggested a context for the action: the design evoked a "mood" period rather than an historical one.

This ambience seems an odd choice when one considers Barton's intentions for the production. John Nettles, who played Bassanio, confirmed Barton's recent fascination with myth (see chapter 9) and said that the director wanted to explore *The Merchant of Venice's* "fairy tale" qualities:

What [Barton] tried to do was restore what he thought were its Elizabethan virtues, that to treat it as a sociological tract was probably wrong, and to over-emphasize the Jews' roles—or to wrongly emphasize the Jews' roles— was to do a disservice to the play. What he wanted to do was to make it into a fairy story which he thought it originally was: it was the story of Bassanio and Portia and their love—the story of the voyage of discovery of the Prince-Hero.[166]

The play was, for Barton, another exploration of the "healing" themes he seeks in the "mythic" plays. To heighten the ritual quality, he used his actors, rather than visual effects, to convey the romance of the play, a successful choice said *The Times:* "In the close space of the RSC's small theatre at Stratford, one might expect the anti-Semitism to be particularly sour. . . . It is quite an achievement, then, that the play becomes lyrical and comic in John Barton's production."[167] Nettles, by the way, mentioned that Barton infused the sense of the lyrical-mythical-romantic tradition into his cast by reading passages from Malory's medieval writings.[168] Six years later Barton himself would play Malory in Gillian Lynne's television adaptation of the medieval stories.

Where, then, do Shylock and the racial undertones associated with his character fit into Barton's fairy-tale schema? Shylock, according to Nettles, was perceived as "the local ogre, the convenient symbol of evil." He was played—in a highly acclaimed performance by Patrick Stewart—not as an evil Jew, but as an evil man who happened to be Jewish. Critics described him as "a thorough-going scoundrel . . . [who] loves his own sardonic jokes"[169] and as "an angry, vengeful man with a chip on his shoulder, arrogantly striding through life . . . worshipping himself and money."[170] In a major analysis of Barton's production for *Shakespeare Quarterly,* Ann Jennalie Cook describes the particulars of the unorthodox Shylock of Stewart:

> Without false nose or earlocks or any other Jewish trappings he deliberately decided to abandon, he created a powerful, subtle, credible Shylock. He tried to strip away centuries of interpretation and get back to the human being represented in the text, and he succeeded to an extraordinary degree. He was disturbing but not tragic, moving but not pathetic. Whether desperate or despicable, Stewart's Shylock remained a man whose greed and meanness of spirit set his athwart the liberal generosity and love of the other characters.[171]

To minimize sympathy for Shylock—but not Jews—Barton devoted particular attention to the Shylock-Tubal scene, which, says J. C. Trewin, has never been so elegantly spoken.[172] Tubal (Tony Church) was impeccably dressed, a refined and cultured gentleman, "a smart Venetian about town."[173] Nettles says Barton was especially concerned "to see that even in the Jewish community Shylock was regarded as an outsider, so he took the curse off his being a Jew."

Another Barton innovation was less successful. After locking his house and giving its keys to Jessica with the admonition to avoid the Christian revels in the streets, Shylock suddenly turned and slapped his daughter, a gesture devised to explain why Jessica would abandon her home and faith. Many felt the slap was gratuitous because it "makes us ask too many irrelevant questions about his dealings for the dead Leah."[174] Stewart explained his action at a Shakespeare Institute Conference in Stratford:

. . . Shylock saw some sign of rebellion in Jessica's eyes (attributable to the impending elopement) which required harsh discipline, but [Stewart] acknowledged that the emotional interchange was not being communicated effectively.[175]

The Christians were no less dispicable for their racial slurs, but their invective was more specifically aimed at Shylock, the man, rather than at Jews in general. In return, Shylock used irony and biting humor as a defense against the Christian taunts. Thus Barton and Stewart found the comedy—though darkling—in the play. Portraying Shylock less sympathetically somewhat diminished the power of the "Hath not a Jews eyes . . . ?" speech (3.1.47ff). According to Nettles, the famous set piece "meant less; it was just generalized pleading." Stewart, however, maintains that the speech is not "a plea for compassion" but is "a calculating, cold-blooded justification of revenge, the complete opposite of its conventional interpretation."

Even in the trial scene Shylock was given less sympathy than one might expect. The trial itself was staged—like the series of casket scenes—with an austere, ritualized formality that focused squarely on the principal debaters: Portia and Shylock. After his defeat to her cunning, Shylock discarded his yamulke and prostrated himself before the judges, "groveling in obsequious acceptance of his enforced baptism . . . a logical response to the offer of continued use of his money."[176] He then exited laughing, an action that B. A. Young suspected might well be the beginning of insanity.[177] Such a supposition makes one think of the downfall and punishment of another Jacobean moneymonger, Giles Overreach, who, like Shylock, is given stern justice for his miserly actions in Massinger's *A New Way to Pay Old Debts.* Perverse skinflints were no strangers to the English stage, and Barton's rendering of Shylock seems far more akin to this tradition than to one of racial humor.

Some believed that Barton's unsympathetic treatment of Shylock realigned the play in Portia's favor.[178] Her "unsentimental hardness and sententiousness" were not softened, and it was clearly established that she was the dominant force in the court: Shylock's plea "Give me leave from hence" (4.1.393) was spoken directly to Portia, not the Duke. Others, however, complained that Marjorie Bland's Portia did nothing to effect her transformation into a male magistrate and that under her reading, "the court room scene becomes less important than in other productions."[179] When the production moved to London, Lisa Harrow played Portia, a move that strengthened the role.

The love scenes sounded the best notes of the production because they were "underplayed beautifully, tempered by restraint."[180] Portia's anxieties were emphasized to promote the underlying seriousness now expected from Barton's comedies. This darker quality was best captured in Portia's emphatic delivery of "I/would/not/lose/you" to Bassanio (3.2.5), and the song "Tell me where is fancy bred," which was sung by Portia herself. Bassanio's choice of the casket was a ritualized dance: he circled the caskets in formal patterns, supported by gentle music. "Here choose I" was an "electric moment," Roger Warren reported, as was the exchange of rings, staged in such a stylized manner that when the ring was later returned to Portia—again in a ritual gesture—at the conclusion of the trial scene, the link between the Belmont and Venice plots was unusually apparent to audiences.[181] The principal "fairy-tale" moment occurred in the finale: the women, hitherto dressed in austere colors, shed their inky cloaks "to emerge resplendent in white at the triple wedding, which takes place among a shower of pink and white flowers."[182]

The joyous ending firmly placed *The Merchant of Venice* in the romantic tradition, and Barton's treatment of the Gobbos suggested another realm of comedy. His clowns were more the descendants of Vladimir and Estragon rather than Will Kemp or Robert Armin; a number of critics noted the Beckettian qualities of the Gobbos.[183] Launcelot provided much of the show's humor and its music with a "one man band." His debate between Conscience and the Fiend (2.2.1–28) was sounded by a concertina and a klaxon horn (à la Harpo Marx). His banter with Jessica helped to establish the tone of the play and made the bigotry bearable; it was playfull irreverent kidding rather than spiteful invective.

The popular and artistic success of Barton's *Merchant of Venice* prompted the RSC to revive it for the 1981 season at Stratford. Most of the values of the studio versions were maintained in the shift to the Royal Shakespeare Theatre. The expanded setting was still intimate (at least by main house standards): a circular platform, placed close to the audience, was backed by a transluscent canopy that accommodated both the Venetian and Belmont locales. The latter evoked memories of *Love's Labour's Lost* (also of the 1978 season) with its falling russet leaves and air of melancholy. Barton further maintained the roughly Chekhovian-Edwardian look of the show's costumes.

Primarily through cast alterations, some values and interpretations changed in 1981, prompting Warren, who had also reviewed the earlier TOP production for *Shakespeare Survey*, to judge that "the impact of the play as a whole was significantly different, and more uneven."[184] David Suchet, himself a Jew, played Shylock as more obviously wealthy and refined than Stewart's shabbily dressed, penurious money-lender. Shylock and Tubal were more discernably "equals" in 1981—the former bent on avenging his ill treatment at the hands of the anti-Semetic Christians, the latter more moderate in his dealings with the Venetians. Warren placed Suchet more in the old tradition of humorous Shylocks, "a loud coarse joker who could still make menace," a contrast to the more subtle portrait of Stewart. When Barton devised "Playing Shakespeare" for British television in 1983, he asked the two actors to discuss their respective approaches to the character, both to illustrate how "things subjective" dictate an interpretation and to validate his notion that ultimately a production is—or at least should be—in the hands of the actors who must bring complex characters to stage life. Barton informed viewers that in the initial rehearsals he gave both Stewart and Suchet "the same directions and made the same points, both in detail and in general." Each actors then accepted, rejected, or refined the director's observations to create a Shylock unique to his imagination and personality. Stewart argued that "to concentrate on the Jewishness can lead to missing the great potential in the character which is its universality," and thus fashioned a Shylock who was "an outsider who *happens* to be a Jew," and whose corresponding malevolence was a universally human trait rather than the byproduct of anti-Semitism. Suchet countered that Shylock was indeed an outsider *because* he is a Jew: "Shakespeare never lets the audience or the other characters forget the Jewish thing. You only have to look at the trial scene where he's only called 'Shylock' six times but 'Jew' twenty-two." Barton judged their divergent performances "equally good," though the media preferred Stewart's more innovative portrait.

Though the 1981 Shylock may have been less revalatory than in 1981, Sinead Cusack's Portia was a well-received improvement on the previous production. Barton added new business in the casket scene (still staged as a ritual) to effect her transformation from a devoted young girl driven to distraction by her father's will to a mature, compassionate woman who knows much about "the quality of mercy." After Bassanio successfully selects the correct casket, Portia tore off the penitential robe she wore as each suitor deliberated on her fate, "and hurled it, caskets, table and all, right off the platform—an exhilarating physical statement of her freedom from shackles."[185]

In one other change of note, Barton recast Launcelot Gobbo into a kind of Feste, scoring changes of mood on his guitar, much the way Emrys James was employed in Barton's *Twelfth Night* a dozen years earlier.

As a general rule, Barton's work on these varied comedies has been governed by several considerations. First, he challenges his actors—and ultimately his audiences—to look beyond traditional interpretations for antithetical responses, thus adding dimension to them. "Violence of contrast," says Barton, "that's what stimulates theatrical excitement."[186] He has shown that it is indeed possible for kings and princesses to be chubby and not altogether "charming," but more human in the process. Sassy serving maids can also be spinsters terrified of growing old alone. One can surely sympathize with boorish young noblemen who do not wish to marry against their will. Viennese dukes can—and do—grow old and perhaps a little senile, both in plays and in life. Ogres can be mocked whatever their race or creed simply because they *are* ogres who *happen* to be of a particular race or creed.

Barton has presented the comedies as a reminder that laughter does inevitably cease and that clowns frequently mask their sadness with jibes and gambols. Collectively, the Barton-directed comedies reflect Shakespeare's notion that comedy and solemnity are integral and often integrated facets of life's experiences.

Finally, Barton accomplished these ends through an intelligent reading of the texts as written. With minor exceptions, the scripts were unaltered and conservatively cut. Little was put in the productions that could not be grounded in the texts, although he and his casts considered the extreme range of possibilities. In short, Barton's restrained, yet extraordinarily imaginative direction of the comedies complemented, rather than competed with, familiar texts and encouraged us to see them with new eyes.

5

"He Who Plays the King":
Richard II (1973–74) and *King John* (1974–75)

When Barton's production of *Richard II* opened at the Brooklyn Academy of Music in the winter of 1974, American critics were perplexed: ". . . why a John of Gaunt so unimpressive, down on his knees for a lackluster deliver of the glorious 'This England?' Why an overhead platform that must all too pointedly lower to the floor while the king upon it roars: 'Down court! Down, King'? Why all that overworked nonsense of riders seated on jogging hopskirt horses?"[1] Similar questions had been asked in England the previous April when *Richard II* opened at Stratford, for this was Barton's most mannered and self-consciously theatrical production to date.

Barton previously worked on the play at Stratford in 1964 and 1966 as part of the *Henriad* cycle, and in a simple Theatregoround (TGR) production with Richard Pasco as the King. Why should Barton suddenly invest the work with a "Greco-Elizabethan"[2] overlay, and why should he follow it with an even more controversial *King John* that obviously contained resonanaces of *Richard II*?

The two productions are best considered in tandem since each is frequently cited as an example of directorial invention at its extreme. Stanley Wells has labeled *Richard II* as perhaps "the most strongly interpretative production of a Shakespeare play" that he has ever seen.[3] The productions invited polar responses. *Richard II* was—with notable exceptions—acclaimed as "an intelligent and outstandingly bold attempt to give the text a life not merely *in* but *of* the theatre."[4] *King John*, on the other hand, was—again with notable exceptions—condemned, even by critics who admired *Richard II*. Harold Hobson of *The Sunday Times* vitriolically declared *King John* "one of the most disgraceful exhibitions ever made in a public theatre by a man of talent."[5] *Richard II* and *King John*, related in thematic and stylistic approach, were conceived and brought to reality within a year's time and are crucial works for understanding Barton's theater vision. Correspondingly, they are among the best documented of his productions.[6]

As rendered by Barton, these histories were bound by a common theme (the king as a player of roles) and production style (an elaborate theatricality grounded in ritual). The director has said that ordinarily he does not carry the ideas of one production into a subsequent effort, nor does he begin with predetermined attitudes:

> I'm not consciously very conceptual. I find I am conceptual when I do the work and it's organic and it's growing when the actors are in front of me. But I start with just notes and hints and ideas and launch myself.[7]

The two productions suggest that there are, in fact, occasions when Barton does approach a play with a predetermined concept. Both *Richard II* and *King John* are too idiosyncratic to be judged otherwise.

Barton's now-famous concept for *Richard II*—alternating the roles of the King and Bolingbroke between two actors—is probably as distinctive as any concept brought to his productions. Ironically, the idea was originally that of another prominent RSC director: Terry Hands. Barton initially disregarded Hands' suggestion, but soon realized it would help him say "something about the nature of the dilemma the two men face as one takes up the crown and the other is deposed."[8] Barton was struck by the symmetry of the drama. The play is rich with imagery focusing on duality. The "bucket" speech in act 4.1 (ll. 184–89)[9] especially aroused Barton's imagination; scene designer Timothy O'Brien identifies the passage as the well-spring of the production.[10]

Barton and his colleagues recognized that "there were complementary aspects of the two characters,"[11] a notion that prompted the production's key artistic decisions. Instead of playing Richard as a martyred king and Bolingbroke as an aggrieved usurper, which necessarily underscores the differences between them, Barton explored their commonality, thus making *both* protagonists in a more universal drama than that suggested by history. Robert Brustein believes Barton's interpretation is the first such exploration on stage.[12] Second, Barton decided to explore the parallels between Richard and Bolingbroke by having the actors exchange roles nightly, less a gimmick than an artistic choice to illustrate that he who wears the crown is necessarily transient in his kingship—"very like an actor who plays a part . . . his run or reign over, he hands it to another."[13] Barton explained his intent in an RSC press release, dated March 26, 1973:

> I believe this doubling of the King and Bolingbroke may help to reveal the nature of the play. Both are characters who consciously assume various roles. I would like the audience to be more than usually aware of this and of a special acting duel between them.[14]

Role-playing and the innate actor in man are favorite Barton themes: examples of this were his *Taming of the Shrew* and the outlandish role assumed by Achilles in *Troilus and Cressida;* further examples will be explored in *King John* and especially in *Hamlet* (see chapter 8). Though it is assuredly a theme that fascinated Barton before he met Anne Righter Barton, his wife deals with the notion extensively in her writings. Barton does not recollect a specific influence of her work on *Richard II*, yet there is, in fact, a passage in *Shakespeare and the Idea of the Play* that suggests another source for his decision to alternate the Richard-Bolingbroke roles. Richard's speech about buckets does not in itself justify the alternation, yet O'Brien says the lines, discussed in a production meeting, are "a means of showing that Kingship in *Richard II* was a role, making an actor of a King as well as a king of an actor." Nor does the speech suggest the theatricality inherent in the script; others are more indicative (e.g., "As in a theatre the eyes of men / After a well-graced actor leaves the stage . . ." 5.2. 23ff). Anne Barton's excellent discussion of the reflexive theatricality of *Richard II*, particularly her analysis of Richard's death at Pomfret Castle, contains a line that seems instrumental in Barton's decision:

Death has, in a curious sense, restored Richard to his throne, giving the lie to his original fears. *He and Bolingbroke have changed places once again;* it is now the latter's turn to find himself in the position of the actor.[15] (Italics mine.)

Her program note for *Richard II* further elaborates upon ideas she set forth a dozen years earlier:

. . . Shakespeare, however, seems to have seized upon and explored the latent parallel between the King and that other twin-natured being, the Actor. Like kings, actors are accustomed to perform before an audience. Like kings, they are required to submerge their own individuality within a role, and for both, the incarnation is temporary and perilous. Like the two kings in *Richard II*, their feelings towards their roles are often ambiguous.[16]

The program note, entitled "The King's Two Bodies," identifies an important source Barton consulted while preparing the production: Ernst Kantorowicz's book of the same title. Barton read the work at the suggestion of his wife, who believed it would help him solidify his thinking about the dual nature of Richard's kingship. The work is a thorough assessment of a difficult Elizabethan doctrine defined by Edward Plowden, who argued that a monarch inhabits two bodies in one: the Body Natural, governed by the same laws of nature to which all men must submit; and the Body Politic, "constituted for the direction of the People, and the Management of the Public Weal."[17] The first is fallible, individual, and subject to death and time, while the latter is flawless, abstract, and immortal. The two natures are fused at the moment of coronation "in a way that deliberately parallels the incarnation of Christ, whose representative on earth—as Richard II continually reminds us—the king henceforth will be." Thus the notion of the King's two bodies was aligned with the medieval doctrine of the devine right of kings, appropriated by Tudor monarchs to strengthen their rule. Unfortunately, these doctrines have little immediacy to modern audiences, a situation recognized by Barton, who said that the play is very difficult to bring off today because "a self-pitying King, indeed the very subject of a King's fall, has far less import than it would have had for the Elizabethans."[18] If nothing else, alternating the roles prompted a useful discussion of "the King's two bodies."

Yet another influence on Barton's concept is suggested by Penny Gold, the director's former assistant. Barton, she says, sees little theater himself but did see a production of Noel Coward's *Private Lives*, which clarified his thinking on *Richard II* because of "its formality, the game-playing that goes on between the characters, the degree to which they are all very conscious of the roles they are supposed to play, the way they act up to those roles but the same time have a distance to them."[19]

Having made his decision to alternate the leading roles, Barton approached two leading RSC actors, Richard Pasco and Ian Richardson. Pasco was first to accept, intrigued by Barton's challenge: "The idea of sharing was very attractive. So was the idea of setting up a theatrical venture, a new theatrical milestone."[20] Richardson four times refused the offer because he had recently established himself in the commercial world, "albeit making a lot of money but artistically rather starving."[21] Pasco begged him to join the venture, and Richardson finally agreed.[22]

Initially, it was agreed that each actor would pursue an individual interpretation of the roles. For Barton, the production was a vivid test of his belief that "a production finally belongs to the actors and not the directors . . . because all directors find their individual views modified by the independent powers of the actors they work with."[23] To insure autonomy Pasco and Richardson agreed that, when possible, neither would watch the other rehearse. Soon they were lingering after rehearsals to discuss concepts, argue alternatives, attack the roles from varying perspectives. Ultimately, they worked side by side, with Barton serving as an enthusiastic mediator. Richardson recalls the rehearsal experience:

> Dickie would say, "I'd like to do it like this." And John Barton would say, "Well, get on with it and show us," and I would sit there . . . making notes. Then I would get up and do it my way. And Dickie would say, "Oh, I don't see it that way at all." And John Barton got very excited and said, "Oh, do keep this differentiation of ideas, because that's what it's all about."[24]

The process led the trio to key discoveries that vindicated Barton's original suspicion that Richard was not the Christ figure nor Bolingbroke the villain that centuries of theater tradition have made them. On the contrary, Bolingbroke was "a rather splendid chap," the King an actor who tries "to find something on which to hang his personality and, because his persona has been so diffused by the constant roles he plays, he has nowhere to hang it."[25]

Very individualized readings of the two roles emerged. Pasco, a more elegaic actor, presented a King akin to the traditional Christlike figure—though Barton encouraged him to counter this aspect with humor and villainy.[26] As an outgrowth of the work he and Barton accomplished with TGR in 1971, Pasco played Richard as a monarch who believed, pathetically, that he could survive because of divine right.[27] Richardson, a skilled technical actor, played the king histrionically, "a preening puppet, a mountebank posing as a monarch."[28] Richardson best describes the varied interpretations he and his colleague evolved:

> I went all the way for the Player King; Dickie went much more for the elegaic aspect, the martyred King. I saw a King with a death wish, if you like, or a King who enjoyed playing King as long as he had all the accoutrements of majesty to play with. . . . Dickie was much more allied to the Christian aspect of it. (Richardson to Gow, p. 12)

If there was a critical consensus, it was that Pasco's Richard was subtler, more moving; Richardson's flamboyant, more technically exciting. James Stredder, however, insists that such comparisons are counterproductive: "The journalistic tendency to compare actors rather misses the point; for anyone seeing both in close succession, it is the idea of kingship that prevails with both actors (through both roles) displaying different facets of the idea against the solid framework of the production and the other characters."[29]

The Bolingbrokes of Pasco and Richardson also differed. Pasco was the brooding usurper, guilt-ridden, aware that his fate is driving him to the same end as the man he overthrows; Richardson, "an ambitious young stallion"[30] out to right the wrongs perpetrated against him. To equalize the roles and to emphasize that this is a twin tragedy, Barton expanded Bolingbroke's role, giving him the soliloquy that Shakespeare withheld until the second part of *Henry IV*. At the beginning of 5.3, Barton inserted the "Uneasy lies the head that wears the crown" speech (3.1.4f) to illustrate that the events that concerned Shakespeare were tragic to the falling king *and* the rising one. Anne Barton's program note clarified the director's intention: "Richard's journey from King to man is balanced by Bolingbroke's progress from a single to a twin-natured being. Both movements involve a gain and a loss. Each, in its own way, is tragic." The actors, by the way, came to the conclusion that Richard is the much more difficult role of the two, even with Barton's enlargement of Bolingbroke's role.

Except for this speech by Bolingbroke, Barton made relatively few adjustments in the script: he did rewrite the "gage scene" to reduce its Bergsonian comicality,[31] enlarged the Queen's speech in 3.4 to build sympathy for her plight, and occasionally reassigned a few speeches to other characters or divided them among a group for choric effect. The cuts and transpositions were conservative when compared to those of *The Wars of the Roses* or, as we shall see, *King John*.[32] For the most part, the cuts were made to reduce the play's running time (or, more accurately, to allow time for Barton's enlargements, particularly the prologue and epilogue), to minimize the confusion arising from the number of small parts, and to delete obscure language or references. Two distinct acting editions were used: the Pasco text and the Richardson. To encourage the actors' freedom of interpretation, Barton allowed each to accept or delete some passages.[33] Pasco cites particular lines spoken to Bushy and Green in which the usurper explains he will execute them because they have

> Disparked my parks and felled my forest woods
> From mine own windows torn my household coat
> Razed out my impress leaving me no signs
> To show the world I am a gentleman.

> (3.1.24–28)

Pasco recalls that Barton wanted the lines cut, but he retained them: "Within my instinctive interpretation of Bolingbroke, I need to say those things . . . he's had his home torn down, his wealth redistributed."[34]

The alteration of the leading actors was a *coup de théâtre* that also emphasized the play's innate theatricality that Barton wished to explore. The acts of its protagonists are often the acts of actors: the Mowbray-Bolingbroke conflict is proclaimed in bravado rhetoric before a court audience; Bolingbroke invests old York with the role of dead Gaunt in 2.3 to abet his rebellious return to England ("Methinks I see in you old Gaunt alive"), and Richard, in the Deposition Scene (4.1), "undecks the pompous body of a King" in ritualistic gestures suggestive of an actor removing his costume. Much of the academic criticism of *Richard II* has centered on its theatricality and the tradition that influenced its author. E. M. W. Tillyard claims that the play's proper antecedent is the morality play,[35] an idea enlarged by Anne Barton, who believes that Richard is "the player king of flawed rule" and Bolingbroke a lord of misrule, a mock king from the folk customs of an earlier England.[36]

Barton seized upon the medieval tradition in his staging: one critic noted he turned "the characters into wooden figures of a medieval morality play . . . a daring gamble which succeeds."[37] Actually, *Richard II* was infused with only a minor degree of medieval sensibilities, whereas *King John* was a full blown exploration of the play in medieval terms.

Barton's theatricality was more Greek than medieval, despite a proliferation of cowled monks. During a discussion of the play at a director's forum in August 1973, Barton admitted that he was aiming at a "Greco-Elizabethan style in acting and production." Barton did not arbitrarily impose the notion on the script, which possesses a distinctively classical quality in its great declamatory speeches and in the general sparsity of the dialogue. The play represents for Shakespeare a break in style and structure from his earlier works; written entirely in verse, it, according to Wells, "implies, obviously, a degree of stylization and artificiality in the language, and one result of this is that a number of characters are so lacking in individuality that they seem mainly or entirely choric in function." The imagery of the play, with its emphasis on symmetry, further suggested to Barton the necessity of mounting the play with more formality than is customary. The style encouraged the sense of high ceremony inherent in the script: the lists at Coventry are framed by incantations of the marshals and combatants; kneeling, hand-kissing, gage-throwing, and other symbolic gestures recur throughout the play.[38]

To effect ritual formality, Barton drilled his actors for almost twelve weeks—an unusually long rehearsal period for the RSC—to adapt them to formal acting, as opposed to the more naturalistic style to which they were accustomed. Stredder, a privileged observer at rehearsals, recalls that in the early stages of work, there was much talk of orchestration, recitatives, arias, and formality.[39] Actors faced the audience, often in scenes where they would normally face each other. Movement was carefully orchestrated; great spaces were maintained between actors (a Barton trademark[40]); lines were often delivered more as incantations than natural speech. The effect was stunning, though it had liabilities: "There was little opportunity for mutual interplay between the actors. Some of the older members of the company, like Sebastian Shaw and Beatrice Lehman as the Duke and Duchess of York, cannot avoid the meed [*sic*] of naturalism that comes naturally to them."[41] The stylization also strained audiences unaccustomed to seeing Shakespeare in such formal patterns.

Such formal acting demanded an equally formal setting. O'Brien lists four additional concerns that motivated his designs: (1) the alternation of the lead roles within the context of an acting company; (2) the idea of Richard II as a compulsive role-player; (3) the image of the play as a bad dream whose central figure is moving towards certain destruction; (4) "the great challenge of the play for any designer, the upper level at Flint Castle (3.3)." He then fashioned a set consisting of two walls that became, in effect, giant ladders on either side of the stage, set at right angles to the forestage. The walls and their oversized steps became visual metaphors for the descending Richard and the rising Bolingbroke, an echo of Richard's notion that Northumberland is "the ladder wherewithal / The mounting Bolingbroke ascends my throne (4.1.29)." Spanning the wall-ladders was the set's most striking—and controversial—piece: a bridge that could be raised or lowered to provide a platform from which Richard could observe the lists or—more spectacularly—the Flint Castle battlements from which the weakened king quite literally was brought to earth in the famous "Down, down I come, like glist'ring Phaethon" speech in 3.3. In the central playing area there was a portable pyramid of golden steps for the throne, and in the dark perimeters of the stage, bleachers on which the acting company sat to watch the play's progress, another reinforcement of the theatricality of Barton's production concept. O'Brien's design seemed a technologically advanced version of the play's opening scene as suggested by the first stage direction of the Cambridge New Shakespeare text:[42] "A great scaffold within the castle of Windsor, with seats thereon, and a space of ground before it."

Some critics believed the design to be in the Brechtian tradition, but Robert Brustein dispelled any notion that Barton and O'Brien were Brechtians: ". . . the name of Brecht has been raised in connection with the production when it features precisely the kind of ostentatious display that used to make Brecht wince. Such a display is more native to Broadway."[43] In actuality, the design was less a Brechtian device than an attempt to create an acting space that approximated Shakespeare's stage (but that was not merely archaeological) and that would offer insight into the play's themes. When the play was revived in 1974, the bridge was deleted and the central pyramid was built up (in a new design by John Napier that also accommodated *King John*). The new design was born of theatric necessity rather than artistic choice: the sight lines at the Aldwych Theatre would not tolerate the tall bridge.

The director prefaced the play with a traditional device to establish a context for his interpretation: the medieval dumbshow. There was, Barton felt, a need for a specific figure to introduce the mime. He considered an Elizabethan prompter (which he used in *Shrew* in 1960), the Lord Chamberlain, even himself as director.[44] Ultimately, he chose the figure of Shakespeare, who became a master of ceremonies for the production. Before the house lights dimmed, "Shakespeare" (patterned after the Droeshout icon) entered, prompt book in hand, and mounted the pyramid at center. Behind him was a "scarecrow" on which hung a golden cloak of kingship, a crown, and a sceptre: the ritual symbols of monarchy. Shakespeare conjured actors with a flourish of the hand, and the company, dressed identically in brown trousers and sweaters, entered in two ceremonial columns to surround the platform. Pasco and Richardson stood before the pyramid, flanking the figure of Shakespeare who held a prop crown tantalizingly above their heads. Each reached for the golden ring and, for a moment, held the crown in the upstage hand (presaging act 4's deposition); Shakespeare bowed to the actor who would play the King that evening. The Lord Marshal of the lists scene dressed that evening's "king," who then inspected his appearance in a large mirror, a portentous gesture. As the King ascended the platform to be formally crowned, the company knelt, chanting "God save the King . . . May the King live forever," a ritual described on page 115 of Anne Barton's book. The actors then donned pieces of costume while retiring to the bleachers to await entrances. The new player-king assumed his role and reign with the drama's opening line, "Old John of Gaunt . . ."

A ring of ever-present monks, in ominously dark cowls, circled the throne pyramid; they were prominent throughout the production (and *King John*), perhaps to underscore the religious elements on which both the play and Richard's reign are based. Though the monks may seem a too obvious choice, here they were an appropriate gesture towards the ritualization of the play.

Other spectres stalked Richard. In 1.2 Barton presented the Duchess of Gloucester as a ghost, literally springing from the grave (via a trap), skull in hand and crying "Blood!" to exhort Gaunt to avenge Gloucester's murder.[45] In early rehearsals she was accompanied by two "Fury-like" attendants who shrieked her words in echo. In Barton's mind she was very much a spirit come to prick the conscience of Old Gaunt, in a stage convention that was typically Elizabethan. Richard David found the elaboration counterproductive,[46] and even Barton thought better of his impulse: in the revival the Duchess entered from the wings and spoke quietly, though she still carried the skull.[47]

The lists at Coventry (1.3) remain among the most memorable moments in Barton's production. This already-dramatic event was made "theatrical" by mounting the combatants on oversized hobby horses. Surprisingly, it was not Barton's idea—originally—to use the horses; nor was it O'Brien's. Richardson claims credit for inspiring the device: "John thought this was a marvelous idea . . . but then he went quite berserk! and he had an oversized white unicorn on skis [actually used for Richard's return to England in 3.2]. And then he decided that Northumberland and all his henchmen . . . should have black stallions."[48] Barton's decision to put the rebels on enormous black horses furthered the nightmarish quality to which O'Brien alluded earlier. The graceful list horses contrasted with "the huge threatening black chargers surely not of this earth . . . the terrifying Four Horsemen of the Apocalypse."[49] Such images are within the script (2.3.58), but Barton's imaginative visualization lingered in the mind's eye long after the aural description faded from the ear.

At the end of the ritual-laden lists scene Barton added yet another ceremony that would be repeated throughout the play. Banished Bolingbroke concludes the scene with a moving speech: "Then England's earth farewell, sweet soil adieu . . ." (306–9). A bowl of English earth was placed on the forestage for the future king to sift on the lines;[50] others with similar lines (Gaunt, the Bishop of Carlisle, the Queen, York, even Richard himself) did likewise elsewhere. Though the business was proclaimed directorial excess by some—"what Shakespeare left implicit was relentlessly italicized"[51]—it was in fact a ritual consistent with the overall concept of the production. Barton's bowl of earth could, to draw an historical parallel, be compared to the *thymele* of the ancient Greek theater.

Ritual unity was further sustained as the rebel lords wore stylized masks and *cothornoi* while plotting the usurpation in 2.1. Barton originally intended to use masks throughout the performance, but it perturbed the actors because the headgear countered all they had been taught about facial expressiveness; finally the masks were used only for moments of portent.[52] To depersonalize the rebels, Barton redistributed as single lines the speeches by Northumberland, Ross, and Willoughby so trhat the scene aurally resembled Greek *stychomythia*. This became particularly effective during the litany of Richard's crimes (2.1.246–62). The choral effect was used elsewhere, notably when Bushy and Greene shared the speech "Each substance of a grief hath twenty thousand shadows" (2.2.14ff). The Captain's speech in 2.4 describing the defection of the Welsh was also redistributed among a chorus of eight actors who formed a half circle at center, backs to audience, to recite the litany of woe to the accompaniment of a plaintive horn.[53]

Elsewhere Barton expanded the role of Sir Pierce of Exton, Richard's eventual assassin, by assigning him Greene's lines about the Bolingbroke rebellion (2.2.49ff). Thus the news of the discord became even more ominous and sinister as Exton, like Northumberland, was played as a force of evil. Barton traced the political repercussions of Richard's decline and Bolingbroke's rise through the character of Exton, who was invested with a sinister, underworld aura.[54] A similarly dark element was introduced in 2.2: the servingman who announces the death of the Duchess of Gloucester wore a death mask.

The respective returns of Bolingbroke from France and Richard from Ireland were visually striking moments in their contrast. The former arrived astride a towering black horse, an apocalyptic image, flanked by monks chanting the *Kyrie Eleison* ("Lord have mercy"—a prayer from the Catholic mass), a union of the nightmarish and religious qualities of Barton's master plan. In contrast Richard returned to England's shores in 3.2., resplendent in white, atop the white unicorn to which Richardson alluded. O'Brien describes his design:

> a poetic image for the return from Ireland in which "roan Barbary" was a life-sized effigy in white trappings with the plumed king astride it in front of a frieze of his followers carrying tall white lances and wearing on their chests shields with the fully modeled heads of horses in white. Thus Richard's cavalry stood motionless like a frozen wave of impotence but "Late tossing on the breaking seas."

Like an icon, the Bishop of Carlisle flanked the white-robed King as he saluted the downstage bowl of earth—"Dear earth I do salute thee with my hand." Richard's pontifical dress and ritual gestures prepared him to discourse on his theological, as well as political, belief that "wordly man cannot depose the deputy elected by the Lord" (56–57). More important, the directorial choices provided a superbly theatrical framework for modern audiences to perceive Richard's message: a set of upstage curtains were ceremoniously parted to reveal Roan Barbary and Richard's white army. Here Barton further expanded Exton's role by assigning him Scroop's lines to remind us that the King's return was not a triumph, but the beginning of his decline—despite a costume that proclaimed otherwise.

The centerpiece of Barton's production was 3.3—the confrontation between Richard and Bolingbroke at Flint Castle. The rebels entered on stilted shoes, dark and ominous, as Bolingbroke speaks in weather metaphors (3.3.54–60). At this point Richard appears on the battlements, high atop the bridge of O'Brien's set. For this, Richard's most spectacular moment as player-King ("Yet looks he like a king!"), Barton costumed the King in a radiant, golden cloak, pleated to unfurl like the feathers of an eagle. Arms spread wide atop the towers, Richard was the sun-king described in the imagery throughout the play: "his golden uncontrolled enfranchisement"; "his fierce blaze of riot"; and "the blushing discontented sun." The historical Richard's coat-of-arms was adorned with sun images, a fact that Shakespeare—and Barton and O'Brien—were surely aware.

Costumed "like a King," Richard delivered his great performance speech: "What must the king do now? must he submit?" The monologue is filled with the oratory of an actor, but the "performance" is rejected by his audience: "Well, well, I talk but idly and you laugh at me . . ." (3.3.170–71). The player-king must relinquish his role, and Barton provided him with a grand exit— "Down, down I come, like glist'ring Phaethon," cried the King, and he was lowered to the stage on the mechanized bridge. The words constitute the formal climax of the play, and the director saved *his* consummate gesture for the moment. Richard the Actor's fall is the product of dramatic necessity (tragedy demands the fall of great men), just as Richard the King's fall is the product of historical inevitability. Barton's theatrical "gimmick" to visualize the actor-King's decline was appropriate to the calculated theatricality of the production and the theme it explored.

Barton placed his first interval after the Flint Castle scene, concluding the first half with a piece of business that showed the "twin buckets" at equal height—albeit one rising, the other descending. Neither Richard nor Bolingbroke was sure who ought to lead the procession offstage as King. Richard bowed politely to Bolingbroke, and they descended the steps of the dias together.

Act 4's Deposition scene is innately theatrical because of Richard's histrionic acts: his divestment and the gesture of shattering the mirror. Thus the scene was relatively unadorned by Barton, allowing Pasco and Richardson to provide the scene's most memorable moments. The climax of the scene occurs when Richard shatters his symbol of earthly vanity, the mirror. Barton highlighted the moment with both a large and a small gesture: first, Bolingbroke's line "the shadow of your sorrow . . ." was repeated and intoned by the entire cast; second, the smashed mirror, framed by a circle of gold, was lifted by Bolingbroke and "placed over Richard's head (a replay of the opening tableau) deliberately enough for us to see it pass from halo to crown, and from crown to noose."[55] Richard wore the prop around his neck for the remainder of the play. Richard was escorted from the stage in a ceremonial procession as Bolingbroke began a new act in the chronicle drama of English kings. The leading actors had again reversed the roles established in the opening pantomime.

The first scene of act 5 contained one of Barton's more controversial choices. The woeful street meeting between Richard and his queen was cut short by the approach of Northumberland, dressed here quite literally as a giant bird-of-prey, clawbeaked, taloned, and feathered in black. Bird images abound in the script, and Barton had shown his sun-king to resemble an eagle at Flint Castle. Apparently he thought it appropriate to extend the metaphor by making

Northumberland a giant bird. The gimmick was universally condemned by critics, and Richardson convinced Barton to cut it when the production moved to London.[56]

Another visual choice was similarly condemned. In 5.2 the York family and their attendants played children's winter games around a prop "mockery king of snow" while singing traditional Christmas carols. Eventually, the snowman melted to reveal Aumerle. Referring to this device and the Northumberland bird, David Nathan chided Barton, suggesting that, had anyone said "You can knock me over with a feather," an ostrich would have galloped on.[57]

Perhaps Barton's most provocative directorial choices occurred in 5.5. Richard, alone at Pomfret Castle—"with no audience and no role to play"[58]— was visited by a Groom, here a cowled monk, who describes Bolingbroke's entry into London astride Richard's favorite Roan Barbary. The groom carried a toy horse, another of the child's fantasy images Barton brought to the production. As the groom's speeches remind us that Bolingbroke has taken Richard's role, Barton's monk lowered his cowl and showed himself to be Bolingbroke. The actors then performed business that probably best typified the statement Barton made with his production: "Bolingbroke as Groom held the empty mirror between his face and Richard's, the mutual reflection of two shadows strutting and fretting their hour upon the stage."[59] O'Brien raises a question that surely evolved in preproduction discussions with the director: Was it the King who saw Bolingbroke in the face of the Groom?

Though Richardson called the moment "a *coup de théâtre* . . . which makes a great deal of sense,"[60] Pasco was skeptical, and it was only when the scene was played before the RSC cast that he was convinced; the stunned reaction of his colleagues showed him that Barton and Richardson (who had immediately sided with Barton) were perfectly right.[61] Others found Barton's expressionistic treatment of the scene a revelation. Both men were ceremonially stripped of all trappings of office—the King in prison garb, Bolingbroke in clerical habit. Thus both were able "to say those things which in the outside political world were disallowable."[62] Though it surely took an enormous liberty with the text, Barton's staging was consistent with the exploration of the parallels between the twin monarchs.

Just as Richard's death speech—"Mount, mount my soul! thy seat is up on high" (5.5.111)—recalls his fall at Flint Castle ("Down, down I come"), Barton's staging of the death recalled the visual impact of the earlier scene. Richard's body was hoisted high in the air by pulleys. While suspended above the stage, he was shot with a cross-bow by Exton, an imposing figure on stilts. His body came to rest on the bridge that had supported him during his bravado display of royal arrogance in 3.2.

The play's final scene, 5.6, begins with the recital of casual slaughters and bloody deeds occasioned by the rebellion—a ritual fulfillment of Carlisle's prophecy in act 4. Another cycle repeats itself: Bolingbroke, king imminent, retires the Bishop of Carlisle, just as Richard had banished Bolingbroke and Mowbray to begin the tragedy. These rituals are interrupted by the appearance of Exton, the executioner, dressed by Barton as a giant infested with snakes, perhaps a response to Bolingbroke's banishment of Exton: "With Cain go wander through shades of night" (5.6.43)—a line that recalls God's banishment of the serpent in the Garden. Barton did not have Exton bear in Richard's coffin according to the original stage direction. The coffin arrived theatrically, descending from the upstage bridge. Speaight noted that Bolingbroke's anguished cry at the sight of the coffin showed "unforgettably what the production was concerned to emphasize—that these antagonists are really *frères ennemis,* moving with a kind of motiveless somnabulism, the one to destruction, the other to despair. If Shakespeare meant us to understand that in politics there is no victory, Barton's production accurately got the message across."[63]

The woeful pageant of *Richard II* ended as it began—with a dumb show in which a new king was crowned. But the new king was not Henry IV. Richard and Bolingbroke flanked the "new" monarch, a nameless member of the company wearing a death mask. The business was surely derived from the text:

> . . . for within the hollow crown
> That rounds the mortal temples of a king,
> Keeps Death his court, and there the antic sits,
> Scoffing his state and grinning his pomp . . .
>
> (3.2.160–64)

Death is, of course, the ultimate usurper of kings, actors, and audiences alike, a grinning audience of one for whom all must perform. Barton's curtain tableau was a theatrical metaphor for this truth: "When Richard dies, it is really the death of all I hold most dear that I am watching; it is I who die with Richard II."[64]

The production played for eighty-four performances at Stratford during the 1973 season, and was then taken to New York the following January, where it was performed twenty more times. The RSC included a slightly revised version in its 1974 repertory because it was popular with audiences and prompted much discussion of Barton's daring.

Barton's version evoked antithetical responses from critics and scholars during its two-year run. It was most often praised for its intelligence, innovation, and the excellence of its verse-speaking. It was most frequently chastised for the literalness of the visual images (for example, the snowman and the hobby horses), the static staging, the flatness of the secondary characters, the lecturelike quality of the presentation, and Barton's textual liberties. Ultimately, whether one approved or disapproved of the production depended on one's openness to experimentation. If nothing else, *Richard II* vindicated Barton's belief that critics "are a mutually contradictory body."

King John, which played in tandem with *Richard II* during the 1974 Stratford season, is also remembered for its extraordinary ideas and visual images. Uncharacteristically, Barton wrote a program note that identifies the seed of his concept:

> Whenever I have seen *King John* on the stage I have been fascinated yet perplexed. When I read it again at the end of 1973, I was struck by how much the play, probably written in 1594, is about England and us *now*. Our world of outward order and inner instability, of shifting ideologies and self-destructive pragmatism, is also the world of *King John*. Even the specific political issues have modern parallels, although I have never seen this emerge fully in performance.[65]

To find answers to this production problem, Barton turned to Shakespeare's probable sources: first, to the anonymous chronicle, *The Troublesome Reign of King John* (c. 1591), and later to Bishop John Bale's politically motivated quasi-morality play, *King Johan* (1539). The director found that "those areas left cloudy by *King John* were more clearly explored in *The Troublesome Reign*, which develops into full speeches, or even scenes, things that in Shakespeare are unexplained references." Barton, the would-be playwright who was first attracted to *King John* while attempting to write a trilogy about the Plantagenets, surmised that "a marriage of the two texts might be fruitful"—better yet, a marriage of three texts would be most fruitful because Bale's play "could add further definition to the Morality theme" Barton felt innate to all three dramas. The combination would ultimately, he hoped, "bring to a production of today something of the starkness of the medieval style which can speak so clearly to a modern audience in this age of Brecht, Arden, and Edward Bond."

Barton reworked, spliced, and edited the three plays: he soon found himself creating something like Frankenstein's monster:

> Having started with very limited plans for cuts and insertions, I found that despite myself, as I worked, and as rehearsal progressed, new leads and possibilities emerged, and these led me to much wider textual changes and additions than initially envisaged. Our final version incorporates many lines from *The Troublesome Raigne*, a few from Bale's *Kynge Johan*, some medieval carols and additions of my own. I hope and believe that my additions do no more than develop and clarify tendencies already in the three plans from which this version is drawn.

Robert Smallwood has tallied[66] the number of lines in the script used at Stratford: of the approximately 2,595 lines in the acting edition, roughly 1,350 were Shakespeare's (some altered, others redistributed); about 600 were from *The Trouble Reign;* and about a dozen from Bale. The remaining 600 lines were Barton's.

The production opened in March, billed as Shakespeare's *King John*. Critics soon referred to the work as "King Barton's John."[67] Harold Hobson was incensed at Barton's "inchoate amalgam of disparate elements presented under a misleading title in the name of an author who did not write it" and intimated that legal action should be taken against the RSC for violation of the Trade Descriptions Act.[68] The critics were not alone in their displeasure: " . . . when I go to Stratford, I not only *expect* to hear Shakespeare's lines, I *want*, and am *entitled* to hear them," wrote one unhappy patron to *The Observer*.[69] Barton emphasizes that he and the RSC did not mean to deceive their patrons: "The whole fuss about *King John* springs from a practical theatre fact. The Publicity Office put out the posters and booking forms before I rewrote the play, and it was too late to change it. And that's why we were clobbered." When the play came to London, it was conspicuously rebilled as "adapted and reworked from the play by William Shakespeare and other sources." That announcement quelled much of the furor: "We put it in huge letters at the Aldwych," Barton remembers, "and everybody was perfectly happy."

There were professed admirers of Barton's revision as well. Michael Billington found the "new" play "infinitely more fascinating than the published Shakespeare version,"[70] while B. A. Young, among the more conservative London critics, said Barton's effort yielded "a positive profit . . . indeed an exciting one."[71] Emrys James, who played John, defended Barton's rewrite: "I found in the adaptation we did were solutions to the problems that had struck me when I did the play towards the end of the Benthall regime at the Old Vic."[72] When the play was revived in 1975, the director's new program note acknowledged the controversy:

> In Stratford our *King John* had an unusually varied reception, provoking both high commendation and total condemnation. My personal view was that neither of these extremes was justified, although of course I understand the feelings of those who condemned the principle of our making an adaptation in the first place. Coming back to the production after its opening, I felt that our version fell somewhat between two stools, and that I should have changed the text either less or more.

The text in its unrevised form is among Shakespeare's least popular plays, both in the theater and in the study. Barton identified some of its problems in 1957 when he and Rylands critiqued Stratford's season for the BBC: " . . . it is hard to grasp what Shakespeare was at with it at first. It seems very episodic . . . the plot is hard to follow and it seems rather perfunctorily set out."[73] The first half of this diffuse play dramatizes the French-Austrian wars; midway through act 3 John becomes a Richard III-like childkiller and thereafter declines as an effective monarch. His weakness eventually leads to his death, for which we are asked to sympathize despite his villainy. Unlike Macbeth he has not a strength of character to offset his foul deeds; unlike Richard III he is not fascinating enough to arouse one's interest.

Just as Richard II's fall is measured and mirrored by the ascent of Bolingbroke, John's is paralleled by the rise of Bastard Falconbridge—a similarity between the two plays that did not go unnoticed by Barton, or his wife, whose program note advised audiences that "it is clear . . . that they [*Richard II* and *King John*] are companion pieces. The two plays set off each other, by exploring similar themes and problems." The Bastard begins the play low in the audience's estimation and, by the play's end, speaks among Shakespeare's most patriotic lines. Were *King John* part of a larger cycle, its diffuseness might be more tolerable, as lesser strands could be developed with more clarity. Actions—whether by John or the factions with which he must contend—are motivated by the doctrine of *commodity* (or expediency), a term whose import may be lost on contemporary audiences.[74] Like *Richard II*, *King John* is also written entirely in verse, much of it bombastic and archaic. These, then, are among the problems Barton confronted when he approached the play in 1974.

Barton's first impulse was to emphasize the contemporaneity of the text. England in the mid-70s was rife with discontent: inflation was eroding the earning power of its people and their confidence in government. The Common Market controversy occupied people's minds. John's lament that

> Our discontented counties do revolt;
> Our people quarrel with obedience,
> Swearing allegiance and the love of soul
> To stranger blood, to foreign royalty

(5.1.10–13)

seemed appropriate to twentieth-century England. Barton interpolated lines of passable Shakespearean pastiche[75] to heighten the play's parallel with modern problems. For instance, Barton's barons were aggrieved that

> This realm is rent asunder quite by faction
> . . . .
> By grievous imposts, duties, tolls and taxes
> The Exchequer eats us quite; the price of goods
> Soars meteor-like unto the louring heavens,
> Whiles that our purses dwindle and decline.[76]

They, much like their counterparts in Eliot's *Murder in the Cathedral,* stepped forward to address the audience, listing their grievances against John's realm—and Barton's England. Thus the revised script and its production were markedly more Brechtian in their political urgency than perhaps any Barton production. Obviously he hoped his audience would heed Bishop Bale's admonition: "For the love of God, look to the state of England." Though Barton customarily avoids overt contemporary political commentary in his stage work, preferring more universally human themes, his statements in *King John* seemed uncharacteristically "topical in the manner of party political broadcasts."[77]

Perhaps to offset the modern references, Barton magnified the morality play elements suggested by Bale's tract, but the ensuing clash of form and content weakened the impact of both. Smallwood judged Barton's fusion of the morality tradition with modern secular themes lacking in "the essential element of religious faith to make it meaningful." Though Barton borrowed *Richard II*'s ubiquitous monks to evoke a religious patina for *King John,* they too seemed a self-conscious imposition on Shakespeare's play.

Barton also added scenes based on the source plays to clarify the ambiguities of Shakespeare's play. First, he devised a long prologue in which the amended will of Richard Coeur-de-Lion was read by a death-masked figure (shades of *Richard II*) to establish John's claim to the throne; this was followed by the first of six coronations. While Barton's prologue is more theatrically impressive than Shakespeare's, it created problems by investing John's reign with an authority that Shakespeare leaves ambiguous. Smallwood lamented Barton's eradication of this "carefully chosen vagueness"; by diminishing it, "John Barton got his play off on the wrong foot."[78]

Barton, who favors ritual and ceremony, padded Shakespeare's *King John* by occasioning six coronations:

1. John (in the Prologue)
2. Arthur (in Barton's scene 2)
3. John (Barton's scene 10; cf. Shakespeare's 4.2)
4. A parodistic coronation of John by the papal legate and cowled monks (in scene 12; cf., Shakespeare's 5.1.)
5. Lewis (scene 13; cf. Shakespeare's 5.2)
6. Prince Henry (closing tableau)

Had one seen *Richard II* at Stratford the previous summer, one would have recognized Richard's pleated golden cloak and mask and the chant "Long live the King," which were prominent in five of the six *King John* coronations.

The fourth crowning, the parody, was a major Barton supplement to the original play. Basing his interpretation on four lines that open Shakespeare's fifth act, he devised an elaborate mockery in which John was humiliated by Pandolph and his ecclesiastical brethren (chanting the *Dies Irae*), who stripped him of this clothing, crowned him with a dunce's cap, and—in a music hall interpolation—smacked him with a custard pie in the face. Theatrically it was entertaining; thematically, it was a comment on the tenuousness of kingship. Richard David labeled it an imposition that "reduced the Protestant conflict to utter triviality."[79]

The most-discussed Barton insertion was John's Death Scene at Swinstead Abbey, orchestrated to suggest da Vinci's *Last Supper,* with John as the Christ figure. Apparently it was devised to encourage greater sympathy for John, now a tyrant guilty of infanticide. The scene was played in a Christmas milieu with the monks singing medieval carols (cf. the York family in act 5 of Barton's

Richard II); John himself sang a sad wassail song before his poisoning. Some felt the addition of the scene, only alluded to at 5.6.29 of Shakespeare's play, "helped to create a human being where before there was little more than a cypher."[80] Others believed the scene was too long,[81] an incorporation more for theatrical effect than dramatic necessity.

Perhaps drawing on discoveries made while working on *Richard II*, Barton and Emrys James rendered a King John who played at being a king—probably because "he does not believe he legitimately is one."[82] Irving Wardle called the Barton-James John "a puny, grinning, jingoistic clown,"[83] an interpretation at odds with any of the kings present in the plays from which Barton drew his inspiration: in *King Johan*, Bale presented a hero sacrificed to papist ruthlessness (the John of Swinstead Abbey in Barton's version); *The Troublesome Reign*'s monarch is partly heroic knight, mostly devious politician, who—whatever his weaknesses—never has his sovereignty questioned; Shakespeare unequivocally questions the legitimacy of John's power in the first scene in his version (1.1.44–45). These three elements that Barton combined were incompatible because their authors had different ends in view and because each used a different medium (i.e., respectively, a didactic play, a history play, and a dramatic play).[84] To accommodate three varying perspectives, Barton created a fourth: a player king, first dazzling the French with heroic histrionics, now a termagant playing the ruthless tyrant when "commodity" demanded it, always a madcap monarch—literally a pretender to the throne.

If John is the foolish ruler of Barton's version, there seems little reason for anyone to follow him, least of all the Bastard Faulconbridge, who ultimately displaces his personal ambition in order to support Prince Henry and the unity of England. As a practicing cynic, the Bastard was intended by Shakespeare to satirize the actions of others, a function that becomes redundant if King John and other courtiers are obvious fools. Where Barton had enlarged the role of usurping Bolingbroke in *Richard II* to make him a more equal match to Richard, he reversed the procedure in *King John* by magnifying the King's already larger role and diminishing that of the play's other focal character. The choice unbalanced the play because audiences could not fully appreciate Faulconbridge's potential as a successor to the throne.[85] Nowhere was Barton's Bastard more at odds with Shakespeare than in the final scene. Barton's penchant for symmetry during this, his "formal" period, dictated another will-reading to close the play. The Bastard read John's will, which named Henry as his successor, but there was every indication that the Bastard was concealing something. After the reading, he tossed the will into John's casket to bury forever the secret of John's intentions, picked up a book from under a Christmas tree, and read the patriotic lines "This England never did, never shall . . ." (5.7.112ff) Finished, he turned and exited whistling. The Brechtian ending, grim and cynical, countered the spirit of national unification that Shakespeare apparently intended.

Barton did not wait until the production moved to London to begin revising his adaptation. Mike Gwilym, a principal in the company, remembers that the director-writer did much rewriting at Stratford because "John was very much finding out as we went along what he wanted to do with the play." As the company showed him what could be done—or what they could not do comfortably—Barton amended the script. *King John* is unquestionably Barton's most "process-oriented" production. Hence, there was a restlessness to the production that discomforted many viewers. Billington, otherwise a staunch admirer of the work, felt that "at times you get the feeling you're watching three different plays running concurrently."[86] Several years after the production closed, Barton was asked whether he might not have let his inspiration get the better of him: "The only time I've done it [rewrite] just following instinct was on *King John*, and I don't necessarily approve of what I did—it was simply the way the instinct went."[87]

"Instinct" gradually led Barton to increase the morality play elements. Partly to infuse a greater sense of the morality tradition, mostly to create a role for Mike Gwilym, then a promising new actor in the RSC for whom Barton and his colleagues wanted to provide work, Barton greatly expanded the role of Peter the Prophet into a death figure. From a single line in Shakespeare's fourth act, Barton created a Nemesis who haunted John for having hanged him. Disguised in various costumes, most frequently a monk, he shadowed John from the prologue to Swinstead, where *he* gave the King the poison chalice. When the production reached the Adlwych in 1975, Peter was a major role, nearly eclipsing that of the Bastard, Pandulph, and Hubert. Gwilym recounts that Barton wanted the Peter-Death figure to serve as a chorus that would, in the morality tradition, serve as a go-between from stage to house. In London, "Death" welcomed the audience with "a marvelous speech" that emphasized Death's unbiased call:[88]

> Yet I do come to all or some
> That be-en under heaven;
> To each state set I a date,
> And make mankind all even.[89]

Speaking on a radio show in the summer of 1975, after *John* had closed its London run, Barton rationalized the morality elements:

> I was particularly struck by the apostrophes to death, which are made in Shakespeare's play, which seem to be picking up the morality tradition, the introduction of Death as an actual character in medieval plays, and I therefore incorporated that bit of thinking in my version. I may have been wrong to do so, I don't know.[90]

That the revival was more clearly devised as a morality play suggests that Barton may have been sensitive to criticism of the political didacticism of the

Stratford script. His revised program note acknowledged the criticism and indicated that the Company would "not take our exploration further . . . not so much to improve a rich but flawed piece of work, as to make it more accessible" by discarding the crassly topical nature of the earlier effort, and enlarging the universal elements of guilt and expiation within a medieval framework. The revival was generally more acceptable to critics for its deletion of the topicality, and for the magnification of Peter the Prophet's role, which gave the work greater focus—even if the work was still not Shakespeare's.

If the scripted revision was never completely accepted, the physical production was on firmer ground. John Napier's set was designed to remind audiences that they were in a theater: it had a raked stage covered by a sloping ceiling, dappled with stars like the Elizabethan "heavens"; the set, dominated by a perspective cross at center, was ringed by lights; a portable black curtain "as in a village hall show"[91] allowed for maskings and revelations. As in *Richard II*, the actors wore all-purpose brown jerkins to which they added selected costume pieces.

Movement was formal and pageantlike, and the delivery was correspondingly stylized, which disconcerted some critics: "Rhetoric is delivered with a wink and a nudge. Actors are encouraged to ogle us, make funny noises, mince about or chorus lines together."[92] Yet Barton offered undeniably strong visual imagery: the coronations; the sackcloth-and-ashes submission of John to Pandulph—"a walking skull encased in scarlet"[93]—and his monks; Arthur's dreamlike escape from death: "As if in a dream, he quietly treads down the steely scaffolding, pronouncing his own death with a wisdom that avoids silliness and becomes magical";[94] the all-white death scene at Swinstead Abbey. Wardle cited the Blanche-Louis wedding-of-convenience as among the production's most memorable images: the "lovers" joylessly take hands while the two kings burst into a flower-bedecked nuptial dance; later, during the dissolution of the marriage, the bride and groom do a sad dance to the sound of gunfire.[95] Ironically, much of the critical pique directed at Barton stemmed from a realization that when the director left Shakespeare intact, he proved "infuriatingly enough that he can still direct it better than anyone else."[96]

The visual excitement of the production could not expiate Barton's extraordinary liberties with the script(s). It is no small irony that the director who had by then established a reputation as perhaps the British theater's most respected illuminators of difficult scripts should be castigated for becoming "the servant not of the play, but of the lazy audience's demand for astringincy and sensation."[97] Wardle surmises that Barton seemed to go out of his way to dispel his donnish reputation by resorting to theatrical, rather than intellectual, means to make *King John* palatable to modern audiences. Most patrons, however, are unfamiliar with the play and probably left the RST or the Aldwych assuming that the play they saw *was* Shakespeare's. Though many of the lines were Shakespeare's, Barton structured his production in such a way as to impose on

Shakespeare "notions about politicians he would not have had and language of which he could never have been guilty."[98]

Barton was successful, for the most part, with *Richard II* because he worked closely within the framework—and the spirit—of the original text. His inventions enhanced the script without competing with it. *King John* was imposed upon from the outset—first by a determination to inject modern parallels into it, then by investing it with a self-consciously medieval overlay.

Barton, ever the playwright seeking to create new texts through his directorial work, has continued to adapt scripts boldly, but since the *King John* experience he has been especially careful to appraise his audiences of his revisions. When *Cymbeline* opened, also in 1974, the RSC program assured us that over 800 lines had been cut and a section had been added by Barton. *The Greeks* (1980) was adapted loosely from the writings of Aeschylus, Sophocles, and Euripides—with major sections added by Barton, but it was advertised as an adaptation and understood to be so from its inception, as was Barton's 1983 adaptation of Ibsen's *The Vikings of Helgeland* and Calderon's *La Vida Es Sueño* (*Life Is a Dream;* also "written" in 1983, in a collaboration with Adrian Mitchell of the National Theatre).

The *King John* experience has also proven of further use to Barton and contemporary directors. Earlier in this century Bernard Shaw suggested a lesson the RSC learned with some difficulty in 1974:

> The moment you admit that the producer's business is to improve Shakespeare by cutting out everything that he himself would not have written, and everything that he thinks the audience will either not like or not understand, and everything that does not make prosaic sense, you are launched on a slope on which there is no stopping until you reach the abyss.[99]

King John, unfortunately, may be considered by some as an "abyss" for Barton and the RSC. Yet it, and *Richard II* with which it is aligned, are among the most important works in Barton's personal history. Here most clearly is the playwright overshadowing the director. With its rewrites, cuts, spectacular visual effects, ritual acting, technical wizardry, mythic resonances, Barton boldly used nearly every theatrical device to realize his intentions. Though they were rooted in his academic background, these productions clearly showed that Barton is much more the creative artist than purely an academic director.

6

"What Country, Friend, Is This?"
Othello (1971) and *Much Ado About Nothing* (1976)

> On the whole I don't approve of changing the period for
> Shakespeare. . . . People do it too glibly without thinking and
> do it to get easy dividends. . . . I think it is often apt to distort
> the play—and turn it into something else (Barton to Adden-
> brooke, *The Royal Shakespeare Company*, 210; personal inter-
> view, November 5, 1980).

Whatever eccentricities he may bring to a *Richard II* or *King John*, Barton
nonetheless maintains recognizably Renaissance externals in his productions,
or on occasion (*Hamlet*, 1980), a generalized timelessness. On two instances,
however, he meticulously recreated specific non-Renaissance worlds for Shakespeare's plays: *Othello* and *Much Ado About Nothing*. In both cases the plays
were transplanted into the Victorian era, which was associated with the height
of the British Empire. Barton's choice established a bond between two plays
not normally associated with each other. Just as important, he illustrated the
benefits—and some liabilities—of playing Shakespeare in other times, other
places.

Though he offered cogent textual reasons for the Victorian ambience, one
suspects that his personal predisposition towards "things English" is a factor to
be considered. Tony Church emphasizes that his friend of thirty years "adores
any form of English eccentricity."[1] The Victorian era remains perhaps *the*
quintessentially English period, and one who revels in English eccentricity
would likely gravitate towards this repository of British grandeur.

As evident in chapter 1, Barton's affinity for "Victorian Shakespeare" began
with *Comedy of Errors*, which he directed at Cambridge in May 1950. It was
hugely popular there and later played at London's Watergate Theatre in August

1951. The farce was embellished by pseudo-Victorian music hall ditties, written by the Reverend Geoffrey Beaumont, chaplain at Trinity College and treasurer of the Amateur Dramatic Club, and wittily stylized sets by Timothy O'Brien. As he would for the tragedy and the comedy in the seventies, Barton found for Shakespeare's characters appropriate Victorian equivalents who were instantly recognizable to his audiences: Aegeon was the soul of gloomy Victorian paternity,[2] speaking with a thick Lancashire accent; the Dromios became saucy Jack Tars singing "My name is Dromio-mio-mio";[3] the twin Antipholi wore high collars and boaters, suggesting "a suitable air of the masher" about them;[4] the Duke was a fussy major (a forerunner of Don Pedro in *Much Ado* a quarter century later?) and the Abbess decidedly Irish. Barton was eager to make Shakespeare's prentice work accessible to audiences more sympathetic to Victorian eccentricity than the broadly sketched characters of Elizabethan low comedy.

With *The Comedy of Errors* Barton may have used his ingenuity as an end in itself; by contrast, the Victorian overlay he applied to *Othello* and *Much Ado* was a means to an end as he sought Eliotesque "objective correlatives" to render plausible troublesome scripts whose plots make unusual demands on an audience's belief. Speaking specifically of *Othello,* though the idea applies to *Much Ado,* Barton said, "I . . . believe that the more naturalistic and the more rooted in reality I made this production, the more the basic difficulty of believing in the improbabilities of the plot might be solved."[5] Hence, for both plays he created minutely detailed worlds of Imperial outposts to account for oppressive societal values innate to Shakespeare's design, but perhaps lost to modern audiences unfamiliar with Elizabethan-Jacobean sociology. Where *The Comedy of Errors* was apparently a "decorative," or decor-oriented, production, *Othello* and *Much Ado About Nothing* were conscientious attempts to explore themes in difficult texts by pitting the values of one society (the particulars of which may be alien to general audiences) with those of another (with which general audiences, it may be assumed, have some knowledge). One may ask why Barton did not stage them in modern dress. Such an enterprise, however, would be counterproductive: the society of the 1970s was much less concerned with sexual innuendo and rigidity of class structure than were the Victorians (or Shakespeare's Venetians on Cyprus or Italians in Messina).

In directing *Othello,* Barton was confronted by an unenviable external problem: the RSC production in 1971 was the first major revival of the tragedy since Olivier's triumph at the then new National Theatre in 1963. "Any director," Ronald Bryden opened his *Observer* review, "could be pardoned for pretending that it was another play, straining to offer a production as different as possible from [director] John Dexter's, dodging comparison at every conceivable point."[6] Barton did not want to examine the racial aspects of the tragedy; hence he opted for a conspicuously Moorish, as opposed to black, protagonist: "That [the blackness] had been totally explored by Olivier. . . . Most important of all, I wanted to get away from the contempoary associations with the black man, Black Power, and so on. To Europeans, he's got to be a barbarian, someone Brabantio would resent his daughter marrying. That's all."[7]

Othello was designed by Julia Trevelyn Oman, who received a preproduction brief from Barton that recounts the thought processes leading to his bold decisions:

> When I try to visualize the play, the image which comes to me most strongly is of the earliest war photographs of the mid-nineteenth century—Fenton's pictures from the Crimea, or Matthew Brady's of the American Civil War. They represent the past, but the near past, and the uniforms and background details still have a poignant reality and emotional appeal for us. There is a kind of doomed romanticism in the air. I see Cyprus as a remote, dusty army outpost cut off from civilization, and Othello himself as a soldier as different in manner and dress from the other professionals in his army as Napoleon or Rommel from theirs. Above all, staging the play in the 1850s could heighten the Othello-Desdemona relationship. When we first see them, they should be rooted in this specific period. In Cyprus, we will give them timeless costumes to set them outside the narrow confines of this period. Othello's nature and idiom set him apart from the naturalistic and domestic texture of the rest of the play.[8]

Barton admits he was hesitant about "taking the plunge into the nineteenth century. I was not sure it would work," but—with directorial hindsight—he thought himself vindicated: "I now believe I was right. What I first went for by instinct makes sense of much that was not otherwise apparent in the text itself."[9] What was readily apparent from the outset was that *Othello* needed a very specific military context. Iago's destructive actions are motivated, in part, because he has been passed over for promotion. Hence, the play, according to Barton, "depends largely on military rank."[10] But the Jacobean age was a period without identifiable uniform; thus it is difficult to express this central issue of the tragedy in purely design terms if one set the action in the early seventeenth century. Furthermore, Barton felt that Renaissance and/or Elizabethan costumes offered yet another problem: "To modern audiences it is fancy dress." Barton wanted to avoid any hint of romanticism in his troops:

> I wanted a world of workaday soldiers, unglamorous, with Iago the norm, and Othello standing out as a romantic figure. . . . The more workaday the norm of the play was, the more it helps to set off Othello as an exotic figure. Again, if it's Renaissance, Othello has no particular extraordinariness, because we haven't got a social sense about the Renaissance.

The designer accommodated Barton's vision by dressing the military in roughly end-of-the-century Austrian uniforms and by rendering a sepia-toned wooden set that suggested both the dark corners of Victorian state rooms in act

1 and, later, an outpost garrison (defined by Moorish drapes, prayer rugs, and tentlike hangings)—a visual realization that "Cyprus shouldn't really be Cyrpus. One should be thinking of somewhere in the Mediterranean that is distant from Venice. . . . I told Julia I wanted the feeling that Desdemona is leaving civilisation and travelling to an outpost of the Empire, a distant stockade." To the visual designs Barton added realistic sound touches for atmosphere: Venetian waltzes wafted through the Duke's council chamber in 1.2; bugle calls regulated garrison life; Arab street musicians played "snakey flute music in the eerie nights;" Iago played a melancholy concertina; the cry of a muezzin punctuated Othello's rising fears of Desdemona's betrayal.[12] Barton's actors further defined the ambience in which the action occurred: soldiers drilled and footstamped their way about the stage; "tousled whores loll[ed] on wooden balconies" overlooking the Cypriot streets;[13] Othello and the members of the Senate smoked cheroots and sipped brandy in the civilized world of the council scene; Roderigo arrived in Venice toting a tennis racket and violin case; Iago took a picture of Othello's wedding party with a Matthew Brady-type gunpowder box camera in 2.1 (after line 209).

Michael Billington felt the *verismo* details enhanced the tragic rhythm of the play: ". . . it proves that if you get the minutiae of the play exactly right, then it becomes easier to accept the psychological improbabilities of the main story. . . . Give everyone a clear-cut social role, as Barton does, and everything else naturally falls into place."[14] Barton's Victorian mantle was, in actuality, an ingenious application of Stanislavski's principle of "given circumstances." It provided a working context from which his actors found motivations for their complex actions. Though they would surely have achieved these ends in a Renaissance context, the Victorian military milieu made the "given circumstances" instantly comprehensible to Stratford audiences.

Iago in particular came into sharper focus in Barton's schema. Played by Emrys James as a balding, somewhat "ugly" little man (who naturally resents that Cassio "hath a daily beauty in his life / That makes me ugly,"), Iago was a disgruntled noncommissioned officer, outraged that others are promoted over him despite his career commitment to army life. James's Iago hid his discontent behind a Kipling type of regimental clown's smile to reconcile the humor with the malevolence in the role. James remembers how he and Barton evolved their interpretation of this pivotal role: "The first decision was that it would be silly to play him as an out-and-out scheming Machiavellian figure because the only way that he can succeed is by concealing that. Therefore I have to be as convincing on stage to my fellow actors as I am to the audience. . . . From that I began to piece together a man who had to be agreeable to his fellows, in order to work his way with them."[15]

Barton had little problem establishing motivations for Iago's malicious destruction of Othello, Desdemona, and Cassio. He discounts critical commentary that posits a "motiveless malignity" for Iago's actions: "There is no reason to disbelieve anything Iago says about why he is doing what he does: that

Othello *has* had his wife, Emilia, and Cassio has, too. The consequence is an Ibsenite tragedy in which a sordid sexual past is coming home to roost for four of the characters, and a fifth, Desdemona, who knows nothing about that."[16] Barton's reference to the Ibsenite quality of the play clarifies even further the director's choice of a Victorian setting.

As Anne Barton's program note suggests, Iago pessimistically sees man as an animal for whom words like "nobility," "honor," and "love" have little meaning. And yet, she argues, "Iago is not quite secure in his cynicism. Styles of life which argue against him constitute a personal affront. To preserve his own self-respect, to avoid becoming ugly even in his own eyes, he must either prove they are hypocritical, or else destroy them."[17] In light of Montaigne's skeptical essays on man—which were just gaining popularity in England as Shakespeare wrote *Othello*—such an interpretation of Iago would work well in the context of the late Renaissance. It worked especially well, however, in Barton's redating of the play's action. Victorian obsession with external shows of virtue and respectability would only fuel Iago's cynicism and his determination to subvert the image of his superiors. This was true particularly as Barton and David Calder presented Cassio: "a Florentine prig visibly wincing at the dirty jokes of his gutter-bred colleagues" in the ranks.[18] If, as Barton maintains, Othello and Cassio *have* been sleeping with Emilia, then Iago has reasons other than his own cuckoldry to seek revenge—he wants to disgrace officers supposed to be the models of British propriety.

Desdemona is a role that, whatever the period setting, invariably seems "Victorian" to modern audiences: demure, innocent, unquestioning. Barton's concept strengthened the exterior image of stage tradition, but he took her a step further and hinted that she was a young woman in the vanguard of the nineteenth century's emancipation movement. Like Hardy's Tess or Fowles's French lieutenant's woman, she felt the awakenings of her sexuality in a society that suppressed a woman's sexual longings. After all, she *does* secretly marry, leave her father, and choose to live on an outpost in a male society. Barton came to the production with definite, if unconventional, ideas about Desdemona's primness:

No critic ever questions her as the epitome of sweet innocence. What I want to get right—what I think Shakespeare intends—is that *she* is the sensualist in her relationship with the great Moor. She is a healthy, passionate Italian girl, deeply in love with Othello, breaking out of the corsets of that Venetian society. And Othello, who is older, has slept around in army camps all his life, had probably never been in love before, is sexually disillusioned. He wants to romanticize and idealize this Venetian princess he's married—in his descriptions of her, and his behavior to her until Iago undermines him, Othello desexualizes her. But she herself is not at all romantic: unlike other Shakespeare heroines, for instance, she has no lyric language.

In this Bradley-inspired interpretation, there is potential tragedy in the Othello-Desdemona relationship: the reality of her innocence falls short of the Moor's ideal, even should Iago not subvert it. Hence, Othello and his bride are not merely dupes to Iago's machinations, but are potentially victims of their own beings. Iago merely exploits truths inherent in the situation. A beautiful woman arrives in an exclusively male society and becomes an instant provocation. Othello, according to Barton, "is soon aware of the atmosphere. And it is made worse for him if, as the text seems to suggest, Desdemona is still a virgin (Iago interrupts their wedding night apparently before the marriage is consummated). So she is more in heat than ever in the middle of the play; which is why it is credible that Othello, without being a fool, can be undermined by Iago."[19] A more sensual Desdemona also better defines the Brabantio-Desdemona-Othello relationship: in this context Brabantio, played as an oppressive, traditional nineteenth-century stage father, showed self-righteous outrage that his respectability had been affronted after discovering that his daughter is not the "prim miss" he thought her to be.

But the play is Othello's, and here Barton and his actor, Brewster Mason, seemed less successful in realizing the production's ambition. Barton cast Mason because his facial qualities suggested the Moorish, rather than Negroid, features the director sought. Barton and Mason chose to play the Moor with pronounced understatement as a gracious and good man who achieved his military authority by quietly yet effectively accommodating the empire builders he serves. Nevertheless, a majority of critics believed Mason's Othello lacked the fire necessary to fulfill the tragedy. When the play was in Iago's hands, the production worked brilliantly, but when its focus shifted to Othello in the final movement, the intensity waned. Derek Mahon best illustrates the reservations given an otherwise highly praised production: "Some vital fire is missing—some edge or arrogance born of an old unease, perhaps, to prepare us for his too swift conviction of Desdemona's guilt. There is too much placidity altogether as he approaches the task of killing her, and his 'Naught did I in hate but all in honour' verges on the priggish."[20] Bryden, conversely, found the Barton-Mason Othello and its eschewing of overt passion and aggression a satisfying counter to the oversized passion displayed by Olivier a decade earlier: "Barton's is an *Othello* for a more hopeful decade, which recognizes how much 'aggression' is simply defensiveness and believes it may be overcome by love."[21]

Barton may have been sensitive to the criticism of his and Mason's handling of the role. When the production moved to the Aldwych Theatre in July 1972 (after a tour to Japan), the director said he wanted to "go further in releasing the primitive animal, charting the breakdown of the man. I changed the whole plan of the costumes, so that [Othello] will gradually revert to his Moorish background having started in European military dress. I wanted to bring out something I didn't bring out before, that he became a Christian, but the Arabic-

Moorish religion begins to break through on him again." Even with modifications, London critics still found Othello tamer than they would have liked:

> . . . Mr. Mason's Othello fails to really catch fire, without providing a satisfying or compelling alternative. He has the dignity, the richly orchestrated voice, great intelligence applied to the lines, but he never lets slip the inward torture and confusion that gratifies Iago's great ambition for emotional chaos. He proves to himself rationally that Desdemona has been unfaithful to him, and ultimately he looks more a fool than one temporarily possessed and mad with jealousy.[22]

If sections of the script failed to catch fire, others were illuminated by Barton's handling of the Desdemona-Othello relationship. If Mason's Moor avoided the primitive passion of Olivier's in favor of fear of betrayal, Lisa Harrow's Desdemona sensed this fear and tried to allay it, to meet it with trust. Bryden found the staging of the "brothel scene" (4.2) one of the production's "most brilliant inventions." Instead of playing it, as is the norm, as a volatile, impassioned tirade, it was played "as a half-naked siesta together, the wife softly trying to calm her husband, make him speak, accept her caresses, and almost succeeding. I've seldom seen acting reach so near the intimate heart of a marriage."[23] That this was a marriage hideously destroyed by a small-minded malcontent was brought out in the play's finale: as Iago was led away to the stockade, he turned to look at the dead bodies on the marriage bed and "cackled" hysterically at the sight of dead Othello and Desdemona.[24] The laugh was a ghoulish parody of the seemingly good-natured giggle that had part of his hail-fellow-well-met act earlier in the play.

With minor dissension, the production concept, if not its total realization, was highly praised, particularly by Barton's theater colleagues. Peter Hall, generally adverse to taking Shakespeare out of his customary period, found Barton's production nonetheless "miraculous": "It suddenly made you understand that there was an important strand in Othello that was about colonial service, the foreignness of Cyprus, being the wife of a fellow on a foreign posting. . . . He opened whole areas of the play I had never noticed myself."[25] David Jones agreed, noting that Barton's daring was "abundantly justified by the way in which tension and gossip of a military frontier community suddenly rationalized all that seems ridiculous or melodramatic in the plot."[26] He did, however, have reservations, noting that the "final tragic resonance" in Othello's performance was missing at Stratford. Though this improved when the production shifted to the Aldwych, Jones felt Barton's new details ("café scenes in Cyprus, Arab street life, additional arms drills for the garrisons") heightened the operatic elements of the Stratford production while obscuring the main emotional drives of the play: "It lost the ring of total truthfulness."

If Barton's relocated Othello failed to maintain the ring of total truthfulness, perhaps it was because the specificity of the altered setting obscured its metaphysical elements. Tragic drama works best in a timeless, almost abstracted state, as the Greeks demonstrated in their great open theaters. By masking *Othello*'s universal qualities with Victorian paneling and Moorish tapestries, Barton perhaps diminished, though not negated, its tragic impact. Instead of becoming the victim of an unyielding universe, Othello became the no-less unfortunate victim of a rigid society: another time, another place and he might have escaped his fate. Over a decade after staging *Othello*, Barton told audiences of "Playing Shakespeare" that, despite his best intentions, he likely had diminished the Moor "by putting him into a world too small for him."

Comedy, on the other hand, is a particularly social genre, or so the theories of Northrop Frye and Suzanne Langer suggest. Perhaps this explains why Barton's transplant of a comedy, *Much Ado About Nothing,* five years later was an unqualified success. Though Barton's contention that "Sometimes one takes a Shakespeare play to be timeless, but *Othello* needs to be rooted in a known society"[27] can be debated, his ideas proved particularly sound when applied to *Much Ado,* a work whose very title suggests considerable community interaction. Roger Warren prefaced his analysis of Barton's staging by citing a 1958 review of the play at Stratford which argues that *Much Ado* is "about the behavior of a largely superficial people in a superficial society: what is important is that the society should be real and recognizable."[28]

Like that of *Othello,* the plot of *Much Ado* hinges on sexual innuendo (the Claudio-Hero affair) against a backdrop of an isolated military outpost on which a malcontented soldier creates chaos to avenge his social exclusion. Also, like *Othello, Much Ado* is written more realistically than most Shakespearean plays: the majority of the work is in prose and, as Anne Barton's program note declares, this is "the least romantic of Shakespeare's mature comedies . . . almost the world of Restoration comedy: witty, fettered by clearly defined special convention."[29] Again Barton turned to the Victorian era and its clearly defined social conventions to help his audiences immediately grasp the play's societal attitudes: "I thought the military life, the social life, would be helped by doing it in the nineteenth century."[30]

Specifically, Barton played the comedy in the Indian Raj of Rudyard Kipling, a propitious choice that accommodated all elements of the multiplotted action. Unfortunately, there is no published record of Barton's brief to his designer (John Napier), as there was with *Othello,* so one cannot be sure what prompted the director's choice. It is worth noting that in 1975—the year before *Much Ado*—Howard Davies directed Brecht's *A Man's a Man* at the RSC's Other Place and set the play in Colonial India. Barton and Barry Kyle shared the theater with Davies while staging Ford's *Perkin Warbeck* and may have gleaned an idea from his colleague. Also, the National Theatre had recently produced Tony Harrison's *Phaedra Britannica,* also set in the Raj.

In 1976 the RSC utilized a single set for its season, a "wooden O" that vaguely suggested the Globe. Barton and Napier masked the timbered façade of the RSC stage with rattan mats, beaded curtains, wicker chairs, muslin awnings, and pampas grass. When one entered the theater—as I did in July 1976—one quickly realized that the RSC had, for the evening, turned travel agents to transport the audience to realms unimagined by Shakespeare. The actors entered: the principal men in smartly decorated Hussar uniforms, the women in drab smocks over Victorian dresses, an immediate reminder that this was, on the surface, a male-dominated world. Other men, tawny-faced, tur-baned, and attired in native Indian costume, served gin rickeys and cigars to the military men who lounged in hammocks and wicker recliners to escape the noonday sun. White women in straw hats scampered about the balconies—eyeing the men coyly while performing domestic tasks. Offstage a cricket match was in progress (Barton is a great lover of cricket), while a military band oom-pahed a march. The "watch" patroled the streets of this Messina-on-Ganges, turbaned *babus,* anyone of whom might have answered to the name of Gunga Din.

It was a meticulous recreation of a world, "a masterpiece of single-minded planning."[31] But for Barton there was a far more serious purpose to the exotic decor. The critics, who generally were as delighted as audiences with Barton's "Shakespeare-wallah," offered a number of explanations for the concept, as is typified by Richard David's rationale:

> . . . the director seeks a milieu in which sex-streaming is normal, and the male club and the female household, the officer's mess and the memsahibs' drawing room are perfectly appropriate habitats for the silly prankishness of the men and the tittle-tattle of the women so graphically portrayed by Shake-speare. . . . The real point of the Indian setting was to create an off-duty, sportive, nothing-much-to-do way of life in which intrigues, the sudden jealousies, the bickerings and back-friends of Shakespeare's plot may become credible.[32]

The boisterous camaraderie of the officer's mess was manifest throughout. For example, in 3.2 Benedick, in the process of becoming a civilized lover, shaves his beard to impress Beatrice. The officers of Barton's army surrounded the once-confirmed bachelor to taunt him. After Claudio's line "Nay, but I know who loves him" (l. 58), the cadre "all counted to ten on their fingers, establish-ing the ritual of debagging in true public school and army officer fashion."[33]

Such rituals were stressed throughout the play and in Anne Barton's pro-gram note: "Post-war Messina is a place full of games-playing and disguise." Barton found occasion to combine both prankishness and disguise: in 2.3—the scene in which "the men" deceive Benedick into thinking Beatrice loves him—Claudio, Leonato, and Don Pedro staged their ruse under the pretext of an amateur theatrical show. On a more serious note, the plotting of Hero's dis-grace by Don John and Borachio in 2.2 was staged against an offstage cricket match from which the bastard—here played as physically awkward and fastidious, "obviously sent out to the army against his will and bitterly resenting it"[34]—has been excluded. Don John, less a villain in Barton's schema than an outsider, was one of the characters whose actions were made more comprehensible by the colonial army setting: "What Mr. Barton makes more clear than I can ever remember is that in this world of privileged impishness, Don John's pointless destructiveness is simply an extension of the prevailing officer's ethical code."[35]

Don John's actions are not the most problematic of the play. Claudio's treatment of Hero is unnerving, and audiences often fail to understand his actions. Furthermore, he not only gets off lightly for his boorish behavior, but he is apparently rewarded by the gift of Hero's "likeness." Perhaps more than anywhere else in the play, it is here that the action needs a strong social context if one is to comprehend the import of Claudio's actions: "The callous treatment of Hero by Claudio . . . appears almost forgivable in this closed, male-dominated environment. . . . His behavior seems more a matter of bad manners than gross cruelty."[36] Hero, the "small daughter" of a sahib Leonato (played as a faithful Indian Civil Servant) and Claudio were clearly from different worlds, a reminder of Anne Barton's contentions that "neither really knows or understands each other—which is why Claudio can behave so badly, and Hero so ineffectually." Instead of confronting his love with his accusation, the young officer merely retreated to the officer's barracks to seek counsel from his commanding officer, Don Pedro, who shared the offense done to the company's honor. Thus Claudio's scheme seemed more a military strategy of retribution for lost honor and less the reaction of a jilted lover.

Barton's staging of the wedding scene (4.1), with little decoration and only a small band of witnesses, quite literally adhered to Leonato's instructions to the Friar that open the scene: "Only to the plain form of marriage . . ." The almost casual atmosphere made Claudio's behavior more disturbing: it was a blaring trumpet in an intimate ensemble. But for Roger Warren of *Shakespeare Survey* the wedding scene did not quite come off: "It was too intimate, too unelaborate a ceremony. Part of the cruelty of the behavior of these honourable men is that Hero is shamed *in public,* 'in the congregation.' Here, there was no congregation; it hardly seemed worth all the effort."[37] The ensuing tomb scene (5.3) was also staged simply, but with a military precision that "exactly fitted the mechanical precision of the text."[38] Claudio and Don Pedro marched in a formal circle, flashing sabres, sheathing them with efficiency. Barton, coincidentally, did not forget the play's title at this solemn moment: it was backed by a military quartet singing a mournful hymn composed by James Walker as "a wicked parody of Victorian sentimentality."[39] In the finale, Hero was reintroduced effectively within the context of the Eastern setting as one of several black-gowned Muslim ladies, her face masked by the traditional veil of the purdah.

Beatrice and Benedick surely play well in any context since theirs is that most elemental of all dramatic confrontations: the witty man versus the equally witty woman. Barton's direction of Shakespeare's most skillfully created lovers was nonetheless revealing. His decision[40] to cast veteran actors Donald Sinden and Judi Dench was a major critical choice in itself. The lovers were necessarily played as mature adults who "swap insults with a sort of desiccated desperation while making us conscious of the fact that they are both getting on a bit and it is almost too late for their dreams to come true."[41] The age of these amorous antagonists lent a particular poignance to the comedy—not unlike that Barton effected with Sir Toby and Maria in *Twelfth Night.* Sinden's Benedick was a Victorian diarist, "languidly stretching out on a wicker chair, musing about the necessary virtues of a future wife at the high noon of chauvinism."[42] That he was an individualist in this regiment of pleasure-seeking officers was evidenced by his academic glasses, stack of books, and diary. But, as Sinden played him, he was hardly stodgy: he played the house magnificently, much like a Brighton music hall comedian. Sinden's playing style, particularly for the soliloquies, suggested that he was the sport of not only his fellow officers and Beatrice— but of the audience as well. His speech in 2.3—"I did not think I should live till I were married" (l. 222)—was delivered as if the house were equally guilty participants in a conspiracy against his bachelorhood. It was a hugely sympathetic portrait of a grizzled army veteran coming to terms with his own value system. Despite its broadness, it was a disciplined performance that complemented Judi Dench's wistful, melancholic Beatrice. The RSC program contained a page of nineteenth-century quotations to familiarize audiences with attitudes of the period. One in particular defined Dench's approach to "Lady Tongue." It was extracted from an 1880 edition of *Punch,* the venerable British humor magazine: "The New Woman of this decade will be the old maid of the next." The Barton-Dench Beatrice seemed especially vulnerable, fully aware that her tartness could earn her a spinsterhood while her juniors found husbands in these foreign climes. She, like Sinden's Benedick, adopted strident wit to mask her vulnerability.

"I think the secret of Barton's success," wrote Michael Billington, "is that he endows his characters with a past as well as a present."[43] From the outset, one was aware that this Beatrice and this Benedick possessed a mutual past that accounted for her especially sour treatment of him in the early scenes. Barton and his actors perhaps found their portraits of the bickering lovers in lines, sometimes overlooked, in the first scene of act 1:

Benedick: [to Beatrice] What, my dear Lady Disdain! are you yet living? [1.1.105: this is his first remark to her and suggests a stormy relationship between them that began long before the play begins.]

And:
    Beatrice: [responding to Don Pedro's suggestion that she has lost the heart of Benedick] Indeed, my lord, he lent it me awhile, and I gave

him use of it . . . Marry, once before he won it of me with false dice. [2.1.275ff]

From this, Barton, Sinden, and Dench projected a past and passionate relationship: the jibes and banter were now bandages to cover emotional bruises. Yet the acerbic masks could not disguise secret longings and furtive glances that produced "an undertow of reluctant affection that gives their ultimate alliance plausibility."[44]

From their first meeting, spoken in hushed tones, during which a native ceremoniously removed Benedick's military leggings, through a show-stopping encounter that saw Beatrice summon Benedick to dinner by emphatically beating a dinner gong in his ear (after which Benedick eyed the house wistfully on "There's a double meaning in that!"), to the conscious similarity of the "o'erhearing scenes" (2.3 and 3.1), which found them hiding behind the same muslin awnings, each encounter was calculated to explore the light and the dark aspects of their relationship. Perhaps the "deception scenes" best illustrated this: Benedick emerged from behind the awning to swear, surprised, that he would be "horribly" in love with Beatrice. It was played broadly to the house—and accepted by the audience in the comic spirit of the play. Beatrice, by contrast, slowly raised the shade and introspectively, even melancholically, considered "the fire in her ears." It underscored the more solemn side of love's commitment and was received by the audience as an equally valid response as Sinden's clowning. The writing of the scenes supports the markedly different reactions: Benedick's soliloquy is written in staccato prose, Beatrice's in measured verse.[45]

Barton's success with the Beatrice-Benedick plot ultimately rested on integrating it logically into the less-credible Hero-Claudio plot. "I cannot remember a production of this comedy when the bantering word-play between Beatrice and Benedick so perfectly synchronized with the attempt to discredit Hero," wrote Milton Shulman.[46] Because each of the mature lovers had been given a well-defined place in the social fabric of Messina, their alliance with the characters of the larger plot was fully plausible: Beatrice, a maternal figure who genuinely cared for the hopeful, younger women in this world of overbearing, insensitive men; Benedick, *of* the colonial cadre, but not *with* them in spirit, attitude, or action. Hence his acceptance of Beatrice's emotional outburst, "Kill Claudio" (4.1.283), was a natural outgrowth of his necessary repudiation of the officer's code. He finally saw what Beatrice knew well: the boorishness of the officers was unbecoming to their position. Anne Barton's note cogently describes the crisis: "She asks Benedick to follow her into the world of real personal relationships. Caught between an old and new loyalty, he finds himself in an awkward position. But he proceeds to do what Claudio could not: he puts his faith in the woman he loves and cuts his ties with the past." Furthermore, the moment of truth allowed Benedick at last to correct past wrongs perpetrated against Beatrice. The scene, which treads the narrow line between romantic comedy and near-tragedy ("I would eat his heart in the market place," 4.1.302), worked well because Barton and his principals consistently found both the light and dark elements of the lovers' complex relationship. One piece of business in the wedding scene superbly captured this duality: Beatrice said "Kill Claudio!" while sadly sweeping up the confetti and flowers of the aborted wedding, crying tears that earlier flowed for Hero's seeming good fortune.

Beatrice's and Benedick's combined move to individuality in a flawed society was illustrated in the production's finale: after the multiple reconciliations—even Don John was reincorporated into Messina's society (paired with Ursula)—the various couples danced off in the *gamos* of traditional comedy, while Beatrice, alone and holding Benedick's sword, was suddenly whisked offstage in an opposite direction by her exbachelor. The finale was daring in its violation of the traditional formula of comic endings: customarily all lovers exit together, suggesting a harmonious rejuvenation of society. That Beatrice and her Benedick deliberately set themselves apart from the social shallowness of their peers was an apt comment that superficial values are yet with us; the bantering lovers had reached a communion of spirit, realizing that love must transcend social constraints and mindless devotion to the show of honor.

Barton also found a credible niche in his Raj rendering for that most English of constables, Dogberry. Barton and actor John Woodvine could have played him as a cockney sergeant whose cousins inhabit any number of British war films and plays. But, according to Barton,[47] Woodvine developed a character that was strikingly fresh and genuinely funny, and—as it turned out—highly controversial: Dogberry, in *this* Messina, was not a noncom brought from Britain, but a native Sikh given just enough military authority and just enough English to keep him perpetually in trouble:

> Dogberry's "point" is that he is inordinately proud of his language, but always gets his idioms wrong: the very formula on which is based the Kiplingesque comic *babu*. The Indian servant of the same tradition is noted for the literalness with which he interprets his instructions and for his gravity he cannot understand the jokes of his flashy masters though he possesses a sly humour of his own. These are the very traits of Shakespeare's watchmen.[48]

Rarely have Dogberry's malapropisms rung so true or been so unforced. Woodvine apparently patterned his caricature after Michael Bates's character on the popular British television series, "It Ain't Half Hot, Mum," a comedy set in colonial India. Woodvine extracted more than verbal humor from the role: physically he was hilarious in his turban, magnificently pompous beard, and bandy legs protruding from oversized jodphurs. He developed a comically patronizing salute; his right hand shot upward, stopping at ear level, palm open, five fingers shimmering with pride. A half turn of the head to the right converted the salute to a thumb-on-nose salute of another kind.

The characterizations of Dogberry and his Watch (who had delightful difficulties manipulating their spears) were warmly embraced by most RSC patrons, but attacked by some critics as racist. The most vitriolic attack came from Harold Hobson of *The Sunday Times,* who had strongly attacked Barton's *King John* two years earlier: "Mr. Barton's premise is that a coloured man is funny merely by being coloured. Ridicule his salaams . . . and too precise forms of speech and you have something that sends audiences into paroxysms of delight . . . it clearly filled the theatre with a comforting sense that if the British have lost an Empire they can at least jeer at those who have gained it."[49] Other critics defended the Woodvine-Barton characterization, including Peter Coveney: "One still meets Indians whose absurd loyalty to the Raj of yester-year informs an attitude of hilarious kowtowing to authority in any shape or form."[50] Barton recalls that he and Woodvine were aware of the dangers of the comic characterization and rehearsed the role first for its realistic, human elements, adding the comic business later.[51]

Though Barton's transliteration consistently accounted for the various plot, character, and thematic elements in *Much Ado,* there was minor critical dissent: "Funny (or rather distinctly unfunny) how producers cannot trust Shakespeare's wit without spoofs or artificial assists."[52] Other cavils were more specific: one wondered if a typically prim Victorian miss could invite her lover to murder the man who hurts her cousin.[53] John Barber missed "the glitter of a sophisticated court,"[54] though it was precisely to overcome the ambiguities of a Renaissance court comedy that Barton transferred *Much Ado* to a more accessible milieu.

Most critics, however, fell into R. B. Marriott's camp; he proclaimed the 1976 Stratford version of *Much Ado About Nothing* the best in England since Sir John Gielgud's memorable celebration at the Phoenix Theatre in the late 1940s.[55] That Barton's production compared favorably with a more traditional—even arguably "definitive"—staging suggests that an intelligent reading of the text applied to an inventive overlay can reap dividends for audiences and actors alike.

The Cambridge director, c. 1952. Courtesy of John Barton.

One of Barton's numerous "old man" roles at Cambridge: "Gramp" in *The Petrified Forest*. Courtesy of John Barton.

One of Barton's favorite political roles: Ulysses in Giradoux's *There Shall Be No War at Troy*. Courtesy of John Barton.

Another favorite political role: The Inquisitor in Shaw's *St. Joan*. Courtesy of John Barton.

John Barton at Eton College, 1947. Courtesy of John Barton.

By Barton-the-Cambridge-Playwright: *That's All One*. Courtesy of John Barton.

By Barton-the-Cambridge-Playwright: *Winterlude* (directed by Peter Hall; Barton, *seated at left,* played the villain). Courtesy of John Barton.

As *Macbeth (left)*. Courtesy of John Barton.

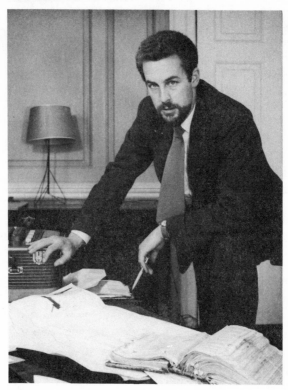

Working on the text for *The Wars of the Roses*, 1963. Courtesy of John Barton.

Barton directs David·Warner, as King Henry VI, in *The Wars of the Roses*, 1963. Courtesy of Shakespeare Birthplace Trust.

The council table which served as the focal point of *The Wars of the Roses*. Peggy Ashcroft (Queen Margaret) and David Warner (King Henry) at center. Courtesy of Shakespeare Birthplace Trust.

Achilles (Alan Howard) and the Myrmidons stalk Hector in *Troilus and Cressida*, 1968. Courtesy of Shakespeare Birthplace Trust.

One of the Barton-staged battle scenes in *The Wars of the Roses*. Courtesy of Shakespeare Birthplace Trust.

Viola (Judi Dench) enters Barton's mysterious Illyria in *Twelfth Night*, 1969. Courtesy of Zoe Dominic Photography.

Twelfth Night's melancholy clowns: Brenda Bruce (Maria), Emrys James (Feste, with lute) Aguecheek (Barry Ingham, with his hapless bagpipes), and Donald Sinden (Malvolio). Courtesy of Shakespeare Birthplace Trust.

"Youth's a stuff will not endure," sings Feste (Emrys James) to Viola (Judi Dench) in *Twelfth Night*. Courtesy of Zoe Dominic Photography.

Othello (Brewster Mason) and Desdemona (Lisa Harrow) are photographed by Iago (Emrys James) upon their arrival in Cyprus; *Othello*, 1971. Photo credit: Tom Holte. Courtesy of Shakespeare Birthplace Trust.

An androgynous Ariel (Ben Kingsley) and "youthful" Prospero (Ian Richardson) in *The Tempest*, 1970. Courtesy of Zoe Dominic Photography.

Richard Pasco as Richard II and Ian Richardson as the controversial "Groom-Bolingbroke" in *Richard II*, 1973. Photo credit: Tom Holte. Courtesy of Shakespeare Birthplace Trust.

The scene of "the Lists" in *Richard II* with Ian Richardson (as Bolingbroke, *at right*) astride the much discussed hobby horse. Note also the twin staircases that dominated Timothy O'Brien's set. Courtesy of Donald Cooper Photography.

RSC actors rehearse on specially constructed stilts in preparation for *Richard II* and the hobby horses. Richard Pasco *(center)* plays the King. Courtesy of Donald Cooper Photography.

Peter the Prophet (Mike Gwilym) confronts King John (Emrys James) at Swindon Abbey in *King John*, 1974. The cowled monks are a favorite Barton visual device. Courtesy of Donald Cooper Photography.

An Indian Dogberry (John Woodvine, *standing*) and Watch in the Raj *Much Ado About Nothing*, 1976. Photo credit: Tom Holte. Courtesy of Shakespeare Birthplace Trust.

A bear dance highlights the folk-tale concept of *A Winter's Tale*, 1976. Roger Rees stands at left. Courtesy of Donald Cooper Photography.

Hermoine (Marilyn Taylerson, *right*) comes to life before the eyes of Leontes (Ian McKellen, *center*) and Perdita (Cheri Lunghi, *kneeling*) in *The Winter's Tale*. Barton calls this the moment in theatre that moves him most. Courtesy of Donald Cooper Photography.

Comedy and melancholy mix freely in an autumnal *Love's Labour's Lost,* 1978. Here Don Armado (David Suchet) suffers ingloriously during The Pageant of the Nine Worthies as the French princess (Carmen Du Sautoy), the King of Navarre (Richard Griffiths), Berowne (Michael Pennington), and Rosaline (Jane Lapotaire, seated at right) look on. Courtesy of Donald Cooper Photography.

The Greeks, 1980: "The most important thing I've done in the theatre." Agamemnon (John Shrapnel) and Iphigenia (Judy Buxton, kneeling at center) are encircled by the chorus in *Iphigenia in Aulis* in Part I. Courtesy of Donald Cooper Photography.

The healing dance of hope between Iphigenia (Judy Buxton) and Orestes (Mike Gwilym) concluded *The Greeks*. Note the wintry clothing worn by the performers. Courtesy of Donald Cooper Photography.

Barton and the RSC create theatre history as Queen Gertrude (Barbara Leigh-Hunt) is forced to look at the Ghost of Old Hamlet (Raymond Westwell) by Hamlet (Michael Pennington), 1980. Courtesy of Donald Cooper Photography.

An intimate, nineteenth-century *Merchant of Venice*, 1981. Portia (Sinead Cusak) and Shylock (David Suchet) during the Act 4 trial scene. Courtesy of Donald Cooper Photography.

Patrick Stewart (as Titus Andronicus) leads a company of neo-Elizabethan actors in the "double bill" of *Titus Andronicus* and *Two Gentlemen of Verona* in 1981. Courtesy of Donald Cooper Photography.

Barton's first professional non-RSC production: *The School for Scandal,* 1983. The "screen scene" was a theatrically powerful moment of recognition between Sir Peter Teazle (Donald Sinden, right) and Lady Teazle (Carol Royle). Courtesy of Zoe Dominic Photography.

"Improbable Fictions":
The Tempest (1970), *Cymbeline* (1975), *The Winter's Tale* (1976), *A Midsummer Night's Dream* (1977), and *Two Gentlemen of Verona/Titus Andronicus* (1981)

English theater critic J. C. Trewin divides productions of *The Tempest* into two types: "plain" and "spangled."[1] The former trusts Shakespeare's poetry to evoke the mystery of Prospero's isle; the "spangled" supplements the playwright's invention with the varied riches of modern stagecraft. While all of Shakespeare's plays can be staged simply or with extraordinary embellishment, *The Tempest* and other fantasies are particularly interesting test cases for the ingenuity and/or excesses of late twentieth-century stage practice. Barton, whose best work has been both plain *(Twelfth Night)* and spangled *(Richard II)*, has accepted the challenge offered by four of Shakespeare's fantastic delights during his twenty-year career at Stratford: *The Tempest* (1970); *Cymbeline* (1975); *The Winter's Tale* (1976); and *A Midsummer Night's Dream* (1977–78). None represented his most memorable interpretative work, yet each is sufficiently provocative and visually stimulating to provide further insight into his problem-solving techniques. If it is true, as Ian McKellan suggests, that Barton is "a great putter-on of shows," then these plays should measure his affinity for theatricality. As important, they are significant stepping stones on his personal journey towards creating a "myth" for himself, since they represent Shakespeare's most conscious attempts to deal with themes of "healing" after chaos has reigned.

   The Tempest opened in October 1970 and ran for a mere nineteen performances. Those who had seen *Troilus and Cressida* in 1968, *Twelfth Night* in 1969, or *Measure for Measure* earlier that summer, likely had high expectations for *The Tempest*, whose textual challenges seemed an ideal test for Barton's acumen. Furthermore, the casting of Ian Richardson suggested that Barton's *Tem-*

pest would have an outstanding Prospero. It did. Whatever reservations the critics and public had about the production, Richardson was lauded for his performance—though not necessarily for the interpretation he and Barton devised.

Another factor affected expectations for an inventive *Tempest*. Peter Brook's popular *A Midsummer Night's Dream* that summer proved that the RSC could imaginatively effect Shakespeare's magic without resorting to purely scenic devices.

Barton himself had long believed that *The Tempest* is best served by avoiding scenic overindulgence. When he and Rylands broadcast their impressions of the 1957 Stratford season for the BBC, Barton theorized why productions of the play frequently failed:

> Time and time again, production of this particular piece has misfired because the producer has succumbed to the temptation to over-decorate it. Now over-decoration is a device which simply increases the audience's suspicion that the piece itself is a bit dull.[2]

Later in the discussion Barton added, "Here, more than anywhere in the canon is a play which appeals to our ear." Apparently Barton's judgment changed little in the thirteen-year interim, and when he brought *The Tempest* to Stratford's stage, he avoided scenic excess. The choice confounded many observers. John Barber's review suggested both Barton's approach to the play and its attendant problems:

> For the new revival set at Stratford John Barton has used his prerogative to set the drama anywhere, and he has elected to set it nowhere. His location is limbo. Apparently following a suggestion that to perform it in the theatre at all is to add unwonted flesh to a work of art ruthlessly paired to the bone, Mr. Barton has devised the most austere *Tempest* within memory."[3]

This "plain" *Tempest* was mounted on an essentially bare stage adorned with only a long, rectangular framework, evocative of a Jacobean banqueting hall, topped by a white roof. The hues of Christopher Morley's design suggested both driftwood and a scrubbed ship's deck. The walls receded "in exaggeratedly converging parallels to a dark space at the back of the deep stage: a cave from which spirits emerge; on either side, deep turquoise hangings, allowing a glimpse of pale spirits encircling the action."[4] This multipurpose structure contributed a spectacular moment in the play's difficult first scene: for the shipwreck, the white ceiling "swooped down towards the stage, and there was an alarming illusion, accompanied by explosions and human shrieks, of a great sail going out of control."

The "spectacle" was provided by the physical appearance of the actors: Ariel entered nearly nude, his body powdered in white and bald except for a long pony tail of blonde hair. Benedict Nightingale judged that he looked "less like an airy spirit than some sly medium's trick version of the spirit guide that is reputed to materialise in seances: solid, Europeanised, slightly censored."[6] Ben Kingsley, who played the sprite and composed the eerie electronic music for the production, spoke in a "childish, sexless chant,"[7] perhaps to accommodate Barton's conviction that the part should be played by a boy.[8]

The act 4 masque was perhaps the production's most controversial moment. Ariel summoned the three "goddesses," who appeared as three males all cast in his own image. Despite a dance to Kingsley's evocative music, the masque was both disappointingly bland and contrary to the script. Ferdinand's ecstatic cry, "This is a most majestic vision, and / Harmonious charmingly!" (4.1.119–20) belied Barton's rendering.[9] Shakespeare's masque was probably intended as a symbol of fertility since Ceres, Iris, and Juno are associated with life-giving elements; the harvest dance is central to the spectacle and theme. The sexless-ness of Barton's apparitions seemed contrary to the spirit of the playwright's design.

The Tempest's other notable strange being, Caliban, was visually impressive. According to Richardson, he was played (by Barry Stanton, perhaps the largest of the RSC actors), as "a great whale, slithering across the stage."[10] *Plays and Players* was even more explicit: ". . . decked out like a moving dung-heep, with a useless leg and an unformed arm, eating raw fish and spitting it out at Miranda, scratching his private parts when he describes her to Stephano, doing fat somersaults across the stage to celebrate his new freedom—before another rope is lashed around his neck."[11] Contrary to this description, Barton per-mitted an unusual degree of pathos for Caliban, particularly when the man-beast unsuccessfully tried to emulate Ariel's singing. The Trinculo-Stephano-Caliban scenes received little emphasis; on the 1957 BBC broadcast Barton dismissed them as "a comic diversion that adds little to the whole." As he often does with scenes in which he has little interest,[12] Barton delegated responsibility for this subplot to his assistant, Robin Phillips.

Barton's deemphasis of the visual and comic elements of *The Tempest* was symptomatic of his approach to the play, and provoked Helen Dawson to say that the director seemed to have "a determination not to elaborate, not to give anything away. . . . And, as a result, though the play's mystery increases, its dramatic reverberations don't."[13]

A clue to the production's austerity may be found in Anne Barton's program note for the production:

> Almost as spare as a myth, it is a work of art ruthlessly pared to the bone. To perform it in the theatre, even to try and talk about it, is inevitably to add to its substance by filling in gaps and silences left deliberately out by the drama-tist. . . . The play constantly invites conjecture and amplification, but it is impossible to be sure of the correct answers to most of the questions posed.[14]

The Tempest is, of course, Prospero's play, and hints of Barton's intentions are found in Richardson's interpretation of the role. The actor was then only thirty-six years old, considerably younger than is customary. There was no attempt to "age" him, either with make-up or costume, here a tattered artist's smock with large pockets—into which the actor thrust his hands frequently in an apparent attempt to deromanticize the magician. Richardson said he played Prospero as "old" to the Elizabethans, and thus accounted for Prospero's obsession with time by inventing a subtext to provide a psychological foundation for his work:

> I played him as a very sick man, perhaps aware of something very sinister wrong inside him. . . . I used it because it built up a terrible tension in the text that *everything* had to be accomplished.

Thus, Prospero's impatience at Caliban's slow progress towards becoming civilized, the anger that prompts him to abort the masque, and his persistent badgering of Ariel to accomplish quickly his commands were explained by a dying man's wish to "get on with it." That may have been the subtext as actor and director understood it, but it did not register with those who assessed the production. Several critics—Barber, Dawson, and Nightingale in particular—extracted a message of despair and self-pitying melancholy from the Barton-Richardson Prospero. Nightingale here represents his colleagues' attitudes:

> Richardson's performance is good . . . but he substitutes resignation for hope, a quiet despair for faith. It is that very word "despair" which is forced to stand out, unnaturally, from what is surely supposed to be a conventional epilogue. . . . I can see no excuse for such an emphasis, and only one explanation: that the director is desperately seeking support, any support, for a dubious reading.[15]

Such a nihilistic reading would account for the sexless, antiregenerative masque that disturbed many viewers. RSC patrons were alerted to the pessimism by Anne Barton's program note:

> A play standing somewhat apart from the other final romances, it seems to reject their essential optimism. . . . What Prospero's art cannot do, however, is the thing which ultimately matters: change the nature and inclinations of the human heart. . . . This is why he abjures it at the end, accepting the limitations of mortality. . . . It seems right and proper now that he should turn to the audience . . . to express an attitude which is basically one of weariness and disillusion, coupled with a desire to rest.

Such a reading seems contrary to the spirit of forgiveness and regeneration suggested by Prospero's last lines: true, the word *despair* is mentioned, but it is subordinated to *mercy* and forgiveness—"As you from your crimes would pardoned be, / Let your indulgence set me free" (epilogue, ll. 19–20)—and to deny the possibility of hope seems unfair to Shakespeare's intent.

Though Barton scarcely cut the text, he did slightly rearrange the ending to accommodate his darker reading. In his provocative essay, "Free Shakespeare," John Russell Brown cites Barton's altered ending as an example of directorial interference: "At the end of *The Tempest*, John Barton found more that he wanted to emphasize in Propsero's farewell to Ariel than in Shakespeare's conclusion . . . the words are transposed, and after a long pause as Antonio and Sebastian *leave* Prospero, the farewell to the spirit is gravely and slowly said as the new conclusion to the play."[16] Furthermore, to emphasize the darker view of the world dominant in 1970, Miranda knelt at the feet of Antonio, the traitorous brother, on the famous line, "O brave new world . . ." (5.1.183–84), which made Prospero's "Tis new to thee" darkly ironic. Barton, according to those who know him well, is an intensely optimistic man, which makes this darker reading seem out of character. As Tony Church has said, " . . . he is the most deeply romantic man I've ever met. What he dreams about are not the dreams of most of us. They are the dreams of Sir Thomas Malory. . . . He is a great optimist, a great believer in the power of goodness."[17]

His love of Malory notwithstanding, Barton's *Tempest* seemed an illustrated lecture of a Montaigne essay (extracted in the RSC program) that wonders whether "it is possible to imagine anything so ridiculous as this miserable and wretched creature, which is not so much as master of himself . . . and yet dares to call himself Master and Emperor of the Universe." Richardson says Barton originally thought to stage the play as a lecture read from a large seaweed-covered book by Prospero, who, while standing at a lectern on the side stage, would manipulate the other characters, like puppets, through the tale.[18] Curiously, elements of this idea were carried into two subsequent productions: Cymbeline, discussed later, was played as an illustrated fairy tale narrated by Cornelius from a large book; *Dr. Faustus* (1974—see chapter 9) presented the necromancer as a puppet master.

Ultimately Barton's *Tempest* lacked a spiritual dimension. In the opinion of Judith Cook it "didn't work at all" because it was merely "a workaday play about magic with no magic in it and, it seemed, no trace of human feeling."[19] Though extreme, Cook's opinion reflects the general disappointment with the production.

Barton himself is dissatisfied with his work on the play: "*The Tempest* beat me. I never wanted to do it. Trevor (Nunn) dropped out, and I hadn't a clue how to do it because it can't be pinned down." Barton admits he yet has a block concerning this, Shakespeare's most enigmatic play: "I don't understand my block about *The Tempest*. I can see logically what's in it, but it doesn't at the moment stir my mythical instincts. I want to go back to it when I know how to solve it."[20] Barton the ironist finds it especially perplexing that Barton the mythmaker cannot come to grips with Shakespeare's most challenging myth-play.

Barton next encountered one of the "myth plays" in 1974 when he performed alchemy on one of Shakespeare's most troublesome scripts, *Cymbeline*.

Here Barton, who staged seven scenes, and codirectors Barry Kyle and Clifford Williams had a clearly defined objective that turned the weakly constructed pastoral into an enchanting fairy tale about the regenerative power of Time, and, apparently, about Britain's coming of age. The production's thematic values, however, are less remembered than Barton's audacious textual work and visual devices. Barton and his colleagues were most intent on "speaking such as sense cannot untie" of Cymbeline's improbable plot.

Barton performed major surgery on *Cymbeline's* imperfect features by revising the original text in two ways: first, he cut 820 lines to tighten the play; second, and of more significance, he expanded the role of Cornelius (a minor character, the Queen's physician) to invent an omniscient storyteller, reading from a large tome of ancient British legends. (It foreshadowed the Barton of the 1980s who would himself turn storyteller.) Barton's program note was forthright in admitting his liberties—perhaps a reaction to the *King John* controversy earlier that season.[22]

Cornelius, now a theatrical device to unify the various strands of the play, gave credence to its fanciful actions, much the way Shakespeare himself used Gower in *Pericles* (written shortly before *Cymbeline* and possibly an influence on Barton's solution to the script's problems). The story-teller introduced the fourteen sections of the new version, vocally establishing an appropriate mood for each. In most cases, critics commended Barton's enterprise, though, predictably, there was dissent. John Elsom believed Cornelius's presence "often seems distractingly unnecessary, a substitute for the stylistic cohesion the production lacks."[24] However, most agreed that the invention provided precisely the "stylistic cohesion" that the play itself lacks. By turning the play—via the narrator—into "an exotic Yeatsian fairy world . . . the skein of fabulous coincidences, so often embarrassingly handled in modern productions, are here delightedly revealed."[25]

Certainly had Shakespeare wanted a narrator for *Cymbeline* he would have written one into the script. But Barton's invention provided a time-honored solution to the play's many problems, particularly the act 5 battle scenes. As Cornelius read the folio stage directions of the battle between the Romans and Britons (see appendix E for Barton's revision), the RSC actors mimed the action beyond a traverse curtain in the misty, upstage recesses of the theater. Critical opinions of this invention varied,[26] but the device was generally received well by critics and audiences alike.

By openly courting the fairy-tale elements, Barton could readily explore the visual impact of the play, something he avoided in *The Tempest*. He and his designers (John Napier, with Martyn Bainbridge and Sue Jenkinson) were somewhat limited by the "house" set the RSC employed that season (which included *Richard II* and *King John*): a square, black, boxlike enclosure with a sloping roof, lights beaming on either side, and traverse curtains drawn for varied purposes at the back. Barton shifted the emphasis to single images, the most celebrated of which was the descent of Jupiter from the RST's "heavens";

the god was lowered in a huge golden egg that opened to reveal Jupiter—symbolizing the restorative powers of nature—perched on a golden eagle; the image folded itself to become the glorious sun of nature's heaven. During the finale, this great golden ring "tilted to form a white halo over Cymbeline's restored court."[27] These *coups de théâtre* were precisely in the spirit of a text written with Jacobean masques as its competetion, and were a studied contrast to Barton's unwieldly "masque" in *The Tempest* several years earlier. More important, they offered visual symbols of the play's thematic concerns. Peter Ansorge's commentary that Barton's ingenuity provided "a splendid moment of cosmic illumination"[28] is not without substance; it suggested that England was rejuvenated after a period of decline under the spell of the sorceress Queen, just as the love of Imogen and Posthumus was revitalized by their long separation and tribulations. *The Tempest* might well have benefitted from such theatrical magic to illuminate similar themes that Shakespeare intended in the last plays.

Since *The Wars of the Roses*, the RSC had developed a reputation for drab costuming.[29] Barton and his designers did much to rectify this notion in *Cymbeline*. Though Iachimo and Cloten retained the darker hues, the Queen was dressed in rainbow silks and crested like a cock; her villainous son, Cloten, was also dressed in feathers, though black, and suggested a bird of prey (a favorite Barton image), perhaps to illustrate Cloten's speech at 2.1.20: " . . . I must go up and down like a cock that nobody can match." The bird image was used elsewhere—while mixing her potion, the Queen crowed, and the announcement of her death was punctuated by the cry of an offstage cock. The most noteworthy costume was that of King Cymbeline: during the reconciliation in the final scene, the old king shed his overgarment to reveal a shimmering, pleated golden cloak of kingship—a visual metaphor of Britain's new glory. It was the same cloak worn by Richard II and the newly crowned Prince Henry in *King John*. Barton seems to have linked the three plays thematically, either as a study of the dual roles a king must play in public and private life, or, as Ansorge suggests, as "an aura of patriotic make-believe."

One other design element merits citation: Imogen's bed, the most important property in the telling of this fancied tale. It was an enormous white bed, "gleaming luxury, admirably serving as a metaphor of the mysterious England depicted in *Cymbeline*—'a great pool, a swan's nest,' a Britain which is *of* the 'world's volume,' but somehow not quite *in* it."[30] To heighten Iachimo's evil intrusion into the sanctity of Imogen's chamber, Barton's designers devised well-conceived business for Ian Richardson's portrayal: the lid of the trunk that the deceiver gives to Imogen was decorated with a wood carving of a nude, headless, hairy male. When the lid was opened, suddenly Richardson's head appeared on the neck—"the violation of the room was obscene."[31] This blatantly theatrical device—a sight gag as old as Aristophanes—was an effective illustration of Anne Barton's observation that "coincidences, implausibility, and theatrical cliché are stressed throughout the play."

Though Barton stressed the play's fairy-tale elements (a courageous choice, given the cynicism of the seventies), he did not let us forget that *Cymbeline* is a moving and bitter account of the separation and reconciliation of Imogen and Posthumus, a mythic depiction of human growth and maturity through suffering and trials unwarranted. *Plays and Players* believed the production succeeded largely because "it comes across as the coupling of experience rather than of innocence—a husband and wife, who have faced a lengthy separation, rather than the parted romantic lovers of Shakespeare's early comedies."[32] To ensure a human foundation amidst the plot's improbabilities, Barton's actors— particularly Susan Fleetwood (Imogen) and Tim Piggot-Smith (Posthumus)— worked naturalistically to reveal the text's emotional truths, a choice that made difficult passages (for example, Imogen's reaction to the discovery of the headless corpse[33]) less susceptible to unsolicited laughter. Michael Billington was especially impressed with the humanity the company found in the characters: "Notorious hurdles . . . are surmounted because they are seen from the character's own point of view. . . . In this way Shakespeare's tall, rambling, geographically restless story is given a mellow humanity, and the final reconciliation seems to be forged through genuine suffering."[34]

How does Barton reconcile an essentially naturalistic playing style with such blatantly formalistic script demands offered by *Cymbeline* (and the other fanciful plays considered in this chapter)? Dichotomies of style do not bother Barton, who told his cast as they assembled to begin work on *The Greeks* five years later: "We need to use naturalistic devices and yet not be naturalistic. There's nothing unusual about that. It's how we approach most classical plays and in particular how we approach Shakespeare. . . . Don't be afraid of this. I find it very attractive. I relish it."[35]

Though the Queen and Cloten were played broadly as written, Iachimo emerged as more than a sinister Machiavellian. Richardson played him in a "deliberately minor key . . . able to put a finger immediately upon the funny side of every situation,"[36] an intelligent, self-assured Italian gentleman whose habit of playing jokes has been developed to offset the boredom of court. Typical of Barton-Richardson interpretations, the portrait of Iachimo countered one's expectation and found humor in situations traditionally played more seriously.

The title role—which Barton called "a thankless part" in 1957—was given unusual prominence within the fairy-tale framework. The program described Cymbeline as "the archetypal king of folklore whose judgment has been inexplicably poisoned at its springs as the result of a second marriage," and Sebastian Shaw presented the King as "almost unreachably senile,"[37] a victim of his Sorceress-Queen. During the last scene he resumed his authority almost magically to provide the finale with "a genuine exhilaration . . . an infectious moment carefully plotted and prepared by Barton's ingenious reading of the play."[38]

If Barton made *Cymbeline* theatrically viable within the context of a fairy tale, in June 1976 he accomplished similar ends by playing *The Winter's Tale* as a folk tale. The production remains a seminal moment in Barton's maturation as a "myth-maker" and story-teller in his own right. Trevor Nunn, who in 1969 had staged one of the century's most successful productions of the play, codirected with Barton.

In 1976 Barton mounted his Indian Raj version of *Much Ado About Nothing* and, on the surface, it appeared that he employed the same device he had used so admirably in April, which was to relocate the action in time and place. But whereas *Much Ado* was placed in a very specific society to account for precise social customs, *The Winter's Tale* was placed in a more purposefully ambiguous milieu. Ostensibly, Sicilia and Bohemia were geographically shifted to a timeless, primitive culture in which the play's improbable events would appear naturally as elaborate folk rituals celebrating the cycle of life. That Barton's ambience was ambiguous is attested by the various cultures to which the critics assigned the action: Finnish; Eskimo; Slavic; Norse; American Indian; Cossack; Serbo-Croatian; Antarctican. One critic even suggested a science-fiction setting: "It looks forwards, not backwards, into the new Ice Age we are being so abundantly promised . . . (Sicily and Bohemia) are now frozen, sterile lands."[39]

The RSC program contained numerous anthropological citations about the folk customs of the Scandanavians. (Remember that Barton also studied for the anthropology tripos at Cambridge, specializing in Nordic cultures; his preparation there no doubt influenced *The Winter's Tale* in 1976, as well as his later work on *The Vikings* and, to be sure, his current myth, which draws on Nordic sagas as well as Greek and Arthurian legends for its impetus.) One note in particular hinted at the directors' decision to shift the play's locale to the North: "Two solstice festivals were celebrated more intensely in Scandinavia than anywhere in the South. The Winter Solstice was called Jul and it marks the darkest day of the year. . . . For the Norsemen, Jul was an essentially family festival and places were even laid for the dead ancestors."

The differences between the first half of the play and the second are as pronounced as those between night and day, winter and summer, and the Barton-Nunn choice of locales heightened the thematic intent of the play. Benedict Nightingale suggested, with some insight, that the RSC shift reflects "a process presumably more dramatic where one solstice is all night and the other all day."[40] Consequently, when Barton staged *The Greeks* in 1980, he marked the progress of the Homeric myth by a similar move from the "green world" of *Iphigenia in Aulis*, which opened the cycle, to the harsh, wintry world of *Iphigenia in Taurus*, which closed it.

On the walls and curtains that covered the RSC's permanent set for the 1976 season were etched primitive folk designs, stick figures, crudely drawn flowers, a matriarchal figure with sunburst headdress, runic writings:[41]

The designs were incorporated into the trim of the costumes and were "etched into everything that will take an image: trees, a shepherd's crook, Autolycus' right thigh."[42] Complementing these primordial drawings, the cast devised a number of ritual games to effect a culture in which the "sad tale" of a jealous husband, his dying wife, and their long-lost daughter would reflect the mysterious changing of the seasons. Robert Cushman, in an adverse review, believed that the hieroglyphs "dehydrated Shakespeare," and that the rituals were probably understood by the cast, but left the audience cold."[43]

The set itself was sparse: at its center stood a single, leafless tree—an emblem of the harsh winter world in which the first half of the play is acted. To convey the family atmosphere of this domestic "tragedy," the stage was strewn with fur rags, folk-woven materials, plump chairs that looked like upholstered bales of cotton. The simplicity of the setting was an asset: the story in which it was acted seemed less complex.

The shift from the wintry landscape of Leontes' court (and his mind, "frozen" with irrational jealousy) to the spring of Bohemia was effected not so much by a change of decor, but by a change in attitude by the performers. Flowers and greenery were more noticeable in the second half, though not as much as some would have liked;[44] the major warmth and contrast was provided by the boisterous behavior of the rustics: juggling, singing, dancing, performing acrobatics, and clowning, a spectacle described by Hobson as "a well-meaning Easter outing trying to revive a Chestertonian Merrie England."[45] Again the RSC provided a note to explain the customs:

For the Nordic peoples, the festival of the Sun (Sol) combined with the festivals further south, which were associated with May Day to make the most joyous celebration of the Nordic year. It was essentially the time dedicated to the young, to dancing, garlands, life and new growth.

The folk tradition that framed this winter's tale provided credible solutions for the play's incredible actions. "Exit (Antigonus) pursued by a bear" is Shakespeare's most taxing stage direction. Though the program acknowledged Sir Arthur Quiller-Couch's suspicion that the Elizabethans had access to a bear from the Southwark pits, Barton and Nunn used the oddity to thematic advantage: the "bear" was actually Time (John Nettles), wearing a headdress, who *escorted*, not chased, Antigonus offstage. Critics either admired or despised the innovation. Roger Warren in *Shakespeare Survey* appreciated the use of "another primitive folk emblem" and thought "it worked, because unnatural shock is the essence of this bizarre scene."[46] Nightingale thought much less kindly of the device: ". . . 'exit pursued by a bear' has been amended to read 'stands, apprehended by a witch doctor.'"[47] J. C. Trewin, the most experienced of British Shakespeare critics, did not pass judgment on the Barton "bear," but did note, significantly, "for the first time in my experience, no one laughed."[48]

A program page entitled "The Bear Facts" suggested why Barton stylized the bear and equated Antigonus's death with the ravages of time. Neville Coghill defines the beast's cosmic significance: "It symbolizes the revenge of Nature on the servant of a corrupted court: it is a thundering surprise."[49] Later, during the sheep-shearing scene, the directors devised a ritualized "bear hunt ballet" in place of Shakespeare's satyr dance. Richard David thought the dance an intrusion that imposed on the play "a unity that is not there."[50]

The other great challenge The Winter's Tale offers directors is, of course, the act 5 "statue scene" in which Hermoine comes to life after sixteen years; Barton calls it one of the moments that moves him most in the theatre. Surely it best embodies the "healing" elements which so strongly appeals to Barton as writer and director. Yet another program note placed Hermione's "death" in a specific social context: "In Scandanavia, a wife's adultery was a serious crime, so much so that some provincial laws gave a husband the right to kill her." Thus her trial (staged as a tribal council meeting under a barren tree) was even more ominous to audiences apprised of this curious custom. The "statue scene" itself was played with ritual solemnity: after Hermione stirred to life, Leontes and his family stood quietly, touching hands in a silent circle of reunion,[51] a gesture that brought the finale a "sense of mystery and strangeness that passes rational explanation or the power of language to describe."[52] It was accompanied by a haunting folk air composed by Woolfenden that Barton calls the most beautiful piece of music he has ever heard in the theater (he used it again in The Vikings). The directors took a theatrically courageous risk when staging the scene: they placed Hermione's "statue" in a corner, *down* stage, and lit it brightly. Thus the gathered court could look directly at the audience, which then experienced the wondrous reincarnation through the eyes of Leontes and his entourage. By placing the actress playing Hermione in such proximity to the audience, the credibility of the scene was taxed. Fortunately, Marilyn Taylerson was equal to the challenge, and the scene worked very well. "Rarely, if ever, can this piece of Shakespearean oddity have been given more credibility," Peter Whitehouse wrote.[53]

Perhaps the most difficult problem to overcome in The Winter's Tale is not the bear, or Hermione's resurrection but Leontes' sudden jealousy. One suspects that Shakespeare merely used the jealousy as a pretext to launch a narrative about the rebirth of a family. In a folk tale we accept this "once-upon-a-time" pretext, but modern audiences want psychologically sound explanations for human actions. Barton, Nunn, and the RSC provided business to justify Leontes' actions. B. A. Young reported that "Polixines certainly is remarkably familiar with Hermione, adjusting her dress over her ankles when she sits, holding her hand as they talk together. . . ."[54] This would account for the Sicilian King's subsequent behavior and reminds us of Barton's treatment of Cassio and Desdemona in the 1971 Othello. To this realistic subtext Nunn added a device he had successfully used in 1969. To show Leontes' descent into madness, the stage lighting shifted dramatically: the major portion of the stage was darkened and an unusual, harsh, white light fell on Leontes (Ian McKellen) to suggest "a weird coldness in order to emphasize the sudden way in which fantasies seize upon Leontes' fevered brain."[55] Though the device countered the simplicity of the folk motif, it did offer two advantages. First, it enabled Leontes to deliver several of the most difficult speeches in Shakespeare with an uncanny clarity; second, the sudden shift in style meant that the actor need not worry about gradually building motivation for the jealousy but could proceed into his tirades with full conviction. Richard David's summary of McKellen's reading and the Barton-Nunn device is useful:

> Even when Leontes emerged from his solipsistic self-communings and engaged with other characters, the remoteness of the dream-world was hardly lessened, sometimes on account of the directors' deliberate manipulation, sometimes in the writing that is Shakespeare's own.[56]

Like *Cymbeline, The Winter's Tale's* universal appeal is derived from its depiction of knowledge acquired from suffering, loss, and regeneration— "healing," to use Barton's favored term. Again the RSC founded its performances on naturalistic acting (Leontes' stylized soliloquies notwithstanding) to underscore the truth of the emotions. The play's three principal women— Hermione (Taylerson), Paulina (Barbara Leigh-Hunt), and Perdita (Cheri Lunghi)—were cited for giving the production a squarely human center, as well as reminding us of the "mother earth" values they symbolize. Leigh-Hunt's Paulina was roundly praised for her contemporary spirit; she, rather than Hermione, was "the fighter . . . who will be bidden by no man if she thinks he is talking, however privileged his position, patently arrant and arrogant nonsense."[57]

If *Cymbeline* and *The Winter's Tale* are about the affirmation of the human spirit, Barton and his codirectors found this hope in their telling of the stories of Imogen, Hermione, Paulina, Perdita, and Mother England herself. Barton believes he did not discover all of *The Winter's Tales* truths, and is anxious to return to the play in the future.

The following year Barton attempted Shakespeare's earliest fantasy, *A Midsummer Night's Dream,* and stymied his critics who were sure that he would offer a curiously different approach to the play. They were almost miffed when he staged instead a rather conventional version of the comedy. One began his review in mock outrage at Barton's uncharacteristic conventionality. The passage defines what Barton did *not* do with *Dream* and suggests the status of his reputation in his seventeenth year at Stratford: "Oh, Mr. Barton, what an unpredictable man you are! . . . Now [you] have given us the biggest surprise of all—a production of *A Midsummer Night's Dream* with no noticeable cuts, no extra bits written in and, most startling of all, no gimmicks."[58] The critic then chastised Barton for *not* waving his magic wand because, in his opinion,

Dream "is a play that badly needs the kind of framework Mr. Barton can provide."

Actually, the unnamed critic missed the point—and by a wide margin. Barton specifically chose not to resort to fanciful gimmicks because he was laboring in the long shadow cast by Brook's inventive *Dream* of 1970. Nunn, now the RSC's artistic director, recounts that for years he could not get anyone to direct the play for fear of comparisons to Brook. Barton eventually accepted the challenge, and in doing so, hopes John Elsom, may have formulated a new policy for the RSC:

> As the months pass we may well look back to this production [of Barton's *Dream*] as one which brought a valuable transfusion of new blood to the RSC and it may have another significance too. It may have scotched the RSC habit of believing that new productions of well-known plays require specific justification for their presence within the repertory.[59]

Elsom's first commendation refers to the young cast Barton employed. Only Patrick Stewart (Oberon) had any significant experience with the RSC prior to this production; the others were apprentices and newcomers to the company. The adventurous casting proved a liability since *Dream* is perhaps the only Barton-directed production severely criticized for the quality of its verse speaking.[60]

What Barton did accomplish, however, was a return of the *Dream* to a more conventional staging. He did not "show us anything different from our normal expectations of the *Dream*, but rather . . . braced up an orthodoxy which was in danger of becoming flabby."[61] Barton eschewed Brook's Meyerholdian gymnastics (though his fairies were commended for their suppleness and physical control), Kott's Freudian eroticism, and other modish overlays in favor of a more workaday approach that evoked "in simplified form the realities of Elizabethan society."[62] To be sure, it was a darker *Dream*, as suggested by the program quotation from Montaigne's essays, which speaks of the "cimmerian darkness" of the dream we call life.

Barton achieved the mystery and even exceeded the enchantment he brought to *Cymbeline* and *The Winter's Tale* without resorting to extensive rewrites, externally imposed narrators, or exotic locales. Essentially his company told the story as Shakespeare wrote it. With the technical wizardry of contemporary theater craftsmen and actors skilled in physical expression, Barton created a mysterious wood outside Athens in which the play's wondrous action could logically, yet magically, occur.

The fairy world created by John Napier's design was evident as RSC patrons entered the theater. Mists rose from all directions, leaves fluttered gracefully down from the flies to the stage floor, shafts of sunlight burst through the dense foliage on the fringes of the stage, and animal noises echoed softly through the forest stillness. A giant plant unfolded, as in a time-lapse nature film, and in the murky light spirits appeared. But these were not the sprites of a Mendelssohn ballet or a Reinhardt spectacular. They were decidedly sixteenth-century spirits defined in David Young's program note:

> . . . a curious mixture of wood sprites and household gods, pagan dieties and local pixies. . . . Through Titania and her train, Shakespeare emphasizes their innocence and delicacy; in Oberon and Puck, he expresses their darker side, potentially malevolent in the lore of the time. . . . The creatures variously called puck . . . as well as other fairies, were dangerous and an Elizabethan audience could not contemplate him or his associates as representatives of the unknown without some apprehensions.[63]

Barton apparently wished to restore this traditional version of fairies; thus they were less attractive, more grotesque, than those associated with Disney. They were bald, with unusual whisks of hair protruding from various parts of their faces; they had pointed ears and paunchy bellies; they had ancient, wizened faces and they possessed "that elusive blend of whimsical and sinister we habitually associate with fairies."[64] Bernard Levin thought they may have been inspired by a fifteenth-century painting, *The Temptation of Saint Anthony*,[65] while another critic cautioned that they might have been too sinister in appearance "for spirits who inhabit muskrose buds and sing a charm *against* sinister creatures."[66] The actors created the illusion of fairy magic as they faded into invisibility by contorting their bodies into the shape of tree stumps and rocks, camouflaged by their physical skills as much as by the coloring of their costumes.

Patrick Stewart, an actor of impressive physique, was a formidable leader of the Fairy Kingdom. Nearly naked, brown-skinned, chanting his lines to effect a primitive lyricism, he was far removed from Alan Howard's unisex Oberon in Brook's version. To begin the second half of the performance, Barton devised an archetypal image: as the lights came up, Oberon was discovered reclining on the leafy floor, playing pan-pipes, "a pastoral god, for all the world like Nijinsky's *Après-midi d'un faune*."[67] Oberon was accompanied in his sinister mischief by the darkly charming Puck, his red hair starched straight back over his forehead in an Elizabethan mohawk.[68]

By contrast, Titania was formally dressed, less an element of the darker forces of the play than an illustration of Dover Wilson's conjecture that "Titania and the Fairies were invented for the world to fall in love with the play."[69] Moth, Mustardseed, and others, were played—as they likely were in Shakespeare's day—by boys, who were "a creepy combination of childish bodies and voices and old men's heads and faces."[70]

Guy Woolfenden composed a haunting score to further the mystery of Athens' magic forest: ". . . the music of this production—an evocative affair of dissonances which somehow become harmonious—helps to reconcile the irreconcilable."[71]

Throughout the production Barton employed many resources of the modern theater to create the magic world of the play. It was hardly a "scholar's approach," though the fairies, presumably, were conceived as a response to his scholarly reading. A truly academic approach to *Dream* would likely make Hippolyta's act 5 observation the touchstone of the production: "It must be your imagination then, not theirs" (5.1.211). That is, the actors should spark the imagination of the audience, which then mentally provides the scenic marvels of the play. An imaginatively rendered production, such as that by Barton-Napier-Woolfenden, it can be argued, does the audience's work by illustrating the script.

The fairyland is only one of the play's worlds. Napier's set reconciled the countryside with the court; the latter consisted of a wooden floor with a central design suggesting Michaelangelo's Renaissance view of man. Theseus, Hippolyta, and the quartet of young lovers were costumed austerely in white and black. The lovers were distinctly courtly youths; several critics thought they detected an influence of Peter Hall's justly famed "Tudor mansion" *Dream* of 1963 in the lovers. Barton allowed his *innamoratti* to succumb to the trendy method of playing the lovers as pratfalling acrobats, a choice criticized by Lloyd Evans, who argued that "Shakespeare's lovers are not, of themselves, funny: they are young romantics to whom funny things happen."[72]

The production was generously praised for its depiction of the mechanicals. Theirs was, by all accounts, a restrained play-within-the play because Barton and his comedians realized that the humor arises from the integrity and intensity that the well-intentioned, if under-talented, thespians bring to it: "All the comedy arises from a matter-of-fact considered application of totally misdirected purpose—it's like watching something that seems perfectly normal becoming utterly ridiculous."[73] Barton unabashedly borrowed a moment from Chekhov to climax the Pyramus-Thisbe play. At Pyramus's death "a thin, silvery woodland chord resounds in sympathetic magic."[74] Billington judged the moment "a touch of directorial genius" that aptly defined the import of the play—"the interpenetration of the mortal and immortal world and the discovery of a universal concorde."

As he had done with Don Armado, Toby Belch, and Aguecheek, Barton found the pathos, as well as the humor, in roles that are traditionally played for their broadest comic values. Richard Griffiths' Bottom joins that list. Griffiths himself initiated the subtler approach:

> At first John Barton wanted me to come on as Bottom in a grand pool of light "down left," while the other mechanicals were lost "up right." I said, "I can't do it like that. Bottom's a man among six others who happens to talk a lot." And that's how I play him, like a real person.[75]

Lloyd Evans called Griffiths work "the best performance of Bottom I have ever seen," and in *Shakespeare Survey* Roger Warren reported that his "quiet, warm, and very human performance was the chief gain of the production's declared policy of using largely untried actors."

There were unfavorable judgments that Barton's *Dream* was too langorous, too deliberate to be effective comedy.[76] A conventional reading of the comedy might well seem tame after Brook's theatrical pyrotechnics. Whatever its flaws, the imagination Barton invested in *Dream*'s visual elements justified the RSC's decision to wait no longer to reintroduce the fantasy to its repertory.

In January 1980 Barton mounted his epic *The Greeks*, whose themes of reconciliation and revitalization after suffering he explored in Shakespeare's fantastic "healing plays." A year later he juxtaposed—at Nunn's request—two of Shakespeare's prentice works, *Two Gentlemen of Verona* and *Titus Andronicus*, into a "twin bill" for an evening's long entertainment at Stratford. Though Barton said the twinning was "a straightforward experiment to see if a double bill of rarities can be good box office"[77] (as it turned out, they were not), there emerged an interesting counterpoint between the two plays that is relevent to the discussion in this chapter. *Titus Andronicus* is a play about revenge and its debilitating powers on the human spirit; *Two Gentlemen of Verona* is about forgiveness of transgressions and its healing powers. Though these themes are central to Barton's interests, he did not deal with them successfully in the double bill by his own admission:[78] "It emerges that when one is doing a play either one hears mythical bells in one's head, or one doesn't. These plays didn't affect me that way." The production's opening night, it must be reported, was rescheduled because the RSC directors felt it needed additional work and a clarification of concept. Nonetheless, the Stratford experiment offered audiences a chance to consider Shakespeare's early efforts with themes that he—and Barton—treated more effectively in the later play.

The unusual billing also serves as an important addendum to Barton's career as he entered his third decade at Stratford. The two plays, staged more as an exercise in theatricality with inferior material than as an exploration of profound issues, were "pure Barton": they were heavily cut (515 lines from the comedy; 850 from the tragedy—which he had previously cut in 1957 for Walter Hudd's double bill of *Titus* and *The Comedy of Errors* at the Old Vic; Barton believed he was improving their imperfections by thus condensing them) and they were staged with maximum theatricality. A single set served both plays. The RSC actors, dressed as an Elizabethan traveling company (Wells notes that Barton wished to define the two plays' Elizabethan qualities), extracted bits and pieces of clothing and props from common trunks and clothes racks to effect Rome and Milano. Actors ringed the playing area and provided sound effects (most notably a variety of bird calls, both comic and plaintive) for the on stage action. Clearly Barton had dipped into his own theatrical trunk to extract devices he had used with some success at Cambridge[79] and in his first (*Taming of the Shrew*, 1960) and most recent (*Hamlet*, 1980) work at Stratford. In one sense the doublebill brought Barton's Stratford work full circle as it reconsidered the director's favorite themes through well-tried textual and staging techniques. But like so many of his efforts, it opened new territory for the RSC, and if it erred, it was on the side of boldness.

8

The Marriage of True Minds:
Hamlet (1980)

Anne Barton's writings have figured prominently in this assessment of John Barton's work, particularly in reference to those plays staged after 1968. In August of that year Barton married Anne Righter (née Bobbi Anne Roesen) in the Stratford Town Hall. Significantly, the ceremony was attended by only two witnesses, each of whom has also figured in the director's career: Muriel C. Bradbrook, Anne Barton's Cambridge mentor, and Timothy O'Brien, the director's schoolfellow who designed a number of Barton productions. Though the Bartons were on the Cambridge campus at the same time—he a fellow at King's College and she working on her dissertation on the legacy of medieval theater to Elizabethan and Jacobean drama—they did not meet until the mid-sixties, appropriately, at a "brain's trust" held during the RSC's summer school.[1]

Anne Barton, American by birth, attended Cambridge in the late 1950s and earned her doctorate under the tutelage of Bradbrook. Her thesis, completed in 1961, was published as *Shakespeare and the Idea of Play* under the name of Anne Righter. It is a perceptive and influential study of reflexive drama that holds art's mirror to itself "to remind the audience that elements of illusion are present in ordinary life, and that between the world and the stage there exists a complicated interplay of resemblence that is part of the perfection and nobility of the drama itself as a form."[2] In the years since the marriage, RSC patrons have also been enriched by Anne Barton's erudite program essays, which provide insight into both Shakespeare's work and Barton's staging of them.

It should be emphasized that Barton does not rely on his wife's critical writings as the source of his production concepts, any more than she relies on his work as the impetus for her essays. Of her influence on his work Barton has said:

> I'm sure I've picked up things from my wife over the years; it's not a very organized or planned thing. I read all her pieces and lectures, and I comment on them. And one picks things out.[3]

But, Barton cautions, he discusses works such as *Hamlet* with his wife "with a certain amount of reserve. I may be passionate to do something she thinks is passionately wrong. That's fair enough, but it doesn't necessarily help me that she should think that." *Hamlet,* which opened in Stratford in the summer of 1980 (and was subsequently moved to the Aldwych in March 1981), is the most prominent example of the interaction between the Bartons. The seeds of the director's production concept for *Hamlet* may be traced to Anne Barton's book and, more specifically, her lengthy and thoughtful introduction to the 1980 New Penguin edition of the play.[4] The latter amplifies ideas from the book, illustrating that *Hamlet* "is unique in the density and pervasiveness of its theatrical self-reference . . . because *Hamlet* as a whole is so concerned to question and cross the boundaries which normally separate dramatic representations from real life."[5]

"When I came to do the play," Barton said in an interview, "I was very keen on the 'player element.' I completely forgot she had touched on it in *Shakespeare and the Idea of the Play,* so whether it was an unconscious memory or not I can't say." Tony Church, who played Polonius, says Barton rarely cites critical theory in the rehearsal room but he frequently referred to Anne Barton's introduction to the New Penguin text in preparation for *Hamlet* "because it was essentially what he wanted to do."[6] Church added that the sequence on Hamlet in *Shakespeare and the Idea of the Play* was "the seedbed of this production without any doubt at all."

One wonders why Barton waited twenty years to accept *Hamlet*'s many challenges since it is a play that has long held his interest. Practical matters precluded him from staging the play:

> . . . there wasn't anybody I wanted to do *Hamlet* with. . . . I wanted to go back to the classic tradition of a lyric-poetic-intellectual-princely Hamlet after twenty years of a British tradition of the boorish lout Hamlet which I didn't like.[7]

The "boorish" Hamlet's to which Barton alludes can be traced back to 1965 and Peter Hall's staging of the play at RSC with David Warner as the Prince, a Kottean existentialist tormented by thoughts of the fundamental absurdity of existence. The Hall-Warner *Hamlet* spawned a brood of surly Danes, notably Nicol Williamson in 1968. In 1980 Barton's version had to contend with a Royal Court production in which Jonathan Pryce's volatile Hamlet did little to diminish the Court's reputation for contemporaneity. At London's Roundhouse Theatre, Stephen Berkoff doubled as actor and director of an eccentrically topical production that gave audiences a skinhead Hamlet who might have been more at home at London's punk-rock Odeon Theatre than the Danish Court. Barton sought an antidote to these petulant princes, products of the social and political turmoil of the sixties and seventies.

To restore the play to its "poetic" roots, Barton turned to yet another Cambridge alumnus: Michael Pennington, who had first acted for him in *Love's Labour's Lost* in 1965. When Barton and Pennington were touring with *The Hollow Crown* in Denmark in 1974, the director suggested that they someday undertake *Hamlet.* Pennington provided Barton with the grace and verse-speaking skills for the interpretation he sought, and Anne Barton, to a degree, provided the critical framework.

Anne Barton's theory that *Hamlet* is "a tragedy dominated by the idea of the play" (*Idea,*159) is not unique. Lionel Abel has made it a touchstone of *Metatheatre;* Nigel Alexander's *Poison, Play, and Duel* and Robert Egan's *Drama Within Drama* also address the issue. Nor is Barton's the first production to demonstrate a traceable influence of Anne Barton's ideas on stage. Trevor Nunn's 1970 version, with Alan Howard as Hamlet, presented a Danish court clad in black and white with "the players singled out as the only characters whose coloured costumes differed from the schematic designs and Hamlet became noticably animated only in their presence."[8] The RSC program for that production extracted quotations from *Shakespeare and the Idea of the Play* to clarify Nunn's use of the Players.

The 1980 *Hamlet* is perhaps the most thorough exploration in stage terms of an "art-life" interpretation of the play's meaning. Like his wife, Barton perceives the theater, represented by the Players whom Fate leads to Elsinor, as the Prince's means of "deciphering a treacherous world in which Claudius can 'smile, and smile, and be a villain,' and everyone except Horatio, may be playing a part" (Intro., 29). Nearly all elements of the RSC staging were geared toward illustrating this Pirandellian view of the play.

Even Barton's editing of the text, though minimal, reflected this subtext. He excised approximately 825 lines of the writer's original 3800, a relatively conservative 21 percent,[9] yet it was not the omissions but an insertion for which the production may well be remembered. Barton interpolated but two words—though Shakespeare's own—which threw the Barton's interpretation into relief. During his epic account of Pyrrhus's attack on Priam in 2.2, the First Player paused to mark the attacker's hesitation at killing the aged King (a moment cited by Anne Barton, Intro., 30):

> So as a painted tyrant Pyrrhus stood,
> And like a neutral to his will and matter . . .

and the attentive Hamlet, recognizing his own inability to kill a king, finished the line for the Player:

Did nothing. (2.2.484–86)

For Hamlet "theatre and life change place."[10] The moment of recognition was shared by the First Player (Bruce Purchase) who, according to Church, "is aware that something strange is happening because he repreats the inflection exactly the way in which Hamlet has given it; he doesn't continue on his own. There is a sense of just watching, knowing by the First Player." Thus Barton purposefully established an ineradicable bond between the Prince, the Players, and their art. The moment reverberated throughout the play: at the conclusion of the "Mousetrap" scene (3.2) Hamlet said, "Leave me, friends" (l. 372)—a line ordinarily delivered with disdain to Rosencrantz and Guildenstern—with great affection to the actors, whom he warmly embraced before they disappeared into the upstage blackness.

The textual enlargement was, however unconsciously, a clarification of an idea suggested by Anne Righter twenty years earlier:

> For the weary reality of Elsinore, the actor substitutes the distant sorrows of Troy; during perhaps 70 lines, the sense of present time is suspended. *Then, at some unidentified point in the speech,* Hamlet himself becomes conscious of the spell. He notices real tears in the eyes of the Player and begins to brood ominously upon the power which the actor can exert over life. . . . (*Idea,* 162. Italics mine).

Though the point at which Hamlet becomes conscious of the spell must remain a mystery for all but the actor who plays him, Barton provided Stratford audiences with a very specific point at which Hamlet became irreversibly involved with the reality of the illusion.

Though Barton opted for a decidedly theatrical *Hamlet,* he did not resort to an elaborate overlay to achieve his ends, say, in the manner in which Peter Brook explored the art of performance in his acclaimed *A Midsummer Night's Dream* (1970). Ironically, the Players were the least overtly theatrical aspect of the production: they were dressed drably and darkly, particularly when set against the almost cartoonish—"stagey"—costumes of Claudius and the Court. They arrived without the customary "the-Players-have-arrived" bravado; they simply walked from the upstage blackness into the world of the play, not unlike Pirandello's six characters. Their acting, in both the First Player's Pyrrhus speech and in the ensuing "Murder of Gonzago," was remarkably underplayed: naturalistic acting in a court of unnatural acts. Barton's version of theatricality reflected the simplicity espoused by Hamlet in his advice to the Players.

Barton's projection of theater metaphors extended well beyond the scenes with the Players. "The stage imagery," Anne Barton writes, "exists independently of the professional actors. . . . it is there from the beginning and remains important in the final movement of the tragedy" (Intro., 24). Barton's exploration of the play's theatricality began even as the audience entered the Royal Shakespeare Theatre. Ralph Koltai's simple design contained its own "stage," a large, slightly elevated, gradually raked platform turned at an angle toward the audience. The artificial stage was surrounded by four benches that became an "audience area" for the spectators in Elsinore's drama: the Court watched the King, Polonius, Voltemand, and Cornelius perform their ceremonial functions at this Danish theater-in-the-round; crazed Ophelia arranged an "audience" in 4.5 around this stage to enact her bawdy incantations while seated in the prop throne of the Players; Hamlet and Horatio crouched against the proscenium to watch the "sorry spectacle" of Ophelia's funeral; the ensuing Hamlet-Laertes duel—with the protagonists wearing masks (fencing headgear)—found a natural space for this last great "maimed rite," an event that Anne Barton describes as a traditional moment in the revenge genre in which "a 'fictional' action, performed by selected characters before an unsuspecting on-stage audience, explodes without warning into real, as opposed to mimic destruction" (Intro., 48). And finally, it was this "stage-upon-the-stage" to which four captains bore the body of dead Hamlet to place it in a pool of light for a final tableau in the production's finest moment.

Behind Koltai's metaphorical stage were theater artifacts from which the RSC cast could draw to tell the story of *Hamlet,* a device used again the following year in his "twin bill" staging of *Two Gentlemen of Verona* and *Titus Andronicus.* At stage left sat a worn prop throne used by Player Kings and kingly Players and mad Ophelia (whose aggrieved mind turned it into a tombstone for her father: as she sang "At his head a green-grass turf / At his heels a stone," she chalked a cross on the chair back). Behind the mock throne stood a thunder sheet on a pole, used by the Players for sound effects during the murder of Gonzago. Hamlet also shook it violently on "the croaking raven doth bellow for revenge" at 3.2.244, as did Ophelia in a pathetic parody of her lover while bewailing the death of her father. At up center was a large wicker basket from which the company extracted costumes and props. At up right stood a suit of armor on a mannequin covered by a tatty blanket, which doubled as an arras when Polonius was audience to the Hamlet-Ophelia or Hamlet-Gertrude dramas. Near the armor was a prop table dominated by an enormous chalice, obviously a stage prop that would figure prominently in the unwinding of the play.

Above the stage hung five naked light bulbs, suspended like theater "ghost lights," which prompted a rehearsal hall atmosphere appropriate to the production concept. Backing the contrived stage area was a vast blackness against which the actors played their drama. This black void was effective for several reasons: it provided focus on the actors since our attention was not induced to wander to irrelevant scenic detail; it promoted simple, theatrical effects to accommodate Barton's concept. For example, the Ghost of Old Hamlet vanished from view as it receded into the blackness, as effective a "dissolve" as one could hope to see in the theater. The RSC Players, like those at Elsinore, conjured effects "wondrous strange" by relying only on the simplest theater devices: a nearly bare stage, Shakespeare's words, and a direct line to the imagination.

Not everyone approved of Koltai's design. Surely some visitors to Stratford expected more elaborate scenic effects from a leading company; one reviewer lamented the failure of RSC design in recent years, as typified in this *Hamlet* design, a fault he ascribed less to the designers than to directors who "are in love with music and couldn't care less about the visual side of a production."[11]

Barton emphatically does care about the visual aspects of production (his 1973 *Richard II* was often condemned for its visual excess), but in *Hamlet* he chose to allow the actors to provide the visual, as well as the aural interest. Barton employed three of Claudius's Switzers in stylized poses as architectural set pieces to suggest changes in locale.

Even Barton's use of music realized the theatricality of the script. For each of Claudius's entrances, there was a garish fanfare, a parody of music associated with the costume epics of earlier days in the theater. Composed by James Walker, the music was almost childishly simple and became more obnoxious as the play progressed. The audience thus experienced some of Hamlet's revulsion for the ostentatious "show" at court. Michael Tubbs, production music director, feels Barton has had "an extraordinary way of using music over the last ten years," and that the *Hamlet* fanfare was "very effective . . . a bit of cardboard flat type of music."[12] In contrast to the "theatrical music" of the court, Barton used simpler music elsewhere to effect: Ophelia strummed a lute and hummed a folk melody (which she later perverted into her bawdy song for the mad scene) to accompany Polonius's advice to Laertes;[13] the second gravedigger played a haunting air on a finger pipe as Hamlet pondered Yorick's skull.

Throughout the performance Barton's actors created business—some obvious, some less so—to reinforce the script's and Anne Barton's predilection for life-as-theater imagery. There may have been occasions when viewers found the production overelaborating on Shakespeare's intent. But to those who knew the play well, it was a unique opportunity to assist at "a sustained attempt to unpack the meaning of the play."[14] More precisely, it was an attempt to unpack *a* meaning of *Hamlet*.

More intimate scenes found characters adopting stage personas to further the action. Polonius, for example, assumed the role of a "director" and treated Laertes, Reynaldo, and Ophelia as if they were actors preparing for roles. He demonstrated how to play societal roles, how to spy on Parisian brothels (to an amused Reynaldo, who applauded the old man's performance, which included assorted character voices), and how maidens ought to enact "devotion's visage and pious actions." When the Players arrived, Polonius donned a fool's cap and sceptre to lead them in and then animatedly engaged Hamlet in a vaudeville routine for which both assumed stage voices (2.2. 394–420). This was indeed a Polonius who acted at the university and who could rightly be counted a good actor.

Though the Players remind Hamlet of "the related and potentially useful ways in which art and life can exchange places" (Intra, 31), the Ghost from the grave aroused that instinct in him long before the Players came to Elsinore. The 1980 Hamlet, the true First Player of this tragedy, knew the power of performance from the outset, an extension of Anne Barton's view of the Prince as "an unrivalled parodist . . . part of a private investigation into how other people structure their experience in words" (Intro., 44).

The actor in Hamlet chose his costumes carefully. His initial appearance prompted one observer to note: ". . . his mourning suggests a mockery; he is wearing what looks like a slept-in dinner jacket."[15] The self-indulgence of the Prince's costume, a frumpy overshirt of "nighted" color, underscored the Queen's questioning of Hamlet's histrionics: "Why *seems* it so with thee?" His explosive reply, which turns into one of the play's most succinct statements on the "actions a man might play," effectively launched the tenor of the production. Later, having determined an antic disposition is a useful action to play, Hamlet dressed in a parody of Renaissance students' garb: a beret, tattered gray gown, bookbag at his side, quill pen tucked behind his ear. After his encounter with the Players, Hamlet admitted the first touches of color to his costume, *in extremis:* a multihued cloak made from swatches of the Players' costumes for the Gonzago melodrama. In 4.4 Hamlet concluded the "How all occasions . . ." soliloquy by wrapping himself, shroudlike, in a torn gray blanket, apparently aware of the role that Providence would eventually assign him. It was the same blanket with which Horatio would cover him at play's end.

Like Polonius, Hamlet too recalled his theater experiences at Wittenburg: "He can give a creditable recitation, without book, of Aeneas' speech to Dido, addresses the First Player familiarly as 'old friend' . . . a connoisseur as it seems of revenge plays, well-acquainted with their conventions and character types" (Intro., 29). Hamlet's acting ability in this production transcended the customary "antic disposition" one immediately associates with the role. There was also an amicable actor in Pennington's Hamlet. When informed that the players were approaching Elsinore, Hamlet entertained Rosencrantz and Guildenstern with deft impersonations of Knights, Lovers, Humourous Men, Clowns, and Ladies (2.2.323–30); Polonius and Hamlet did a series of music hall "turns" during the Jepthah exchange, and later Hamlet played a willing straight man to the Gravedigger's one-liners as the two teamed to entertain Horatio. Hamlet's scurrilous jests at Ophelia's expense in 3.2 emphasized the double entrendres in the manner of a leering burlesque comedian, which might have seemed overdone in another context. Not all of Hamlet's "performances" were successful: the "rogue and peasant slave" soliloquy featured a garishly melodramatic outburst as Pennington—who otherwise had played the role with marked reserve when not intentionally "performing" for other characters—swirled a cape and brandished a sword at "Bloody, bawdy villain / Remorseless, treacherous, leacherous, kindless villain! O vengeance!" He sank to his knees and back to reality at "Why, what an ass am I," said as a self-mocking realization that he indeed was not a Vendice or Hieronimo, that "experienced playgoer though he is . . . in real life he cannot reduce his own complexity and awareness to that of the conventional stage revenger" (Intro., 41). Few moments in the production better bonded Anne Barton's analysis of Hamlet's dilemma with its realization in theater terms.

The soliloquies as a whole were treated by Barton and Pennington for exactly what they have become: well-known, eagerly anticipated set pieces. With the exception of the first ("O, that this too too sullied flesh"),[16] which began on an upstage bench and moved to the center of the stage's stage, the soliloquies were played at center, full-front as the solo tour-de-forces that nearly four centuries of great actors have made them. This was particularly true of the "To be or not to be" soliloquy, among the most difficult entrances an actor must make. There was a Barton once who might have altered the script to facilitate a more psychologically satisfying placement of the soliloquy, but in the theatrical context in which it was played, Pennington simply ran on, stopped at center, and began the soliloguy. *The Sunday Times* critic was bemused by the entrance, which he surmised may have been borrowed from ballet:

> Mr. Pennington leaps in from the wings, lands in the center of the stage and exclaims: "To be or not to be. *That* is the question!" Then he pauses a moment as if to say: *"There! I've said it."*[17]

The moment was not as facetious as the description suggests. Because it was consistent with the production's premise, the soliloquy played true, as did Pennington's use of a mask, discarded by the First Player, during the "rogue and peasant slave" soliloguy. The mask incidentally, was then left onstage by Hamlet and picked up by Claudius (Derek Godfrey) in the following scene. The king held the white, highly stylized mask over his heart during the "How smart a lash" speech (3.1. 49–54) in one of the production's most self-conscious moments.

Barton chose Pennington to play Hamlet because he wanted a prince who was a poet as well as an actor. Throughout the evening one was conscious of this Hamlet's enjoyment of the aesthetic and connotative value of words. This was perhaps most obvious in the "What a piece of work is a Man" speech in 2.2. Pennington began the address sitting against the prop trunk, but as he (and we) became entranced by the evocative power of the poetry, he was drawn to center stage. Pennington's Hamlet enjoyed words and coining a phrase even more. Words and phrases such as "caviar to the general" and "as adders fanged" were invariably "set off" as if in inverted commas. Audiences thus savoured afresh expressions dulled by overfamiliarity. Church says this is very much part of Barton's verse-speaking, at least for Shakespeare's most aesthetic characters such as Hamlet and Richard II:

> I do think that sometimes John encourages people to pick a word out. He's frightfully concerned, and I think he's very right, that one should be coining the phrases one uses. . . . John is famous for savouring an unusual phrase, which is fine if it doesn't hold up the work.

Much of the television show, "Playing Shakespeare," illustrates this element of the Barton verse-speaking technique.

There were other significant innovations by Barton and his company that extended beyond the theatrical motif. This recreation should not imply that the RSC reduced its exploration of *Hamlet* to a single issue (nor did Anne Barton's introduction, which does much to define the play's relationship to the dramatic tradition that preceded it.) Even without its application of a particular interpretation, the Stratford production would likely be memorable for at least two other "discoveries": Gertrude's relationship to the Ghost, and the personality of Polonius.

Under Barton's guidance, Barbara Leigh-Hunt's Queen Gertrude was a far more dominating figure than is perhaps customary. "The Mousetrap" incited her wrath more pointedly than the King's, which, thought Peter Jenkins, turns Claudius into another player king, "a usurper trying to live up to the part."[18] Her famous retort to Hamlet—"The lady doth protest too much methinks"— was sternly and aggressively said, nose-to-nose with Hamlet, a marked contrast to the meek evasions one usually hears. Barton himself may have heightened the Queen's displeasure by restructuring the Player Queen's speeches to underscore Gertrude's incestuous guilt. He placed the couplet "In second husband let me be accurst / None wed the second, but who killed the first" *after* its companion couplet three lines later. The revised exchange, which has lines 181–82 cut in the Barton acting edition, now reads:

Player Queen:	O, confound the rest!
	Such love must needs be treason to my breast.
Hamlet:	That's wormwood, wormwood.
Player Queen:	A second time I kill my huband dead,
	When second husband kisses me in bed.
	In second husband let me be accurst,
	None wed the second, but who killed the first.

Though reordering Shakespeare's words is a debatable practice, one can see the efficacy of Barton's revision, which produced a curious staccato in its repetition of "second." That, coupled wiht the Player Queen's recitation while kneeling at the feet of her adulterous counterpart, doubtless accounted for Gertrude's ire.

The intensity of the Hamlet-Gertrude clash in 3.2 made for even greater explosiveness in 3.4. From its outset the closet scene was indeed a clash of mighty opposites. The coup de théâtre, however, occurred midway in the scene. In what may be a theatrical first,[19] the Barton production permitted Gertrude to see the Ghost during the closet scene, or at least strongly suggested that she did so. As Hamlet knelt facing his mother, the Ghost entered behind her. Hamlet's fixation on the apparition prompted Gertrude, with an assist from her son at "Why, look you *there*" (3.4. 134), to turn and face the Ghost. As Old Hamlet reached out to touch her, she fainted, and the spirit stalked off into the upstage blackness. Church describes the rehearsal process that led to the innovation:

No one has ever brought forward a convincing explanation, except on a literary basis or a history of literary convention, as to why she doesn't see the

Ghost. . . . What Barbara said was, "I think she does see him" but what they [Barton, Pennington, and Leigh-Hunt] arrived at was—and I think this is quite brilliant—is that she *doesn't* see him when she says she doesn't see him, but Hamlet turns her head and makes her see him. Then something happens entirely in her mind . . . the Ghost approaches her and puts his hand on her as a sort of blessing . . . and she passes out. But when she comes round, Hamlet says "Didn't you see it?" and she says, "Oh, I don't know what you're talking about." She doesn't actually deny it. It doesn't interfere with text and you can make a very good case that she eventually did see the Ghost but that she certainly wouldn't admit to it. . . . It's extraordinary that she *doesn't* see him. And it is so extraordinarily obvious that surely every Gertrude has asked the question in rehearsal.

Of this RSC "act of textual defiance," Irving Wardle noted, "you can hear the ice cracking all round, but thanks to the preparation that has gone into it, the surface just holds." The bold choice reaped benefits for the remainder of the scene. The interplay between mother and son was especially warm (*not* in any of the Freudian implications of some twentieth-century productions[20]) as there was a sense of a "shared" experience between two similarly tormented humans. Barton further increased the intensity of the scene by splicing it to 4.1 and deleting the King's first speech. The Queen knelt numbly as Claudius entered her chamber, and because of what had just transpired in our presence, her line "Ah, mine own lord, what I have seen tonight" (4.1. 5) was especially potent.

The closet scene was notable, too, for its opening moments. The death of Polonius was interpreted differently from most productions, largely because Polonius himself had been interpreted differently throughout the play. In contrast to the two most popular methods at present of portraying the king's counselor (i.e., either as a ruthless manipulator whose power is founded on duplicity, or literally as a "foolish prating knave," hardly a fit counselor for the majesty of Denmark) Barton and Church sought a benevolent man. Church said Barton saw in Polonius's family in general, and in the old man in particular, "the one, good productive thing in the play which Hamlet destroys. His central position with me as Polonius in *Hamlet* is—which I shouldn't think anyone has ever told me before[21]—is that Polonius actually is the good old man that he is described as being by the Queen and the King. Not just a good statesman, but actually a genuinely good person." Thus when Polonius is killed by Hamlet, the Prince, the audience feels a genuine loss. Pennington cradled Polonius's dying body in his arms and nearly wept through the "wretched, rash, intruding fool" speech, which added greatly to the poignancy because it reflected the irony of the moment: Hamlet knows he has erred by killing a good man, meddler though he was, and recognizes his error will not go unpunished by the Divinity that shapes our ends. Church ascribes Polonius's meddling to an "actor's curiosity" about human nature: "His joy in the highways and byways of human nature eventually leads him to hiding behind arrasses to find out more about it, and it's hiding behind arrasses that kills him."

While Church's Polonius (which received the most enthusiastic critical acclaim of any in the company) worked well throughout most of the performance, the overwhelming benevolence of the character betrayed one of the most
problematic scenes in the play. One wonders, even in the most neutral productions, why Polonius—if he does care a jot about his daughter's welfare—does
not intercede when Hamlet abuses her during the nunnery scene. Pennington,
in an action more akin to the "boorish Hamlets," brutally slapped her face at
"it hath made me mad." Given Polonius's extreme concern in previous scenes,
it seemed inconceivable that so caring a father would not immediately rush
forth to protect his daughter. But Polonius and Claudius waited until Hamlet
had left the room *and* until Ophelia finished her "noble mind" soliloquy before
venturing forth. One questions the delay, particularly since Polonius and
Claudius, only partially hidden by the armor, were visible to a portion of the
audience. Church argued the point with Barton, who dismissed his objections
with the assumption that "people never ask the question." *"But they do,"*
emphasized Church, who cited discussions of the production with over eighty
student groups, virtually every one of which asked precisely that question.
Despite this instance when an otherwise thoughtful interpretation worked
against itself, one hopes the portrait will establish a benevolent precedent for
subsequent actors.[22]

If there was a common criticism of the production, it was of the apparent
lack of political ambience. Cuts were made to diminish the political thrust of
the tragedy. Anne Barton labels the Fortinbras subplot "a politic distraction" in
the play (Intro., 23) and the director concurred in his dimunition of the role.
Within Elsinore's walls there was also a sense that politics were a distraction.
For example, Barton cut Hamlet's catalogue of Claudius's sins in 5.2 (ll. 63–
70), which includes the Prince's complaint that the usurping king "popped in
between th'election and my hopes" When Hamlet finally smote Claudius in the
aborted fencing match, the court did not cry "Treason! Treason!" Barton cut
the line. He had also cut "the Court" throughout, save a couple of inconspicu-
ous attendants. With the exception of Voltemand and Cornelius (who doubled
as the usually anonymous lords who bring news of Ophelia's madness), there
was "no palace life going on around Hamlet. There was no sense of a court."[23]
Barton's decision to diminish the court's role seemed compatible with the
narrative focus of his production, which, for him, was the tragedy of two
families rather than one of the body politic. If he downplayed Hamlet's *social*
context, it was to accommodate more fundamental concerns that had themselves been diminished by nearly two decades of political activism. Also, Barton said that this choice to cut the political portions of the story was dictated by
purely practical considerations: he wanted to reduce the play's running time to
insure that his audience was out of the theater by eleven o'clock.

Irving Wardle found the production's "overwhelming virtue" to be "a
theoretical exploration of the play by a man who knows that no theory can
contain it." As surely as any essay on *Hamlet,* Barton's staging probed a point

of view and by most accounts probed it successfully. In the last analysis, what may indeed be the "overwhelming virtue" of the RSC's 1980 *Hamlet,* in deference to Mr. Wardle's perceptive commentary, was its ability to tread the narrow path between a purely academic exploration of *one* of the play's meanings and a realization of its narrative strengths. On occasion Barton has obscured the narrative lines of a play with an elaborate overlay of symbolism and stylization while testing a theory about its meaning. *Richard II* and *King John* are the most frequently cited examples. With *Hamlet,* however, he showed that a production could remain coherent on its own terms and still explore a major theoretical question.

9

Beyond Shakespeare:
Doctor Faustus (1974), *Perkin Warbeck* (1975), *The Pillars of the Community* (1977), *The Way of the World* (1978), *The School for Scandal* (1983), and *La Ronde* (1982)

John Barton is unique among contemporary British directors in that he has limited his directorial work almost exclusively to the plays of Shakespeare and the English Renaissance. Michael Bogdanov, an RSC and National Theatre director, feels that Barton's parochial interests are not without liability:

> Most directors have had a much more catholic background than John has. He's very rarified. John would benefit from doing theatre other than classic theatre. He wouldn't agree with this, but he would benefit by going away and relearning while working with somebody else who could give him another approach.[1]

Of late Barton has indeed extended his directorial vistas, and a brief survey of his non-Shakespearean work indicates his thematic interests.

At Cambridge Barton worked with dramatists other than Shakespeare, but even then his efforts were most clearly centered on the Elizabethan-Jacobean age. He achieved notable success with Marlowe's *Edward II*, which eventually transferred to London's Lyric Theatre. He also staged Jonson, Greene, and other of Shakespeare's contemporaries. Rarely, however, did he approach dramas of the modern era, other than original scripts written by classmates, a renowned version of Chekhov's *The Three Sisters* ("the most important thing I did at Cambridge"), and Anouilh's *Antigone*, the single play by an established twentieth-century playwright. Unlike his colleagues Peter Hall and Trevor Nunn, who have enhanced the RSC's reputation by staging the works of Pinter, O'Casey, and other moderns, Barton has—with the exception of Schnitzler—avoided twentieth-century playwrights: "I don't myself feel the same challenge with modern drama; its problems and opportunities seem to me more limited."[2] In a *Flourish* interview he established his preference for the classics:

> In order to handle something I feel strongly about . . . my instinct is to work within the framework of some existing myth or history. If I try to express or make sense of my own feelings about politics *in vacuo* I end up in a morass. This leads one to work within the formal confines (plot, diction, dialectical argument) of a classical text. . . . I feel that classic drama when it deals with politics and history can provide a sense of proportion about modern dilemmas which seems lacking in some of the extreme theories and esoteric practices of the twentieth-century theatre. When one throws out narrative, for example, one risks baffling the majority of the audience. They can't relate anymore. Strength of narrative, intensity of argument—these can still quicken a really diverse audience, despite social and educational divisions.[3]

Barton's comments here are useful, not only as a rationale for his predilection for classic dramas, but because they provide insight into his production choices in the contemporary theater. Barton's almost exclusive involvement with Shakespeare has also been dictated by practical considerations: "I've never had any wish to avoid other plays. It was just that one was usually needed to do the Shakespeare season. . . . For many years it was difficult to get directors for the Main House, or do Shakespeare—but that's changing now. I always felt an obligation to do it, but I'm quite happy to move away from it."[4]

In his early days at Stratford, Barton provided the RSC with non-Shakespearean scripts, primarily anthologies such as *The Hollow Crown, The Vagaries of Love,* and a macabre collection of poetic commentaries on death, *Respice Finem.* Also, drawing on his "First Stage" experience with the BBC, he and Hall planned an epic version of medieval plays. A 1966 announcement in *The Bristol Evening Post* suggests what might have been: "The final Stratford productions this year were to have been an adaptation of the major medieval miracle plays into two plays, prepared by John Barton and directed by Peter Hall or Peter Brook. But work on the massive text is not far enough advanced, so these productions are postponed until next year."[5] The following year Hall assumed the directorship of the National Theatre and the project never reached fruition. For some years Barton harbored the notion of doing the medieval cycle, but has lately reconsidered the project: "It's technically frightfully difficult to do the medieval style and the rhyme scheme . . . and I question whether doing the cycles in this day isn't quaint." He does, however, acknowledge that the National Theatre's recent staging of *The Passion Play* showed that there is indeed theatrical life in medieval drama and he may yet mount a medieval cycle.

Barton did provide the RSC with a script for *The Second Shepherd's Play,* adding sections from the Wakefield cycle to the traditional script to enhance the Christmas story. In an inventive touch, he arranged for the Angel Gabriel, in early music hall style, to teach the audience *"Gloria in Excelsis Deo"* with the aid of a medieval song sheet which he unrolled from the hollow of his staff.[7] Tony Church, who directed the play at Barton's request in 1964, calls the play "a joyous experience . . . the words and imagination of it all." Barton looks back on the adaptation as among the best scripts he has produced in his "play-writing" career.

Trevor Nunn established his reputation with the RSC in 1966 by staging Cyril Tourneur's difficult and macabre melodrama, *The Revenger's Tragedy.* The production was hailed as Stratford's most remarkable non-Shakespearean work to date: "Certainly the effect was to reveal a play which commanded greater stature than anyone had supposed."[8] A portion of its success belongs to Barton, who adapted the text from a 1965 edition by Gamini Salgado.[9] Critics ascribed the playability of the text to Barton's editorial skills.[10] Barton cut the verbose script, altered the scene order for continuity and clarity, and added about 150 lines of his devising, most of which were necessitated by actors' requests for clarification of troublesome passages. One insertion in particular exemplifies Barton's skill in composing classical verse. In this exchange between Spurio and the Duchess (3.5.120) Barton devised a conceit appropriate to the drama and the characters, who are devious, self-centered and lustful:

Duchess: So: let's try out [other] countries
                  And learn new ways to climb.
Spurio: Aye, to the mountain.
Duchess: There's many ways.
Spurio: Yet all meet i' the shrine
                  Where torches kiss, thus, i' the fiery circle.
Duchess: Hot brands should be thus brandished and enmixt.
Spurio: And cold sheets warm'd thus by the twain betwixt.
                  This place is cold and craveth such fire.
Duchess: Cold as the icicle i' the old Duke's bed,
                  Whose touch is loathsome to me. Come, you're afire.
                  Here is a vault for your vaulting.

Stanley Wells found Barton's textual contributions to the production useful because they "add to the cruelty and sexuality of the original text. They do not, it seems to me, add to its comedy or increase the element of self-parody that Tourneur himself allows to his characters." *The Revenger's Tragedy,* Barton's most ambitious revision since *The Wars of the Roses,* solidified his reputation as both textual scholar and script doctor; it also satisfied his appetite to write plays for the time being.

Barton's first non-Shakespearean directorial work with the RSC came in 1974. To be sure, he did not stray far from Shakespeare: he selected Marlowe's *Dr. Faustus.* And fittingly, in a year in which he busied himself revising Shakespeare's texts (*King John* and *Cymbeline*), he significantly altered Marlowe's script.

When *Faustus* opened at the Aldwych in September 1974—after previews in Nottingham, Newcastle, and the Edinburgh Festival—Barton inserted a prominent note in the program to explain the "new" script: the two extant texts—the "A" text (1604) and the "B" (1616)—have led scholars to conclude that of the play's original 3,120 lines, only 825 are Marlowe's. Barton combined the two versions into a working text that included slightly more than 1,100 lines from the originals, 800 of them Marlowe's. The excisions included most of the comic subplots because, Barton thought, "they tend to trivialize the tone of the play itself."[11] The cuts were offset by the addition of about 550 lines from Marlowe's source, *The History of the Damnable Life of Dr. Faustus*, commonly called the English Faust-Book: "There is hardly a passage in the Marlowe sections of the play which do not derive from the Faust-Book. Thus I believe that many passages from it can illuminate Marlowe's text and accord it better than can many of the non-Marlovian sections we cut in this production." For example, in Barton's eleventh scene, Beelzebub introduces the final action, which covers Faust's last three months on earth, by reading from the Faust-Book:

He lived an epicurrish and swinish life. . . . And so time ran way with Faustus, as the hour glass, and now was Good Friday past, and he had but a day and a night to come of his four and twenty years.[12]

Elsewhere Barton added some few lines of his own based on incidents from the source material. The most notable of these was a seductive encounter between Faustus and the Duchess of Vanholt, a bawdy scene in which the Doctor uses his powers to seduce the pregnant woman by concocting an aphrodisiac. Theatrically, it was one of the most satisfying scenes in the production. Barton also added a tag to the final speech in the play, something about "learned scholars having more to say about Faustus' life and death."[13] The actual description of Faust's death was derived from a contemporary description of Marlowe's own death to draw parallels between the playwright and his most famous creation.

Critical reaction to Barton's revisions was mixed. J. C. Trewin judged them "amply justified,"[14] while Michael Billington proclaimed that they transformed "Marlowe's broken-backed theological treatise into a thrilling theatrical event" and that the Barton text had "paradoxically given the play an astonishing evenness of tone."[15] Anthony Seymour admitted that the revision was indeed arresting, but he still believed that such editing is "a practice to be deplored" because "it becomes the conception of a modern company, not that of a Renaissance freethinker."[16] The most articulate condemnation of Barton's revision came from John Barber in *The Daily Telegraph*.[17] Though he admitted that the new text achieved a consistency of style and language more accessible to moderns, Barber offered several worthy objections:

First, no one knows exactly how much Marlowe wrote, hence it is presumptuous for a modern editor-director to revise the text merely on the supposition that most of it is not Marlowe's anyway. Barber cites Sir Walter Gregg, Goethe, and T. S. Eliot to support his thinking.

Barber next argued that the comic scenes should not have been cut and replaced with incidents "from a source the poet knew, doubtless considered, and certainly rejected." Finally, Barton's alterations and production effects diminished "the ambiguity at the heart of the play." Barber believed Barton's interpretation reduced Faustus from a humanistic freethinker to "a deluded nut, snivelling over a toy model of the nativity, and not a magnificent over-reacher doomed to the fate of Icarus."

Rather than exploring the power and the use (or abuses) to which new learning can be put, Barton focused on the psychological elements of Faust's dilemma. An Anne Barton program note suggested that Mephistophilis's line— "Why *this* is hell, nor am I out of it"—evoked a "curiously modern, Sartean sense of a state of mind." Thus the director confined his action to Faustus's study, designed by Michael Annals as an extension of the doctor's mind. Barton justified his decision on purely textual grounds: ". . . bearing in mind that the bulk of the scenes most certainly written by Marlowe are set in Faustus' study, I decided to present the whole play as taking place there." An unnamed critic for *The Manchester Evening News* found the narrowed setting, depleted of the broader comedy, "a bit mean for an entertainment centered around the Catholic universe of Heaven and Hell."[18] In another article, Barber found Barton's focus reductive and claimed that it "presents the drama as a grim cautionary tale rather than a tragedy of divine discontent."[19] Others found the innovation revealing. Confining the action, said *The Sunday Telegraph*, evoked an "hallucinatory" aura for the play and rendered the protagonist in more contemporary terms.[20]

To suggest the workings of Faust's mind, Barton devised a metaphor to visualize his consciousness. The Good and Bad Angels were played, not by actors, but by hand puppets that Faustus himself (Ian McKellen) manipulated. McKellen, who studied ventriloquism, projected his voice into a black voodoo doll for the Bad Angel, a white Christmas cherub for the Good. Again Barton's choice was explained by his wife's program essay: ". . . the Good and Bad Angels are objectively real emissaries of Faustus' personality; voices from within his own mind." The director originally intended for McKellen to play both Faustus and Mephistophilis, but the idea was too complicated to translate satisfactorily into theatrical terms.[21]

Puppets were integral throughout the play: thirteen of the original fifty roles were "played" by life-size Bunraku puppets manipulated by black-cowled devils. Patrick Tucker (Barton's co-director) traced the history of *Faustus* as a puppet play in a program note. Apparently the Thirty Years' War created a shortage of actors and puppets became the mainstay of live entertainment. Given the magical and mysterious subject matter of Faustus, the play became a popular vehicle for German *Puppenspeils;* "certainly in Germany the *Faust* puppet play is as popular and traditional as *Punch and Judy* is in England."[22] Furthermore, Barton staged *Faustus* at a time when he was relying on blatantly theatrical devices in *Richard II* and *King John,* thus it is not surprising that the director employed puppets.

The puppets were not used indiscriminately; thematically they illustrated in purely visual terms that Faust's desires were illusory. The Seven Deadly Sins were portrayed by puppets to show "the grotesqueries of vice more than any mortal could."[23] More impressive was Helen of Troy, "no more than a blonde wig, mask, and nightdress borne in by Mephistophilis."[24] Faust performed a bizarre dance of death with the doll, in effect a shrouded corpse, which thereby made the seduction scene "a chilling act of necrophelia."[25] Though most observers applauded the inventive use of puppets, others were less sure they were a judicious choice. Barber argued that making the vision of Helen "a paltry marionette sterilizes the ineluctable lure of flesh-and-blood sensuality." Garry O'Connor, writing for *Plays and Players,* offers one of the most cogent commentaries on Barton's puppets:

> Faustus and Mephistophilis may more easily be envisaged as puppets than Helen of Troy, for it is Faustus' soul that is being jerked on the end of a string, not the nature of temptation. Although use of such an interesting and imaginative device on the stage is to be applauded, the puppets are a further contradiction in style. It is as if Baudelaire's debauched images were to be removed in favor of Sartre's aphorisms.[26]

Faustus's satanic spirits were also questioned. Lines normally spoken by the Chorus of Learned Doctors were reassigned to the Devils. The play's moral was spoken by Lucifer himself. "Contradiction," wrote Anne Barton, "is the informing principle of this tragedy," and the director's decision to have the Devil warn the audience not to sin embodied the spirit of contradiction. Barber thought the choice was Faustian in its arrogance: "Perversion can go no further than this . . . all the lovely ambivalence of the play is lost." Trewin, on the contrary, thought the ending "more menacing for the implacable authority of the three devils." Robert Cushman felt Barton's play was darker than even Marlowe intended:

> . . . in [the Devils] mouths the chorus' traditional exhortations and moralizations sound decidedly wry. The intention may have been only to provide ironic *frisson;* but if taken seriously, it suggests that the whole moral system which Faustus transgresses is diabolically controlled.[27]

Barton's *Faustus* placed extraordinary demands on McKellen, who was playing his first role with the RSC. He came to the company after his stint with the Actor's Company expressly to work with Barton, whom McKellen believed would extend his range.[28] He and Barton chose a decidedly anti-Marlovian rendering of Faust; rather than a larger-than-life "overreacher," he was a modern man doomed by wrong choices, "a sad case of existential decay."[29] McKellen refuted critics who found this modern reading ignoble:

> ... I don't find him a very noble person. His intentions may be high-minded early on in the play, but they are very soon corrupted, and he falls very quickly into something much less than his intentions. That's true of many great figures, Coriolanus, Macbeth. They may be striving to be better than they are, but it's in the nature of their failing to reach the heights that we understand and care about them.[30]

Though opinion of Barton's *Doctor Faustus* was divided, the production remains among his most provocative. It is quintessentially a Barton work in its textual adjustments, strongly theatrical base, and controversial yet enlightening interpretation. Trewin summarizes the production's import to Barton's career and style: "*Doctor Faustus* is inventive and scholarly: it shows what a man of the theatre John Barton can be."

The following year Barton and Barry Kyle staged John Ford's rarely seen *Perkin Warbeck* in the RSC's studio theater, The Other Place. The play, which deals with a pretender to the throne of Henry VII, is a study of the nature of the public king and the private self, themes that Barton explored in *Richard II* and *King John*. Michael Coveney's *Financial Times* review noted the similarities in approach between the Shakespeare and Ford plays:

> Warbeck casts himself as a martyr to the idea of monarchy, and just as Mr. Barton has discovered striking theatrical imagery for that "idea" in *Richard II, King John* and, indeed, *Cymbeline,* so he does here. With the aid of mock processions, elaborate cloaks, and token banners we are transported to a regal side show in which to "appear" a prince is as good, almost as to be one.[31]

Among his least known directorial projects, *Perkin Warbeck* is significant because it reflects favored Barton themes: appearance-reality, role-playing and the overlap between life and the theater, and guilt and expiation. Asked if these themes have led him to work on selected plays, Barton answered, "I think it's probably true, but I don't think it's very conscious. I don't conceptualize a great deal; it's something that happens when I'm actually working."[32]

Of late Barton has shown a special interest in the guilt-expiation theme. In the summer of 1977, for instance, he staged Ibsen's early play, *The Pillars of the Community*, at the Aldwych Theatre. Among other things, the drama deals with communal guilt and the rot that tears at the fabric of a smug, self-satisfied society in its depiction of an unscrupulous boat builder who provides profits to his small community at the expense of innocent lives. Barton rarely uses the stage to promote political beliefs, so he was drawn to the play not by its indictment of misguided capitalism but by the characters' individual and collective guilt.

Pillars of the Community was a significant production on several accounts. It was the first professional staging of the play in London in fifty years, and it marked the one-hundredth anniversary of the play's composition, for which Barton asked Inga-Stina Ewbank to provide the RSC with a new translation. Most important, it was Barton's first professional staging of a non-Elizabethan-Jacobean play, his first RSC attempt at a "contemporary" prose play.

The cast was headed by Ian McKellen (Bernick), Judi Dench (Lona Hessel), and Tony Church (Rorlund, the schoolmaster). Mike Gwilym, another principal, believed that Barton's primary contribution to the production was the creation of "the sort of world and the sort of atmosphere in which the events could take place."[33] Critics suggested that work's strength was the manner in which the director and his actors overcame the deficiencies of the text: "John Barton's production is so firmly based and the entire cast so expert at manipulating details of gesture so as to serve the whole that such considerations [of the play's weaknesses] do not enter the mind."[34] Only David Zane Mairowitz felt Barton's approach to be weak: ". . . Barton chooses to concentrate on the character dilemmas, thereby playing directly into the drama's weakness. *Pillars of the Community* here becomes the lonely pilgrimage into truth of one previously corrupt man—its most obvious and trite and poorly constructed level—which minimizes the thorough ruthlessness of the main character."[35]

Mairowitz may have underestimated Barton's design. The ending of the play—in which Bernick confesses his duplicity—was not necessarily played as a journey through purifying fire that puts Bernick on the road to truth. John Peter praised Barton for suggesting that Bernick's confession need not be the cathartic exorcism many suspected: "Under its tone of moral fervor lies a landscape of personal and general corruption exposed beyond possibility of forgiveness or cover-up."[36] Peter compared the ending in tone and attitude to Barton's purposefully ambiguous handling of the finale of *Measure for Measure*. Other critics suggested that McKellen's reading of the speech—punctuated by conspiratorial glances to the audience—was not a confession but another "con job" comparable to Richard Nixon's infamous "Checkers speech."[37] Such interpretative extremes suggest that the production's finale indeed captured the ambiguity proposed by Ewbank's program note: "The ending of the play leaves us doubting how far its chief Pillar has actually been transformed by the Spirit of Truth."[38]

The following year Barton tackled another non-Shakespearean drama that also dealt with another tightly knit, morally obtuse society: William Congreve's Restoration comedy, *The Way of the World.* It should not go unnoticed that Barton's RSC offering in the main house that season was *Love's Labour's Lost,* also about an artificial, wit-oriented society. Michael Pennington played

Berowne in the Shakespeare comedy, Mirabell in Congreve's. The actor recalls Barton's comments about the approach the latter production should take. The director cautioned his cast to remember the society for which the play was written—"vicious, dirty, divided, and dirt-ridden"[39]—qualities hidden beneath a façade of elegance, gaiety, and wit.

As with Ibsen's play, Barton was again confronted by a script notorious for its plot complexities, which Anne Barton outlined in the RSC program. In particular, she cited the complicated relationship(s) "both formal and unacknowledged, which binds these people together in groupings so intricate and closely knit as to be claustrophobic."[40] The critics were unanimous in their praise of Barton's delineation of plot and character relationships. Eric Shorter proclaimed the production "a triumph of balance and integrity," emphasizing that "no one is usually expected to follow Congreve's plot, not even the cast. This time, Mr. Barton makes us believe that we are doing so."[41]

Though *The Way of the World* is among the finest comedies in the English language, the production also recognized its darker side. Irving Wardle informed *Times* readers that "it has been left to John Barton . . . to examine our greatest prose comedy for traces of sober meaning—the result is by far the best I've seen."[42] Pennington relates his director's intentions as they began work on the play:

> In *The Way of the World* John was very concerned that there is always something left out at the end. . . . Mrs. Fainall is left out. The tying up of loose ends is miraculous, but it does leave one person out in the cold. That's what John wished to establish in the play—the whole question of Restoration values and those brilliant people with their squalid morals.[43]

The production therefore avoided the garrishly artificial mannerisms frequently associated with Restoration comedy. The sets and costumes (though elaborate) were muted, to suit the more naturalistic playing style. Benedict Nightingale found Barton's deromanticized version stimulating and modern: "Barton banishes gratuitous style and show . . . and offers instead a group of plausible worldlings in plausibly domestic surroundings trying simultaneously to hide and fulfill desires both pecuniary and sexual. . . . It might be London now, a guileful wrangling place where it is dangerous to display emotional vulnerability, and unsophisticated and embarrassing to advertise any but the most formal affection."[44]

Though most observers applauded the forthrightness of the production, there were reservations. The less obviously comic attitude was criticized by those who preferred their Restoration comedy done more traditionally: " . . . it imperturbably and fatally presumes to demonstrate overtly the seriousness of Congreve's satire. The glum dance with which [Barton] ends the proceedings is a saraband for the death of comedy."[45]

Pennington's Mirabel was played differently than is perhaps customary. He did not aggressively compete with Millimant in their verbal duels, but "instead he relaxed in a cool acceptance of his own powers and concentrates on the lover rather than the intriguer. He knows he will win in the end. . . . The unnerving thing about Mr. Pennington's performance is its apparent sincerity."[46] The actor suggested that his work with Barton on *Troilus and Cressida* two years earlier helped his perception of Mirabel. He refuted those who questioned the understatement of the role:[47]

> I think that if you made Mirabell as much of a peacock, as extrovert and brilliant as the people surrounding him, you'd have no anchor for the play at all. His function with Millamant is not that of two brilliant wits competing— it's a case of a brilliant woman and a foil, a man who bides his time.[48]

Judi Dench's Millimant did much to eradicate memories of Edith Evans's portrait of Congreve's heroine. J. C. Trewin offered her acting his highest praise: "Judi Dench has created the part for our stage. . . . It is the living Millimant, not for one moment the self-conscious exercise in coquetry we have often had to substitute."[49] Hers was a thoroughly modern interpretation—"an anticipation of Shaw's New Woman, demanding with quiet insistence her right to independence and dignity within marriage."[50] The justly famous "proposal scene" (act 4), in which the sparring lovers draw up a contract of marriage, was judged "the jewel of the production" by Wardle. Furthermore, the years of training in verse-speaking at the RSC acting studio brought extraordinarily high praise to the company for its manipulation of Congreve's language: "I have never seen this play performed with such crisp clarity, nor heard its language . . . spoken with such lucid perfection."[51]

In January 1983 Barton returned to eighteenth-century British high comedy when he staged Sheridan's *The School for Scandal* at London's Haymarket Theatre, a notable production if for no other reason that it marks his first professional directorial work outside the RSC. Much of the cast was composed of veteran Barton performers from the RSC: Donald Sinden (Sir Peter Teazle), Sebastian Shaw, Beryl Reid, and Judy Buxton. It was Sinden who pressed Barton to undertake the play. Barton accepted, partly because of his "devotion" to Sinden (who had served him well as Malvolio, Benedick, and others), but mostly because he was attracted to the "Shakespeare" in Sheridan: "(The play) has that mixture, which you get in Shakepeare, of naturalistic language muddled up with heightened, formal, antithetical language which has to be relished and savoured if it is to communicate itself."[52] On the whole, however, *The School for Scandal* is not a play that "excited my inner juices because it is not a play of great depth and resonance."

For his production of Sheridan's comedy, Barton added both the Prologue and Epilogue inserted by Garrick and Coleman for the original performance. Barton favored the Epilogue because he felt it diminishes the sentimentality of the play's contrived ending. Throughout the work, Barton said he tried to imbue Sheridan's characters with more humanity than eighteenth-century comedy characteristically allows; he felt his best work involved clarifying the relationship between Sir Peter and Lady Teazle. To achieve his ends, Barton borrowed techniques that had served him well in his earlier work. He infused a Chekovian melancholia into the script, particularly for the Teazle scenes (climaxed by a superb "screen scene" that hinted of tragic recognition in the extraordinarily long silence that followed the collapse of Sir Joseph's screen) and for the customarily rowdy drinking scene of act 3. The understated playing style caused the production to receive little enthusiasm from the critics. Nightingale dismissed it as "a pretty shallow, showy production,"[53] while Wardle found it "a piece of slow practice," performed with perhaps too much "measured deliberation."[54] Nonetheless the play was a popular success; it was revived at the Duke of York's Theatre for a long West End run in late 1983, and scheduled for a tour of the Continent in 1984.

These productions, and the 1980 epic, *The Greeks* (see chapter 10), are yet pre-twentieth-century works. Only with Arthur Schnitzler's *La Ronde* has Barton directed a play written in this century (1903). The bittersweet comedy of love and sex—and its provocative analysis of the distinction between the two—has long fascinated Barton, who calls it "a minor masterpiece." He had wanted to stage it since his Cambridge days, but an unusual copyright restriction did not allow his dream to become a reality until January 1982. Barton worked from his own adaptation (which he wrote from a literal translation by Sally Davies, wife of Barton's RSC colleague, director Howard Davies), and rendered a production that explored the play's Chekhovian elements, which, as one should expect, drew him to the Viennese comedy—"loneliness, lying, relationships." To the Chekhovian wistfulness, Barton added a theatrical element of high stylization; for example, the scene changes that marked the ten trysts were choreographed Viennese ballets. The production received mixed notices. Its theatricality and poignancy were applauded—"Barton makes the comedy broader than one might have expected, but the dying fall can be heard all the way through"[55]—but it was ultimately dismissed for failing to offer "any coherent view of the material,"[56] perhaps a criticism aimed more at the play than the production.[57] Nonetheless, the project offered hope that Barton's first effort with a twentieth-century play will induce him to investigate other dramatists of this age. John Whiting's 1961 drama, *The Devils,* will be staged by Barton in The Pit at the Barbican Centre in the summer of 1984, and certainly one can expect a Chekhov in the near future, but—as we shall see in the next chapter—his current fascination with myth and making modern myths may forestall Barton-the-Director from working on plays created in this time. It is more likely that Barton-the-Playwright will add to the chronicle of twentieth-century drama.

10
"To Sing a Song That Old Was Sung": *The Greeks* (1980)

Throughout this survey of his career, it has been apparent that John Barton has long been at war with himself: the director has often had to confront the aspiring playwright who is steeped in classical literature and the myths from which it is drawn: "I *had* to rewrite these texts that I came upon. They have to do with some mythical depths in myself. I don't understand it, and I don't know why. . . ."[1] With *The Greeks*, produced by the RSC at the Aldwych Theatre in January 1980, the warring strains in Barton fused to create what he considers the most important project of his career. "Important" because, first, it provided theater audiences an unparalleled opportunity to experience both the high drama and the innate theatricality of the Trojan War from a modern perspective. Not since *The Wars of the Roses* has the RSC, nor Barton, tackled an enterprise of such magnitude. In many ways *The Greeks* was a more formidable challenge. Unlike *The Wars of the Roses*—and even the RSC's latest epic, Trevor Nunn's *Nicholas Nickleby*—both of which at least derive from a single source with which most audiences have some familiarity, the compilation of many plays by different authors with varied philosophies was indeed a Protean task. One critic believed that Barton's project was more significant than *The Wars*: "*The Greeks* is superior (as well as more necessary than) Mr. Barton's previous essay, *The Wars of the Roses*. As a production it is less accomplished—which is forgivable; there is no tradition to work from."[2]

Second, and perhaps more important here, *The Greeks* satisfied a creative urge that has driven Barton for over a quarter century: "I found something that was crucially right for me. I was dealing with something that affected me deeply. . . . At Cambridge I tried to work out my religious beliefs but got absolutely no where. I suppose that came out twenty-five years later in *The Greeks.*" For Barton, *The Greeks*—and the sources that inspired his adaptation—became a liberating experience that helped him define a personal philosophy of life and provided him with a direction in which to channel his creative energies. In theatrical terms, *The Greeks* was a major climax in Barton's personal drama, a recognition of what his past career has meant, a reversal of the writing block that has stifled his goals for years.

Since his Cambridge days he has been drawn to classic myths because they

209

give this age "a series of political and human archetypes which we can still recognize."[3] Despite his medieval sensibilities, Barton felt that the Greek material was more immediate to twentieth-century audiences: "It is more fertile and resonant in the modern sense in a way the medieval isn't. . . . There is something wonderfully healthy about the Greek material." Furthermore, from a purely theatrical perspective, the Greeks offered Barton elements that appeal to him as a stage director: "What I love in the material, and what I tried to distill in the version, is that there is something wonderfully simple and direct about 'I'm unhappy, I'm happy.' 'What is truth?' 'What is good and evil?' that appeals to one. It's got the simplicity and sense of the medieval cycles. I tried to keep *The Greeks* simple, yet complex and reverberant."

Barton has long wanted to stage a number of the original Greek tragedies; *The Bacchae* and the Oedipus trilogy topped his list. In the early days of the RSC, he gathered members of the company during the 1965 Stratford season to explore the classic world with studio productions in different styles, exercises, discussions, debates, all leading to great enthusiasm but no public performance. The winter (1965) edition of *Flourish* contained a short "filler" article about a company workshop that presaged work to be completed fifteen years later:

> This year, under the direction of John Barton, all energies will be focused on one major undertaking: an exploration of the Greek experience. Barton, who for weeks has been hidden behind mountains of scholarly tomes and translations, wants to cover the full spectrum—not just the plays, but Platonic dialogues, science, religion, philosophy, cosmology.[4]

From this material Barton devised another anthology piece, "The Peloponnesian Wars," which "tried to examine political man more closely by incorporating within it a Socratic dialogue, *The Alcibiades*."[5] The document is important because it perhaps best defines Barton's political philosophy. Barton does not subscribe to any of the current "-isms" on the political spectrum, but rather considers himself a Thucydidean. His philosophy is summarized in a speech that he wrote into the early pages of "The Poloponnesian Wars"; it occurs during a debate among the Athenians about the desirability of entering into war with Sparta. The italicized passages were written by Barton; the others came from the original Greek sources:

> *In theory, politics are concerned with disposing events. Unfortunately, in practice, events happen first, and politics becomes the art of making the best of them and trying to undo harm already done. We are all apt to act for the moment, and it is not until we suffer or are plunged into chaos that we begin to think of ways out. We all know that things have gradually gone wrong since the Persian Wars, but we believe that nothing has happened which is necessarily fatal, and which cannot be dealt with by reasonable discussion. We* urge you, *therefore,* while both *sides are* still free to make sensible decisions, *to* settle our differences by arbitration.[6]

Barton's career has been marked by productions of plays that illustrate the dangers of violating the spirit of these lines: *Troilus and Cressida* and *The Greeks* are the foremost examples. In 1967 Barton and David Jones staged an "Adlwych Sunday Night" production of "The Peloponnesian Wars," to which Jones added a condensed version of the Fulbright hearings on Viet Nam.

In these explorations of Greek material, Barton was as concerned about the form in which they were presented as the content of the material. His encounters with traditionally staged Greek works left him certain that he and his actors needed to explore new forms:

> I agree that everything the Greeks did is pretty well dead for us: masks, men playing women's parts, buskins, the vast area, the singing and dancing. What I'm trying to do [with *The Greeks*] is to tell the story in our tradition, not ape what we know of theirs. One of the reasons I want to do *The Greeks* is because I've always been dissatisfied when I've actually seen performances of their plays. I've never really been happy because the production style and the acting seemed inflated and tried to make something cosmic and earnest out of the material that was much simpler and lighter.[7]

Barton's work on *Troilus and Cressida* in 1968 and 1976 fueled his desire to coalesce the sprawling story of the Trojan War into a unified dramatic experience. He filled notebooks with Greek plays, both edited versions of the Attic masters and some of his own writing. In 1977 he hinted at the frustrations of devising a playable Greek script, but received little encouragement from his RSC colleagues. Nunn and Terry Hands warned him of the liabilities of such a project, intimating that Greek plays in the modern theater are "ghastly."[8] But Barton persevered and with the help of Kenneth Cavander, a Greek scholar, translator, and poet-playwright, after six attempts produced a mammoth script, consisting of ten plays tracing the decline of the great civilization because of the atrocities of the Trojan War.

From the outset Barton was keen that the newly wrought script avoid the "elaborate, poetic, and ornate" style one associates with Greek drama, a style he feels "probably derives from the high poetic idiom of *The Orestia*."[9] Barton preferred the swiftness and terseness of Euripides. Cavender told Barton that it is difficult to translate the Greek idiom without expanding it because "the immediate sensual experience of hearing and speaking this verse as a native tongue is forever lost to us. When the words out of which it is constructed are translated literally, or line by line, they come out . . . disconcertingly flat."[10] Barton described the language of the finished product in a *Sunday Times* interview:

> What we've gone for is a very terse, chatty style, pared of imagery or ornateness. I've chucked out the heightened because I've always found the heightened a wallow, a self-indulgence. If characters moan about their great

suffering, that is not a moving experience in the theatre. It is something boring and dead. I suspect it.[11]

In the television special, "Playing Shakespeare," Barton further instructs his actors and his television audience about the need to moderate emotional outbursts, a lesson he applies to Shakespeare and Greek work in equal measure: "If the actor lets his emotions carry him away, we [the audience] will start to *observe* him rather than to *share* with him." The precept dictated his writing for *The Greeks,* and Barton cites Iphigenia's last speech in the cycle as an important example of what he tried to achieve:

> O Artemis and you gods
> Who may or may not be wise,
> I have suffered enough.
> So has my brother.
> Look, look on us
> And on all human people.
> Please take away our hatred.
> Please take away our anguish,
> Please take away our fear.
> Please heal my brother
> And make me whole again.
> Let me live in the world
> As a free and loving woman,
> Sharing some good man's bed
> And let me give milk to my son.
> Give us back our sureness.
> Give us back our courage.
> We search and we know nothing.
> We fight and we are defeated.
> We suffer and it dulls us.
> We are brief . . . but you endure.[12]

Of the speech Barton says, "I think I caught it [i.e., the simplicity of emotion] as a writer. It is cool on the surface, not inflated, not obviously passionate, but it is very emotive." Generally the language was praised for precisely the qualities Barton sought and Cavander achieved. Billington devoted a paragraph of his *Guardian* review to the language of *The Greeks,* praising it because it is always specific and concrete. He offered a side-by-side comparison of a speech from the New Penguin edition of *Andromache* and Cavander's efforts to illustrate his point. The speech is by Thetis, the sea nymph, to ancient Peleus. In the Penguin edition she invites him to "wait until I come out of the sea with fifty dancing nymphs to escort you home." Cavander and Barton amplify her command theatrically:

Do you remember? Where you wooed me long ago
And where you made me happy.
And where we will dance the wedding dance
And I will turn myself
Into a thousand creatures
Fishes, sea-beasts, serpents
That roll and revel and wriggle
And you shall be lord of them all.

(*Andromache*, 266)

Billington judged the latter version superior because it "incorporates a sense of recollected happiness and sensual invitation."[13] Other lines were perhaps too terse and self-consciously rendered:

They cut the meat
From the hands and feet
And gave it to my father to eat.

(*Agamemnon*, 150)

More than the language, Barton was interested in the great tales themselves: "The narrative excitement is terrific, which is one of my reasons for doing the whole myth."[14] Barton was concerned that the present generation has lost contact with these myths and devised *The Greeks* to remedy this cultural gap:

It is quite easy to find intelligent and informed people to whom the names of Agamemnon and Orestes mean nothing. It was this that gave me the idea of putting together a cycle of diverse material that would tell their story in full. As far as I know this story has not been told before in one single dramatic work. . . . We wanted to tell the story as clearly and simply as possible. . . . The narrative is, we hope, the thing.[15]

Barton hoped to present the entire cycle in a single day when the occasion permitted, yet he wanted each play to stand by itself dramatically. Hence, generous cutting, editing, and rewriting of the originals became necessary. To provide exposition and to bridge the gap between plays, Barton found it necessary to write one play himself (*Achilles*). The ten plays in the ultimate acting edition were divided according to a general theme and subject matter:

Part I: *The Wars* (which deals with the theme of Sin)
    1. *Iphigenia in Aulis* (Euripides)
    2. *Achilles* (from Homer, written by Barton)
    3. *The Trojan Women* (Euripides)
Part II: *The Murders* (which deals with the theme of Punishment)
    1. *Hecuba* (Euripides)

Barton cites the Greeks themselves as the first great adapters and rearrangers of the Homeric myths, and he noted that "Euripides, in particular, was famous, or notorious, for his startling adaptations of the traditional myths. . . . If *The Greeks* has an overall tone, I hope it is his."[16] Because Barton approached the Greek myths with the intention of heightening the humanity of the characters and exploring the fallibility of the gods, it was natural that he should rely most heavily on the Euripidean viewpoint, since his plays most deflate the overblown qualities of Greek tragedy that troubled Barton. Nightingale questioned the degree to which the production was actually Euripidean:

> . . . what disturbs me most is the extent to which Barton amplifies what is, admittedly, the cycle's running debate on the nature of the gods, making the characters' skepticism more explicit and categorical than it properly should be. . . . What we're left with is not Aeschylus . . . and his customary attitude to the gods. . . . We are certainly not offered Sophocles . . . his priestly belief in an inscrutable cosmic justice is nowhere to be found. Nor do we quite get Euripides. . . . Rather we have a contemporary agnostic's attempt to refashion Euripides in his own furrowed, flustered image.[17]

Barton acknowledges that the critics are not without justification in some of their reservations about *The Greeks,* especially about the "debasing" of the gods. He feels it was a "good idea which I did wrong. I wanted the trilogy to be about myth getting debased; therefore I quite deliberately undercut myself. In performance we went too far." Mike Gwilym, who played both Achilles and Orestes in the production, confirms that "by the end John was coming round to thinking maybe he'd gone too far," but cites Apollo's speech in *Orestes* as a confirmation of the Euripidean viewpoint.

In actuality, Barton placed *Iphigenia in Taurus* last in his sequence to blunt the cynicism: the cycle ended with the reunion of Orestes with Iphigenia and the two led the company in a dance of healing which suggested that the Greeks had survived the chaos and looked forward to better times. Billington maintained that the strength of the production was its restorative elements that expose "the running sore of human conflict but that finally resolve it in a plea for balance, harmony and order," themes central to Barton's political philosophy. Perhaps the most quoted line from the production was Athene's admonition to the strife-ridden factions in *Iphigenia in Taurus:*

You must find a way
Between freedom and compulsion.
You must accept that
Order, harmony, and meaning
Only come to men in fragments.

In his comparison of *The Wars of the Roses* with *The Greeks,* Irving Wardle noted the events of the former happened "as one damn thing after another: it had an 'it' construction." With *The Greeks,* "It is always 'because.' "[18] The opening line of the cycle is "Who is to blame?" In context, the chorus is discussing the creation of the world, but the question reverberates throughout the ten plays. By the conclusion, it is painfully apparent that everyone is to blame, yet no one is to blame—a paradox suggested by Apollo himself to Orestes: "What you did was just, and also it was not just" (*Orestes,* 236). The questions "Who is to blame?" and "What is the meaning?" have similarly haunted Barton throughout his work. It is currently driving him to write his "story," and may cause him to write an addition to *The Greeks:* "Somewhere there's a play to be written," says Barton, "about something I've not solved with *The Greeks.* I brooded a long time whether to build into the whole thing Aeschylus's *Eumenides,* the trial of Orestes. I decided not to because of the obvious reason that it's totally out of style with the rest of the material." Yet Barton instinctively feels that his ending leaves the question of responsibility unresolved. His ending, which assuages the pain of Iphigenia by reuniting her with Orestes, does not satisfactorily account for Orestes' guilt. "I think the answer is that Orestes should be tried and acquitted [as in *The Eumenides*], but not healed because I think the problem is insoluble. *That*'s the ending I want to write." Barton thinks he may have the ever-present chorus of women, who have observed first-hand the horrors of the war and its resultant chaos, cast the votes in favor of or against Orestes' guilt—"it should be exactly what happens in Aeschylus: the votes would be even and Athene would cast her vote. I think with a bit of playmaking I might do that." (Barton may indeed have an opportunity to revise *The Greeks:* plans are afoot to revive the production and to film it in 1986. American producer Joseph Strick is behind this project.)

The Greeks was structured to chart the decline of civilization. The first portion of the trilogy showed the Greeks as idealistic, romantic, and primitive; Barton compared the effect to the attitudes with which Europe entered World War I. It was, in large measure, this "doomed romanticism" that caused Barton to undertake *The Greeks:* "Being romantic isn't interesting as such: it's the dialectic between romanticism and disillusionment, between purity and ambiguity, between aspiration and despair. It's that theme that excites and was a crucial element in my mind in *The Greeks.*" Thus, by the end of Part III the mood had shifted to disillusionment and uncertainty. Barton charted the change in two ways. Visually the clothing became more modern: the first play presented Greeks dressed in classic attire; by *Orestes,* the protagonists were in jeans and khaki jackets, toting sten guns like modern guerilla terrorists. Barton defended the anachronisms, surmising they would "help the impact of the gods' final arrival."[19]

Barton best effected the change from a vibrant, optimistic society to a bitter, disillusioned one through an effective use of the chorus of women, which provided the commentary throughout the ten plays. Throughout the cycle Barton was emphatic that the RSC actors "tell the story from the women's point of view. We should see the men *using* the women. . . . Over and over we see women without men, or women longing for their men, or women being used by men and wanting to be free. This has an obvious relevance for us today . . ." (p. xiii). In the first play the chorus of women were seen as giggling, giddy, spirited young women racing to the seaport to watch the launching of the war ships. By the trilogy's final hour the same women, "ravaged by seventeen years of sacrifice and war and bereavement and murder and rape and madness, [are] told by one of the gods who have destroyed their lives that, all in all, the best idea is compromise."[20]

Barton individualized members of the chorus to sustain his goal of humanizing Greek drama. Rarely did they speak in unison, and each was given a specific function in the ancient Homeric world. James Fenton, who has reservations about other elements of the production, admired Barton's handling of the chorus: "People thought in advance that the project would founder on the chorus, but it was often saved by them."[21] Barton was keenly aware of the liabilities of presenting a chorus to modern audiences and took special care to make them interesting: "One is nervous about the chorus. I think the great thing is to ration the amount you have of them; a little of them goes a long way. . . . The women will be working—I want them as unpretentious as possible. I tell the actors: 'Be Hobbit-like . . . you're simple folk!'"[22]

The Greeks was played on a simple, nearly bare set that complemented the sparseness of the language. John Napier designed a raked stage, the center piece of which was an open, circular area with an earthen floor (cf. the 1960 *Troilus and Cressida*). Stalks of corn suggested locale; masks of gods and goddesses dominated the background,[23] omnipresent reminders of the supernatural beings who shaped the lives of the protagonists. Gwilym said that the set and properties were chosen by Barton and Napier for a feeling of timelessness, with some props inserted to evoke the modern era. The setting was complemented by "daringly modern" music composed by Nick Bicat. Typically, Barton requested dominant themes—the Greeks had a jaunty march tune, the Trojans a melancholy strain. Barton used the music ironically to counterpoint the action. "When the worst things were happening," Gwilym recalls, "there was a little uplifting lilt of a tune going on in the background. It would throw everything out of keel for an instant and you would have to stand back from it." Also,

Barton prudently used the timeless sound of the sea to underscore the action, a device that served him well in *Twelfth Night.*

As he had done with so many of Shakespeare's plays—notably the romances described in chapter 7—Barton instructed his actors to found their work upon a naturalistic acting style, coupled with a judicious use of the formal, to contemporize the tone of the production. At their first cast meeting, Barton gave his actors very specific instructions about their mission:

> We must always find a balance between what is *naturalistic* and what is *formal.* The plays are often domestic in scale and this is what we should stress . . . we must never be heavy or earnest or solemn or pretentious, or anything that savours of a heavy, inflated style. We must never forget that *The Greeks* is at bottom a reaction against that tradition. . . . In this respect, Hamlet's advice to the Players is as true as ever it was. So let us be passionate, by all means, but let us not be heavy. (xvi–xvii.)

As with *The Wars of the Roses,* the RSC desired to present the entire cycle in a single day on selected occasions. Events began at ten o'clock in the morning with the launching of Agamemnon's fleet and ended at almost eleven with the expiation of the curse on the House of Atreus. A play-by-play consideration of Barton's odyssey suggests that *The Greeks* was indeed an undertaking of "a certain magnitude."

I. The Wars

Most observers agreed that the first portion of the trilogy was the most successful, primarily because it possessed a narrative drive and benefitted from a freshness of interest.[24] Also, the atrocities of war are more universal than the familial murders of the second section or the devine chaos of the last. Part I contained two of Euripides' most moving plays: *Iphigenia in Aulis* and *The Trojan Women.*

Play 1: Iphigenia in Aulis

From an idyllic beginning with a chorus of excited maidens awaiting the launch of Agamemnon's armada, the play suddenly changed its tone to horror as Iphigenia, dressed in a yellow wedding gown, is led away by her father to be sacrificed. The play established a trend for the cycle: mood and atmosphere are subject to change at a moment's notice. Barton told his cast that this was an integral part of *The Greeks'* design: "We could say that *The Greeks* offers a coherent picture of something incoherent. . . . Should we not perhaps rejoice at such diversity and contradiction? Doesn't it relate to our own experience? We should play each moment for what it is and allow a complex, contradictory picture to build up. We have to be boldly discordant, and savour the contradictions" (xvi).

The first play introduced central characters to the cycle: Agamemnon (John

Shrapnel), "a father who knows he will be diminished in his humanity but must do his political duty"[25]; Clytemnestra (Janet Suzman—in the most-praised performance of the trilogy), integral to Part II; and Iphigenia (Judy Buxton), who would ultimately effect the healing of the final play.

Play 2: Achilles

Though Barton followed Homer's account of the Achilles-Patroclus relationship and Hector's death, one suspects that he drew heavily on his several experiences with *Troilus and Cressida* in the writing of this play. Not only did it bridge the chronological gap between the first and third plays to give a picture of life *during* the Trojan War, but it introduced one of the cycle's major themes: the subjugation of women. The plot of this play sprang entirely from Achilles and Agamemnon arguing over their mistresses and illustrates that "a woman was an object that a man could do what he liked with" (xii). Such attitudes would culminate in the following play, *The Trojan Women*, the most graphic depiction in Barton's cycle of the brutalization of women by men. *Achilles* also sounded another note that would reverberate throughout the cycle: sardonic laughter. Wardle describes the effect:

> The first note of the living play inside the prearranged scheme is struck . . . with the appearance of the hero's immortal mother, Thetis, delivering a suit of armour from Zeus. Annie Lambert brings it to him on a shield, as if she is serving a hot dinner. The sound of astonished laughter rang around the Aldwych, and from that moment, comedy started growing out of the tragic entrails.

Play 3: The Trojan Women

The final play of Part I is perhaps the best known of any in the ten-play cycle. It provided the thematic climax of Agamemnon's notion that women in particular must suffer the dictates of Necessity—which he had invoked to sanction his earlier abduction of Iphigenia. To show the subjugation of women, the captive chorus was brutally branded and locked in chains in one of the most memorable effects of the production. The trilogy ended as the enslaved women drummed the floor while evoking the names of their dead and as Troy perished in flames behind them. The perimeter of the dust-bowl stage was ringed by the skeletons of the war's victims. The meaning of Barton's theatrical, shocking ending was not lost on Peter Jenkins: "It is an event for the ancient world comparable to the Fall itself in the Judeo-Christian tradition,"[26] the embodiment of Barton's title for part I, "Sin."

II. The Murders

From sin comes more sin, and the second phase of *The Greeks* focused on acts of self-perpetrating revenge by Hecuba, Clytemnestra, and Electra. Thematically it explored the cycle's opening line, "Who is to blame?" Jenkins judged Part II weaker than the first because the narrative thread began to sag.

Play 4: Hecuba

Jenkins specifically cited *Hecuba* as being out of place: "It is really a sequel to *The Trojan Women* and, in any case, a digressionary sub-plot to the Agamemnon story." Essentially, the play was prologue to the middle plays since it recapped the action for those who missed Part I and established the savagery of revenge: Hecuba brutally plucked out the eyes of a Thracian king who killed her remaining son.

Play 5: Agamemnon

Agamemnon probably would have provided a more logical bridge between the first two parts of the trilogy, particularly as Barton staged the King's "triumphant" return by having the enslaved Trojan women draw him on in a chariot that looked like an "anti-tank" vehicle with tongs made from machine gun barrels. Though the text was written by Aeschylus, Barton and Cavander were guided by the spirit of Euripides in their version of *Agamemnon* (and of Sophocles' *Electra*). Jenkins found the Euripidean overlay on the works of the earlier playwrights unsatisfactory: "Although Barton tries to breathe the more human spirit of Euripides into them, they stand out more starkly than the rest, and . . . fail to carry forward the argument with the gods which was for me the main driving force of the whole production."[27] In a more earthy, less elevated style than Aeschylus's, the play seemed more a domestic conflict, less a cosmic tragedy of doom and horror.

Play 6: Electra

Barton used the Sophoclean *Electra*, rather than Euripides' version because its action occurs outside the palace, as does *The Agamemnon*, and he wished to preserve a continuity of setting. He did, however, retain Euripides' tone. As rendered by Barton and Lynn Dearth, *The Greeks'* Electra emerged as "a punk Electra"[28] and "a grinning, razor cut nihilist."[29] Dearth explains the choices she and her director made for the character: "You can play [her] two ways . . . either as the injured tragic heroine with enormous cause for grief [the Sophoclean tradition], or as the self-indulgent neurotic who lives and feeds on revenge. We've chosen the latter interpretation. I haven't made her likeable, but I hope she's understandable. People who are unlikeable are sometimes the most tragic."[30] If Barton and Dearth erred it was to impose the attitudes of one playwright on another one whose ideas are not necessarily compatible. *Electra*'s finale previewed Part III: Orestes and Electra propelled the action into the twentieth century, dressed as modern-day terrorists in the Baader-Meinhoff tradition.

III. The Gods

If Part I was essentially tragic in tone and Part II melodramatic, the final part of Barton's trilogy was "absurdist, reductive, ironic, unglorious, untragic, and discreetly contemporary."[31] Its title was ironic because the four plays questioned the wisdom—not to mention the compassion—of the dieties whose petty quarrels precipitated the Trojan War. Barton was keenly aware of the problems the gods present to modern audiences:

> Trying to make the audience accept the gods is a challenge I welcome. I try to stress that in the beginning men are in touch with the gods. The gods come down to a wedding, for instance—then gradually in our cycle men lose touch with the gods. They lose their belief in them. Do they exist? They start questioning them; then finally, in the last modern evening, the gods turn up. That's the challenge, a modern 1980-ish evening in which the gods arrive and confront our day and age.[32]

For Barton there were three choices for a depiction of the gods: first, benevolent beings who bring us Order, Justice, Meaning, and Harmony; second, an opposite view that denies order and views the gods as random, chaotic, and arbitrary. Barton opted for a third view—"probably the view we should rest on: there is truth in both of these views" (xiv–xv).

Play 7: Helen

No play in the cycle, including Barton's own, received as much critical attention as *Helen*, Euripides' little-known "comedy," which shows that Helen never went to Troy but spent the war sunning herself in Egypt. Euripides exploded the Homeric myth and Barton seized it to underscore the ultimate horror of the Trojan War: not only was it fought for a woman of temporal beauty, but it was fought for a woman who avoided the war. The dead at Troy were victims of a cruel hoax by the gods.

Helen was played for high camp to set its tone: Janet Suzman, as Helen, wore a gaudy blonde wig and beach towel while reclining on a sarcophagus to annoint herself with suntan oil.[33] She was eventually "rescued" by a bumbling Menelaus (Tony Church). Both the inclusion of the play itself and the parodistic manner in which it was played were debated by the critics. Though he enjoyed the "cabaret skit" atmosphere of the piece, Jenkins felt it damaged the overall design of the final evening: "[It] commits Barton to a tone and style which he cannot sustain, except at the expense of everything he seemed to be trying to do in Parts One and Two."[34] James Fenton's *Sunday Times* essay provided an alternative to Barton's choice: "It would have been much better to concentrate on the more important feature of Menelaus, the fact that he is evil. This would have made more sense of the later *Orestes* and given the whole epic the necessary weight and purpose it lacked."

Play 8: Orestes

Unlike *Helen, Orestes* is a familiar play and audiences were perhaps better prepared for its cynical treatment of both gods and Greek "heroes." Furthermore, the play's action—Orestes, Electra, and Pylades pursue their course of revenge against Helen—was a logical continuation of the previous events, whereas Helen seemed a diversion. Objections were aimed at the staging rather than at the play: the three avengers ran "berserk with machine guns on a stage occupied by old Tyndareus in full classical armour."[35] If such a description is jarring in print, one can only imagine what effect Barton's staging had on his audiences. Fenton suggests why the concept was attacked by even the production's most ardent admirers: "The *Orestes* would have reminded us irresistibly of modern terrorism if it had not been played in such a way as to remind us of modern terrorism." (Ironically, Barton had cautioned his cast about not over-stressing the "women's rights" theme that ran throughout the cycle: "This has obvious relevance for us today but I don't think we need to do anything about it. The point makes itself without us stressing it. Let's trust the plays themselves and let them have their life" [xiii].) Billington argued, not without cause, that "modern urban terrorists are motivated by a frenzied political animus: Orestes and Electra by a vengeful hatred of Helen, the source of their misery." The other principal objection to the play was the depiction of Apollo, comically played by Shrapnel. The god was shown as the most inept of *dei ex machinae*, "a Monty Python parody." Gwilym recalls that RSC audiences were taken aback by the irreverent treatment of the gods, but Billington found the iconoclasm revealing because it "underscores Euripides' own cynicism about devine justice . . . and makes the crucial point that whatever confusion and contradiction there is on earth is also amply reflected in the heavens." Nonetheless, Barton himself feels that perhaps he allowed Shrapnel too much latitude in his "send up" of Apollo.

Play 9: Andromache

Barton says he is especially stirred by *Andromache*'s "absurdist, reductive ending" and used it to continue the tone established in the first two plays of the final section. Hermione's costume reflected Barton's intentions: a close-fitted dress from the thirties with ruffles at the bottom, very high-heeled shoes on which she tottered, and bright red patches on her cheeks to match her hair. Andromache's opening monologue about women's capacity for enjoyment being enlarged by their proneness to suffering ("Weeping my woes to heaven / We women love that"—p. 243) was played comically; later she sang the Trojan theme song over picnic baskets full of dismembered bodies. Primarily, the play reunited many of the central characters in preparation for the finale.

Play 10: Iphigenia in Taurus

The final play, in which Orestes is reunited with Iphigenia—who, in another surprising turn of events, was not killed by Agamemnon but saved—was serious in tone, but the previous plays diminished the dignity of the finale.[36] John Barber thought Barton's attempt to restore order and invest the cycle with meaning—in other words, healing must lead us from chaos—allowed the play to sink under the weight of its "soggy wisdom." Gwilym reports the company's own reservations about the sententious ending:

> I think that the feeling of the whole cast was that the end . . . restated what we had already made clear many times. We all petitioned John to cut it. And it was just a simple case of John saying, "Believe me. It works." I don't think it ever entirely worked, but what can you say? It is that man's vision and it's years of his work. (Personal interview, November 1980.)

The final play was staged in a timeless, frozen wasteland in which the company wore furs. Barton told his cast he wished to explore "the theme of men's and women's love of the sun and the light and their great dread of going under the earth into darkness. This ties up with our theme of the decay of civilisation" (x). Cushman suggested that the visual image was probably meant to remind audiences of "that other enigmatic comedy of reconciliation, *The Winter's Tale*, which Barton had also set in an Icelandic milieu four years earlier. The director acknowledges that he was indeed struck by the parallels between the two plays (Iphigenia is like Perdita, "the child who is destroyed and yet she's not destroyed—that's deeply mythological matter that gets me somewhere inside"), and he affirms that is why he set *Iphigenia* in the snow. The frozen wasteland melted as brother and sister were reunited, and the play and the cycle at large ended with a Greek song and dance of reconciliation.

The very scope of *The Greeks* insured a variety of critical commentary. Virtually every writer lauded Barton's ambition and vision. Other than the interpretation of several roles (Hermione, Apollo, Helen), the company was praised for the quality (and quantity!) of the acting and for the clarity with which the story was told.

Most of the negative criticism centered on two points. The indulgence of some of the stage business—notably the machine-gun-toting terrorists, the anachronistic Helen who looked like a tourist at a Club Med, the campy *deus ex machina*—was questioned, but generally accepted because the business was consistent and well executed. Barton, who originally intended to share the direction with Gillian Lynne (who could not undertake the task because of illness), admits that he did "not direct it marvelously well . . . I was too involved with the writing. I entirely agree with some of the comments about what we got wrong."

More significant, critics pointed to the unevenness of tone and dramatic quality; the ironies and comic tone were ultimately reductive because they prevented the plays from reaching, in Fenton's eyes, "a mature conclusion," a possibility that—as we have seen—Barton is considering as he ponders a revision of the plays. Fenton further suspected that Barton's close association with

Shakespeare may have tempted the director to impose a Shakespearean overlay on *The Greeks:*

> My point is that Shakespearean tragedy was not a mere successor to classical tragedy; it was a vigorous alternative which the classicists rightly saw as inimical to their ideals. The dislike is mutual. Mr. Barton cherished the idea of telling the whole story of the House of Atreus through the medium of the Greek tragedies. But when he came to do so, his allegiance to Shakespeare proved too strong. He could not help but mar the plays. It was as if Shakespeare was the Fury, pursuing the director and punishing him for a temporary defection.[37]

Though Barton may have "marred the plays" in their original form, he succeeded in accomplishing his larger intention: to create a moving story that encompassed a spectrum of human experience and cast light on our lives in the late twentieth century.

The import of the production, whatever its flaws, has been detailed by Colin Ludlow in a *London Magazine* appraisal of *The Greeks'* worth:

> Over three evenings, *The Greeks* builds up a catalogue of experience, and whatever the ironies or complexities involved, when Orestes and Iphigenia look back across the final play, we, with 2,000 years of similar history behind us, are able to share their sad and moving sense of missed opportunities, of happiness having proved elusive and suffering and waste occupying its place instead. The vision is sufficiently resonant and compelling for the audience, whenever a character or the chorus offers any comment, to lean forward and listen. If there is a measure to Barton's achievement, that is it.[38]

The success of *The Greeks* has enticed Barton to attempt other episodic works from varied cultures. At the request of Norwegian theater artists, Barton went to Bergen, Ibsen's native city, to adapt and stage the rarely produced *Vikings of Helgeland* in June 1983. Three years earlier Barton had conducted a Shakespeare seminar in Norway, where the project was first discussed. Actually, *The Vikings* had been tempting Barton for years. Calling the work "a flawed masterpiece," Barton was drawn to the work because "it seemed to capture and embody the world of the sagas," on the one hand, and because "it mixes Ibsenite relationships and marriage problems with a mythical, fairy tale plot" on the other. About 1978 Barton mentioned the prospect of *The Vikings* to Nunn, but nothing came of his idea until the Norwegians asked him to direct the work. Inga Stina-Ewbank provided Barton with a literal translation of Ibsen's prentice work, and he wrote a simple, poetic text, utilizing the writing techniques that served him well on *The Greeks.* The finished product consists of short verse lines, three stresses to the line. "They think I've invented a new verse form," Barton proudly notes.

The production, which incorporated Norse songs and word games in which people make up rhymes, was staged—like *The Winter's Tale* and *Iphigenia in Taurus*—in a snowy setting (to be accurate, a "salty" setting: Barton found that salt was "extraordinary for making snow"). It was sparse, simple, yet encompassed a wide spectrum of human activity.

Barton particularly enjoyed his relationship with the Norwegian actors. His keen ear for sound delighted in the natural lilt of the Norwegian language: "The Norwegians are very good at relishing words, even better than English actors. I could actually direct it better textually in Norwegian than in English." Barton was especially impressed with his actors' ability to take up the text "and make it their own," a challenge he offers to his actors, and a technique he explores in some depth in "Playing Shakespeare."

"I learned quite a lot, and it was quite an important experience for me," says Barton of *The Vikings* production. Perhaps the most salutory lesson he derived in Norway, coupled with his *Greeks* project, was that he needed to create a "myth" of his own. From the Greek legends, the Norse sagas, and Malory's Arthurian tales, Barton is attempting to create a composite myth, a narrative written "in a sound-made language that I hope will be very poetic." Barton likens his story to J. R. R. Tolkien's Hobbit sagas, but says his work will go beyond Tolkien, particularly in its treatment of female characters:

> I reacted against the ignoring of the women in the Tolkien books, and I've gone very far in the other direction because *The Greeks* is based on women. The way I've done the story is to reverse things: it's a matriarchy and the women go on Quests as well as the men. The center of the story is about women's quests. I don't know why.

When one considers that Barton's best directorial work has frequently centered upon plays that deal with "questing women" who triumph over chaos—i.e., *Twelfth Night, Love's Labour's Lost, All's Well That Ends Well, The Merchant of Venice, The Winter's Tale,* and even some elements of *The Greeks*—one can appreciate Barton's predisposition for such subject matter. Concomitantly, one can also appreciate why Barton's success with such works has been so pronounced: certainly those "mythical bells" to which Barton frequently refers sound clearly in his ears when directing these plays.

While Barton is creating his new myth, he yet remains active in the theater. In November 1983 he staged his adaptation of Calderon's complex—and highly mythical—*La Vida Es Sueño (Life's a Dream)*. Like *The Greeks* and *The Vikings,* it is a project he has long desired to embrace. In 1980 he completed an English version of the play but was not satisfied with it. He joined forces with Adrian Mitchell, a director and translator with England's National Theatre. Mitchell, too, had translated the Calderon work, and he and Barton combined their resources for the production at The Other Place in Stratford and The Pit at the RSC's new London home, The Barbican Centre. Mitchell, says Barton, "is everything I am not: left wing, socially conscious, a very prolific writer. I am deliberately putting myself in the hands of somebody different to stir myself up a bit (personal interview, June 1983)."

That Barton should be strongly attracted to *Life's a Dream* is not surprising. Though written in Spain in the midseventeenth century, the play resonates with archetypal characters, situations, and images that dominate the greatest dramatic myths of Western theater, such as Prometheus, Oedipus, and Hamlet. Its intricate plot owes much to the allegorical religious drama of the Middle Ages, the intrigue of the revenge tragedy, and the restorative power of reconciliation explored in Shakespeare's last plays. Thematically, the drama poses questions that drew Barton to *The Greeks* in 1980:

> What is the worst fate the gods can give?
> Some say to die, while others say to live.

And the resultant performance on Christopher Morley's small, sparse stage conjured images from previous Barton productions: the heroine, Rosaura (Barbara Kellermann), was discovered as the lights came up astride the black hobby horse used in *Richard II* ten years earlier; later, she entered with skull in hand, brandishing a dagger, a black-cloaked parody of Michael Pennington's actor-Hamlet. The King of Poland (Charles Kay) wore an enormous black cape, adorned with silver stars and crescents, that literally covered the entire floor space of the stage; one could not help but recall other mythic kings favored by Barton, particularly *Cymbeline.* The protagonist, Sigismund (Miles Anderson, in a justly praised performance), embodied the "flawed knight" principle that attracts Barton. His move from ignorance to knowledge is achieved by role playing, hence the production was uncompromisingly theatrical, though simple. Actors sat among the audience when not performing; characters selected crowns, jewelry, and weapons from an omnipresent prop table; an offstage orchestra underscored the action with satiric flourishes (very reminiscent of the 1980–81 *Hamlet*) and melancholic airs; the action was stage-managed by a wise fool (Anthony O'Donnell) clothed in the motley of a jester. Thematically and theatrically, *Life's a Dream* was unmistakably a Barton enterprise; its ingenuity was revealing, its acting clear, and its appeal to audiences enormous as they, like Barton, rediscovered the contemporary viability of a too-long neglected masterpiece.

With *The Greeks, The Vikings,* and *Life's a Dream* and the evolving "mythic" works (which may include Byron's massive *Cain* in the near future), Barton has indeed been "stirring himself up." But what is important to realize at this point in his career is that these new works do not necessarily represent a new direction for Barton: they are the long-awaited culmination of a quest that started thirty-five years ago in Cambridge.

11

"His Hour Upon the Stage": Barton Anatomized

There are two John Bartons in one body. There is Barton-Mephistophilis, responsible in his time for some memorable atrocities. . . . There is also the white angel, Barton-Faust. He is here clearly steeped in the text, equipped with a rich visual imagination.
—Bernard Levin, *The Sunday Times* (London), May 15, 1977.

He's like a lot of geniuses: he's either absolutely stunning . . . or he's absolutely awful.

—Ian Richardson, Santa Barbara, California, February 16, 1980.

Antithetical responses from critics and colleagues are not unusual when John Barton is the subject of conversation. Barton himself is as seemingly contradictory as the critical commentary his work has prompted. He is acknowledged as the most erudite and intellectually potent of the contemporary directors at Stratford, yet stories of his absent-mindedness are legendary: he has been known to step into paint buckets on otherwise empty stages; while giving cast notes, he has managed to insert his chair leg into a coffee cup; it is not uncommon to see him driving around Stratford with his car door wide open; he invariably has a half-dozen cigarettes lit at one time during a rehearsal because he has forgotten where he has laid each one. He has provided some of the most cogent insights into Shakespeare's most demanding plays, but feels inadequate to discuss them in other than rehearsal situations. He has "dared" to rewrite Shakespeare, the Greek masters, Ibsen, and others, but he is self-effacing about his contributions to contemporary stage practice. Researching his career is often a frustrating experience because while there is abundant material on his colleagues—notably Peter Hall and Trevor Nunn—there is relatively little on Barton, who discourages interviews and personal publicity. He is not aloof or uncooperative; while talking with him one senses a genuine willingness to accommodate, but he seems unable to discuss his ideas because he truly believes them insignificant and secondary to the plays themselves. John Nettles emphasizes that "everything is peripheral and beside the point" to Barton's desire to discover the mysteries of Shakespeare's plays—and that discovery takes place only in rehearsal and production.[1]

The "voyage of discovery"—a favorite Barton term for the process—is not always launched under favorable circumstances. In an address to the Seventeenth International Shakespeare Conference at Stratford in 1976, Barton identified four elements that "make a theatre director tick."[2] His catalogue suggests the liabilities of his profession and serves as a framework from which to discuss Barton's style, its strength and its weaknesses.

1. *"Conceptualizing the play and considering the thematic impact."* Surprisingly, Barton adds that this is often a minor point. "Conceptualizing," for Barton, is an instinctive, rather than purely intellectual process: "One launches the idea instinctively, intuitively . . . one says to the actors, 'Wouldn't it be a good idea if . . . ?'" To those who assume that Barton as a matter of course relies on an intellectual, scholarly approach to direction, he states:

> Directing, of course, calls for a mixture of intuition and intellect. But I believe that intuition is the more important of the two. . . . The intuitions come first, and then one's intellect tries to analyze them. It works that way round.[3]

2. *". . . the practical theatre problem."* This, says Barton, is the most important of the four elements. "When I direct an actor, it primarily is influenced by one's knowledge of that actor. I find myself saying the part should be played like this, but with this actor it should be played like that." When confronted by academics and others about specific production choices, his standard answer is "the reason is always theatrical—like that actor couldn't play something any other way. That's what happens all the time in rehearsal. I often give up my view about something because if the actor doesn't agree with it, I can't make him do it."[4] This is an ideal statement which is subject to alternate opinion, but there are examples to illustrate Barton's contention. The 1978 and 1981 productions of *The Merchant of Venice* both sprang from Barton's vision of the play as a romantic fairy tale, but the temperaments and talents of Patrick Stewart and David Suchet, who played Shylock, created quite different interpretations of the role. Barton was so fascinated by this divergence that he included a discussion between these actors in the television series, "Playing Shakespeare." One other example from Barton's career illustrates that practical theater problems often deter his preconceptions: when *Richard II* was transferred to the Aldwych Theatre in 1974, Barton wanted to retain the con-

troversial bridge O'Brien had designed for the Stratford production, but sight lines at the Aldwych would not permit the high bridge and Barton was forced to find an alternative.

3. "*. . . the problem of the theatre space.*" Barton, as a rule, prefers an austere setting that focuses attention on the actor and the words of the playwright. Thus his work at the RSC has not been particularly limited by the problems of the theater space—other than the size of the auditorium of the main house.

4. "*. . . suggestions from actors.*" John Barber wrote in *The Daily Telegraph* that Barton is "very much an actor's director. . . . For him the production begins only when it is off the printed page and in rehearsal, when he seizes eagerly on what individual players have to offer him."[5] Because no director has ever pleased every actor with whom he works, there are those who question Barber's assessment; dissenting views will be considered later. In general, however, most actors with whom I talked concur with Barton's description of his methodology and his reliance on actors:

> When I work on a play, I first of all read and think about it very hard. But when I go into rehearsal, my initial step is to say to the actors, "Do something; let's put the scene on its feet; you give me something and I will respond to it." I find that when I do that, new thoughts come that have never occurred to me in the study; I call into question things that I had previously believed, or decide that they are wrong for this particular actor because his persona cannot embody it.[6]

Ultimately, the role of the director, in Barton's estimation, is that of a "chairman negotiating between interested parties."[7]

Asked if there is indeed a "John Barton style," the director answered, "Yes, I think it's probably true, but I think it's hard to define. I couldn't say what it is."[8] Peter Hall, who knows Barton's work as well as anyone, is not hesitant to describe the style of his Cambridge fellow:

> I could recognize a John Barton production in a minute flat. . . . Dispositions of the actors on stage, the way the groups are closed, the focus on the person who is speaking. In his early years he used to make actors do quite arbitrary moves, which actors cannot stand doing. Now he is more adroit. John's productions are always carefully weighted and sometimes, mostly, that is miraculous. Sometimes it leads to over-emphatic delivery.[9]

Barton agrees that his style and approach have changed during his twenty-year professional career, but notes, "I don't think I've changed very consciously or deliberately. I think it's been a gradual, subliminal thing."[10] Nonetheless, there are identifiable constants that help define a Barton production:

The quality of the verse-speaking

"If it's a classical text, I do think you notice a difference in the verse-speaking. It hurts him to hear the verse chopped."[11] "The value of the spoken word—that is always a prime consideration for him." Such comments from Gwilym and Nettles, respectively, are indicative of responses from actors and critics asked to define Barton's distinctive qualities. Wardle recalls a British television show for Weekend TV in which Barton demonstrated verse techniques with actors:

> It was a real, penetrating observation of each word, with a distinct sort of acting, with a distinct clue to the actor about how to play it. That is his advice to the actor all the time, "Trust the verse, trust the verse."[12]

Melvin Bragg, who produced that Southbank show, persuaded Barton to develop the ideas of the original show into a complete series that would explore the RSC's techniques of "Playing Shakespeare." Barton obliged and spent most of 1982 devising the script for the series. The result is a twelve-part work that allows audiences to experience firsthand the verse-speaking techniques that Barton brought to Stratford in 1960 and that have become the mainstay of the RSC style of speaking verse.[13] Fortunately, the shows have been transcribed and prepared in book form because Barton believes that "a book which reflects the way actors think about Shakespeare is now needed." Methuen will publish the book which will be released to coincide with the telecasts of "Playing Shakespeare," in July 1984.

Barton divides his concerns into two broad categories: "Things Objective," which deal with the rules governing poetry and Shakespeare's writing style; and "Things Subjective," which reflect one's subjective response to a text, that is, one's interpretation. In all cases Barton emphasizes that most of the material is bound by commonsense rather than anything esoteric or mysterious. The twelve discussions of "Playing Shakespeare" are briefly summarized here because collectively they best reflect Barton's verse-speaking techniques, surely the most important element of "the Barton style":

1. "The Two Traditions." Barton maintains that there should be no problem reconciling the language-oriented tradition of the Elizabethans with the naturalistic acting tradition espoused by Stanislavski: ". . . in Shakespeare our two traditions, Modern and Elizabethan, come together. I believe our tradition actually derives from him. . . . Shakespeare wrote for the Elizabethan theatre and wrote infinitely rich and complex plays of great psychological depth. I believe he both accepted this theatre and transformed it. In a sense he is the inventor of both characterisation and naturalistic speech."

2. "Using the Verse." RSC actors have learned that the verse is there "to *help* the actors. It's full of little hints from Shakespeare about how to act a given speech or scene. It is a stage direction in shorthand." Here Barton addresses the cornerstone of his teaching methods: he emphasizes, both in private conversation and on the television show, that Shakespeare uses blank verse and its normal metric patterns as a means of alerting actors to significant moments in a script: "Shakespeare gets his dramatic effects by *setting up* that norm and then significantly *breaking* it. Where he breaks it an added stress is provided." Thus Barton's actors are trained to look for the contrapuntal breaks and give stressed words special color. The monosyllabic line merits special attention in Barton's method because it "has an extraordinary power to move." "In sooth, I know not why I am so sad," "You do me wrong to take me out o' the grave," and particularly Emilia's admonition to Iago, "I will not" (*Othello:* 5.2.224) are favorite Barton examples of Shakespeare's use of monosyllabic lines to create emotion and tension.

3. *"Language and Character."* Originally titled "Heightened Language," this segment details how Shakespeare and his contemporaries loved words, how "they relished them and played with them." Using techniques he had learned from Rylands, who wrote a book on precisely this topic, Barton instructs his actors to note how Shakespeare's language is most often shaped by the words that complement or contrast with other words around it. To this end, he offers actors what he feels is the most useful advice in his methodology: "If I had to restrict myself to one single bit of advice to an actor new to Shakespeare's text, I'm not sure it wouldn't be . . . *look for the antitheses and play them.* . . . Shakespeare was deeply imbued with a sense of it. He thought antithetically. It was the way his sentences over and over found their shape and meaning."

4. *"Using the Prose."* Barton judges this program—which was not telecast—as less successful than others; nonetheless, it is useful for its delineation of prose ("Just over twenty-eight percent of Shakespeare's plays are in prose," he began) as another kind of "shorthand" that the actor must decipher as surely as the verse: "If there is a golden rule for prose it is this: look for the strong stresses and sense the rhythm from that." Ultimately, Barton effectively illustrates that Shakespearean prose can often be as heightened as the poetry; conversely, he argues that verse can be as naturalistic as prose.

5. *"Set Speeches and Soliloquies."* One of the most interesting of the programs, this segment details how actors can maximize the effect of the long speeches that frequent Shakespeare's plays. His discussion tells much about his staging techniques and spatial relationships, such as those employed in *Hamlet:* "I personally believe that it is right ninety-nine times out of a hundred to share the speech [i.e., soliloquy, but in Barton productions extraordinarily long speeches are most frequently played to the audience] with the audience and a grave distortion of Shakespeare's intention to do it to oneself. If the actor follows that note, the speech will work. If he doesn't, it will be dissipated and disap-

pear. The audience won't listen properly." Here, too, Barton has much to say about "coining phrases" so that the audience hears these speeches afresh, a technique he and Pennington used so effectively in *Hamlet* (whose "To be or not to be" soliloquy was used by Barton and that actor to illustrate this point on television).

6. *Using the Sonnet.* Although it was deleted from the final telecast, the sixth discussion was a working summary of the earlier segments. Barton has long maintained that sonnets, compact and complete in themselves, offer the same challenges encountered in the full texts: "Give me an actor, a sonnet, and fifteen minutes, and I can learn what I need to know about an actor." Accordingly, he introduced sonnet classes, the backbone of the RSC actor training program, in 1960.

7. *"Irony and Ambiguity."* Because Barton believes antithesis is central to playing Shakespeare, he devoted an entire program, the first in the "subjective" explorations of the text, to the topic. Noting that today "we are not very good at irony . . . most of us use it rarely, if at all," Barton instructed his actors to find the irony and ambiguity in Shakespeare by using hints from the text and, as important, by developing the intellectual facility of "being at once inside and outside the situation" in which one finds oneself on stage. Having found "loaded and ambiguous words," actors then ought to put them "into a kind of inverted commas."

Correspondingly, some of the negative criticism of Barton's verse-speaking technique seems to stem from this last advice. In his essay "Shakespeare on the Modern Stage," Eric Salmon defines a liability of Barton's approach:

> John Barton's productions for the RSC . . . are always distinguished by the extreme intelligence of the verse speaking; the meaning of every word is made clear. But sometimes this is done at the expense of verbal excitement, so that the spoken texts sounds almost like spoken footnotes on itself.[14]

In "Free Shakespeare" John Russell Brown cites Barton as one who abuses language: "John Barton is particularly fond of enforcing his view of the play by breaking speeches with silences or by heavy emphasis on a few words."[15]

8. *"Passion and Coolness."* Probably the most useful segment for understanding Barton's direction philosophy, "Passion and Coolness" emphasized the need for "balance" in the emotional and intellectual demands of the text. Using Hamlet's famous act 3, scene 2, advice to the Players, Barton argues that Shakespeare asks "for what we would call coolness in playing passion." Therefore, in production and in "Playing Shakespeare," Barton constantly admonishes his actors to moderate their passions because "if the actor lets his emotions carry him away, we will start to *observe* him rather than to *share* with

him." Barton maintains that the language of the text is emotional enough to sway an audience: "Perhaps the moral is that it's sometimes more important to make the text resonate than to be moved oneself." (Refer to Barton's instruction to Mike Gwilym in *Troilus and Cressida*, chapter 3, for a practical example of this philosophy.)

9. *"Rehearsing the Text."* As its title implies, the program was a functional demonstration in which Barton, Pasco, and Dench rehearsed a scene from *Twelfth Night*. Throughout Barton stressed the need to use the text as the primary means of shaping the scene: "If the textual points are ignored, it is pretty certain that Shakespeare's intentions will be ignored or twisted. Something else will be put in their place . . . an alternative, which might be rich and exciting in its own right, but not a realisation of Shakespeare."

10. *"Exploring a Character.* Here Barton returned to his much-praised productions of *The Merchant of Venice* with the actors who played Shylock: Patrick Stewart (1978) and David Suchet (1981; see chapter 4). The three discussed the discernably different interpretations of the money-lender, and—in the process—validated Barton's contention that ultimately a production belongs to the actors. That was the most graphic illustration of Barton's notion that "subjective things" are as crucial in playing Shakespeare as "objective things."

11. *"Contemporary Shakespeare."* Barton and Ian McKellen consider the most valid means of making Shakespeare relevant to modern audiences. Though their comments have little to do with verse-speaking, the segment, deleted in the telecast version, is nonetheless useful for its delineation of Jan Kott's thesis that contemporary actors, directors, and audiences must use Shakespeare's texts to get at their own experience, rather than imposing modern experiences on the texts.

12. *"Poetry and Hidden Poetry."* More philosophical than practical, the final segment featured Barton and seven actors (Ashcroft, Harrow, Howard, Kingsley, McKellen, Sinden, and Suchet) discussing the often frustrating gap between the ideals espoused in Barton's schema for playing Shakespeare and their realization in practical stage production. Barton admits that he feels "a deep sense of failure . . . as a director because I haven't found a way of helping actors fully" to bridge this gap. Fortunately for us, he has perhaps come closer to realizing this aspiration than most who have attempted it.

To summarize the twelve segments, Barton composed a pithy passage in blank verse that encapsules what he and the RSC actors sought to accomplish on British television:

We've talked of possibilities, not rules.
Of questions, balances, not absolutes.

So, are there any rules? Yes, try to find
What *goes on* in the text and ask yourselves
If you can *use* it. You must not eject it
Until you've smelt it out and asked the questions.
Never forget that the verse is there to help you.
It can be heightened. And yet very often
It's close to our own humdrum speech.
We often use it but we never notice . . .

Though his intentions here were humorous, the piece is a succinct catalogue
that defines Barton's greatest directorial strength: eliciting well-spoken verse
from his actors.

Other Barton directorial traits include:

Formal movement and blocking patterns

Hall's remark on the Barton style (see p. 228) suggests that Barton's disposition of actors on stage is highly calculated. Some productions—*Richard II*
comes to mind—are exceptionally formal in their pictorializations. Other
plays, such as the 1980 *Hamlet,* employ blocking patterns that are formal even
in an essentially naturalisic acting style. In 1.3, for example, Polonius and
Ophelia discussed Hamlet's condition while sitting on benches across the stage
from each other. Though their speaking was conversational in tone, one was
constantly aware of the great space between them. Gwilym acknowledges that
such conspicuously stylized blocking is an outgrowth of Barton's theory of
verse-speaking:

[Barton] believes that a lot of problems are solved on stage by relationships—
physical relationships between actors. He's always a great one, for instance,
if there is a dense piece of language, of creating space between actors just on
the simple feeling—and it seems to work—that if you have to convey a
message fifteen feet from the person you're talking to, you're probably going
to have to use the language better and more accurately than if you're mum-
bling in their ear. . . .

A constant note from Barton is, "Give it space, give it space."
Church describes the technique in similar terms ("He believes greatly in
giving something 'air'—a phrase he uses again and again"—and which he used
frequently in "Playing Shakespeare"). Key speeches are thus staged with a
minimum of distraction:

He has a great tendency to just plunk all the major moments of the play dead
center, which is absolutely different from Terry Hands who uses all sorts of
areas. . . . John increasingly goes for a totally blank, open stage with the least
possible realistic detail in it. . . . He always insists on maximum dramatic
focus at a given point . . . so much so that you find almost everybody gets
center stage to make the major points, and it is always basically facing front.[16]

Theatricality

While he generally disdains distracting scenic detail, Barton frequently embellishes the actors' work with carefully selected theatric devices. His fondness for sound and music effects are best remembered in the sounds of the sea in *Twelfth Night* and *The Greeks;* the pervasive echo of metal on metal in *The Wars of the Roses;* the plaintive cry of a mufti in *Othello,* and the wistful call of the owl in *Love's Labour's Lost.* Gwilym remembers Barton's theatrical use of sound in *The Greeks,* which helped him overcome a difficult passage of text in *Achilles:*

> There are always huge strides forward in John's productions just before opening, and it's partly to do with the surprises he has up his sleeve for you . . . In *Achilles* I was to have this "hot line" to the gods . . . and it's something an actor thinks about because it's a big thing to ask the audience to accept. And yet Barton gets you to stand out on the stage and you're talking to Zeus. And Zeus answers with these amazing, huge, frightening thunderclaps. And you just think: this is easy, he's done it for you.

Nettles concurs that Barton is "a man of the theatre through and through." Consider Richard II's appearance atop the walls of Flint Castle, the ballet of death in *Troilus and Cressida,* any number of battle sequences in the histories, the descent of Jupiter in *Cymbeline,* and the coronations of *King John.* Wardle suspects that Barton may use theatrical overlays to counter his academic reputation: "He seems very keen to prove that he is not a dry, thick old Don and is as theatrical as anybody else . . . Barton will use any old barnstorming trick if it's going to make a point he wants to make."

Strong narrative line

In recent years Barton has demonstrated a concern for the clear delineation of the plot line. In a 1981 *Times* interview he stressed that "the first job of any director at Stratford is to tell the story and help the audience find its way about the plot—and that is not as easy as it sounds. It is a matter of focusing, selecting, and removing the superfluous."[17] In his program note for *The Greeks* Barton told his audiences that "the narrative is the thing," and judging from the critical commentary on such densely plotted plays as *Cymbeline, Pillars of the Community, The Way of the World,* and *The Greeks,* he has succeeded in accomplishing the task of telling a good story in his works.[18] Nettles defines a virtue of a Barton production as being the "lovely shape" the director gives to them: "They have a beginning, a middle, and an end—and what an end sometimes." The actor further declares that Barton has an extraordinary ability "to hold the whole shape of the play in his head while doing any one scene."

Characterization

Sheila Bannock, writing for the *Stratford Herald,* identified Barton's rendering of stage personalities as an integral part of his work:

For me, the most striking characteristic of John Barton's recent productions for the RSC has been his flair for revealing character and for showing in the most diverse circumstances how action and motivation spring from the personalities involved. His Shakespeare productions have been the most humane and perceptive from this point of view of any at Stratford and of most elsewhere that I have seen.[19]

Peter Hall maintains that, in general, characterization is among Barton's finest virtues. At its worst he says, "it is caricature and simplification" but at its best, it makes audiences "absolutely understand what the play is about."[20] Stanley Wells adds that one of Barton's directorial strengths is his "capacity to make you feel that the characters had a relationship before the play began." To effect these qualities in his productions, Barton consciously seeks opposite traits within characters whom we thought we knew well:

Again and again, a character who seems to be foolish or cruel or stupid turns up with something completely the opposite of one's first view of him; and that seems to me to be not a chaotic view of human nature, but a faithful and realistic one. It is something which Shakespeare tapped in a way that no writer before him had done, except fitfully.[21]

Strong critical statements

Tyrone Guthrie once noted that "one of the minor tragedies of the historical development of European culture has been the divorce between theatrical performance and the literary study of drama."[22] Barton's productions have done much to bridge this gap, not so much because he has purposefully imposed a critical interpretation on the plays, but because he and his actors fully explore the texts themselves for new insights. This has on occasion led to excess, but in the main Barton has illustrated that plays previously thought "unplayable" (for example, *All's Well That Ends Well* and *Troilus and Cressida*) indeed possessed strong and manageable story lines and, more important, themes that spoke meaningfully to audiences in the late twentieth century. And, in most cases (*King John* is perhaps the notable exception) Barton has extracted such values from the text itself: Barton, says Irving Wardle, "is a text man in the sense that he does seem to have the conviction that the secret to everything about a performance of a play is concealed like a buried treasure inside the text." Barton productions are anticipated because of the critical insights one expects from them. Gordon Parsons wrote in 1974 that "perhaps a dozen of Shakespeare's plays reflect the fully matured genius of his vision. John Barton has done more than any other director to reveal the exciting contemporary relevance of many of these."[23]

Humanistic content

Barton does not have a pronounced political, religious, or social philosophy that dominates his productions. He explains his lack of a philosophic basis: "I'd

like very much to have one of those consistent philosophies—Marxist, Freudian, Catholic, or what you will—that answers every question, but I find people
and things too complicated for that."[24] He disdains labels, but allows that he
agrees with the "humanist" viewpoint,[25] perhaps an outgrowth of his affinity
for the literature and ideas of the late Middle Ages and the Renaissance. Even in
his darkest works, such as *Troilus and Cressida* and *The Greeks,* Barton sees the
plays as examinations of the violation of order and goodness and a longing for
something better. "He is pro-civilization," says Wardle, "and anti-anything
that imperils it. That was one of the things he wanted to do with *The Greeks*—
to show how fragile what we call humanity is." Pennington defines this as
another of Barton's strengths: "That's why John Barton is so good with plays
like *Love's Labour's Lost* and *The Way of the World*—he instinctively looks for
the morality in a play."[26] Tony Church, who knows Barton well as both man
and director, describes his colleague's moral foundation: "John has a massive
interest in goodness and the power of goodness. He is a deeply, I think,
religious man without accepting that he is religious at all . . . I have never met
anybody else with stronger morals. He really does believe in a moral force, a
force for goodness." Barton, who laments the modern tendency of playwrights
and some directors to look for the pejorative view of human beings, says, "I
tend to look for the humanity in evil people . . . I believe that is the Shakespearean thing: to find a touch of humanity at the least expected moment
(personal interview, June 1983)."

Textual revisions
    Much of Barton's reputation rests on his alteration of texts to suit his needs
for a production. Stanley Wells notes that "it is paradoxical that the Shakespearean director with the highest qualifications in English literature is the one
who has been most free in his handling of the text,"[27] but it is precisely because
Barton has the academic credentials that he feels justified in his revisions:

> There is a great paradox behind the work of Shakespearean scholarship,
> especially textual scholarship. Its aim is to establish as accurately as possible
> what Shakespeare actually wrote. But the more the texts are studied, the
> more it becomes clear that individual texts are full of cuts, insertions and
> alterations, made in the Elizabethan theatre. Such study in fact calls in ques-
> tion the very idea of the sacrosanct text. . . . In a sense, I believe that the
> work of textual scholarship sanctions our rehandling of the plays more than
> anything, since it demonstrates that the Quarto and even the Folio texts are
> the fruit of a complex and often corrupting stage history.[28]

In fact, Barton sees "writing" as another of the director's functions:

> The writing function in directing remains very important to me, whether its
> the actual writing of words (e.g., *The Wars of the Roses*) or the script editing
> that's necessary with many Shakespearean texts; bodying out what may be

crudely constructed, bald stage directions which must be developed into complex actions, battles, processions. The director in this aspect of his job is a kind of writer.[29]

According to Ian Richardson, many of Barton's alterations occur on the rehearsal room floor: "If one of the actors said, 'This strikes me as rather awkward,' the pencil would come out and Barton would say, 'Let me see,' and he rewrites Shakespeare. 'This is wormwood, wormwood,' he would say of the offending passage.'" When one attends a Barton production, one expects that the acting edition is a modification of the original text: this is as much a part of the Barton style as any element of this catalogue. And, as is evident throughout this study, Barton's proclivity to rewrite stems from a latent desire to write plays of his own. His adaptations, for better or worse, are an integral part of his creative process.

"Cold-starters"

Because Barton places a primary emphasis on discovering submerged truths in the plays, his productions have a reputation for being what Gareth Lloyd Evans refers to as "cold-starters."[30] A number of critics have mentioned this,[31] and Barton himself is aware of this according to Wells: "He would be known to be still reworking [a production] and reworking it, and he would say that it would be much better when it got to London." His actors, too, are aware of this process of maturation. Nettles confides that this is very much part of Barton's approach: "His productions . . . often start off very cold because all the ideas haven't been worked out or fully dramatized. As they go along they get better. It's not there to get good reviews: it's there to explore a bit of Shakespeare." Peter Roberts has suggested that what may seem a liability of Barton's methods is actually a benefit: "It's as well to remember that a Barton production seems to especially participate in the theatre's strongest suit: the fact that it is a living organism capable of development in a way denied pre-packaged entertainment."[32] If there is indeed an academic strain running through Barton's work, it is in his perception of the theater as a laboratory in which the process is as important as the product, if not more so.

The process by which Barton arrives at "his product" begins in his study, where he steeps himself in the text of the proposed play: "I read the play a great deal, immersing myself in it and getting to know it as well as I possibly can. But I never find my way very far before I start rehearsing."[33] Barton maintains that he does not conceptualize, but merely starts "with notes, and hints, and ideas."[34] Penny Gold, his former assistant, describes the director's approach in similar terms:

He will read it over and over again until he can tell you where any line comes from, unlike those people who have to turn the pages over and over to find what's said in the next speech even in the rehearsal room. He does emphatically know more than most directors about the text. There are very few questions an actor can ask John that he cannot completely, honestly, and assuredly answer from that text. He's not bluffing his way through, which is very reassuring to an actor.[35]

To what extent does Barton rely on the vast body of critical material available to him in the preparation of a production? "I read very little [criticism]. I do occasionally if I feel the need, but on the whole I just read the play."[36] On the other hand, there do seem to be influences traceable to specific critics in various productions such as *Hamlet, Richard II,* and *Measure for Measure.* The actors with whom Barton works agree that he does not customarily cite the available scholarship in rehearsal. "He's not interested in scholarship for its own sake," said Tony Church, "but he is very well aware of the scholarship of the period . . . he doesn't believe in academic notes at rehearsals." Barton himself provides the reason for this attitude: "I think that, whatever one thinks about a play academically or privately, it becomes something completely different when one's working with a living actor."[37]

Barton has frequently compared the work of the critic with that of the director, and he has noted the dissimilarities as well:

> I think the critic exists in an at times enviable isolation where there is just himself and the text and he can respond directly to it. Whereas a director is responding to individual human beings, to the invention and imagination and instincts of the individual actor, and that's the raw material he's got to deal with. He has to accept it before he tries to mold it. And though his previous knowledge of the play helps him in defining it, in shaping it for the actor, the basic starting point is not just the text. It's a text plus the creation and invention of the actors; which makes it a completely different experience.[38]

Barton customarily relies on his actors as the impetus for an interpretation, but—says Nettles—he varies his methods according to the play and its demands:

> I've been in three productions with John Barton and in each case he's taken a different stance. Sometimes he can be autocratic and very dictatorial about what he wants [Nettles cites the 1976 *Troilus and Cressida,* a restaging of the 1968 version, as an example], and at other times he can say, "It's your decision; you've got to do it. Let's arrive at this decision together" . . . Other times he just splits the difference—he pretends to initiate a democratic discussion, but all the time he leads you to where he wants you to be. He'll lead you to some land he's already charted.

Nettles said *The Merchant of Venice* (1979) was very much a communal enterprise: most decisions resulted from intense company discussions about the play, with Barton functioning only as arbiter.

Barton will not give line readings to actors, a point he stresses in "Playing Shakespeare":

I am sometime tempted to but I suspect it. I think the prejudice against it in our modern acting tradition is healthy. It would make the actor a mimic. He would be playing a set tune rather than spontaneous interpretations. He wouldn't feel *real*. Anyway, why should I think I could do it better?

Barton's rehearsals are among the most demanding in the RSC. He customarily begins at 10:00 A.M. and works without stopping until at least 7:30 in the evening, six days a week. He rarely lectures the company, even at the outset of a production, though he broke tradition and talked at some length at the beginning of rehearsals for *The Greeks*. Fortunately, the published edition of that text (Heinemann, 1981) provides a unique opportunity to sit in on a Barton rehearsal lecture.

Asked to define his rehearsal process, Barton answered:

It is very difficult to define the process that goes on in the rehearsal room: instinct is a great matter—directors and actors work together on instinctive ideas which bubble up from day to day, which they then test with their reason. We sometimes cut things out because we think they are an overlay on the text, and sometimes leave them in, hoping and trusting that they are an embodiment of something implicit in the text. This process is certainly influenced by the fact that we are people living in the twentieth century. But as often as not we also try to modify our modern responses by asking, "What does Shakespeare *really* mean here? Are we distorting him by doing something which we *want* him to mean, because it appeals to us.?"[39]

Actors who work with Barton say that he does not usually give specific details about how he wishes a scene to work. Gwilym offers an analogy between Barton's directorial methods and the child's game of "Connect-the-Dots":

He will let a scene take its own emotional shape, I think. Not because he's not interested in the emotional shape, but because I don't think he would really know how to plan that. I don't think he'd think that was his job. What he would do is—do you know those games where you have to mark in the dots to complete the picture?—what he would do is give you the dots but leave it to you to join them.

Barton sees himself as a psychological guide for his actors: "What I have to do is to answer their questions about the individual characters. . . . The exploration of character is not the only objective of rehearsals, but it is at the heart of the acting tradition in England, and one has to work within that tradition."[40]

Most actors feel secure with Barton's methods because he allows them latitude to explore character, yet he coaxes them in directions they might not see. Richard Pasco is a Barton admirer:

John Barton is a very gentle "coaxer." He has given me enormous help by his scholarship, by his sensitivity, and by his ability to "feed" the inner meanings of the text to me like no director I've ever known. I adore working with John: he's an inspiration to me.[41]

As part of his preparation for a production, Barton customarily works with actors on individual speeches outside the rehearsal room. After allowing them to explore these ideas, he adds perceptive comments that enhance their work. Gwilym describes this pivotal moment in the Barton rehearsal process:

> . . . you have a quite presentable performance of your scene a couple of weeks into rehearsal. And you might go on with that for many weeks, just fiddling around with that, and think that that's it. Sometimes you might feel despair because you think you haven't explored the possibilities of the scene and John seems to be happy with it. And then later on, he will say something terribly simple that will completely transform the scene.

There are, however, reports of dissension among some of his actors. Judith Cook, in a feature article on Barton in *Plays and Players,* reported that one of the principals in the *Twelfth Night* cast termed the production "an unhappy time," adding that a feeling existed that there was no communication between actor and director, that the success of the production was only "a happy coincidence." She then identified a common criticism of Barton from some of his actors: ". . . an actor, even if she or he has worked with him before, can suddenly find no common tongue in which to communicate. 'As if,' one said, 'we were both talking in different languages.'"[42] Barton challenges Cook's remarks, calling them "absolute nonsense," particularly in light of the *Twelfth Night* experience: "I would have said that the contrary was true, that it was not an 'unhappy time.' The intercommunication was very good." Yet there remains some objections to Barton's methods from actors who admire him. Sebastian Shaw says that on occasion Barton can "forget actors are human."[43] Such complaints stem from several sources. Shaw, who worked with Barton on *Richard II,* felt that the formality with which the director invested that play in 1973 forced the actors into a rather mechanical performance. Michael Bogdanov, recalling his term as Barton's assistant director in 1970, agreed: "Yes . . . [he treats actors] mechanically. He just maneuvers them around, through the text. That's his problem, and that's what we mean when we say he's pedantic."[44] Nettles says that actors often resent that he destroys their security by suddenly recognizing a new idea buried in the script and making drastic changes in their interpretation late in the rehearsal period: "Just about the time you're getting secure, then he'll smash it all and finally arise and create something new." That actor again attributes this practice to Barton's unswerving desire to make new discoveries in the script. Guy Woolfenden, who has composed more musical scores for Barton than anyone in the RSC, cites similar frustrations while working with his long-time colleague; at times, says Woolfenden, "you feel brow-beaten because [you feel] nothing will be accepted."[45] Gwilym agrees that the director can be "absolutely infuriating," but emphasized, "When that happens, you just have to say, 'Well, the one thing I do know is that John Barton cares about this production, cares about my part, and wants me to do good.'"

When Barton does commit himself to a course of action, it can be difficult to dissuade him from his concept. "John sticks his heels in," said Gwilym. Michael Tubbs, who has served as music director for several Barton productions, agrees that stubbornness is a Barton trademark: "Yes, yes, yes. It's always been a characteristic. So often he might try a lot of things but somehow you know that however widely he might try things, the chances have always been that he will come back to his original point."[46] Tony Church agrees that it is difficult to argue with Barton:

> He's very difficult because John is a very ingenious man with a dialectic. He will always argue a case and he's very difficult to argue with. I've seen him again and again in meetings and he's very difficult to defeat. [Laughter] Ah, that's what makes it fun!

Barton is not despotic. *If* an actor can show him that a scene will in fact work, Barton will embrace the idea. Gwilym explains: "He's a great one for getting actors to prove that their ideas will work. He will not accept an idea in the abstract, and so it is quite often dangerous to tell him what you're going to do *until* you've found a way of doing it."

If one remembers that Barton's career with the RSC began amid the problems of *The Taming of the Shrew* (in which he was accused of telling his actors *too much*), one can understand why Barton may have subsequently adopted a posture that seems uncommunicative. In 1972 Barton told a journalist: "A director never really has complete control of what happens and shouldn't have. He isn't like the conductor of an orchestra taking players through a symphony. Actors have their own understanding of their parts and their performance varies from night to night."[47] Barton feels that the manner in which he works with actors marks one of the substantial developments in his directing career:

> I've changed, grown, developed—and I've become more experienced . . . . The main change is probably in how I put things to actors. It's not enough to have the right idea; unless one can find the right and helpful way of expressing it, then the idea is valueless. I've perhaps learned how to help actors, and to be flexible in approach.[48]

Those remarks were made in 1974; more recently Church has commented that Barton "has become a great deal more relaxed and easy in the way he works with actors." Whatever cavils artists may raise about his methods must be judged in the context of the productions, which, as we have seen, are noted for the strength and insight of their characterizations. And, it must be reported, virtually all of the artists with whom I talked, whatever negative feelings they may have had about specific methods employed by the director, emphasized their admiration and respect for Barton.

Despite the seemingly contradictory statements about his rehearsal methods by those who work with him—and even by Barton himself—the picture that emerges suggests that a Barton production is indeed the result of a consortium between a director who knows the script exceptionally well and a company of inventive actors who are encouraged to develop their creative insights. In his best work (such as *All's Well, Twelfth Night*, the 1978 *Love's Labour's Lost*, the 1968 *Troilus and Cressida*), Barton placed the burden of interpretation squarely on the actors' shoulders and served as a resourceful guide who hones their interpretations. In his more excessive works—*King John*, the 1976 *Troilus*, and, some would argue, *Richard II* (particularly characters other than Richard and Bolingbroke)—the actor was secondary to his vision, and, consequently, both performer and production were somewhat diminished.

In addition to the quality of the verse-speaking, the well-defined narrative line, and the perceptive characterizations for which his works are widely respected and that form part of his emerging style, there are additional strengths that merit discussion:

—*Intelligence of approach:* "Nothing unthought happens in a play directed by John Barton," wrote Peter Thomson in *Shakespeare Survey* in 1971.[49] Partly on the strength of his academic background, mostly through the quality of the insights he brings to production after production, Barton is regarded as perhaps the most perceptive of the contemporary British directors. However they might feel about a particular work, critics invariably note that Barton has caused them to "rethink" a play.

—*Simplicity:* Barton's best work is marked by a simplicity of style and execution. Part of this may be attributed to the austerity of design favored by the director. A greater measure of his success here rests in the clarity of language he extracts from his actors. A *Birmingham Post* article on the accomplishments of the Royal Shakespeare Company recognizes this facet of Barton's direction:

> Trevor Nunn . . . has spoken of the importance of the word in Shakespeare and a number of productions—especially those by John Barton—have been given a simple, quasi-Elizabethan setting with a minimum of fuss and frippery intervening between the speaking actor and the audience.[50]

In "Playing Shakespeare" Barton stressed that "in acting and directing we must see the complexities but try to be simple." With some notable exceptions, his work at the RSC has been bound by this precept.

—*Theatrical daring:* It may seem paradoxical to include this element after a discussion of his simplicity, but when he uses his effects judiciously and in support of the text, Barton has provided some of the most memorable theatrical effects in contemporary stage practice. Barton, says Nettles, "has an eye for theatrical effects which is nonpareil," which is an opinion echoed by *Sunday Times* critic J. W. Lambert, who has written of the director's "dazzling theatrical flair which is a joy in itself."[51]

—*Play selection:* Barton has gained a reputation for his ability and willingness to accept the challenge of difficult scripts, Shakespearean and otherwise, that do not necessarily have mass audience appeal. "He's got an instinct for the right play at the right time, and one of his preoccupations is to find the right play for the right time," said Irving Wardle during a discussion of Barton's contributions to modern theater practice. His play selection reflects an instinct for contemporary sensibilities, as well as universal concerns embraced by the great myths of the past. To his credit, Barton rarely relies on external means to make four-hundred-year-old plays relevant to modern audiences.

Barton's weaknesses as a director generally fall into one of three categories:

—*Anti-emotional:* Barton's greatest flaw, suggests Judith Cook in *Plays and Players,* "seems to be a fear of emotion. Even the portrayal of feeling on stage and an emotional performance from an actor, which can bring tears to the eyes, worries him. . . . To avoid feeling, he often escapes into the wilderness of the text."[52] In a review questioning the lack of emotional impact in the 1971 *Othello,* an often-cited example of this "weakness," Robert Cushman declared that "there is sometimes a feeling that having taken the play apart, Barton has failed to put it together again."[53] Confronted with these observations, Barton responded: "I don't suppose it has ever crossed my mind. I think it's possible that I would treat the emotions more cooly than some directors. . . ."[54] The seventh program of "Playing Shakespeare," as we have seen, describes in much detail the rationale and practice behind Barton's "cool" treatment of emotion on stage; invariably his instructions to temper passionate outbursts can be reduced to a belief that an audience will *observe* rather than *share* an experience if the actor permits too much emotional involvement in a speech or scene. Characteristically, Barton returns to Shakespeare's text to support his contention, citing Hamlet's advice to the Players—"In the very whirlwind of your passion you must acquire and beget a temperence that will give it smoothness"—as a case in point. "It is pretty clear where Shakespeare's sympathies lie," says Barton on matters of "coolness and passion." Gwilym clarifies why Barton treats emotions "cooly":

I don't think he's afraid of emotion. I think he finds it boring. I mean, once you've declared an absolute grief which is weighing you down to the ground, there is nothing to ever grab hold of the audience's attention again. But if one—according to John's theory—can find the irony in it, and the bitter humor in it, you will keep the audience with you much better and much longer. I think that tends to work in his productions very well.

Tangentially, Wardle suggests that Barton must approach "direct human experience" by roundabout means, that he needs a complex and intellectually challenging work to come to grips with these feelings. Doubtless Barton is better known for his intellectual revelations, but there are nonetheless extraordinary examples of the director finding deep-felt emotion in scenes where we might not expect it: the Toby-Maria "betrothal" scene in *Twelfth Night;* Falstaff's midnight encounter with Doll Tearsheet in *2 Henry IV;* and the Richard-Bolingbroke exchange at Pomfret Castle (though, admittedly, Barton took textual liberties to bring them together); the joyful reunion and celebratory dance of reconciliation that concluded *The Greeks* cycle. One wonders how valid the charges of "anti-emotionalism" are, but enough critics have commented upon it to warrant inclusion here.

—*Textual liberties:* While analyzing contemporary trends in Shakespearean stage production, Richard David identifies "overproducing" and "reshaping texts in accordance with one's own temperament and predilections" as a general weakness of the current generation of British stage directors.[55] Any discussion of textual "editing"—either through revisions and rewrites or through inventive interpretations—invariably includes Barton as an exemplar of such practices. Certainly there has always been the frustrated playwright in Barton who releases his creative energies through various script revisions. Stanley Wells maintains, however, that one of Barton's genuine weaknesses is "not quite measuring up to the text as it is and . . . getting around interpretative problems by rewriting them. In a sense it's an admission of failure—but *only* in certain productions."[56]

—*Underlining, gimmickry, forced interpretations:* Perhaps the most consistent criticism leveled at Barton's work involves "over-visualization" of the text to make an interpretative point. Barton's friend and fellow academician Inga-Stina Ewbank describes the phenomenon in a general discussion of the strengths and weaknesses of modern stage practice:

> . . . we are perhaps in an era of *visual* theatre never equalled since the days of the masque. I, for one, have often recently come away from a performance with the impression that it is by visual means—sometimes decor, choreography, even dumb-shows—that the producer has tried to "demonstrate" the matter of the play, "more pregnantly than by words"; indeed, that the stage picture, like Hamlet's actors, must "tell all."[57]

Though Ewbank is speaking generally here, images from Barton productions come to mind: the black Northumberland bird in *Richard II,* Cressida's harlot's mask in the 1976 *Troilus,* Bernardine's sacrilege with the crucifix and chamber pot in *Measure for Measure.* John Russell Brown cites Barton frequently in a scathing attack on modern directorial abuse. He argues that

"Shakespeare is not free" because "directors are working . . . to make their own *answers* abundantly clear, by underlining with all the contrivance of set, costume, lighting, sound and the drilling of actors, by placing of visual emphasis, by grouping and movement, by verbal emphasis and by elaborate programs and public relations operations."[58] To charges of underlining, Barton answers: "Directors are always underlining; most directors do. I don't think that's anything exceptional."[59] And as far as gimmicks are concerned, Barton says, "I think the question is whether an individual piece of business is an inventive overlay, or whether it's a truthful bodying-out of what's implicit in the text. But perhaps in the end it rather comes down to a question of taste."[60]

Actors, and Church is one, are also aware that Barton can be too inventive in his resolve to make clear the meaning of the text:

> He still has a tendency, I think, to be frightened of things that aren't going to work. And then he will "screw it down," physically. . . . I think a criticism which has been legitimately used against John is that if the text is making a point quite strongly, he will sometimes underline it.

Speaking specifically about the 1976 *Troilus,* noted for its visual effects, Nettles intimated that Barton does not always trust the script and therefore relies on theatrical effects: "John Barton has no sense of economy. He'll try and make all the effects at once. . . . He sees in the text all the possibilities, all of them extraordinary and exciting and wonderful. And he can't choose between them." Barton is alert to such criticisms and has, on several occasions, deleted what originally seemed to be "a good idea." Of such ideas Barton says: "The trouble is when one has an idea you can't really tell until the last moment, maybe until first night, whether the idea is good or not. . . . There is no such thing as certainty."[61] Like many modern directors, Barton occasionally succumbs to the temptation to overemphasize a particular thematic strand. Lambert's evaluation of Barton's contributions to the RSC defines the problem: ". . . Barton's influence in applying a searching understanding into the play has been wholly stimulating—even if occasionally the proud discovery of a subtext has led to its being over-exposed, as if a surgeon were demonstrating that a beautiful woman has a bowel by cutting her open to show us."[62] Barton defends himself by asking from critics the same privileges that they enjoy in their studies:

> . . . if a director sees a particular meaning which he wishes to explore, he is surely engaged in an act of critical interpretation analogous to that which the scholar makes in the study. He does not think his interpretation definitive and he realises that it is selective.[63]

It is Barton's last sentence that is important. He has always maintained that his work represents but one man's attempt to explore the myriad meanings of the plays.

Of late there has been a call for "neutral productions" that offer no distinct interpretation of a script, bur rather a "neutral" reading, so that the audience may attach whatever meaning *they* wish to the production instead of having a director lead them through the text as a museum guide might take tourists through a gallery. Barton disdains any notion about the possibility of a "neutral" reading, though his *Tempest* and *Measure for Measure* were sometimes judged as examples of such phenomena:

> I think it is certainly impossible, and I question whether it's desirable. . . . You have to be specific with actors. When one reads a play in the study, one can say again and again of a given line, "I'm not sure what Shakespeare intends here; it could be this or it could be that." But, however unsure one may be, one can't leave things uncertain for the actor . . . one's got to choose a specific reading for the actor to play.[64]

Though one cannot call them "weaknesses" per se, there are gaps in Barton's development as a director that want filling. He has—as much as any director in the century—mastered the so-called problem plays: *All's Well That Ends Well*, *Troilus and Cressida*, and—to a lesser extent—*Measure for Measure*. But, to the disappointment of many, he has not attempted *Lear* on his own own (he assisted Trevor Nunn in 1976), nor has he done *Macbeth*, perhaps the most notoriously difficult play to conquor. (There are reports that the 1980 Brian Forbes–Peter O'Toole *Macbeth* at the Old Vic so appalled Barton that he is eager to stage the tragedy.[65]) Barton has perhaps limited himself too much to the works of Shakespeare and has only recently professionally directed plays written in this century (*La Ronde*, 1982 and *The Devils*, 1984), an indication of a broadening of his artistic vistas.

Despite these deficiencies, Barton has in his twenty years with the RSC built a rich legacy that is matched by few theater artists in this century. In an age of specialization, Barton stands out as a theatrical Renaissance man: acting teacher, writer, editor, scholar, director, critic.

Barton's work as an acting teacher at the RSC Acting Studio has done much to raise the standard of classical acting in England and, consequently, throughout the English-speaking world. His influence extends beyond his actors: his fellow directors, such as Clifford Williams, acknowledge their indebtedness to his guidance—"You can't be at Stratford near John Barton . . . and not know what the ground rules of verse speaking are."[66] It is not uncommon for directors to enlist Barton as a verse coach. Peter Hall, looking back on the accomplishments of the RSC, says, "We caused a revolution in the speaking of Shakespeare's verse. . . . I would say that's the best thing I've done in my life."[67] If Hall was the general of that revolution, then Barton was its mastermind. "Playing Shakespeare" will doubtless stand for years to come as the visual legacy of the RSC's heritage.

As one of the founding members of the Royal Shakespeare Company, Barton merits a niche in the history of the English theater. He has provided stability and continuity in the development of the company's style, as well as in its repertory. Hall has called Barton "the moral conscience" of the organization"[68] because of his insistence on raising the standard of stage production.

Barton will also be remembered for his varied works on the texts of Shakespeare, Tourneur, Ford, and Marlowe that have promoted new interest in textual scholarship. Probably no director since Granville Barker has done as much to create interest in the practical application of this discipline. Barton himself has indicated the importance of bridging the gap between the work of the practicing theater artist and the scholar:

> The ideal of the director/scholar is a good one, but since each profession is a full life in itself, I doubt any man can completely exert in both fields. . . . But of course the more directors are in touch with scholarship, and scholars are in touch with the theatre, the better for Shakespearean production.[69]

It is very much a part of Barton's legacy that he has taken a step towards reaching the goal he describes. In addition to his textual work, Barton's dramatic anthologies, particularly *The Hollow Crown*, are meritorious. Of their kind, Wells judges that Barton's are "far and away the best anyone has done." More recently, his adaptations of the Greek tragedies, *The Vikings*, Schnitzler, and Calderon have renewed interest in important but commercially neglected works. His evolving personal myth may itself provide new insight about myths we thought we knew well.

The synthesis between the intellectual insight of the academic and the inventive theatricality of the artist has altered stage production drastically in the late twentieth century. The year before Barton arrived at Stratford, Richard David wrote an essay for *Shakespeare Survey* that called for a more concerted effort between performers and scholars: "In truth . . . both are essential if the plays are to be presented so as to reveal the true 'form and pressure' of Shakespeare's intentions . . . . What he had to say was said not merely in literary terms but specifically in terms of the theatre."[70] Barton has, in the intervening years, realized David's ideal.

Whatever his other accomplishments and present aspirations, Barton is yet regarded as a director who has consistently invested his work with stimulating insights into complex texts and encased them in imaginative theatrical designs. His productions, Wells believes, "at their boldest have been the best we've had in the last twenty years."

Asked what his legacy might be, Barton, almost embarrassed by the question, replied, "It's—by its nature—very, very emphemeral indeed. . . . My work will be totally forgotten, one would think."[71] But the theater's memory is long: one still talks about the work of Garrick, of Macready, of Irving. Barton himself frequently refers to Granville Barker. Reminded that the theater's work is not as ephemeral as he supposed, Barton reconsidered the question, "Of what are you most proud in your career with the RSC?" and answered:

Doing Shakespeare justly, doing it better. I think the general standard of Shakespeare production in the 1950s was dreadful. . . . So I suppose I think about a kind of standard. But it's such a funny business. You put everything into it, the work, the rehearsal period, and then as soon as it opens, I have a feeling that it has nothing to do with me—it's not mine anymore. What I feel at bottom is that if I'm any good, whatever I make, the work is the thing that's valuable.

Appendix A
"Profile"

The following "Profile" appeared in *The Varsity* (Cambridge), May 12, 1951:

Profile
JOHN BARTON
President of the A.D.C.

By directing Julian Slade's forthcoming *Lady May*, John Barton adds Musical Comedy to his wide range of experience as a producer, actor, and writer. His first venture, *Henry IV, Part 1*, took place in his last half at Eton where, although "play-acting" was frowned upon, the success of the enterprise was such that John's confidence in himself was confirmed and Shakespearean production has remained a leading passion with him ever since.

Coming up to King's, he joined the A.D.C. and concentrated upon acting immediately in order to establish himself in a position where he could fulfill his ambitions as a producer. Amongst the twenty-five parts he has interpreted, he was imperiled to play ten Old Men successively. He is easily distinguished for certain mannerisms of voice and movement, which practically every member of the A.D.C. can imitate to some degree. He, however, is unique in being able to imitate no one.

His first leading part came in the Marlowe Society's *Twelfth Night*, when his Toby Belch gave him the necessary impetus to launch a risky, but worthwhile, double bill of *The Critic* and *Macbeth* at the beginning of the next fall term. It had a mixed reception from the Cambridge critics, but he found their judgments on the whole "stimulating." In material results the project paid its way, rather a rarity at the time, and won him much experience both as producer and actor, although *Macbeth* doled out its traditional ill-luck with facial wounds incurred in the battles.

He now turned Secretary of the A.D.C. to consider the club's organizational and financial position. A disinterested business sense, inherited from his father, drove him to investigating the club's balance sheets from 1939 onwards. The yearly deficit which had tended to grow since the war was thus eradicated, and John has clarified and reorganized the accounts, budgeting carefully for expenditures before each production, initiating new members into the club's organization as soon as possible to ensure continuity of policy. It has been found depressingly necessary on occasion to hold Committee meetings as frequently as twice a week, spending long hours in details of administration and interviewing caretaker, solicitor, or accountant. But in spite of his continued attention to these matters, he probably remains a better producer than economist.

It has been sometimes objected that the running of the Cambridge dramatics is in the hands of a small group. Whether or not this is ideally desirable, he is convinced that it is an administrative necessity, for few people have the time or experience to cope with the little seen and unglamorous side of owning a theatre, which is one of John's wildest ambitions. He is a strong advocate of communal criticism within the theatrical circle, a body which is always in danger of lapsing into sprightly, but unhelpful cattiness on the one hand, or excessive praise for mediocrity on the other.

As President he tries to encourage a high standard of performance in the A.D.C. Theatre. He refuses to air his criticisms in the Press, as he feels himself far too much involved in Cambridge Drama to sit in public judgment of his colleagues. But he usually makes private criticisms after unsatisfactory productions, and it is to his credit that he makes no enemies with his candour. He has found that adverse criticism is of more practical help than congratulations, while the most encouraging form of praise is the interest everyone shows in the production.

The contention that Cambridge Theatre consists of a half-a-dozen people intent on always giving one another the main parts he feels is a slight on his impartiality. At the beginning of this year, he produced independently his own play, *That's All One*, in which he gave leading parts to a number of untried actors, while refusing to type-cast those more experienced. The play, a whimsical mixture of pastoral, fantasy, and poetry, was received with mixed enthusiasm. But it showed that he could create characters and taught him humility, by "having to obliterate purple passages that made my actors moan." A second play, *Brown Ptarmigan*, was runner-up in the Young Writers Competition this year. At the moment he is in the middle of writing a thesis which relates *Beowulf* to Shakespeare. His Norse and Anglo-Saxon studies are interrupted by a number of commitments in the coming Cambridge Festival. His masterly production of *A Comedy of Errors* of last May Week is probably to be revived at the Watergate Theatre [London] this summer.

As President, John's work on the A.D.C. and Coordinating Committees has won him admiration and respect. But his all-embracing efforts to maintain a high standard at Cambridge amateur dramatics have not been achieved without his being accused of "professionalism." While asthma prevented him from maintaining the customary maturity of outlook in H.M. Forces, his dislike of publicity and his shy, almost embarrassed manner with strangers often means that he is misunderstood. He prefers his own company and it is perhaps a weakness that he lives too much in a world of his own ideas. To appreciate John fully, you must know him, and that is not easy. Yet he is no recluse. His conversation is stimulating to those who know him, and he has an ability to get what he wants.

There is a possibility that he will stay for a fourth year to write a thesis on the staging of Shakespeare. Whether this would help his other writing is to be doubted, but those who know him and will also be up next year, sincerely hope he will stay to serve Cambridge Dramatics in the future as he has in the past.

—J. B. M.

Appendix B

Programs for the BBC broadcasts of *The First Stage: A Chronicle of the Development of English Drama from Its Beginning to the 1580s*
Arranged and introduced by John Barton; produced by Raymond Raikes.

Program 1: Week of 18 November 1956
—John Barton describes the scope of the series with extracts;
—"The Beginnings of English Drama: X–IV Centuries."
Program 2: Week of 25 November 1956
—Mystery Plays of the Old Testament:
>   1. "The Creation and Fall" (from Norwich, Chester, York, Wakefield, and Hegge plays)
>   2. "Noah's Flood" (from Newcastle, Chester, Wakefield, and Hegge plays)
>   3. "Abraham and Isaac" (from Brome, Chester, and Wakefield plays)

Program 3: Week of 23 December 1956
—Mystery Plays:
>   1. "The Nativity" (from the Wakefield *Prima* and *Secunda Pastorum* and extracts from other cycles)

Program 4: Week of 20 January 1957
—Mystery Plays:
>   1. "The Betrayal, the Trial, and the Crucifixion" (from York, Wakefield, Chester and Hegge plays)

Program 5: Week of 17 February 1957
—Mystery, Miracle, and Morality Plays:
>   1. "The Resurrection" (mainly from the York cycle)
>   2. Extracts from "Mary Magdalene" (XV Century)
>   3. "The Play of the Sacrament" (1461)

Program 6: Week of 17 March 1957
—Moralities and Allegorical Drama
>   1. "The Pride of Life" (c. 1405)
>   2. Extracts from: *The Castle of Perseverance*" (c. 1425) and "Mind, Will, and Understanding" (c. 1460)
>   3. *Mankind* (c. 1475)
>   4. *Everyman* (c. 1495)

Program 7: Week of 14 April 1957
—Moral Interludes and Secular Entertainment
    1. *Fulgens and Lucrece* (Henry Medwall; c. 1497)
    2. Extracts from *Mundus et Infans* (before 1522)
    3. Extracts from *Hickscorner* (before 1512)
    4. The first part of *Magnyfycence* (John Skelton; c. 1516)
Program 8: Week of 12 May 1957
—Mere Interludes: The More Group
    1. "Calisto and Melibaea" (John Rastell; c. 1530)
    2. "Johan the Husband, Tyb the Wyfe, and Sir Johan the Priest" and "The Play of the Weather" (John Haywood; c. 1521–31)
Program 9: Week of 9 June 1957
    1. "The Nice Wanton" (c. 1547–53)
    2. *King Johan* (John Bale; c. 1547)
Program 10: Week of 7 July 1957
—Drama in the Schools: The Classical Influence on English Comedy
    1. "Jacob and Esau" (c. 1557)
    2. *Ralph Royster-Doister* (Nicholas Udall; c. 1553)
Program 11: Week of 4 August 1957
—Drama at the Universities and the Inns of Court
    1. *Gammer Gurton's Needle* (c. 1550)
    2. *Gorbuduc* (Thomas Sackville and Thomas Norton; c. 1562)
Program 12: Week of 8 September 1957
—Popular Theatre
    1. *The Spanish Tragedy* (Thomas Kyd; 1585–87)
    2. *The Jig of Rowland* (Will Kemp; from the German)
Program 13: Week of 15 September 1957
—Concluding talk: "The Rise and Fall of English Didactic Drama"
—John Barton reviews the series.

Appendix C
Barton's Revision of the "Gage Scene"

The following is Barton's revision of the "gage scene" in *Richard II* (4.1.1–90). Lines that Barton rewrote or rephrased have been italicized.

Bolingbroke:	*Go call him forth . . .* Now, freely speak thy mind, What thou dost know of noble Gloucester's death.
Northumberland: (formerly Bolingbroke's line)	Who wrought it with the king, and who performed The bloody office of this timeless end.
Exton: (formerly Bagot's)	Then set before my face the Lord Aumerle.
Bolingbroke:	Cousin, stand forth, and look upon that man.
Exton: (formerly Bagot's)	My Lord Aumerle, I know your daring tongue Scorns to unsay what once it hath delivered. In that dead time when Gloucester's death was plotted, I heard you say, "Is not my arm of length, That reacheth from the restful English court As far as Calais, to my uncle's head?" Amongst much other talk that very time I heard you say that you had rather refuse The offer of an hundred thousand crowns Than Bolingbroke's return to England— Adding withal, how blest this land would be, In this your cousin's death.
Aumerle:	Princes and noble lords, What answer shall I make to this base man? [Delete ll. 21–24] There is my gage, the manual seal of death, That marks thee out for hell! I say thou liest, And will maintain what thou has said is false

254

	In thy heart-blood, though being all too base
	To stain the temper of my knightly sword.
Bolingbroke:	*Sirrah*, forbear, thou shalt not take it up.

[Delete Aumerle's reply, ll. 31–32]

Ross:	If that thy valour stand on sympathy,
(formerly Fitzwater's)	There is my gage, Aumerle, in gage to thine:
	[Delete l. 35]
	I heard thee say, and vauntingly thou speak'st it,
	Thou caused Gloucester's death.
	If thou deny'st it twenty times, thou liest.
	[Delete ll. 39–42]

| Aumerle: | My Lord of Ross, thou art damned to hell for |
| | this. |

Willoughby:	Aumerle, thou liest, his honor is as true
(formerly Percy's)	In this appeal as thou art all unjust,
	And that thou art so, there I throw my gage,
	To prove it on thee [Delete two half-lines]—
	Seize it if thou dar'st.

| Aumerle: | An if I do not, may my hands rot off. |
| | [Delete 50–51] |

Hotspur:	I task the earth to the like, forsworn Aumerle,
(formerly "Another	And spur thee on with as many lies
Lord's")	As may be halloaed in thy treacherous ear
	From sun to sun: there is mine honour's pawn—[1]
	Engage it to trial if thou darest.

[Delete Aumerle's reply, ll. 57–59]

| Salisbury: | My Lord *Aumerle*, I do remember well |
| (formerly Surrey's) | The very time you and *Ross* did talk.[2] |

| Aumerle: | [Delete l. 62] |
| (formerly Fitzwater's) | You can witness with me this is true. |

| Salisbury: | As false, by heaven, as heaven itself is true. |

| Ross: | *Salisbury*, thou liest. |
| (formerly Fitzwater's) | |

Salisbury:	*Thou dost dishonour me!* Dishounourable boy!
(formerly Surrey's)	[Delete ll. 66–72, except for:]
	. . . There is mine honour's pawn!

Ross:	If I dare eat, or drink, or breathe, or live
(formerly Fitzwater's)	I dare meet *Salisbury* in a wilderness,
	And spit upon him, whilst I say he lies,
	And lies, and lies. [Delete ll. 76.5–79]
	Besides, I heard the banished Norfolk say,
	That thou, Aumerle, didst send two of thy men
	To execute the noble duke at Calais.

Aumerle: [Delete ll. 83–85; substitute:]
                            I have a thousand spirits in one breast
                            To answer twenty thousand such as you.
                            By heaven I'll throw it all!

Bolingbroke: These differences shall all rest under gage,
                            Till Norfolk be replaced . . .
                            [Continue scene as written; delete l. 94]

Source: Official RSC Prompt Book for *Richard II*, Shakespeare Centre Library, Stratford-upon-Avon.

Notes

1. James Stredder notes that Hotspur acted with "deliberate hesitation" before throwing his gage ("*Richard II* at Stratford, 1973," Master's thesis, University of Birmingham, 1973), 65.

2. I have taken these alterations from the prompt book; however, the lines may have been mistranscribed by the stage manager. The lines would make more sense if "Aumerle" and "Ross" were reversed.

Appendix D
Barton's Prologue to *King John*

(Enter Death as Presenter, before the curtains.)

Death: Now peace to all who be in hall
    Or lieth under Heaven:
And peace abide this Christmastide
    Now give you all good even.

Gentles, perchance you know me not
    A fellow I am of fame;
I am that king whereof they sing
    But I tell you not my name.

Yet I do come to all or some
    That be-en under heaven;
To each estate set I a date,
    And make mankind all even.

Be ye a losel or a lord,
    Be ye a man or child,
Be ye a Knight or a lowly wight,
    Or a lady sweet and mild;

Be ye a holy churchman great
    Or a Duke of high degree
Be ye a Prince, or perchance a King,
    Anon you must dance with me.

In very sooth, I am come this night
    To lay a King to rest,
Hight Richard, one of mickle might
    In Christendom the best.

When Kings be graven in the green
    And lie all under mold,

Source: Official RSC Prompt Book for *King John*, Shakespeare Centre Library, Stratford-upon-Avon.

Then little recketh, I ween,
   Their gay crown of gold.

God save the King, that he may win
   His kingdom joy and mirth;
For if that a King should fall to sin
   His realm shall rue his birth.

Then pray you all God save the King
   From all attaint and treason;
And you may see another spring,
   As is both right and reason.

Now, gentles, must our game begin;
   Therefore be merry, all:
Remember well what I you tell,
   And come when I you call.

Appendix E
Barton's Interpolation of Battle Scene for *Cymbeline*

Barton's interpolation of Folio stage directions into the act 5 battle sequence in *Cymbeline* (5.2). The lines were spoken by Cornelius, who read from a large book while actors mimed the battle behind him.

> The battle beginneth. Enter from one side Lucius,
> Iachimo and the Roman army and from the other side
> Cymbeline and the British army whom Posthumus
> Leonatus followeth like a poor soldier [*sic*]. Having
> saluted one another they go forth and the hurly soon
> spreadeth itself all about Milford Haven most bloody
> and most furious.
> Posthumus encountereth Iachimo in a skirmish whom,
> after some little strife, he vanquisheth and so leaveth.
> Yet n'er the less the Romans thrive in their assaults
> so thet [*sic*] the Britons fly and Cymbeline is taken
> to the great shame of the army.
> And now in sooth must the Romans have conquered had not
> a rescue come in time, by the appointment 'tis thought
> of Almighty Jove. Enter to the King's rescue
> Belarius, Guiderius and Arviragus and then Posthumus
> Leonatus who seconds them.
> They rescue Cymbeline,
> and betake themselves to a certain lane
> and stand o'erthwart the same and so obstruct it
> that the Britons may no longer fly but at length
> rally and drive the Romans from the field with great
> slaughter so that Lucius himself and Fidele, his page,
> are taken by the victors.
> The battle endeth.

Source: Official RSC Prompt Book for *Cymbeline*, Shakespeare Centre Library, Stratford-upon-Avon.

Appendix F
A Chronology of John Barton's Work with the Royal Shakespeare Company, 1960–1984

1960

January	Invited to join the RSC by Peter Hall as an assistant director.
June 21	Directed *The Taming of the Shrew.*
July 26	Assisted Peter Hall with *Troilus and Cressida.*
	Adapted, staged, and performed in *The Hollow Crown* (revived in 1961–62).

1961

	The Hollow Crown
November 15	Directed *Carmen* at Sadler's Wells, London (non-RSC production).

1962

	Devised *The Vagaries of Love.*
March 19	Adapted and directed *The Art of Seduction;* played the Narrator.

1963

July 17	Adapted and codirected (with Peter Hall and Frank Evans) *The Wars of the Roses:* —*Henry VI* —*Edward IV* —*Richard III*

1964

Winter	Appointed associate director of the RSC.

1964

April 3   Codirector (with Peter Hall and Clifford Williams) of *The Henriad:*
                   —*Richard II*
                   —*Henry IV, Part 1*
                   —*Henry IV, Part 2*
                   —*Henry V*

August 12   Codirected the revival of *The Wars of the Roses.*

1965

April 7   Directed *Love's Labour's Lost.*

May 27   Directed *Henry V* (a restaging of the 1964 production at the Aldwych Theatre, London; assisted by Trevor Nunn).

1966

April 6:   Codirected (with Clifford Williams and Trevor Nunn) *Henry IV, Part 1* (a restaging of the 1964 production).

April 14   Codirected *Henry IV, Part 2.*

June 22   Devised and directed *The Battle of Agincourt for* Theatregoround.

August 11   Codirected *Henry V.*

1967

February 26   Devised and directed (with David Jones) *Two Open Debates on War (The Peloponnesian Wars)* at Aldwych Theatre.

April 12   Directed *Coriolanus.*

June 1   Directed *All's Well That Ends Well.*

1968

January 17   Directed *All's Well That Ends Well* at Aldwych Theatre.

April 3   Directed *Julius Caesar.*

August 8   Directed *Troilus and Cressida.*

September 24–   Directed *Julius Caesar* for provincial tour (prior to revival at
November 6   Aldwych).

1969

March 19   Devised and directed *When Thou Art King* for Thea-
and 28   tregoround (assisted by Gareth Morgan).

June 19   Directed *Troilus and Cressida* (Aldwych Theatre; followed by European tour).

August 21   Directed *Twelfth Night.*

1970

February 12–   Directed Australian tour of *Twelfth Night.*
April 18

April 1   Directed *Measure for Measure.*

July 3   Directed *When Thou Art King* for Theatregoround (assisted by Gareth Morgan).

August 6   Directed *Twelfth Night,* Aldwych Theatre.

August 26   Directed *When Thou Art King* (Part 3) for Theatregoround.

October 15   Directed *The Tempest,*

1971

March 29   Directed *Richard II* for Theatregoround (also at Stratford and the Aldwych Theatre).

April 8   Directed *Twelfth Night* (revival of 1969 production).

April 12   Directed *Henry V* for Theatregoround (also at Stratford and the Aldwych Theatre).

September 9   Directed *Othello.*

1972

January 18   Directed *Othello* at Aldwych Theatre.

April–October   Assisted Trevor Nunn with "Romans cycle."

1973

April 10   Directed *Richard II.*

1974

January 9–27   Directed *Richard II* at Brooklyn Academy of Music in New York.

March 20   Adapted and directed *King John* (assisted by Barry Kyle).

April 10   Directed *Richard II* (revival of 1973 production).

June 4   Directed *Cymbeline* (assisted by Barry Kyle and Clifford Williams).

August 13–31   Adapted and directed *Doctor Faustus* for provincial tour.

September 5   Directed *Doctor Faustus* at Aldwych Theatre.

September 18   Directed *Richard II* at Aldwych Theatre.

December 19   Directed *Cymbeline* at Aldwych Theatre.

1975

January 9	Directed *King John* at Aldwych Theatre (revival of 1974 production with major script revisions).
January 27	Directed *Doctor Faustus* for provincial tour and Stratford (revival of 1974 production).
August 5	Directed *Perkin Warbeck* at The Other Place, Stratford (assisted by Barry Kyle).

1976

April 8	Directed *Much Ado About Nothing.*
June 3	Directed *The Winter's Tale* (with Trevor Nunn)
August 3	Directed *Troilus and Cressida* (with Barry Kyle)
November 4	Assisted Trevor Nunn and Barry Kyle with *King Lear.*

1977

March 10	Directed *Much Ado About Nothing* at Newcastle Theatre Royal (revival of 1976 production).
June 30	Directed *Much Ado About Nothing* at Aldwych Theatre (revival of 1976 production restaged by Peter Stevenson).

1977

March 22	Directed *Troilus and Cressida* at Newcastle Theatre Royal (revival of 1976 production).
May 6	Directed *A Midsummer Night's Dream* (with Gillian Lynne).
June 25	Directed *A Midsummer Night's Dream* at Aldwych Theatre.
August 1	Directed *The Pillars of the Community* at Aldwych Theatre.

1978

Winter	Appointed director of the RSC.
January 27	Directed *The Way of the World* at the Aldwych Theatre.
March 22–April 15	Directed *A Midsummer Night's Dream* (with Gillian Lynne; revival of the 1977 production).
May 11	Directed *The Merchant of Venice* at The Other Place, Stratford.
August 11	Directed *Love's Labour's Lost.*

1979

February 26	Directed *The Merchant of Venice* at Gulbenkian Studio, Newcastle.
March 6	Directed *Love's Labour's Lost* at Newcastle Theatre Royal.
April 12	Directed *Love's Labour's Lost* at Aldwych Theatre.

May 2	Directed *The Merchant of Venice* at The Warehouse Theatre, London.

1980

February 1	Adapted and directed *The Greeks* at Aldwych Theatre.
July 2	Directed *Hamlet.*

1981

April 4	Directed *Hamlet.*
April 6	Directed *The Merchant of Venice.*
July 1	Directed *The Hollow Crown* at the Fortune Theatre, London.
July 16	Directed *The Merchant of Venice* at the Aldwych Theatre.
September 3	Directed the "Double Bill:" *Two Gentlemen of Verona* and *Titus Adronicus*
September 17	Directed *Hamlet* at the Aldwych Theatre.

1982

January 10	Adapted and directed (with Gillian Lynne) *La Ronde* at the Aldwych Theatre.
March 23	Directed the "Double Bill" at Newcastle.
	Devised "Playing Shakespeare," featuring twenty-two RSC actors, for Weekend TV.

1983

January 6	Directed (with Peter Stevenson) *The School for Scandal* at Haymarket Theatre, London. (Non-RSC production.)
June	Adapted and directed *The Vikings* at *Den Nationaler Scene,* Bergen, Norway (from Inga Stina-Ewbank's translation of Ibsen's *The Vikings of Hegeland*).
November 23	Adapted (with Adrian Mitchell) and directed *Life's a Dream* at The Other Place, Stratford-upon-Avon.
December 15	Directed (with Peter Stevenson) *School for Scandal* at the Duke of York's Theatre, London.

1984

May 2	Directed *Life's a Dream* at The Pit, Barbican Centre, London.
May 5	Performed the role of Sir Thomas Malory in Gillian Lynne's telecast of *Le Mort D'Arthur,* ITV.
July–August	Hosted telecast of "Playing Shakespeare," Weekend TV.
August 17	Directed *The Devils* (John Whiting), The Pit, Barbican Centre, London.

Notes

Chapter 1. Ambition's Ladder

1. Interview with John Barton, London, November 5, 1980. All Barton quotations in this chapter are from this interview unless noted. See also: "Profile: John Barton of the ADC," *Varsity* (Cambridge), May 12, 1951, 4 (see appendix A).

2. Charles Marowitz, "From Prodigy to Professional," *New York Times Magazine,* November 24, 1968, 62–63.

3. Interview with Tony Church, RSC actor, Stratford-upon-Avon, November 20, 1970. All Church quotations in this chapter are from this interview unless noted. Church entered Cambridge in 1950 and worked with Barton on a number of productions there; he later followed Barton into the professional theater, first with the Oxford-Cambridge players, then with the RSC. He has worked with Barton more than any other actor has.

4. Kenneth Muir, "Fifty Years of Shakespearean Criticism: 1900–1950," *Shakespeare Survey* 4 (1951): 25.

5. George Rylands, *Words and Poetry* (New York: Payson and Clark, 1928), 16.

6. Rylands, "The Poet and the Playwright," *Shakespeare Survey* 7 (1954): 34.

7. "Leading Lecturers," *Varsity* (Cambridge), December 2, 1950, 4.

8. From "Playing Shakespeare" television script, John Barton, 1983.

9. Peter Hall, quoted by David Addenbrooke, *The Royal Shakespeare Company: The Peter Hall Years* (London: William Kimber, 1974), 26.

10. Ian Richardson, RSC Workshop, University of California, Santa Barbara, February 16, 1980.

11. "Leading Lecturers," 4.

12. Addenbrooke, *Royal Shakespeare Company,* 26.

13. Barton, quoted by Gareth Lloyd Evans, "Directing Problem Plays: John Barton Talks to Gareth Lloyd Evans," *Shakespeare Survey* 25 (1972): 68.

14. Penny Gold, quoted by Judith Cook, *Directors' Theatre* (London: Harrap, 1974), 68.

15. Barton, quoted by Terry Coleman, "Elizabethan Manner," *Guardian* (Manchester), September 4, 1972.

16. Barton, "Too Much Drama," *Varsity,* February 8, 1952, 6.

17. "Profile," 4.

18. Hillary Usill, "Our Revels Now Are Ended," *Records and Recordings,* April 1964.

19. "Profile," 4. The article notes that Barton is "unique in being able to imitate no one."

20. Curiously, Barton's first production at Stratford (*Taming of the Shrew*) used a similar concept.

21. Peter Marris, "The Alchemist," *Varsity,* December 2, 1950.

22. Unfortunately *Edward II* played at the end of the fall term and was not reviewed in *Varsity* because of the Christmas break. Church remembers the production as being "marvelous."

23. Barton, quoted in Lloyd Evans, "Directing Problem Plays," 66.

24. Barton, quoted in Addenbrooke, *The Royal Shakespeare Company,* 206.

25. Barton, quoted by Ronald Hayman, "John Barton," *Times* (London), September 9, 1972, 11.

26. I am quoting Church here; the text reverses the sentence (1.3.20). Other variations from the text are also quoted from Church's reconstruction of the production. He was trying to recreate the experience of the Cambridge version rather than a verbatim recitation of the text.

27. Barton, quoted in Hayman, "John Barton," 11.

28. "Cambridge Diary," *Varsity*, February 23, 1952.

29. Dr. John Sullivan of the Classics Department, University of California, Santa Barbara, was a student at Cambridge in 1952 and remembers Barton's *Caesar* vividly. I am indebted to his account of the production.

30. "Ay Met a Lay-on," *Guardian* (Manchester), March 13, 1952.

31. "Julius Caesar," *Observer*, March 16, 1952.

32. Church, lecture at the University of California, Santa Barbara, February 19, 1981.

33. Addenbrooke, *The Royal Shakespeare Company*, 28.

34. Richard Mayne, "That's All One," *Varsity*, October 28, 1950, 4.

35. Mark Amory, "John Barton Brings His Gift to the Greeks," *Sunday Times Magazine* (London), February 3, 1980, 42.

36. John Wilders, "A Preview," *Varsity*, April 18, 1953, 3.

37. Paul Almond, "Dramatic Adventure," *Varsity*, November 1, 1952, 6.

38. David Friedman, "The Day Is Yours," *Varsity*, November 8, 1952, 6.

39. Michael MacOwan, "New Elizabethan Actors," *Radio Times*, May 15, 1953.

40. "The Westminster Henry V," *Stage*, July 16, 1953. Reviews of *Henry V* are in the Birmingham Central Library Shakespeare Collection.

41. "Henry V," *Times* (London), July 10, 1953.

42. John Bourne, "King Hal," *Yorkshire Post*, May 22, 1953.

43. R.G., "Well Balanced," *Daily Telegraph*, July 10, 1953.

44. "Henry V."

45. Barton, quoted by Vincent Guy, "Director in Interview: John Barton," *Plays and Players* 17 (November 1970): 40.

46. Barton, quoted by Janet Watts, "Pillar of the RSC," *Guardian Weekly* (Manchester), August 14, 1977. Barton says he first recognized his inability to discuss plays when, after directing *Henry IV* in 1966, he was asked to speak to a group. He remembers that he stood up and heard "a little voice saying, 'I have no views on *Henry IV*.' I paused for a long time, and said, 'Any questions?'"

47. Amory, "John Barton Brings His Gift," 43.

48. Barton, *The First Stage: A Chronicle of the Development of English Drama From Its Beginnings to the 1580s* (London: BBC Press, 1957); all Barton quotations concerning medieval drama and its influence on the Elizabethans are from this source.

49. *The First Stage* broadcasts have been preserved on records and can be obtained at most university and public libraries (Phonodisc: The Spoken Word, 99705–99722, 1968). Barton emphasizes that he had nothing to do with the broadcast performances (although he is credited as the director on the recordings): "I thought they were terrible."

50. The Shakespeare Collection at the Birmingham Central Library contains the complete transcripts of these broadcasts. Barton's relationship with the BBC continued: in 1963 he did two broadcasts, one a defense of his adaptation of *Henry VI*, the other an examination of Greene's *Edward III* in which he argued, through a linguistic analysis, that sections of Greene's history were actually written by Shakespeare.

51. Barton, "Midland Critics: *King John*," BBC Broadcast, May 9, 1957.

52. Barton, "Midland Critics: *The Tempest*," BBC Broadcast, August 15, 1957.

53. Barton, "Midland Critics: *Cymbeline*," BBC Broadcast, July 15, 1957.

54. Barton eventually added other anthologies to his repertory: *The Art of Seduction* (1962), based on Laclos's *Les Liaisons Dangereuses*; *The Vagaries of Love* (1962), which attempted to

answer Raleigh's immortal question, "What is love?" Barton's script offered forty solutions to the query, drawing responses from Shakespeare, Keats, Marvel, Dryden, Hardy, Yeats, Lawrence, and others. In May 1962 Barton, Max Adrian, and Peggy Ashcroft read the work at the Coventry Theatre Festival.

55. Barton, quoted by Judith Cook, "Uneasy Lies the Head," *Birmingham Post*, September 14, 1971.

56. Interview with Michael Bogdanov, San Diego, California, August 13, 1980.

57. Peter Hall, "Avoiding a Method," in *The Royal Shakespeare Company: The Crucial Years*, (Stratford-upon-Avon: Max Reinhardt, 1963), 16–17.

58. Edmond Gardner, "Stratford 1960: A New Era," *Shire and Spire*, April 1960.

59. John Russell Brown, "The RSC 1965," *Shakespeare Survey* 19 (1966): 112.

60. Interview with Mike Gwilym, RSC actor, London, December 9, 1980.

61. Addenbrooke, *The Royal Shakespeare Company*, 90.

62. "Royal Shakespeare Company," *Flourish* 2 (Autumn–Winter 1964–65): 7.

63. Amory, "John Barton Brings His Gift," 43.

64. Ibid.

65. Ivor Brown, program note for *The Taming of the Shrew*, Royal Shakespeare Theatre, 1960.

66. Bernard Levin, "The Murder of Shakespeare in Five Acts," *Daily Express* (London), June 22, 1960.

67. "Lively Farce in Stratford," *Morning Advertiser* (London), June 22, 1960.

68. Gareth Lloyd Evans, "Breezily Efficient, Though Not a Collector's Item," *Stratford-upon-Avon Herald*, June 24, 1960.

69. Kenneth Tynan, "The Economics of Murder," *Observer*, June 26, 1960.

70. Cheryl Brahms, "The Taming of O'Toole," *John O'London*, June 30, 1960.

Chapter 2. "Feats of Broils and Arms"

1. Edmund Gardner, "The Enterprising Mr. Hall," *Stratford-upon-Avon Herald*, January 25, 1963.

2. Peter Hall, Introduction to *The Wars of the Roses* (London: BBC Press, 1970), xvi. All Hall quotations regarding *The Wars* are from this source, unless noted, and will hereafter be cited parenthetically in the text.

3. "Atticus," *Sunday Times* (London), August 18, 1963.

4. Barton, "The Making of the Adaptation," *The Wars of the Roses* (London: BBC Press, 1970), xxii. All Barton quotations concerning *The Wars*, unless noted, are from this source and will be cited parenthetically.

5. P. xvi. The *Henry VI* cycle had been offered twice within recent memory: Douglas Seale and Barry Jackson staged it for the Birmingham Repertory Company from 1951 to 1953 and later transferred them to the Old Vic in 1957; *Richard III* was not included in the cycle, and, Barton remembers, the trilogy seemed "oddly incomplete" without it.

6. Barton to Gareth Lloyd Evans, "How Far Can You Cut Shakespeare?" *Guardian* (Manchester), November 26, 1964, 8.

7. Coleman, "Elizabethan Manner."

8. Hall to Charles Marowitz, "The Director and the Permanent Company," in *Theatre at Work*, ed. Charles Marowitz and Simon Trussler (New York: Hill and Wang, 1967), 152.

9. Barton to Addenbrooke, *The Royal Shakespeare Company*, 205.

10. J. C. Trewin, "Sequence Opens at Royal Shakespeare Theatre," *Birmingham Post*, July 18, 1963.

11. Hall, "Blood Will Have Blood," RSC Program for *Richard III*, RST, August 1963, n.p.

12. Barton, *The Wars of the Roses*, sc. 63. Hereafter, all quotations from *The Wars* will be cited by scene numbers in the text. Barton's text does not contain line numbers.

13. Hall to Amory, "Barton Brings His Gift," 42.

14. Interview with John Barton, London, November 5, 1980.

15. Barton to Hayman, "John Barton," 11.

16. Barton, "King John," *Listener*, August 21, 1975.

17. Hall emphasized that it was "no part of our business to father Shakespeare with purple passages fit for anthologies. I therefore tried to keep Barton's rewrites to bare narrative. . . . If the version therefore sometimes reads flatly, it is my responsibility, not Barton's" (xi).

18. Barton interview. He further admitted that it was a personal source of satisfaction to have his work mistaken for Shakespeare's. I asked Barton if he had any thoughts of writing a "modern" Elizabethan or Jacobean play in that manner. "No, no," he quickly replied.

19. Coleman, "Elizabethan Manner."

20. Stanley Wells, "The Academic and the Theatre," in *The Triple Bond*, ed. Joseph G. Price (University Park, Penn.: Pennsylvania State University Press, 1977), 11.

21. Barbara Hodgdon, "*The Wars of the Roses:* Scholarship Speaks on Stage," *Deutsche Shakespeare-Gesellschaft West Jahrbuch 1972* (Heidelberg: Quelle and Meyer, 1972), 170. Not all of the 1,144 lines were of Barton's invention: many were incorporated from Holinshed and other of Shakespeare's sources.

22. Hodgdon's *Jahrbuch* analysis (see above) is the most thorough of such analyses. I am indebted to her scholarship, which I found very useful as a basis for my discussion.

23. Roger Gellert, "Barton's Bard," *New Statesman*, July 26, 1963, 121.

24. "Shakespearean Histories for the Modern Audience," *Times* (London), January 13, 1964.

25. Kenneth Tynan, "Gang War in Armour," *Observer Weekend Review*, July 21, 1963.

26. Barton to Lloyd Evans, "How Far. . . ?"

27. Muir, as quoted by Lloyd Evans, "How Far . . . ?" *Guardian*, November 26, 1964, 8.

28. "Shakespeare on TV," *Times* (London), April 21, 1965.

29. Barton to Lloyd Evans, "How Far . . . ?"

30. Jan Kott, *Shakespeare Our Contemporary*, trans. Boleslaw Taborski (Garden City, N.Y.: Anchor Books, 1966), 45. All quotations from Kott are from this source and will be cited parenthetically in the text.

31. Interview with Barton, November 5, 1980.

32. Trevor Nunn to Jim Hiley, "A Company with Direction," *Plays and Players* 25 (October 1977): 17. Although *Shakespeare Our Contemporary* was not published in Polish until 1964 and in English until 1966 (both after the RSC production of *The Wars*), Hall had a proof copy in February 1963. An even earlier copy was apparently in RSC hands as early as 1962: Peter Brook's much-discussed production of *King Lear* seems indebted, in part at least, to Kott's essay on that tragedy—"King Lear or Endgame?" (127–68 of *Shakespeare Our Contemporary*).

33. Gareth Lloyd Evans, "Stratford Round Up," *Guardian Weekly* (Manchester), December 26, 1963.

34. Hodgdon, "Scholarship Speaks on Stage," 178.

35. Hall, "Blood Will Have Blood."

36. Dame Peggy Ashcroft to Addenbrooke, *The Royal Shakespeare Company*, 193.

37. Felix Barker, "No Thorns in This Glorious War of Roses," *Evening News* (London), July 18, 1963.

38. Editorial, *Times* (London) August 24, 1963, 7.

39. Harold Hobson, "What Shakespeare Believed," *Sunday Times* (London), April 19, 1964.

40. Amory, "John Barton Brings His Gift," 43.

41. Barton to Ronald Hayman, "John Barton," 11.

42. Richard Kee, "Plays," *Queen*, August 28, 1963. Dr. Robert Potter of the University of California, Santa Barbara, saw the production during his student days in England and remembers vividly the excitement and "danger" of the combat scenes, particularly those with great broad swords. I am indebted to his reconstruction of these moments.

The battle scenes began an RSC tradition of "smoke-filled" combats, which has become something of a Barton trademark. During a discussion of Barton's style with Michael Tubbs, an RSC music director and composer, Tubbs jokingly noted that Barton "has a good nose for smoke" (interview, Stratford, November 21, 1980).

43. Clifford Williams to Addenbrooke, *The Royal Shakespeare Company*, 249.

44. "Atticus," *Sunday Times*, August 18, 1963.

45. Lloyd Evans, "How Far . . . ?" 9.

46. Ibid., 8.

47. Bury to Addenbrooke, *The Royal Shakespeare Company*, 212.

48. Phillip Hope-Wallace, "The Wars of the Roses at Stratford-upon-Avon," *Guardian* (Manchester), July 18, 1963.

49. Trewin, "Sequence Opens. . . ."

50. Ken Griffin, "So History Was Made at Stratford," *Leamington Spa Courier*, July 18, 1963.

51. John Bury, "Against Falsehood," *Flourish* 5 (Winter 1965): 6.

52. Robert Speaight, *Shakespeare on the Stage* (London: Collins, 1973), 288.

53. J. C. Trewin, "Stratford Gives All Day Long War of the Roses Session," *Birmingham Post*, January 13, 1964. Trewin believes that these gory details were deleted from the Aldwych revival in 1964.

54. Lloyd Evans, "Stratford Round Up."

55. Hall, "Blood Will Have Blood."

56. Dame Peggy Ashcroft, "Margaret of Anjou," in *Deutsche Shakespeare—Gesellschaft West Jahrbuch 1974* (Heidelberg: Quelle and Meyer, 1974).

57. Ibid., 9.

58. Hope-Wallace, "The Wars of the Roses."

59. Hobson, "What Shakespeare Believed."

60. These figures are based on prompt books contained in the Shakespeare Centre Library at Stratford-upon-Avon. They are approximate figures because of the large number of prose lines in the *Henry* plays and because Barton cut words and phrases from whole lines.

61. "Divine Right and the King of Vanity," RSC Program for *Richard II*, RST, April 1964.

62. Hall, "The Empirical Empire," RSC Program for *Henry V*, RST, April 1964.

63. Trevor Nunn, in Ralph Berry, *On Directing Shakespeare: Interviews with Contemporary Directors* (London: Croom Helm, 1977), 57–58.

64. Milton Shulman, "Theatre," *Evening Standard* (London), June 4, 1964.

65. Ray Seaton, "This Richard Almost Saintly," *Wolverhampton Express and Star*, April 16, 1964.

66. Alexander Leggatt, "The Extra Dimension: Shakespeare in Performance," *Mosaic* 10 (1977): 45.

67. "The Morality Tradition and the Rejection of Vanity," RSC Program for *Henry IV, Part 1*, RST, April 1964.

68. Robert Speaight, "Shakespeare in Britain, 1964," *Shakespeare Quarterly* 15 (1964): 382.

69. "Polished Pertubation and Golden Care," RSC Program Note for *Henry IV, Part 2*, RST, April 1964.

70. Speaight, "Shakespeare in Britain, 1964," 385.

71. J. C. Trewin, "A Little Touch of Harry in the Night," *Birmingham Post*, June 4, 1964.

72. B. A. Young, "Henry V," *Financial Times* (London), June 4, 1964.

73. Alan Brien, "A Henry for Our Generation," *Sunday Telegraph* (London), July 7, 1964.

74. "Recast Henry IV Is More Intense," *Times* (London), April 7, 1966. This paper's critic lamented, "Financially this is a difficult year for the Royal Shakespeare Company, and one can appreciate their need to play safe; nevertheless, this production puts some strain on sympathies."

75. Ronald Bryden, "Next Stage," *New Statesman* 69 (June 4, 1965): 891.

76. Gareth Lloyd Evans, "The Chap in Charge Is Shakespeare," *Guardian* (Manchester), April 21, 1966.

77. Gareth Lloyd Evans, "Henry V's Army Clobbers Its Way Through France with Grim Realism," *Stratford-upon-Avon Herald*, August 19, 1966.

78. Gareth Lloyd Evans, "Grandeur Makes *Henry IV* Memorable," *Stratford Herald,* April 15, 1966.

79. Typical of the comments on Hotspur was the judgment of "W.B.," writing for *Yorkshire Post* (April 7, 1966): "He has brought into the play an essential quality of fiery nobility, dangerous wit, and brash courage, without giving the extrovert performance in which his predecessor mistook antics for acting."

80. Ray Seaton, "Paul Rogers' Definite Portrait of Falstaff," *Wolverhampton Express and Star,* April 16, 1966.

81. Alan Brien, "An Intellectual Falstaff," *Sunday Telegraph* (London), April 10, 1966.

82. Ian Richardson to Gordon Gow, "Through the Right Doorway: Ian Richardson in Interview with Gordon Gow," *Plays and Players* 29 (September 1979): 10.

83. Peter Roberts, "The RSC's First Decade," in *Theatre 71,* ed. Sheridan Morley (London: Hutchinson, 1971), 130.

84. "Royal Shakespeare Company" *(Times),* 11.

85. John Coe, "The Wars Make Sense at Last," *Bristol Evening Post,* July 20, 1963.

Chapter 3. Wars and Lechery

1. A. P. Rossiter, *Angel with Horns* (Cambridge: At the University Press, 1962), 129.

2. C. B. Young, "The Stage History of *Troilus and Cressida,*" *Troilus and Cressida,* ed. Alice Walker (Cambridge: At the University Press, 1969), lv. (All quotations from the play are from this text.)

3. These principal stagings—by Poel, MacOwan, Guthrie, Hall, and Barton—have been meticulously detailed by James Christie in his doctoral dissertation, *Five Twentieth-Century Productions of Troilus and Cressida* (Stanford University, 1972).

4. John Barton to Gareth Lloyd Evans, "Directing Problem Plays: John Barton Talks to Gareth Lloyd Evans," *Shakespeare Survey* 25 (1972): 64. Barton qualifies his enthusiasm: ". . . but that may be because of what I am, rather than what the play is. I would hesitate to make absolute judgment, but it's extraordinary to me that anybody could think of *Romeo and Juliet,* for instance, as being a better play that *Troilus and Cressida.*"

5. See Joyce Carol Oates, "Essence and Existence," in *Shakespeare: Troilus and Cressida, A Casebook,* ed. Priscilla Martin (London: MacMillan & Co., 1976), 167ff.

6. Una Ellis-Fermor, "Discord in the Spheres," in *Discussions of Shakespeare's Problem Comedies,* ed. Robert Ornstein (Boston: D.C. Heath and Company, 1961), 21.

7. Barton, "The Director's Notes in Rehearsal," Official RSC Program for *Troilus and Cressida,* RST, August 1968. All Barton comments on *Troilus and Cressida* are from this source unless otherwise noted.

8. Peter Hall, Program Note, Official RSC Program for *Troilus and Cressida,* RST, April 1960.

9. Barton, quoted by Addenbrooke, *The Royal Shakespeare Company,* 204.

10. J. C. Trewin, *Shakespeare on the English Stage: 1900–1964* (London: Barrie and Rockliffe, 1964), 246.

11. Barton, quoted in Addenbrooke, *The Royal Shakespeare Company,* 203. J. L. Styan surmises that the concept might have been "prompted by Brecht's white circle of light for acting his *Antigone* in 1948" (*The Shakespeake Revolution,* Cambridge: At the University Press, 1977, 209).

12. J. C. Trewin, *Going to Shakespeare* (London: George Allen and Unwin, 1978), 189. Elsewhere Trewin cites Cressida's words "As false as sandy earth" as a possible inspiration for the concept (*Shakespeare on the English Stage,* 246).

13. Alan Brien, "Eden's War," *Spectator,* July 29, 1960.

14. Robert Speaight, "Shakespeare in Britain," *Shakespeare Quarterly* 11 (1960): 451.

15. Tony Church, quoted by Addenbrooke, *The Royal Shakespeare Company,* 118.

16. Christy, "Five Twentieth-Century Productions", 224–25.

17. Rossiter, *Angel with Horns,* 131.
18. Vesnica Pistotnik, "Aspects of the 1968 and 1976 Productions *of Troilus and Cressida,"* (Master's thesis, University of Birmingham, 1980), 56. Given the density of the language, this is a relatively small number of cuts. More than a few critics felt the text could have been trimmed even more.
19. Barton, quoted in Addenbrooke, *The Royal Shakespeare Company,* 205. The prompt book for the production, however, suggests that Barton's responsibilities may have been more extensive. Before each scene is a notation—either "P. H." or "J. B."—which apparently identifies which director had primary responsibility for a scene. Hall seems to have staged the "love plot" (i.e., the Troilus and Cressida scenes), Barton the "war plot." Barton says he is sure that he did not direct as many scenes as the prompt suggests; of the notations he said, "It was probably a preliminary breakdown of responsibilities that was never done" (interview, June 17, 1983, London).
20. "Good Production of Troilus," *Times* (London), July 27, 1960.
21. Christy, "Five Twentieth-Century Productions," 299.
22. The directors may have been influenced by their Cambridge mentor, Rylands, who staged *Troilus* for a 1954 BBC broadcast; in a *Radio Times* interview he defined the importance of Pandarus and Thersites to the play:

Each side has a chorus. Thersites squatting and scavaging among the tents symbolizes the bestial elements of war . . . . Within Troy's walls, an interior which is civilized, a little oriental, lurks Uncle Pandarus.

Douglas Allen, "The Knell of Chivalry," *Radio Times,* September 17, 1954. Quoted by Michael E. Kimberley, *"Troilus and Cressida* on the English Stage" (Master's thesis, University of Birmingham, 1968), 112.
23. Anthony Alvarez, "The Straight and Narrow," *New Statesman and Nation* 60 (July 30, 1960): 155.
24. Kimberley, *"Troilus and Cressida,"* 130.
25. Edmund Gardner, "Sand and Smoke—And Some Fine Acting in Troilus and Cressida," *Stratford-upon-Avon Herald,* July 29, 1960.
26. Alvarez, "The Straight and Narrow."
27. Speaight, "Shakespeare in Britain [1960]," 451.
28. Christy, "Five Twentieth-Century Productions," 248.
29. Robert Speaight praised Barton's battles for defining their thematic and theatrical importance to the play: ". . . they form the conclusion to an exceedingly protracted argument." Specifically, he lauded the quality of the combat: "I have never seen anything more sinister than the slaying of Hector. And the playing of the different lights through the smoke of a pardonably anachronistic cannon gave a lurid chiaroscuro to the scene" (Speaight, "Shakespeare in Britain [1960]," 451–52).
30. Ian Richardson, quoted by Gow, "Through the Right Doorway," 10.
31. Bryan Magee, "Shakespeare at Home," *Listener,* May 25, 1967.
32. Peter Roberts, "Home Grown," *Plays and Players* 14 (June 1967): 19.
33. F. W. D., "A Coriolanus to Rank with the Best," *Oxford Times,* April 21, 1967.
34. Jeremy Kingston, "Theatre," *Punch* May 3, 1967, 653.
35. Milton Shulman, "The Unmasking of a President, Roman Fashion," *Evening Standard* (London), April 14, 1968. To be fair, there were favorable reviews: Hillary Spurling, *Spectator,* April 12, 1968, and J. C. Trewin, *Birmingham Post,* praised Barton's *Caesar.* But the majority of critics judged the production tedious. When *Caesar* moved to the Aldwych in November, it was judged significantly improved.
36. Peter Roberts, "Power Politics," *Plays and Players* 15 (June 1968): 18.
37. B. A. Young, *"Julius Caesar," Financial Times* (London), April 4, 1968.
38. D. R., *"Julius Caesar," Solihull News,* April 4, 1968.
39. Peter Lewis, "The Most Boring Roman of Them All," *Daily Mail* (London), April 4, 1968.

40. Gareth Lloyd Evans, "The Reason Why: The Royal Shakespeare Company 1968 Reviewed," *Shakespeare Survey* 22 (1969): 140. It is Lloyd Evans who supposes that Barton chose to explore the Casca-Caesar relationship. He does not elaborate upon this idea in his review.

41. Barton, quoted by Ronald Hastings, "Trevor Nunn Moves in at Stratford," *Daily Telegraph* (London), March 30, 1968.

42. Ian Richardson to Gareth Lloyd Evans, "Shakespeare and the Actors," *Shakespeare Survey* 21 (1968): 123.

43. R. B. Marriott, "Julius Caesar Made Dull by the RSC," *Stage and Television Today*, April 6, 1968.

44. Peter Lewis called the stage fights "the worst I have seen in a long time" (*Watford Evening News*, April 6, 1968), and Phillip Hope Wallace judged them among the "feeblest" he had seen (*Guardian*, November 21, 1968). Hope Wallace referred to the original Stratford staging of the play while noting that they had been improved when the production shifted to London that autumn.

45. "Troilus and Cressida," *Sunday Telegraph* (London), June 22, 1969.

46. Frank Cox, "*Troilus and Cressida,*" *Plays and Players* 16 (August 1969): 49. Ronald Bryden concurred in his review in *The Observer:* "I've seldom seen a Shakespearean text so searchingly explored" (June 22, 1969).

47. Barton, "Director's Notes," RSC Program. Irving Wardle correctly identified Barton's emphasis. "(The play) is shown through Thersites' eyes, and for once it becomes savagely coherent" (*Times*, August 9, 1968).

48. Interview with John Nettles, RSC Actor, Santa Barbara, California, February 15, 1980; all Nettles comments regarding *Troilus* are from this interview.

49. Ray Seaton, "Troilus . . . With a Freudian Touch," *Wolverhampton Express and Star*, August 19, 1968.

50. Benedict Nightingale, "Nothing But Wars and Lechery," *New Statesman* 76 (August 16, 1968): 208.

51. Barton to Guy, "Director in Interview," 49.

52. Richard David, *Shakespeare in the Theatre* (Cambridge: At the University Press, 1978), 119.

53. B. A. Young, "*Troilus and Cressida,*" *Financial Times* (London), August 9, 1968.

54. Ronald Bryden, "Stratford's House Style," *Observer*, August 11, 1968.

55. D. A. N. Jones, "Mars 'n Venus," *Listener*, August 15, 1968.

56. Irving Wardle, "Rhythm and Passion," *Times* (London), June 20, 1969, 7.

57. Interview with Sebastian Shaw, Santa Barbara, California, February 14, 1980.

58. Basil Boothroyd, "Theatre," *Punch* 255 (August 21, 1968): 270.

59. Grenville Robinson, "The Royal Shakespeare Company Has a Way with It," *Daily Sketch*, June 20, 1969.

60. Craig Raine, "All Change," *New Statesman* 92 (August 27, 1976): 286.

61. Bryden, "Stratford's House Style."

62. Harold Hobson, "Heroes, Heels, and Hypocrisy," *Sunday Times* (London), August 17, 1969.

63. Milton Shulman, "Meanwhile Back at the Trojan Camp," *Evening Standard* (London), August 9, 1968.

64. David Jones, "What's with the Aldwych," *Flourish* 2 (Summer 1969): n.p.

65. Lloyd Evans, "The Reason Why," 143–44.

66. Barton's RSC program note read:

The play is to some extent an attack on our cosy habit of generalising. We use abstract words like Honor, Fame, Beauty, and Truth to sanction what we do and give ourselves a sense of order and meaning. We need these to smooth over the confusion of life, and to avoid acknowledging the chaos within ourselves. Ulysses does this a great deal . . . .

67. Kott, *Shakespeare Our Contemporary,* 71.

68. When I interviewed Church at Stratford (November 20, 1980), he spoke at length about Barton's search for "the good" in Troilus:

Where would he find the forces of good? In the heroic ideals which the play smashes. . . . Certainly Nestor he would regard as an absolute, a good old man whose dream of a wonderful world of chivalry is destroyed. And Hector is the representative of that dream and is shown to have feet of clay in the end. . . . Once again [Barton] doesn't ask that the theatre has to come to an optimistic conclusion. What he is saying is that Shakespeare is actually stating that there is a force for good and it is being smashed. . . .

69. Jones, "Mars 'n Venus."

70. Lawrence, *Shakespeare's Problem Plays,* 167.

71. Sebastian Shaw, quoted by Christy, "Five Twentieth-Century Productions," 283.

72. Anne Righter, *Shakespeare and the Idea of the Play* (London: Chatto and Windus, 1962), 182.

73. Wardle, "Sex and Warfare in Stratford."

74. W. A. Darlington, "A Matter of Principle," *Daily Telegraph* (London), June 30, 1969. This is a review of the Aldwych revival, but Darlington applied the same criticism to the Stratford production.

75. W. A. Darlington, "A Queer Twist to Shakespeare," *Daily Telegraph* (London), September 19, 1968.

76. Barton, quoted in Lloyd Evans, "Directing Problem Plays," 70.

77. Rosemary Say, "So Thersites Was Right," *Sunday Telegraph,* August 11, 1968.

78. Nightingale, "Nothing But Wars and Lechery," 208.

79. Jones, "Mars'n Venus."

80. "A Death That Made It All Worthwhile," *Leamington Spa Courier,* August 16, 1968.

81. I am indebted to Dr. Robert Egan of the University of California, Santa Barbara, for his account of this moment. He saw the 1969 Aldwych revival of the production.

82. Christy, "Five Twentieth-Century Productions," 301.

83. Ibid.

84.

[Mirren] makes the girl shallow-pated rather than wicked and establishes this in her first scene with Pandarus. During her love scenes with Troilus she convinces herself of her own sincerity and is all the more vehement in its defense because she really knows how little depth it has.

W. A. Darlington, "Acting of Cressida Clear and Original," *Daily Telegraph* (London), August 9, 1968.

85. Helen Mirren, quoted by Ian Woodward, "A Very Leading Lady," *Guardian* (Manchester), September 3, 1969.

86. Say, "So Thersites Was Right."

87. Rossiter, *Angel with Horns,* 136–37.

88. See Christy's account of Troilus's transition, "Five Twentieth-Century Productions," 306.

89. *"Troilus and Cressida" Sunday Telegraph* (London), August 22, 1968.

90. Ellen Kalman, "John Barton's Brilliant Coup de Theatre," *Today's Cinema,* August 13, 1969. Barton used similar effects elsewhere in the production: the prophecies of Cassandra were echoed electronically (Brown, *Sheffield Telegraph,* June 20, 1969).

91. "A Death That Made It All Worthwhile."

92. Frank Cox's assessment of Barton's *Troilus* is worth quoting since it illustrates the respect given the production by a number of his colleagues:

John Barton's approach is not flawless—not quite, anyway—but after two viewings of his complex, persuasive treatment I for one am frankly so impressed by its combination of scholarship and theatricality that I could in all humility cross *Troilus and Cressida* off an over-crowded list of plays to be seen and puzzled over. Why? Because, for my money, its questions are answered *("Troilus and Cressida,"* 49).

93. Lloyd Evans, "The Reason Why," 144.

94. "Persuasive 'Cressida' Is Marred by Gimmicks," *The Scotsman,* June 23, 1969.

95. Hillary Spurling, "Good Company," *Spectator,* June 28, 1969. Peter Lews of *The Daily Mail* (London) noted that the homosexual overtones had been toned down since Stratford (June 20, 1969).

96. Interview with Michael Tubbs, RSC Music Director, Stratford-upon-Avon, November 21, 1980. Tubbs rewrote Woolfenden's score because the original music book was lost; Tubbs had to reconstruct the score from tape recording of the 1968 production.

97. Frank Marcus, "War and The Other," *Sunday Telegraph* (London), August 22, 1976. Michael Billington (*Guardian,* August 19, 1976) and J. C. Trewin (*Birmingham Post,* August 19, 1976) disagreed and found the 1976 production more interesting than the 1968 one. In general, however, most reviewers preferred the earlier production.

98. Interview with Mike Gwilym, RSC Actor, London, November 9, 1980. All Gwilym comments regarding *Troilus and Cressida* are from this interview.

99. Interview with Barton, London, November 5, 1980.

100. J. W. Lambert, "Castles in the Cuban Air," *Sunday Times* (London), August 22, 1976, 35.

101. John Elsom, *"Troilus and Cressida,"* Listener, August 26, 1976.

102. Roger Warren, "Theory and Practice at Stratford, 1976," *Shakespeare Survey* 30 (1977): 175. Barton apparently thought better of the idea: the mask was eventually dropped and was replaced by "a cackling laugh" (David, *Shakespeare in the Theatre,* 120).

103. Elsom, *"Troilus and Cressida."*

104. Official RSC Prompt Book for the 1976 production of *Troilus and Cressida,* Shakespeare Center Library, Stratford-upon-Avon. The prompt contains the following directions for the kissing scene:
"Achilles unveils Helen doll" (70)
"Doll goes for Achilles' balls" (72)
"All circle for dance"

105. David Zane Mairowitz, *"Troilus and Cressida,"* Plays and Players 24 (October 1976): 20.

106. David, *Shakespeare in the Theatre,* 120.

107. Prompt Book and production photographs of the 1976 production. Masks were worn by Hector (Lion); Helenus (Griffin); Paris (Goat); and Troilus (Horse).

108. Michael Billington (*"Troilus and Cressida"* [review], *Guardian,* August 18, 1976); Robert Cushman (*Observer,* August 22, 1976); J. C. Trewin (*Birmingham Post,* August 28, 1976); R. B. Marriott (*Stage and Television Today,* August 26, 1976); and Roger Warren ("Theory and Practice at Stratford," 176) all believed the production to be less tied to a specific production than the 1968 one.

109. Gareth Lloyd Evans, "Troilus and Cressida Together at Last," *Stratford-upon-Avon Herald,* August 20, 1976.

110. B. A. Young, *"Troilus and Cressida,"* Financial Times (London), August 18, 1976.

111. David, *Shakespeare in the Theatre,* 121. The frying pan business was cut in later performances.

112. Mairowitz, *"Troilus and Cressida,"* 21.

113. David Isaacs, "Love, War, Etc.," *Coventry Evening Telegraph,* August 18, 1976.

114. Michael Pennington to Ellen Goodman, "Interview with Michael Pennington," *RSC Newspaper,* Spring 1980, 5.

115. Irving Wardle, *Times,* "Irreconcilable Clashes On Stage," August 18, 1976, 5. Gwilym remembers the scene as the most troublesome in the production; neither the director nor the actors

were never really happy with it. He said the scene was changed in rehearsal frequently and several times in performance in an attempt to find a solution to its complexities. "I don't think there is an answer," he concluded.

116. Barton, quoted in Lloyd Evans, "Directing Problem Plays," 67–68.

117. Warren, "Theory and Practice" 175.

118. Billington, *Troilus and Cressida*," 6.

119. RSC Prompt Book. Pistotnik notes that Barton cut almost 200 more lines from the 1976 production than the 1968 play ("Aspects," 5). There was considerable criticism of the production's length in 1968.

120. Warren, "Theory and Practice," 175.

121. David, *Shakespeare in the Theatre*, 125.

Chapter 4. "The Owl and the Cuckoo"

1. J. W. Lambert, "The Wind and the Rain," *Sunday Times* (London), August 24, 1969.

2. Gareth Lloyd Evans, "Interpretation or Experience: Shakespeare at Stratford," *Shakespeare Survey* 23 (1970): 135.

3. John Barton, "Elizabethan Tragedy and Artifice," *Flourish* 5 (Spring 1965): 10.

4. Barton, "The Owl and the Cuckoo," RSC Program for *Love's Labour's Lost*, RST, April 1965. All Barton comments regarding *Love's Labour's Lost* are from this essay unless otherwise noted.

5. Barton, "Elizabethan Tragedy and Artifice," 10.

6. John Russell Brown, "The Royal Shakespeare Company 1965," *Shakespeare Survey* 19 (1966): 117.

7. Geoffrey Lane, "A Winner to Begin With," *Wolverhampton Express and Star*, April 8, 1965.

8. W. A. Darlington, "Fine Style and Speech, Yet Bewildering," *Daily Telegraph* (London), April 4, 1965.

9. R. B. Marriott, "Melancholy Shrouds the Summer of Love's Labour's Lost," *Stage and Television Today*, April 15, 1965.

10. Michael Pennington to Ellen Goodman, "Interview with Michael Pennington," *RSC Newspaper*, Spring 1980, p. 5. All Pennington quotes are from this interview.

11. Barton to Lloyd Evans, "How Far . . .?"

12. Apparently there is some tradition for reassigning the line. Trewin notes that in 1948 Peter Brook, in his acclaimed production, gave the line to the French Princess (*Going to Shakespeare*, 70). In 1978 Barton returned the line to Don Armado.

13. B. A. Young, *"Love's Labour's Lost"* (review), *Financial Times*, April 8, 1965.

14. L. W. Lambert, *Drama in Britain, 1964–1973* (London: Longman Group, 1974), 25.

15. Alexander Leggatt, "The Extra Dimension: Shakespeare in Performance," *Mosaic* 10 (1977): 47.

16. Pennington to Gordon Gow, "A State of Mind and Body," *Plays and Players* 26 (May 1979): 15.

17. John Peter, "Edward Bond Goes to War," *Sunday Times* (London), August 13, 1978.

18. Irving Wardle, *"Love's Labour's Lost,"* *Times* (London), August 14, 1978.

19. Anne Barton, Program Note for *Love's Labour's Lost*, RST, August 1978. The note was an abridgment of her introduction to the Riverside Shakespeare edition.

20. Roger Warren, "A Year of Comedies at Stratford," *Shakespeare Survey* 32 (1979): 209.

21. Peter, "Edward Bond."

22. Jane Ellison, "Barton Bright," *Evening Standard* (London), August 15, 1978.

23. Warren, "A Year of Comedies," 208.

24. Official prompt book for *Love's Labour's Lost* (1978), Shakespeare Center Library, Stratford-upon-Avon.

25. Michael Billington, *Guardian,* *"Love's Labour's Lost"* (review), August 14, 1978.

26. B.A. Young, *"Love's Labour's Lost"* (review), *Financial Times,* August 14, 1978.

27. Wardle, *"Love's Labour's Lost."*.

28. Barton to Guy, "Director in Interview," 49.

29. Ronald Bryden, "In Illyrian Neverland," *Observer,* August 24, 1969.

30. Stanley Wells, *Royal Shakespeare* (Manchester: Manchester University Press, 1976), 44–45. Specifically, the performances were divided as follows:

Year	Place	Number of Performances
1969	Stratford	30
1970	Aldwych	47
	Australia	40
1971	Stratford	71
1972	Japan	14

31. Judith Cook, "King John Barton," *Plays and Players* 21 (June 1974): 27.

32. Speaight, ("Shakespeare in Britain," *Shakespeare Quarterly* 20 [1969]: 438) noted the similarities. Stanley Wells, in *Royal Shakespeare,* [Manchester: At the University Press, 1977] prefaces his discussion of Barton's production by establishing Hall's staging of *Twelfth Night* as a point of reference.

33. Felix Barker, "Misses the Gay Touch," *Evening News* (London), April 22, 1958.

34. Trevor Nunn to Barry, *On Directing Shakespeare,* 60.

35. Wells, *Royal Shakespeare,* 47.

36. Anne Barton, *"As You Like It* and *Twelfth Night:* Shakespeare's Sense of an Ending," in *Stratford-upon-Avon Studies 14,* ed. David Palmer and Malcolm Bradbury (New York: Crane, Russar and Company, 1972), 173–76 passim. Other were less easily convinced, notably playwright-critic Frank Marcus, who argued that the Bartons' thesis that *Twelfth Night* prefigured the final romances is "an intellectual notion, unsupported by evidence. . . . It takes a man of exceptional intelligence and erudition to turn the sunny enchantment of *Twelfth Night* into a bleak and turgid elegy. John Barton at Stratford is such a man" (*Sunday Telegraph,* August 24, 1969). Robert Cushman's *Plays and Players* review echoed Marcus's concern: ". . . if you take *Twelfth Night* to be a dramatised Feast of Misrule . . . and your lady-wife backs you with a closely argued programme note, the one quality your production cannot afford is tameness. But here inertia, so to speak, runs riot" *"Twelfth Night,"* *Plays and Players* 17 (October 1969): 20). These comments were distinctively counter to the general opinion, which saw Barton's deliberate reading of the play as revelatory.

37. Christine Avern-Carr, *"Twelfth Night* at Stratford-upon-Avon: 1958–1974," (Masters thesis, University of Birmingham, 1975), 19.

38. Judi Dench to Gareth Lloyd Evans, "Judi Dench Talks to Gareth Lloyd Evans," *Shakespeare Survey* 27 (1974): 141.

39. John Barber, "Team of Fine Actors in *Twelfth Night,"* *Daily Telegraph,* August 21, 1969. Roger Williams, of the *Coventry Evening Telegraph,* concurred: "The Humour is not played down. In fact it is thrown into added relief by the lingering treatment of many poignant moments" (August 22, 1969).

40. Interview with Tony Church, Stratford-upon-Avon, November 20, 1980. In an interview with Mark Amory of *The Sunday Times Magazine* (February 3, 1980), Church also said of Barton's *Twelfth Night:* "It *was* poetic. It *was* elegaic. But it *was* funny. The laughs were bigger than I've ever heard them because they came out of something."

41. G.R.A., *"Twelfth Night,"* *Evening Telegraph* (Coventry), April 23, 1969.

42. Sheila Bannock, "Dream *Twelfth Night* Has Inspired Comic Malvolio," *Stratford-upon-Avon Herald,* August 29, 1969, 2.

43. Barber, "Team of Fine Actors."

44. Nunn, quoted in Berry, *On Directing Shakespeare*, 60.

45. Cushman, *"Twelfth Night,"* 21.

46. Leggatt, "The Extra Dimension," 43.

47. Bannock, "Dream *Twelfth Night*," 2.

48. J. C. Trewin, *"Twelfth Night," Birmingham Post*, August 22, 1969. Trewin is, of course, referring to Barton's propensity for smoke effects, typified by the *Troilus* production. The "smoke" was actually a "sea mist."

49. C.J.W., "Impressive *Twelfth Night* at Stratford," *Evesham Journal*, August 28, 1969.

50. Doreen Tanner, "A Bittersweet Play Produced with Colour," *Liverpool Post*, August 22, 1969.

51. Richard David, "Of an Age and For All Time: Shakespeare at Stratford," *Shakespeare Survey* (1972): 167.

52. Church to Amory, "John Barton Brings His Gift," 45.

53. Interview with Michael Tubbs, RSC Music Director, Stratford-upon-Avon, November 21, 1980. All Tubbs comments are from this interview.

54. The song is still in the RSC repertory. Terry Hands used it in his 1979 production of *Twelfth Night*. Guy Woolfenden said that Barton considers the song the "most perfect" show song he has heard (interview, New York City, August 16, 1982).

55. "Barton is taking Shakespeare's Imagery and What It Tells Us altogether too solemnly. Such punctillious underlining can only render the words ridiculous," wrote Robert Cushman in *"Twelfth Night,"* 20.

56. Wells, *Royal Shakespeare*, 49.

57. Barton to Guy, "Director in Interview," 49.

58. Speaight, "Shakespeare in Britain [1969]," 438.

59. Bryden, "In Illyrian Neverland."

60. Lambert, *Drama in Britain*, 58.

61. Jeremy Kingston, "Theatre," *Punch*, September 3, 1969.

62. M. M. Mahood, quoted in RSC Program Note for *Twelfth Night*, RST, August 1969. All Mahood quotations are from this source.

63. J.C. Trewin, *"Twelfth Night"* (review), *Birmingham Post*, August 23, 1969.

64. Bryden, "In Illyrian Neverland."

65. David, "Of an Age and For All Time," 167.

66. Wells, "The Academic and the Theatre," 13.

67. Lambert, "The Wind and the Rain."

68. Simon Gray, "Morally Superior," *New Statesman* 78 (August 29, 1969): 285.

69. Lloyd Evans, "Interpretation or Experience," 135.

70. Barton cut slightly less than 100 lines from the play. His other major textual alteration was the transposition of 2.2 with 2.1 to provide continuity for the Viola-Malvolio ring exchange. This is not unusual (Hall did it in 1958). Also, speaking as one who has transposed the scenes while directing the play, I found an additional advantage: if the transposed scenes follow each other, Viola exits with the line "Time, thou must untangle this, not I / It is too hard a knot for me t'untie," and—in the repositioned scene—is followed on by Sebastian. Since Time can only untangle the knot by eventually reuniting Viola and Sebastian, thus clearing up their mistaken identities and resolving the improbable love alignments, it is an effective counterpoint to have Sebastian—Time's instrument of reconciliation—appear immediately after Viola's supplication.

71. Richard David thought it was not sensible "to make Maria a puritan maypole when everything in the text indicates a jolly little bundle." Otherwise David's review was one of the most favorable of the production ("Of an Age and For All Time," 167).

72. Harold Hobson, *"Twelfth Night," Christian Science Monitor*, April 17, 1971.

73. "Memorable *Twelfth Night*," *Glasgow Herald*, August 25, 1969.

74. Ibid.

75. Wells, *Royal Shakespeare*, 52.

76. Bryden, "In Illyrian Never." Bryden noted that the costume helped Sinden effect "the

comic highpoint of the evening": when Olivia gave him the ring and instructed him to "run" after Caesario, he responded, "Run, Madam?" in outraged dignity, and broke into a "Zulu lope" to carry out the order.

77. Ray Seaton, "Graceful Evening of Sadness and Mirth," *Wolverhampton Express and Star,* August 22, 1969.

78. Speaight, "Shakespeare in Britain [1969]," 438–39.

79. Milton Shulman, *"Twelfth Night*—Pretty But Taken Too Seriously," *Evening Standard* (London), August 22, 1969.

80. B. A. Young, *"Twelfth Night"* (review), *Financial Times,* August 21, 1969.

81. Bryden, "In Illyrian Neverland."

82. Seaton, "Graceful Evening."

83. Gray, "Morally Superior," 285.

84. Wells, *Royal Shakespeare,* 57–58.

85. R. B. Marriott, "Feste, the Hero of Royal Shakespeare *Twelfth Night,*" *Stage and Television Today,* August 28, 1969.

86. Wells, *Royal Shakespeare,* 62.

87. Ian Richardson, RSC Workshop, University of California, Santa Barbara, February 16, 1980.

88. Barton to Lloyd Evans, "Directing Problem Plays," 66.

89. Sheila Bannock, "Topical Appeal Makes 'All's Well' Speak Directly to Modern Society," *Stratford-upon-Avon Herald,* June 9, 1967.

90. Robert Speaight, "Shakespeare in Britain [1967]," *Shakespeare Quarterly* 18 (1967): 392.

91. A. P. Rossiter, quoted in RSC Program for *All's Well That Ends Well,* RST, June 1967.

92. "Colour and Pace at Stratford," *Glasgow Citizen,* June 3, 1967.

93. Desmond Pratt, "Frustration of Age and Youth in *All's Well,*" *Yorkshire Post,* June 2, 1967.

94. Peter Ansorge, "Contemporary Shakespeare," *Plays and Players* 14 (August 1967): 37. See Trevor Nunn's comments on the RSC goals in *On Directing Shakespeare,* 56.

95. Herbert Kretzmer, "All's Well on Stage But Not in Silly Program," *Daily Express* (London), June 2, 1967.

96. Hillary Spurling, "Et in Arcadia Philpotts," *Spectator,* June 9, 1967.

97. Pratt, "Frustration."

98. Charles Godden, "Fast and Furious Life," *Morning Star* (London) June 3, 1967.

99. J. C. Trewin, "Setting to . . . ," *Illustrated London News,* June 10, 1967.

100. John Peter, "Producer's Triumph Over Material," *Times,* June 2, 1967, 8.

101. Milton Shulman, "Poor Bertram—He Just Didn't Want to Get Hitched!" *Evening Standard* (London), June 2, 1967.

102. In 1967 Richardson also played Vendice in Tourneur's *The Revenger's Tragedy* (directed by Trevor Nunn, from a script heavily edited—and rewritten in part—by John Barton: see chapter 9). Here, too, critics praised Richardson's playing for the humor he brought to the role.

103. Spurling, "Et in Arcadia Philpotts."

104. Both quotations are from the RSC Program for *All's Well That Ends Well,* RST, June 1967.

105. Peter, "Producer's Triumph."

106. B. A. Young, *"All's Well That Ends Well,"* *Financial Times* (London), June 2, 1967.

107. Peter, "Producer's Triumph."

108. R. B. Marriott, *"All's Well That Ends Well"* (review), *Stage and Television Today,* June 8, 1967.

109. Barton, as quoted by Lloyd Evans, "Directing Problem Plays," 67.

110. Ansorge, "Contemporary Shakespeare," 37.

111. Ibid.

112. Ibid.

113. Peter, "Producer's Triumph," 8.

114. Bannock, "Topical Appeal."

115. Pratt, "Frustration."

116. Young, *"All's Well."*

117. Stanley Wells, "Directors' Shakespeare," *Deutsche Shakespeare-Gesellschaft West Jahrbuch 1976,* (Heidelberg: Quelle and Meyer, 1976), 71.

118. Interview with Sebastian Shaw, Santa Barbara, California, February 14, 1980. A. P. Rossiter, who, it has been noted, is admired by Barton, is quoted in the RSC Program for *Measure for Measure* (RST, April 1970) as saying, "I do not know what to make of the Duke."

119. Interview with John Barton, London, November 5, 1980.

120. Barton, as quoted by Lloyd Evans, "Directing Problem Plays," 64–65.

121. J. M. Nosworthy, quoted in RSC Program for *Measure for Measure.* John Barber (*Daily Telegraph,* April 6, 1970) wrote that Nosworthy's views were extracted from the preface of his New Arden edition to the play. Nosworthy argues that Shakespeare's characters exhibit "a kind of Strindbergian moral ambiguity." Barber concludes that "the preface has certainly influenced John Barton's revival of the play."

122. Barton, as quoted by Lloyd Evans, "Directing Problem Plays," 65. Anne Barton's Program Note informed RSC patrons that *"Measure for Measure* has proved more critical disagreement, a greater number of conflicting readings than any other Shakespearean comedy."

123. Jane Williamson, "The Duke and Isabella on the Modern Stage," in *The Triple Bond,* ed. Joseph G. Price (University Park, Penn.: Pennsylvania State University Press, 1975), 165.

124. Milton Shulman, "Comedy . . . , At Its Best When Broad," *Evening Standard* (London), April 2, 1970.

125. Benedict Nightingale, "A Bit of a Drag," *New Statesman* 79 (April 10, 1970): 524.

126. Robert Speaight, "Shakespeare in Britain," *Shakespeare Quarterly* 21 (1970): 444.

127. Sebastian Shaw to Terry Coleman, "An Age of Kings," *Guardian* (Manchester), April 13, 1970.

128. D. A. N. Jones, "Hard Cases, Bad Laws," *Listener,* April 9, 1970.

129. Barton, as quoted by Lloyd Evans, "Directing Problem Plays," 65–66.

130. Speaight, "Shakespeare in Britain [1970]," 444. Marriott said it was Barton's "best moment" (*"Measure for Measure"* (review), *Stage and TV Today,* April 9, 1970).

131. J. C. Trewin, "Bonfires on Ice," *Illustrated London News,* April 11, 1970, 30. W. T. of *The Nottingham Evening Post* (April 2, 1970) suggested a "lack of faith" in the play may have accounted for the ambiguous ending. John Russell Brown, in his provocative essay "Free Shakespeare" (*Shakespeare Survey* 24 [1971]: 129), cites the moment as an example of directorial abuse; his major complaint was that the business marked Isabella "undeniably as the odd one out."

132. Irving Wardle, "Stratford Integrity," *Times* (London), April 2, 1970, 12.

133. Peter Thomson, "A Necessary Theatre: The RSC Season 1970 Reviewed," *Shakespeare Survey* 24 (1971): 124–25.

134. Peter Brook, quoted by John Barber, "True (Or Too True) to Life?" *Daily Telegraph* (London), April 6, 1970.

135. Ronald Bryden, *"Measure for Measure"* (review), *Observer,* April 5, 1970.

136. Interview with Michael Bogdanov, RSC director, San Diego, California, August 13, 1980. All Bogdanov quotations concerning Barton's *Measure for Measure* are from this interview.

137. Jones, "Hard Cases, Bad Laws." Jones noted that the business "is more strident then we want—but perhaps Shakespearean in a bloody-minded way."

138. John Barber, "Curtain Up at Stratford," *Daily Telegraph,* April 1, 1970.

139. Ian Richardson to Ronald Hayman, "Baring the Nerve Ends," *Times* (London), March 21, 1970, iii (Arts Section).

140. Ibid. Jones "Hard Cases, Bad Laws" wrote that Angelo and Isabella indeed seemed to be "seducing each other while they talk of justice and mercy."

141. Thomson, "A Necessary Theatre," 124.

142. "Scholarly Impact," *Cambridge Daily News,* April 10, 1970.

143. Helen Dawson, *"Measure for Measure,"* Plays and Players 17 (May 1970): 35.

144. Thomson, "A Necessary Theatre," 123.

145. Dawson, *"Measure for Measure,"* 35.

146. Williamson, "The Duke and Isabella," 167.

147. M.A.B., "Problems for the Seeker of Moral Guidance," *Leicester Mercury,* April 2, 1970. Wardle ("Stratford Integrity") also noted Isabella's sexuality: "She has a range of direct emotions; impulse and sheer coyness that make the big scenes with Angelo and Claudio exceptionally rich in moment to moment development." Dawson (*"Measure for Measure,"* 35), in a negative vein, wrote that Miss Kohler was altogether "too blue and pinched about her chastity" when she should have been "not only afraid of sex, but almost psychotically hate the thought of it."

148. Thomson, "A Necessary Theatre," 123.

149. Barton, as quoted by Lloyd Evans, "Directing Problem Plays," 65.

150. Thomson, "A Necessary Theatre," 123.

151. Shaw to Coleman, "An Age of Kings."

152. "Challenger to Chastity," *Sunday Telegraph* (London), April 5, 1970.

153. Wardle, "Stratford Integrity," 12.

154. Bryden, *"Measure for Measure."*

155. Thomson, "A Necessary Theatre," 123–24.

156. Barber, "True (Or Too True) to Life?"

157. Interview with Barton, London, November 5, 1980.

158. Dawson, *"Measure for Measure,"* 34.

159. Speaight, "Shakespeare in Britain [1970]," 445.

160. Barton, as quoted by Lloyd Evans, "Directing Problem Plays," 65.

161. Harley Granville Barker, quoted by John L. Styan, *The Shakespeare Revolution* (Cambridge: At the University Press, 1977), 2.

162. A larger production of the play opened at the Aldwych, London, in the spring of 1981; it was included in the Main House repertory at Stratford later that year with David Suchet as Shylock.

163. Roger Warren, "A Year of Comedies at Stratford," *Shakespeare Survey* 32 (1979): 204.

164. Ibid.

165. Nicholas DeJongh, *"The Merchant of Venice,"* *Guardian* (Manchester), May 12, 1978, 12.

166. Interview with John Nettles, Santa Barbara, California, February 14, 1978. All Nettles comments regarding Barton's *Merchant* are from this interview.

167. Ned Chaillet, *"The Merchant of Venice,"* *Times,* May 13, 1978, 7.

168. In interviews with the author, Tony Church and Mike Gwilym both also spoke of Barton's fondness for Malory. Church suggested that Barton "lives in Malory's world."

169. John Barber, *"The Merchant of Venice"* (review), *Daily Telegraph,* May 3, 1979.

170. Malcolm Rees, "Vengeful Arrogant Shylock," *South Wales Argus,* May 16, 1978.

171. Ann Jennalie Cook, *"The Merchant of Venice* at The Other Place," *Shakespeare Quarterly* 30 (1979): 159.

172. J. C. Trewin, "New Plays," *The Lady,* May 24, 1979.

173. Warren, "A Year of Comedies," 205.

174. Sally Aire, *"The Merchant of Venice,"* *Plays and Players* 25 (July 1978): 33.

175. Cook, *"Merchant of Venice,"* 159.

176. Ibid.

177. B. A. Young, *"Merchant of Venice"* (review), *Financial Times,* May 3, 1979.

178. "So Much to Like," *Morning Star* (London), May 16, 1978.

179. Chaillet, *"Merchant of Venice,"* 7. Malcolm Rees wrote that Bland was "inclined to treat her love scenes and the famous courtroom scene with the same attack and determination, taking the edge off her role as a woman in the play" ("Vengeful Arrogant Shylock").

180. Peter McGarry, "Sparkling Merchandise," *Coventry Evening Telegraph,* May 12, 1978.

181. Warren, "A Year of Comedies," 205.

182. Aire, *"Merchant of Venice,"* 33.

183. Chaillet, DeJongh, and Eric Shorter (*"Merchant of Venice"* [review], *The Star,* May 15, 1978) all referred to Beckett in their discussion of the Gobbos. The latter complained that they were "too emphatically like fugitives from Godot."

184. Roger Warren, "Interpretations of Shakespearian Comedy," *Shakespeare Survey* 35 (1982): 141.

185. Ibid., 142.

186. Barton to John Higgins, "The Realistic Economies of Doctoring Shakespeare," *Times* (London), August 26, 1981, 9.

Chapter 5. "He Who Plays the King"

1. Jerry Tallmer, "The Royal Shakespeare Company," *New York Post,* February 11, 1974. In *New York Theatre Critics Reviews* 36 (1975): 379.

2. John Barton, speaking at a "Director's Forum," August 23, 1974, Shakespeare Institute, Stratford-upon-Avon. Quoted by James Stredder, "John Barton's Production of *Richard II* at Stratford-upon-Avon, 1973," *Deutsche Shakespeare-Gesellschaft West Jahrbuch 1976* (Heidelberg: Quelle and Meyer, 1976), 29.

3. Stanley Wells, *Royal Shakespeare* (Manchester: At the University Press, 1977), 65. All Wells's comments on this play are from this source.

4. Peter Thomson, "Shakespeare Straight and Crooked: A Review of the 1973 Season at Stratford," *Shakespeare Survey* 27 (1974): 154.

5. Harold Hobson, "The Hollow Crown," *Sunday Times* (London), March 24, 1974.

6. James Stredder's master's thesis (University of Birmingham, 1973) has been condensed into an excellent account of the production in *Deutsche Shakespeare-Gesellschaft West Jahrbuch 1976* (see n. 2 above); in the same edition is an analysis of Barton's *King John.* Stanley Wells *(Royal Shakespeare)* and Richard David *(Shakespeare in the Theatre,* chap. 10) also discuss the plays in some depth. I am indebted to these men for their perceptions, and to Dr. Robert Egan of the University of California at Santa Barbara faculty who saw *Richard II* at Brooklyn Academy of Music in January 1974. I also was a privileged audience member at a performance of *Richard II* at Stratford in July 1973.

7. Interview with John Barton, London, November 5, 1980. All Barton quotations concerning *Richard II* are from this interview unless otherwise noted.

8. *The Coventry Evening Telegraph Stratford 73 Extra,* p. 2, quoted by Stredder, "John Barton's Production of *Richard II,*" 25.

9. All quotations from *Richard II* are taken from the New Shakespeare, ed. J. Dover Wilson (Cambridge: At the University Press, 1971).

10. Timothy O'Brien, "Designing a Shakespeare Play: *Richard II,*" *Deutsche Shakespeare-Gesellschaft West Jahrbuch 1974* (Heidelberg: Quelle and Meyer, 1974), 112. All O'Brien quotations are from this source.

11. Ibid., 113.

12. Robert Brustein, "A Surfeit of Regal Splendour," *Observer,* April 15, 1973.

13. Felix Barker, *"Richard II,"* *Evening News* (London), April 12, 1973.

14. Stredder, "John Barton's Production of *Richard II,*" 29.

15. Anne Righter, *Shakespeare and the Idea of the Play* (London: Chatto and Windus, 1961), 116.

16. Anne Barton, "The King's Two Bodies," RSC program note for *Richard II,* RST, April 1973.

17. Ernst Kantorwicz, *The King's Two Bodies* (Princeton, N.J.: Princeton University Press, 1957), 7.

18. Barton to Lloyd Evans, "Directing Problem Plays," 64.

19. Penny Gold, quoted by Cook, *Directors' Theatre,* 11.

20. Eileen Totten, "A Pair of Kings," *Plays and Players* 20 (June 1973): 28. All comments by Pasco and Richardson about *Richard II* are from this source unless noted.

21. Hugh Herbert, *"Richard II* Squared," *Guardian Weekly* (Manchester), May 5, 1973.

22. In the interview with Totten, Richardson said: ". . . it's only conjecture on my part . . .

they wanted me back in the Company and they wanted to provide an attractive offer. The whole idea (of double casting) was born out of necessity rather than artistic integrity . . . which has paid off a hundred per cent."

23. Barton, as quoted by Lloyd Evans, "Directing Problem Plays," 71.

24. Richardson to Gordon Gow, "Through the Right Doorway: Ian Richardson in Interview with Gordon Gow," *Plays and Players* 29 (September 1979): 12.

25. Ian Richardson, quoted by Hugh Herbert, "A Pair of Kings Squared," *Guardian Weekly*, May 5, 1973.

26. Stredder, "John Barton's Production of *Richard II*," 27.

27. W.H.Y., "Such a Compact Richard II," *Birmingham Evening Mail*, June 8, 1971.

28. Barker, "*Richard II.*"

29. Stredder, "John Barton's Production of *Richard II*," 31.

30. Charles Lewsen, "*Richard II*," *Times* (London), April 12, 1973.

31. Barton rewrote the "gage scene" to heighten the tension among the feuding lords and to diminish the comic tendencies of the quarrel. Several critics commented that the scene, for the first time in their memories, was received seriously by audiences undistracted by the absurdity of the repetitive tossing of the gages. See appendix C for the revision.

32. Stredder, "John Barton's Production of *Richard II*," 32, compares Barton's cuts for the 1973 *Richard II* with his other stagings of the play:

	1964 New Temple	1971 New Penguin	1973 New Penguin
Cuts (in lines)	−328	−484	−523
Losses/gains through alterations and "telescoping" of lines	−	−2	−6
Additions to text	+1	+2	+55
Total effect of Alterations	−327	−482	−474

33. Stredder notes the following variations in the text for Pasco and Richardson ("John Barton's Production of *Richard II*," 27):

Pasco spoke these lines, which Richardson omitted:

3.1.23–25 (Bolingbroke)

3.1.27 (Bolingbroke)

3.2.130–31 (Richard)

3.3.162 (Richard)

Richardson spoke these lines, which Pasco omitted:

3.2.11 (Richard)

3.2.45 (Richard)

(All references are to the New Penguin edition of the text.)

34. Richard, Pasco, quoted by Herbert, "A Pair of Kings Squared."

35. E. M. Tillyard, "Shakespeare's History Plays," in *Shakespeare and His Critics*, ed. A. M. Eastman and G. G. Harrison (Ann Arbor: University of Michigan Press, 1964), 45–46.

36. Righter, *Shakespeare and the Idea of the Play*, 122–23.

37. "Shakespearean Giggles," *South London Press*, October 15, 1974.

38. Considerable critical support exists for Barton's use of ritual in *Richard II*. See Dover Wilson's introduction to the Cambridge edition, which emphasizes that the play ought to be played as ritual: "As a work of art it stands far closer to the Catholic service of the Mass" (p. xiii). The idea, derived from Walter Pater's nineteenth-century exploration of the play, was quoted verbatim in Rossiter's *Angel with Horns* (38). Anne Barton discusses the rituals of the play in the context of Cambridge anthropologist Sir James Frazer's *The Golden Bough*; Barton's prologue

parallels that described by Frazer (and Anne Barton). In an interview with Barton, the director said he did not read these sources in his preparation for the play. See also Margaret Loftus Renald, "The Degradation of Richard II: An Inquiry into the Ritual Backgrounds," *English Literary Renaissance* 7 (1977): 170–96.

39. Stredder, *"Richard II,"* 32.

40. Interview with Mike Gwilym, London, November 9, 1980. Gwilym said that in rehearsals Barton constantly prods his actors to "give it space, give it space," meaning that they should open up distances between them. Barton believes that actors communicate more effectively if they have to project distances over greater spaces.

41. B. A Young, *"Richard II,"* *Financial Times* (London), April 12, 1973. Young stated that the formalism was curiously effective—though he would not like to see "the manner magnified into a house style."

42. Barton used the New Penguin edition for this production, though his customary preference is the Cambridge New Shakespeare.

43. Brustein, "A Surfeit of Regal Splendour."

44. Stredder, *"Richard II,"* 73.

45. The Gloucester murder was the subject of an earlier chronicle play, *Woodstock*, about which Rossiter has written extensively. He claims many of *Richard II*'s ambiguities can be resolved if we, like Shakespeare's audience, understand that Richard's fall is in part retribution for his involvement in Woodstock's murder. See *Angel with Horns*, 29–36.

46. David, *Shakespeare in the Theatre*, 166.

47. Wells, *Royal Shakespeare*, 69. Wells felt Barton "appropriately presented her stylized" in 1973, but acknowledged that her entrance "created a melodramatic impression which exemplified the dangers of stylization."

48. Richardson, RSC Workshop, University of California, Santa Barbara, February 16, 1980.

49. Harold Hobson, "Power Behind the Throne," *Sunday Times* (London), April 15, 1973, 35.

50. The RSC Program contained an excerpt from "Symphonic Imagery in *Richard II*," by Richard Attick (*PMLA* 62 [June 1947]). Attick saw the duality of the symbol of earth: "Earth, while it emblematizes the foundation of kingly pride and power, is also a familiar symbol of the vanity of human life and of what, in the Middle Ages was an illustration of that vanity—the fall of kings."

51. Benedict Nightingale, "Royal Shakespeare Company," in *Theatre 74*, ed. Sherian Morley (London: Hutchinson, 1974), 82.

52. O'Brien, "Designing a Shakespeare Play," 116.

53. Barton likely found Wells's introductory remarks to the New Penguin text of *Richard II* a useful support for his staging. Wells argues that the Captain is more important for his representative quality than for personal characteristics.

54. Stredder, "John Barton's Production of *Richard II*," 38–39.

55. Thomson, "Shakespeare Straight and Crooked," 152.

56. Richardson, RSC Workshop. John Nettles interrupted this narrative to say that Barton had attempted to get him to wear the bird costume as Thersites in the 1976 *Troilus*.

57. David Nathan, *"Richard II"* (review), *Jewish Chronicle*, April 20, 1973.

58. Stanley Wells, RSC Program for *Richard II*, 17.

59. Thomson, "Shakespeare Straight and Crooked," 153.

60. Richardson, RSC Workshop.

61. Totten, "A Pair of Kings," 28.

62. Cook, *Director's Theatre*, 12.

63. Robert Speaight, "Shakespeare in Britain," *Shakespeare Quarterly* 25 (1974): 391.

64. Eugene Ionesco, RSC Program for *Richard II*, 17.

65. John Barton, "Sources and Issues," RSC Program for *King John*, RST, March 1974, 8. All Barton quotations regarding *King John* and the two source plays are from this note unless otherwise noted.

66. Robert Smallwood, "Shakespeare Unbalanced: The Royal Shakespeare Company's *King John*, 1974–75," *Deutsche Shakespeare-Gesellschaft West Jahrbuch 1976* (Heidelberg: Quelle and Meyer, 1976), 83.

67. Robert Cushman, "King Barton's John," *Observer,* March 24, 1974. He seems to be the first to have used the term. Others have used it since then.

68. Harold Hobson, "Captive Bard," *Sunday Times* (London), March 31, 1974. Hobson's anger prompted two articles on Barton's "abuses."

69. Barry Hillman, "Mr. B as Bard" (letter to the editor), *Observer,* March 31, 1974.

70. Michael Billington, *"King John,"* *Guardian* (Manchester), March 30, 1974.

71. B. A. Young, *"King John,"* *Financial Times* (London), March 22, 1974.

72. Emrys James, quoted by Tom Sutcliffe, "King James Version," *Guardian* (Manchester), June 24, 1975.

73. John Barton, "Midland Critics: *King John,*" BBC Radio, May 9, 1957.

74. When Peter Brook and Barry Jackson staged *King John* in 1945, they added five words to clarify the concept of *commodity,* which sparked a controversy; little wonder Barton met with hostility. See Trewin, *Going to Shakespeare,* 77, for an account of Brook's emendation.

75. Peter Thomson, writing for *Shakespeare Survey,* appraised the quality of Barton's writing in *King John:* "Barton is not a great writer (neither was Bale), and it would have been wiser to invite a better dramatist to do the radical reworking . . . *if he felt such reworking was necessary"* (*Shakespeare Survey* 28 [1975]: 140).

76. Smallwood, "Shakespeare Unbalanced," 92. The "meteor" line, perhaps the most frequently cited Bartonism, was cut in the 1975 revival.

77. Frank Marcus, "In All Directions," *Sunday Telegraph (London),* March 24, 1974.

78. Smallwood, "Shakespeare Unbalanced."

79. David, *Shakespeare in the Theatre,* 179.

80. Christopher Hudson, *"King John* Carry-On," *Evening Standard,* March 21, 1974.

81. Coincidentally, in 1957 Barton criticized Robert Harris for "an unconscionable time in dying" during King John's death scene. BBC Radio, May 9, 1957.

82. Jeremey Kingston, "Bitter Orange," *Punch* 268 (January 22, 1975): 159.

83. Irving Wardle, *"King John,"* *Times* (London), January 10, 1975.

84. David, *Shakespeare in the Theatre,* 175–76.

85. Smallwood ("Shakespeare Unbalanced," 95) charts the line distribution between John and the Bastard. In acts 4 and 5 of Shakespeare's play, John speaks 62 lines, the Bastard 208. In Barton's version, John has 186 lines and the Bastard 118. Most of John's lines were gained in the submission scene with Pandoulph, and in the Swinstead Abbey scene.

86. Billington, *"King John."*

87. Barton to Watts, "Pillar of the RSC."

88. Interview with Gwilym. Barton proudly notes that Gwilym received a "best actor" in a small-part award from the London theater critics in a role "which had been entirely created to get him into the Company." Barton said Gwilym was "brilliant" in the new role.

89. Official RSC Prompt Book for *King John,* 1975 Aldwych Theatre production. The entire speech may be found in appendix D.

90. Barton, "The Sources of Shakespeare," BBC Radio, reported in *Listener,* August 21, 1975.

91. V.J.D., *"King John* as Morality Play," *Evesham Journal,* March 28, 1974. Peter Thomson's essay in *Shakespeare Survey* offers a complete description of the set ("The Smallest Season: The RSC at Stratford, 1974," *Shakespeare Survey* 28 (1975): 138.

92. John Barber, "Emrys James as a Pursy Neurotic," *Daily Telegraph,* January 10, 1975.

93. Cushman, "King Barton's John."

94. Peter Coveney, *"King John"* (review), *Financial Times,* September 20, 1974.

95. Irving Wardle, "Good and Evil Doubly Projected in Stratford's New *King John,*" *Times* (London), March 21, 1974.

96. Cushman, "King Barton's John."

97. John Barber, *"King John"* (review), *Daily Telegraph,* January 10, 1975.

98. Thomson, "The Smallest Season," 138.

99. Bernard Shaw, "On Cutting Shakespeare," in *Shaw on Shakespeare*, ed. Edwin Wilson (New York: E. P. Dutton and Co., 1961), 265.

Chapter 6. "What Country, Friend, Is This?"

1. Interview with Tony Church, Stratford-upon-Avon, November 20, 1980. All quotations from Church in this chapter are from that interview.

2. T.B., *"Comedy of Errors," Varsity* (Cambridge), June 10, 1950.

3. *"Comedy of Errors," Sketch* (London), September 12, 1951. This review (and the next) was found in scrapbooks contained in the Shakespeare Collection at the Birmingham Central Library.

4. *"Comedy of Errors* with Music," *Times* (London), August 24, 1951.

5. Barton, quoted by Addenbrooke, *The Royal Shakespeare Company*, 210.

6. Ronald Bryden, "A Moor for the Seventies," *Observer*, September 12, 1971, 498.

7. Barton, quoted by A. C. H. Smith, "The Romantic and the Sensualist," *Flourish* (1972): 1. All Barton comments concerning *Othello* are from this source, unless noted.

8. Barton, RSC Program for *Othello*, RST, September 1971.

9. Barton, as quoted by Smith, "The Romantic and Sensualist," 1. Furthermore, according to Addenbrooke (210), Barton "had a hunch that after doing so many Elizabethan productions, I could work more imaginatively and richly by taking a different context."

10. Barton to Ronald Hayman, "John Barton," *Times* (London), September 9, 1972, 11.

11. Bryden, "Moor," 498.

12. Derek Mahon, "Theatre," *Listener*, September 16, 1971.

13. Bryden, "Moor," 498.

14. Michael Billington, *"Othello," Guardian* (Manchester), July 19, 1972.

15. Emrys James, quoted by Smith, "Finding Acting in Myself," *Flourish* 1 (1972): 8.

16. Barton, as quoted by Smith, "The Romantic and Sensualist," 1.

17. Anne Barton, "Hell and Night," RSC Program for *Othello*, RST, September 1971.

18. Billington, *"Othello."*

19. Barton, paraphrased by Smith, "The Romantic and Sensualist," 5. I have quoted Smith's paraphrase, which I assume is based closely on Barton's comments.

20. Mahon, "Theatre." Other critics who felt the Barton-Mason interpretation of Othello "lacked fire" included Robert Cushman, *"Othello," Plays and Players* 19 (November 1971): 32; Don Chapman, *Oxford Mail* (September 9, 1971); Eric Salmon, "Shakespeare on the Modern Stage: The Need for New Approaches," *Modern Drama* 15 (1972–73): 305–19; and Benedict Nightingale, "The RSC Ascendant," in *Theatre 72*, ed. Sheridan Morley (London: Hutchinson, 1972), 63–75.

21. Bryden, "Moor," 498.

22. B. A. Young, *"Othello," Financial Times* (London), July 19, 1972.

23. Bryden, "Moor," 498.

24. Milton Shulman, "Milton Shulman at Stratford," *Evening Standard* (London), September 9, 1971.

25. Peter Hall, quoted by Amory, "John Barton Brings His Gift," 45.

26. David Jones [and Trevor Nunn], "Written on Sand," in *Theatre 73*, ed. Sheridan Morley (London: Hutchinson, 1973), 63.

27. Barton, as quoted by Ronald Hayman, "John Barton," *Times*, September 9, 1972, 11.

28. *Leamington Spa Courier*, August 28, 1958, quoted by Roger Warren in "Theory and Practice at Stratford, 1976," *Shakespeare Survey* 30 (1977): 171.

29. Anne Barton, *"Much Ado About Nothing,"* RSC Program for *Much Ado About Nothing*, RST, April 1976.

30. Interview with John Barton, London, November 5, 1980.

31. Sheridan Morley, "Barton Tailoring," *Punch*, April 21, 1976.

32. David, *Shakespeare in the Theatre*, 216–18, passim.

33. Pamela Mason, "*Much Ado* at Stratford, 1949–1976," (Master's thesis, University of Birmingham, 1976), 123. Mason meticulously recreates Barton's production and I am indebted to her account for stimulating my memory of the production.

34. Robert Cushman, "*Much Ado* in India," *Observer*, April 11, 1976.

35. Michael Billington, "*Much Ado About Nothing*," *Guardian* (Manchester), April 9, 1976, 9.

36. Milton Shulman, "Review," *Evening Standard* (London), April 9, 1976. In his subsequent review of the Aldwych revival the following summer, Shulman added that Barton's Indian setting "fits the plot like a tailored sari. These Victorian officers, particularly serving in a foreign clime, would be especially demanding and suspicious about the virginity of their prospective brides" (*Evening Standard*, July 11, 1977).

37. Warren, "Theory and Practice at Stratford," 171.

38. Ibid.

39. B. A. Young, "*Much Ado About Nothing*," *Financial Times* (London), July 1, 1977.

40. Trevor Nunn was listed as Barton's assistant director on *Much Ado* and likely had some say in the casting. Coincidentally, Nunn directed *King Lear* at the RSC's Other Place that season. Barton was listed as his assistant. That production was also set in the late nineteenth century, but it was more Bismarck's Germany than Victorian England. The concept was apparently Nunn's, but Barton seems to have had some influence on the choice of setting (see "Playing King Lear: Donald Sinden Talks to J. W. R. Meadowcroft," *Shakespeare Survey* 33 (1980): 81–88) for commentary on Barton's contributions to that production. Barton has never staged *King Lear* as principal director: "I've never had an urge to do [*Lear*]. I think *Lear* is a wonderful play, but it's awfully clear and I have nothing to say about it" (interview, London, November 5, 1980).

41. Peter Lewis, "Thanks, Bard, for Cheering Me Up," *Evening Mail* (London), April 9, 1976.

42. Felix Barker, "Much Ado About the British, Sahib," *Evening News* (London), April 9, 1976.

43. Michael Billington, "*Much Ado About Nothing*," *Guardian*, July 1, 1977.

44. Kenneth Hurren, "Indian Mutiny," *Spectator*, April 17, 1976.

45. Richard David found "both soliloquies delightful and effective in themselves and doubly so in contrast" (*Shakespeare in the Theatre*, 220).

46. Shulman, "Review."

47. "John Barton on Race Relations," *Stratford-upon-Avon Herald*, April 30, 1976.

48. David, *Shakespeare in the Theatre*, 216–17.

49. Harold Hobson, "Shakespeare's Stage," *Sunday Times* (London), April 11, 1976, 37.

50. Peter Coveney, "*Much Ado About Nothing*," *Plays and Players* 23 (June 1976): 21.

51. "John Barton on Race Relations."

52. Tom Sutcliffe, "Simple Stratford," *Vogue*, June 1976.

53. Benedict Nightingale, "Indian Summer," *New Statesman* 91 (April 16, 1976): 516.

54. John Barber, "Much Ado in Messina Under British Raj," *Daily Telegraph*, April 9, 1976.

55. R. B. Marriott, "*Much Ado About Nothing* at Stratford-upon-Avon," *Stage and Television Today*, April 15, 1976.

Chapter 7. "Improbable Fictions"

1. J. C. Trewin, *Going to Shakespeare* (London: George Allen and Unwin, 1978), 268.

2. John Barton, "Midland Critics: *The Tempest*," BBC, August 15, 1957.

3. John Barber, "Embittered Propsero in Austere Limbo," *Daily Telegraph*, October 17, 1970.

4. D. A. N. Jones, "Celler-work," *Listener*, October 22, 1970.

5. Helen Dawson, "*The Tempest*," *Plays and Players* 18 (November 1970): 38.

6. Benedict Nightingale, "Prosperless," *New Statesman* 80 (October 23, 1970): 542. Other writers felt this Ariel may have been "our old friend, Renaissance Man" (Trewin, *Birmingham Post*,

October 16, 1970); or "a figure straight off a Greek vase or an Etruscan tomb or from William Blake" (W.S., *Gloucester Citizen,* October 18, 1970).

7. John Higgins, "A Touch of Autumn," *Times* (London), October 16, 1970, 13.

8. Barton, "Midland Critics: *The Tempest.*"

9. In 1957 Barton criticized Brook's masque for being "completely contradictory to anything the text could suggest." He then defined what he then thought the masque should be, citing Ferdinand's exclamation as evidence: "Brook gave us a modern sophistication. A Masque is a simple, formal affair written with a definite convention in mind. It is pageant-like."

10. Ian Richardson, RSC Workshop, University of California, Santa Barbara, February 16, 1980. All Richardson comments concerning *The Tempest* are from this discussion, unless noted.

11. Dawson, "The Tempest," 39.

12. Interview with Michael Bogdanov, San Diego, California; August 13, 1980.

13. Dawson, "The Tempest," 39.

14. Anne Barton, *"The Tempest,"* RSC Program for *The Tempest* RST, October 1970.

15. Nightingale, "Prosperless," 542.

16. John Russell Brown, "Free Shakespeare," *Shakespeare Survey* 24 (1971): 130–31.

17. Interview with Tony Church, Stratford-upon-Avon, November 20, 1980. Michael Tubbs, a music director for the RSC, and Dr. Stanley Wells also attested to Barton's romantic optimism in other interviews with the author.

18. Richardson said Barton "chickened out" and dismissed the idea as merely illustrative talk. Richardson nevertheless found it useful in his creation of the role:

I said, "No, no, no . . . it may be just talk, but the idea that a man could have a book of knowledge and wisdom, and put it on a lectern and dictate what the people in the action could do is very good for me to carry in mind as Prospero."

19. Cook, "King John Barton," 25.

20. Personal interview, London, June 17, 1983.

21. Barton, "Midland Critics: *Cymbeline,*" BBC, July 15, 1957.

22. Anne Barton, *"Cymbeline,"* RSC Program for *Cymbeline,* RST, June 1974.

23. The Free Cast List for *Cymbeline* read:

The text for this production contains cuts of 820 lines. The part of Cornelius has been expanded to include the lines of the first gentleman of I. i and the Roman soothsayer in V. v, together with some stage directions from the First Folio and lines drawn from Shakespeare's sources.

24. John Elsom, "Courtly Romances," *Listener,* June 13, 1974.

25. Gordon Parsons, "Barton's Offering," *Morning Star* (London), June 5, 1974.

26. Irving Wardle judged the Barton battle plan to be "a distinct improvement on the scrambled confusion of the battle dialogue" (*Times* [London], June 5, 1974, 7). Contrarily, Robert Cushman argued in *The Observer* (December 29, 1974):

Here I quarrel with Mr. Barton; the battle is a decisive factor in the action, and in the destinies of many of the characters, and whatever the difficulties (and they are immense) we need to get a good look at it. We need, for example, to see the disarming and partial repentance of Iachimo, if only so that we may be reminded of his existence before the end.

27. Peter Thomson, "The Smallest Season: The RSC at Stratford," *Shakespeare Survey* 27 (1974): 143.

28. Peter Ansorge, *"Cymbeline,"* Plays and Players 21 (July 1974): 40.

29. Robert Speaight theorizes that the RSC believes "that if you dress a character in even moderately bright colors, he or she ceases to be a human being" ("Shakespeare in Britain [1974]," 390).

30. Ansorge, *"Cymbeline,"* 40.

31. Thomson, "Smallest Season," 144.

32. Ansorge, "*Cymbeline*," 40.

33. See David, *Shakespeare in the Theatre*, 186, for a detailed account of Susan Fleetwood's handling of this sequence. David notes that she involved "the audience in the nightmare quality of the experience and its power, so that detached and critical spectatorship was impossible."

34. Michael Billington, "*Cymbeline*," *Guardian* (Manchester), June 5, 1974.

35. John Barton and Kenneth Cavender, *The Greeks* (London: Heinemann, 1981), xiii.

36. Ansorge, "*Cymbeline*," 41.

37. Wardle, "*Cymbeline*" (review) *Times*, June 5, 1974, 7.

38. Ansorge, "*Cymbeline*," 41.

39. Harold Hobson, "Banners Bright," *Sunday Times* (London), June 6, 1976, 35.

40. Benedict Nightingale, "Well-Seasoned," *New Statesman* 91 (June 11, 1976): 790.

41. These designs were copied from production photographs of *The Winter's Tale* contained in the library at the Shakespeare Center, Stratford-upon-Avon. There are more pictures of the nearly bare set than is customary for RSC production photos, an indication of the unusual nature of this particular set.

42. Peter Whitehouse, "Primeval Love and Jealousy," *Sunday Mercury* (Birmingham), June 6, 1976.

43. Robert Cushman, "Theatre," *Observer*, June 13, 1976.

44. Desmond Pratt, "*The Winter's Tale*" (review), *Yorkshire Post*, June 5, 1976.

45. Hobson, "Banners Bright," 35.

46. Warren, "Theory and Practice at Stratford, 1976," 174.

47. Nightingale, "Well-Seasoned," 790.

48. J. C. Trewin, "*The Winter's Tale*," *Birmingham Post*, June 7, 1976.

49. Amid program descriptions of cultural practices of the Nordic peoples, there was a note that put the bear in the time-life cycle:

In the Far North when Winter made the ground too frozen hard to bury the dead and food too scarce to feed the old, the aged dead and dying were put on the ice flows to become food for the bears. The bears, thus sustained through the hardest months, became prey for hunters in the spring.

50. David, *Shakespeare in the Theatre*, 223.

51. Warren, "Theory and Practice at Stratford, 1976," 174. Warren says that similar business was used in Nunn's 1969 production.

52. Michael Billington, "*The Winter's Tale*," *Guardian* (Manchester), June 4, 1976, 10.

53. Whitehouse, "Primeval Love and Jealousy."

54. B. A. Young, "*The Winter's Tale*," *Financial Times* (London), June 7, 1976.

55. Warren, "Theory and Practice at Stratford, 1976," 173.

56. David, *Shakespeare in the Theatre*, 223.

57. F.W.D., *Oxford Times*, June 11, 1976.

58. V.J.D., "A Young Team of Triers Present 'New Shakespeare,'" *Evesham Journal*, May 12, 1977.

59. John Elsom, "Family Dreams," *Listener*, May 19, 1977.

60. Gareth Lloyd Evans, "Blessed Return," *Stratford-upon-Avon Herald*, May 11, 1977. The courtiers were singled out for poor verse-speaking—"of all people Mr. Barton here fails not only to induce his players to embrace anything except a certain pertness of tone but even, in one case, audibility." A number of other critics also noted the weak quality of the verse-speaking.

61. Elsom, "Family Dreams."

62. Anthony Everitt, "*Midsummer Night's Dream*," *Birmingham Post*, May 9, 1977.

63. David Young, quoted in the RSC Program for *A Midsummer Night's Dream*, RST, May 1977. Young's ideas were extracted from his study of the play, *Something of Great Constancy: The Art of a Midsummer Night's Dream* (New Haven, Conn.: Yale University Press, 1966).

64. Lloyd Evans, "Blessed Return."

65. Bernard Levin, "Lullabies of Broadway," *Sunday Times* (London), May 15, 1977. Levin called Barton's fairies "atrocities . . . hideous, bald freaks."

66. Roger Warren, "Comedies and Histories at Stratford, 1977," *Shakespeare Survey* 31 (1978): 141.

67. Ibid., 142.

68. Tony Stark, "Shades of Tolkien at Stratford," *Redditch Indicator Weekly,* May 20, 1977.

69. RSC Program for *A Midsummer Night's Dream,* RST, May 1977.

70. Sally Aire, *"A Midsummer Night's Dream,"* *Plays and Players* 24 (July 1977): 22.

71. Lloyd Evans, "Blessed Return."

72. Ibid.

73. Ibid.

74. Billington, *"A Midsummer Night's Dream"* (review), *Guardian,* May 9, 1977, 9.

75. Richard Griffiths to Jim Hiley, "A Company with Direction," *Plays and Players* 25 (October 1977): 20.

76. An unsigned review in *The Tatler and Bystander* (July–August 1977) said: "Intent on evoking the atmosphere of a mesmerizing dream, Mr. Barton lulls his audience into a state of somnambulance." Everitt (*Birmingham Post,* May 9, 1977) concurred: "In sum, although Mr. Barton does not ruin the *Dream* for those who are fond of it, he manages to make it boring."

77. Barton to John Higgins, "The Realistic Economics of Doctoring Shakespeare," *Times* (London), August 26, 1981. All Barton comments on the "twin bill" are from this source.

78. For instance, Stanley Wells assessed the impact of the twin bill: "This Stratford evening lacks the elements of complete contrast, the suggestion of a necessary escape from high seriousness into frivolity . . . nor does the juxtaposition of the two plays cast unexpected illumination upon either" (*Times Literary Supplement,* September 18, 1981, 1071).

79. Barton has staged *Two Gentlemen of Verona* and *Titus Andronicus* on twin bills at Cambridge—but not with each other. The comedy was paired with Marlowe's *Faustus,* the tragedy with Greene's fanciful *Friar Bacon and Friar Bungay.* Barton does not recall if his cutting of the plays, particularly *Titus,* at Cambridge influenced his 1981 cuts.

Chapter 8. The Marriage of True Minds

1. "Stratford Producer Marries," *Birmingham Post,* August 10, 1968.

2. Anne Righter, *Shakespeare and the Idea of the Play.* (London: Chatto and Windus, 1962), 86. Hereafter cited parenthetically as *Idea.*

3. Interview with John Barton, London, November 5, 1980. All Barton comments regarding *Hamlet* are from this interview unless otherwise noted.

4. Anne Barton, introduction, to *Hamlet,* ed. T. J. B. Spencer (Hammondsworth: New Penguin, 1980). Hereafter cited paranthetically in the text as *Intro.*

5. Intro., 28. This quotation—and others relating to the self-conscious theatricality of *Hamlet*—comprised the two-page program note in the RSC Program for the production (RST, July 1980).

6. Interview with Tony Church, Stratford-upon-Avon, November 20, 1980. All Church comments regarding Barton and *Hamlet* are from this interview.

7. Ian Richardson, another renowned RSC "poetic" actor, said that Barton wanted him to play Hamlet in the late 1960s, but film commitments prevented him from accepting the role (Richardson: RSC Workshop, University of California, Santa Barbara, February 16, 1980).

8. Addenbrooke, *The Royal Shakespeare Company,* 172.

9. These figures are based on deletions made in the Assistant Stage Manager's Prompt Book at the Royal Shakespeare Theatre, which the company manager, Mr. Nick Jones, graciously allowed me to examine; he believed the cuts to be accurate. Barton believes my figures to be inaccurate,

citing a study he did of the three previous *Hamlet*'s at the RSC (1965: Peter Hall; 1970: Trevor Nunn; 1975: Buzz Goodbody). Barton believes he cut the play slightly more than 1000 lines and found that his edition represented the mean average of the RSC cuts. Barton said his cutting was dictated by the desire to finish the play by 11:00. Barton, incidentally, did not use the New Penguin text, which was not yet published when rehearsals began; he used the New Shakespeare (Cambridge, 1971).

10. Irving Wardle, "A Theatrical, But Gentle, Prince," *Times* (London), July 3, 1980. Wardle's account of the moment errs by stating that Hamlet "echoes" the First Player's line. He precedes the Player. Interestingly, Church said that in early rehearsals Pennington repeated the line after the Player, but before the production opened, the line was initiated by Hamlet and repeated by the Player.

11. James Fenton, "Hamlet, Prune of Denmark," *Sunday Times* (London), July 6, 1980.

12. Interview with Michael Tubbs, RSC Music Director, Stratford-upon-Avon, November 21, 1980. Tubbs composed the music for Barton's highly praised *Twelfth Night* (see chapter 5).

13. Michael Billington cited the moment as an example of Barton's "great achievement as a director: the creation of an absolutely consistent psychological world full of echoes and reverberations" (*The Guardian* [Manchester], July 3, 1980).

14. T. P. Matheson, "The Gentlest of Princes," *Times Literary Supplement*, July 11, 1980, 782.

15. B. A. Young, "Hamlet," *Financial Times* (London), July 3, 1980.

16. Benedict Nightingale (*New Statesman*, July 11, 1980) castigated Pennington's use of "sullied" instead of "solid" flesh, "a reading that could appeal only to the very deaf, grossly unimaginative, or obtusely pedantic." Barton hears well, and could never be accused of a lack of imagination (though the contrary charge has been applied to his work). He has, of course, been accused of pedantry. But the textual note of the New Shakespeare text (pp. 151–52) offers such a convincing argument for "sullied" that one wonders who is being the pedant, Barton or Nightingale.

17. Fenton, "Hamlet, Prune of Denmark."

18. Peter Jenkins, "Coherent," *Spectator* 245 (July 12, 1980): 24.

19. Church said he researched the Gertrude-Ghost relationship in some depth at the Shakespeare Center Library, Stratford, but could find no record of the Queen actually seeing the Ghost in a performance of note.

20. Correspondingly, Barton cut Hamlet's reference to Nero in the soliloquy at 3.2.393–97. The lines have been used to suggest that *Hamlet* may have incestuous designs on his mother, as it was Nero who raped his mother before killing her.

21. Church has played Polonius on several occasions, most notably in the 1965 Peter Hall–David Warner *Hamlet* for the RSC. For Hall, Church played the counselor as "an absolute bastard and found it very difficult to accept." Curiously, Barton remembers that production for "the best Polonius, Gertrude, and Claudius I've ever seen" (Barton, quoted by Addenbrooke, *The Royal Shakespeare Company*, 208).

22. Hume Cronyn's Polonius in the Gielgud *Hamlet* (1963) was generally benevolent, if somewhat foolish.

23. Fenton, "Hamlet, Prune of Denmark."

Chapter 9. Beyond Shakespeare

1. Interview with Michael Bogdanov, San Diego, California, August 13, 1980.

2. John Barton to Guy, "Director in Interview," 48.

3. Barton to Michael Kustow, "Synthesis," *Flourish* (1967): 14.

4. Interview with John Barton, London, November 5, 1980.

5. "Seventeenth-Century Drama to Be Revived," *Bristol Evening Post*, May 14, 1966. The title of this article refers to *The Revenger's Tragedy*.

6. Interview with Barton.

7. Tony Church, "The Shepherd's Play," *RSC Newsletter* (Autumn 1978), 4. This business was added to the 1967 version, which Barton retitled "The Shepherd's Play."

8. J. W. Lambert, *Theatre in Britain, 1963–1974* (London: Longman Group, 1974), 28.

9. Stanley Wells, *"The Revenger's Tragedy* Revived," in *The Elizabethan Theatre VI*, ed. G. R. Hibbard (Hamden, Conn.: Archer, 1972), 109. Wells reconstructs the production and includes Barton's revisions.

10. S.B., of *Stage and Television Today* (October 13, 1966), wrote: "The text contains darkly magnificent poetry which has been skillfully and imaginatively edited by John Barton to bring out the trenchant quality of the verse."

11. Barton, "Marlowe's Text," RSC Program for *Doctor Faustus*, Aldwych Theatre, September 1974. All Barton comments on *Doctor Faustus* are from this essay, unless otherwise noted.

12. Official RSC Prompt Copy for *Doctor Faustus*, Shakespeare Center Library, Stratford-upon-Avon.

13. Sheila Bannock, "What the Doctor Ordered," *Stratford-upon-Avon Herald*, February 28, 1975. The Barton addition, spoken by Lucifer, tells how scholars sought Faustus's body, but instead "found this history written by him, saving only his end, which was after by the Scholars thereto added" (RSC Prompt Book for Doctor Faustus).

14. J. C. Trewin, "Unmeasured Shakespeare," *Illustrated London News*, November 1974.

15. Michael Billington, "Doctor Faustus," *Guardian* (Manchester) September 6, 1974.

16. Anthony Seymour, "Repair Job Brilliant, But Wrong," *Yorkshire Post*, September 9, 1974.

17. John Barber, "Deviled Dish of Mock Marlowe," *Daily Telegraph*, September 9, 1974.

18. "Morality Play in a Low Key," *Manchester Evening News*, September 11, 1974.

19. John Barber, "Masks and Marionettes in Doctor Faustus," *Daily Telegraph*, August 27, 1974.

20. "Doctor Faustus," *Sunday Telegraph*, September 9, 1974.

21. Interview with Irving Wardle, London, November 19, 1980. The *Times*'s critic had interviewed McKellen prior to the production.

22. Patrick Tucker, "Faustus as a Puppet Play," RSC Program for *Doctor Faustus*, Aldwych Theatre, August 1974.

23. P.B., *Warwick Advertiser*, February 20, 1975.

24. Alan Riddell, "Edinburgh Shock," *Sunday Telegraph* (London), September 1, 1974. Riddell's description echoes Anne Barton's program description of Helen: ". . . a phantom created by the devils."

25. Geoff Ward, "Faustus Is So Well Balanced," *Evening News* (London), February 20, 1975.

26. Garry O'Connor, "Doctor Faustus," *Plays and Players* 20 (October 1974): 37.

27. Robert Cushman, "Going to the Devil," *Observer*, September 1, 1974.

28. Ian McKellen to Gordon Gow, "Reaching for the Heights," *Plays and Players* 22 (October 1974): 17.

29. Benedict Nightingale, "Plays for All Seasons," *New Statesman* 88 (September 13, 1974): 356.

30. McKellen to Gow, "Reaching," 17.

31. Michael Coveney, "Perkin Warbeck," *Financial Times*, August 9, 1975.

32. Interview with Barton, London, June 17, 1983.

33. Interview with Mike Gwilym, London, November 5, 1980. All Gwilym comments in this chapter are from this interview.

34. Ivor Lewis, "London Theatre: Ibsen's *Pillars of the Community*," *Scotsman*, August 3, 1977.

35. David Zane Mairowitz, *"Pillars of the Community*," *Plays and Players* 25 (October 1977): 24.

36. John Peter, "A Great Bomb of a Play," *Sunday Times* (London), August 7, 1977, 33.

37. Jack Tinker, "Sheer Dazzle from Dench," *Daily Mirror* (London), August 3, 1977.

38. Inga-Stina Ewbank, "Do You Know What We Are . . . We Pillars of the Community?" RSC Program for *Pillars of the Community*, Aldwych Theatre, August 1977.

39. "Way of the Actor," *Guardian* (Manchester), January 27, 1978.

40. Anne Barton, *"The Way of the World,"* RSC Program for *The Way of the World,* Aldwych Theatre, January 1978.

41. Eric Shorter, "Beryl Reed Glitters in Restoration Play," *The Daily Telegraph,* January 30, 1978. J. C. Trewin, (*Lady,* February 9, 1978) said that Barton "clarified the plot as much as any director can." Wardle (*Times,* January 28, 1978, 11) agreed: "The ramifications of the intrigue are most carefull attenuated and the plot takes shape with startling coherence."

42. Wardle, *"The Way of the World"* (review), 11.

43. Michael Pennington to Ellen Goodman, "Interview with Michael Pennington," *RSC Newspaper* (Spring 1980), 5.

44. Benedict Nightingale, "Larfing [sic] Matters," *New Statesman* 95 (February 3, 1978): 161. Jeremy Kingston (*Sunday Times,* January 29, 1978) had similar perceptions: "Barton opens the proceedings at a measured, conversational pace, slowly untangling Congreve's labrynthian plot and revealing an everyday world of solid objects, calculating relationships, and palpable people."

45. "No Way," *What's On in London,* February 5, 1978.

46. Wardle, *"The Way of the World,"* 11.

47. *The Observer* said that "Mr. Pennington has all of Mirabell's controlling intelligence, but not much of his controlling personality" (February 5, 1978).

48. Michael Pennington to Gordon Gow, "A State of Mind and Body," *Plays and Players* 26 (May 1979): 16. Pennington added at the end of his "defense": ". . . if we were to do it again, we might reconsider. I don't know, maybe some of the tones were washed out. But fundamentally I think we had the right interpretation."

49. J. C. Trewin, "New Plays," *Lady,* February 9, 1978.

50. Rosemary Say, "Rules and Rituals," *Sunday Telegraph,* February 5, 1978.

51. Wardle, *"The Way of the World,"* 11.

52. Barton to Lucy Hughes-Hallet, "Putting Vigour Back into Sheridan," *Times* (London), January 6, 1983, 8.

53. Benedict Nightingale, "Theatre," *New Statesman,* January 14, 1983, 30. The critic also expressed disappointment in the lack of an ensemble performance: ". . . where is the detail, the nuance, the give-and-take between actor and actor that one had expected?"

54. Irving Wardle, "Laughter Versus Deliberation," *Times* (London), January 7, 1983, 9. Wardle said, "All kinds of intelligent and comically promising details have been introduced to enlarge and articulate the dialogue, but they are apt to smother laughter with measured deliberation." Wardle's colleague at *The Times,* James Fenton, dismissed the production as "unnecessarily slow . . . unnecessarily mannered" (*Sunday Times,* January 9, 1983, 41).

55. Gabriele Annan, "The Melancholy Round," *Times Literary Supplement,* January 22, 1982, 79. Irving Wardle judged that there was too much melancholy and that the production was "doused under glib melancholy" (*Times* [London], January 12, 1982, 9).

56. Wardle, *"La Ronde"* (review), *Times* (London), January 12, 1982, 9. James Fenton was more blunt: "The production as whole was a mess . . ." (*Sunday Times,* January 17, 1982, 40).

57. Barton said the reviews of *La Ronde* were generally much kinder to the production than to the play itself. He, who dearly loves *La Ronde,* wistfully added, "And my wife tells me it's a terrible play."

Chapter 10. "To Sing a Song That Old Was Sung"

1. Personal interview with John Barton, London, June 17, 1983. All comments by Barton are from this interview unless otherwise noted.

2. Robert Cushman, "Wars, Murders, and Gods," *Observer,* February 10, 1980.

3. Barton to Kustow, "Synthesis," 14.

4. "Socrates Comes to Stratford," *Flourish* 5 (Winter 1965): 7.

5. Barton to Kustow, "Synthesis," 14.

6. "The Peloponnesian Wars," adapted by John Barton (unpublished manuscript, 1967). Mr. Barton graciously provided this script for me because he believed it best represented his political attitudes.

7. Barton to Amory, "John Barton Brings His Gift," 40.

8. Ibid.

9. Barton, "The Greeks," RSC Program for *The Greeks*, Aldwych Theatre, February 1980.

10. Kenneth Cavander, "Introduction to *The Greeks:* The Translation," *The Greeks* (London: Heinemann, 1981), xix.

11. Barton to Amory, "John Barton Brings His Gift," 41.

12. Barton and Cavander, *The Greeks*, 284–85. Quotes from the play will hereafter be cited parenthetically in the text.

13. Michael Billington, "How They Worked Like Trojans to Bring Triumph to 'The Greeks'," *Guardian* (Manchester, February 4, 1980).

14. Barton to Amory, "John Barton Brings His Gift," 40.

15. Barton, "The Greeks," program note.

16. Ibid. Barton defended his liberal adaptation: "Any changes we have made in the original stories are far less than the changes the Greek dramatists themselves made to their own legends."

17. Benedict Nightingale, "Deadly Diet," *New Statesman* 99 (February 8, 1980): 221.

18. Wardle, *"The Greeks"* (review), *Times* (London), February 4, 1980.

19. Barton, "Introduction to *The Greeks:* From a Preliminary Talk to the Actors," *The Greeks*, xviii. Other Barton quotations from this source will hereafter be cited parenthetically in the text.

20. Sheridan Morley, "Pieces of Atrium," *Punch*, February 13, 1980, 278.

21. James Fenton, "How the Greeks Won the War," *Sunday Times* (London), February 10, 1980, 39.

22. Barton to Amory, "John Barton Brings His Gift," 41.

23. Thurman W. Stanback, *"The Greeks," Theatre Journal* 32 (December 1980): 525.

24. Peter Jenkins, "Ancient and Modern," *Spectator* 244 (February 9, 1980): 23.

25. John Barber, *"The Greeks," Daily Telegraph*, February 4, 1980.

26. Jenkins, "Ancient and Modern," 23.

27. Stanback, *"The Greeks,"* 525.

28. Ian Jack, "Will Electra See Her Name in Lights?" *Sunday Times*, February 10, 1980, 39.

29. Wardle, *"The Greeks."*

30. Lynn Dearth to Jack, "Will Electra. . . ?" 39.

31. Amory, "John Barton Brings His Gift," 42. Amory's catalogue was based on a conversation with Barton about *The Greeks.*

32. Ibid., 41.

33. Cushman. Barton intended the suntan lotion business to be a "timeless" gesture. Irving Wardle relates an amusing anecdote about Helen and her suntan oil. While Barton was preparing *The Greeks,* Wardle interviewed him:

> He was talking about the degree of anachronistic license to which they were going to commit themselves. And he took examples from the play of *Helen* . . . and he said, "The way we'll do this—sunbathing is a timeless activity—so we'll have her come on and sunbathe, and she'll have a towel. That's fine, but she wouldn't have dark glasses." Come the event, she had dark glasses; not only that, she had an atomizer and was spraying herself with sun tan oil. (Interview with Wardle, London, November 19, 1980.)

34. Jenkins, "Ancient and Modern," 23. Benedict Nightingale had similar feelings: "The silliness of it infected the subsequent proceedings and . . . exhausted the audience. Euripides' mood is sometimes ironic, even sardonic, the most 'modern' in Greek drama; yet Aristotle thought him the most tragic of the poets, and he never, I think, trivialized pain" ("Deadly Diet," 221).

35. Wardle, *"The Greeks."*

36. Jenkins said, "In the final play Barton needs to round off his epic in a serious and dignified fashion, but it's too late for that" ("Ancient and Modern").

37. Fenton, "How the Greeks Won the War," 39. Fenton, recalling the Hands-Nunn advice to forgo Greek tragedy, further stated: "What those who tried to warn John Barton should have said was: revive Greek tragedy by all means, but do not attempt at the same time to revive, or invent, Greek comedy."

38. Colin Ludlow, "Theatre," *London Magazine* 20 (August–September 1980): 114.

Chapter 11. "His Hour Upon the Stage"

1. Interview with John Nettles, Santa Barbara, California, February 15, 1980. All Nettles comments are from this interview unless otherwise noted.

2. John Barton, quoted by Annabel Ferriman, "Director's Four Facets of Theatre Success," *Times* (London), August 28, 1976, 12.

3. Personal interview, London, June 17, 1983.

4. Barton to Watts, "Pillar of the RSC."

5. John Barber, "Curtain Up at Stratford," *Daily Telegraph* (London), April 1, 1970.

6. Barton to Lloyd Evans, "Directing Problem Plays," 70.

7. Barton quoted in "Hal's Pals," *Stratford-upon-Avon Herald,* September 3, 1976.

8. Interview with John Barton, London, November 5, 1980.

9. Peter Hall to Amory, "John Barton Brings His Gift," 45.

10. Interview with Barton, November 5, 1980.

11. Interview with Mike Gwilym, London, November 5, 1980. All Gwilym comments are from this interview.

12. Interview with Irving Wardle, London, November 20, 1980. The show was "The Southbank Show"; Barton and Terry Hands, with a group of RSC actors, demonstrated acting techniques. All Wardle comments in this chapter are from this interview unless otherwise noted.

13. Barton enlisted the aid of twenty-one of the RSC's finest actors to illustrate his ideas: Dame Peggy Ashcroft, Tony Church, Sinead Cusack, Judi Dench, Susan Fleetwood, Mike Gwilym, Sheila Hancock, Lisa Harrow, Alan Howard, Ben Kingsley, Jane Lapotaire, Barbara Leigh-Hunt, Ian McKellen, Richard Pasco, Michael Pennington, Roger Rees, Norman Rodway, Donald Sinden, Patrick Stewart, David Suchet, and Michael Williams. The list is significant because these actors have figured prominently in Barton's best work; Ian Richardson was asked to participate but was unavailable for the telecasts.

14. Eric Salmon, "Shakespeare on the Modern Stage," *Modern Drama* 15 (1972–73): 318–19.

15. Brown, "Free Shakespeare," 18.

16. Interview with Tony Church, Stratford-upon-Avon, November 21, 1980. All Church comments are from this interview.

17. Barton, as quoted by Higgins, "The Realistic Economies of Doctoring Shakespeare," *The Times* (London), August 26, 1981, 9.

18. In a discussion of Barton's work, Stanley Wells, who has seen most of Barton's productions, said: "That seems to be a Barton strength—the strong narrative line" (interview, Oxford, November 28, 1980; all Wells comments are from this interview unless noted).

19. Sheila Bannock, "Dreamy *Twelfth Night* Has Inspired Comic Malvolio," *Stratford-upon-Avon Herald,* August 29, 1969, 2.

20. Hall to Amory, "John Barton Brings His Gift," 45.

21. Barton to Lloyd Evans, "Directing Problem Plays," 68.

22. Tyrone Guthrie, quoted by John L. Styan, *The Shakespeare Revolution* (Cambridge: At the University Press, 1977), 180.

23. Gordon Parsons, "Fresh Respect for the Original," *Morning Star,* March 22, 1974.

24. Barton to Guy, "Director in Interview," 49.

25. Interview with Barton, November 5, 1980.

26. Michael Pennington to Ellen Goodman, "Interview with Michael Pennington," *RSC Newspaper* (Spring 1980), 8.

27. Stanley Wells, "The Academic and the Theatre," in *The Triple Bond,* ed. Joseph G. Price (University Park, Penn.: Pennsylvania State University Press, 1977), 10–11.

28. Barton to Lloyd Evans, "How Far Can We Improve Shakespeare?" *Guardian* (Manchester), November 26, 1964.

29. Barton to Guy, "Director in Interview," 48.

30. Lloyd Evans, "Troilus and Cressida Together at Last."

31. For example, Irving Wardle began his review of *Measure for Measure:* "Barton's productions are apt to mature and reach a peak much in excess of their initial promise" (*Times,* April 2, 1970). Robert Cushman recalled that neither *All's Well That Ends Well* nor *Twelfth Night,* two of Barton's finest works, "came into glory until they arrived at the Aldwych" (*Observer,* June 9, 1974).

32. Peter Roberts, "Power Politics," *Plays and Players* 15 (June 1968): 18.

33. Barton to Addenbrooke, *The Royal Shakespeare Company: The Peter Hall Years,* 208–9.

34. Interview with Barton, November 5, 1980.

35. Penny Gold to Cook, *Directors' Theatre,* 9.

36. Interview with Barton.

37. Barton to Lloyd Evans, "Directing Problem Plays," 70.

38. Ibid.

39. Ibid.

40. Ibid.

41. Pasco to Addenbrooke, *The Royal Shakespeare Company,* 104–5.

42. Cook, "King John Barton," 25.

43. Interview with Sebastian Shaw, who emphasized that he admires and respects Barton as both a director and a person, Santa Barbara, California, February 14, 1980.

44. Interview with Michael Bogdanov, San Diego, California, August 13, 1980. All Bogdanov quotations are from this source unless otherwise noted.

45. Interview with Guy Woolfenden, New York, August 16, 1982.

46. Interview with Michael Tubbs, Stratford-upon-Avon, November 21, 1980. All Tubbs quotations are from this source unless otherwise noted.

47. Barton to Terry Coleman, "Elizabethan Manner," *Guardian* (Manchester), September 4, 1972, 8.

48. Barton, *The RSC,* p. 209.

49. Thomson, "A Necessary Theatre," 123.

50. Anthony Everitt, "Why Stratford Faces Tough Times Ahead," *Birmingham Post,* October 19, 1974. Irving Wardle also praised Barton's ability to make "strong, simple statements out of complicated works" (interview).

51. J. W. Lambert, "The Wind and the Rain," *Sunday Times* (London), August 24, 1969.

52. Cook, "King John Barton," 26.

53. Robert Cushman, *"Othello," Plays and Players* 19 (November 1971): p. 32.

54. Interview with Barton, November 5, 1980.

55. David, *Shakespeare in the Theatre,* 241.

56. Stanley Wells said that there are two sides to Barton: the Barton who is faithful to the text and the Barton "who is a fair writer and who wants to write his own plays. What he did with *King John* is partly an example of this" (interview).

57. Inga-Stina Ewbank, "More Pregnantly Than Words: Some Uses and Limitations of Visual Symbolism," *Shakespeare Survey* 24 (1971): 13.

58. Brown, "Free Shakespeare," 128.

59. Interview with Barton, November 5, 1980.

60. Barton to Lloyd Evans, "Directing Problem Plays," 66.

61. Interview with Barton, November 5, 1980.

62. Lambert, *Drama in Britain, 1964–1973*, 24.

63. Barton, as quoted by Lloyd Evans, "How Far Can We Improve Shakespeare?" *The Guardian*, November 26, 1964.

64. Barton to Lloyd Evans, "Directing Problem Plays," 69–70.

65. Interview with Wells. The O'Toole Macbeth was indeed appalling.

66. Clifford Williams, *Directors' Theatre*, 144.

67. Hall to Addenbrooke, *The Royal Shakespeare Company*, 90.

68. Hall to Amory, "John Barton Brings His Gift," 45.

69. Barton, *Guardian* (Manchester), November 26, 1964.

70. David, "Actors and Scholars: A View of Shakespeare in the Modern Theatre," *Shakespeare Survey* 12 (1959): 77.

71. Interview with Barton, November 5, 1980.

Sources Consulted

A. Interviews with the Author

Barton, John. RSC Director. London. Interviews, November 5, 1980, and June 17, 1983.

Bogdanov, Michael. RSC Director. San Diego, California. Interview, August 13, 1980.

Church, Tony. RSC Actor. Stratford-upon-Avon, England. Interview, November 20, 1980.

Daniels, Maurice. RSC Director. New York, N.Y. Interview, August 16, 1982.

Firbank, Anne. RSC Actress. Santa Barbara, California. Interview, February 14, 1980.

Gwilym, Mike. RSC Actor. London. Interview, November 5, 1980.

Nettles, John. RSC Actor. Santa Barbara, California. Interview, February 14–15, 1980. RSC Workshop, University of California, Santa Barbara. Interview, February 16, 1980.

Richardson, Ian. RSC Actor. RSC Workshop, University of California, Santa Barbara. Interview, February 16, 1980.

Shaw, Sebastian. RSC Actor. Santa Barbara, California. Interview, February 14, 1980.

Tubbs, Michael. RSC Music Director and Composer. Stratford-upon-Avon, England. November 21, 1980.

Wardle, Irving. Drama Critic, *The Times* (London). London. Interview, November 19, 1980.

Wells, Stanley. Editor, *Shakespeare Survey.* Oxford, England. Interview, November 28, 1980.

Woolfenden, Guy. RSC Musical Director. New York, N.Y. Interview, August 16, 1982.

B. Published Interviews with John Barton

Addenbrooke, David. *The Royal Shakespeare Company: The Peter Hall Years.* London: William Kimber, 1974.

Amory, Mark. "John Barton Brings His Gift to the Greeks." *Sunday Times Magazine,* February 3, 1980, 40–46.

Coleman, Terry. "Elizabethan Manner." *The Guardian* (Manchester), September 4, 1972.

Cook, Judith. *Directors' Theatre.* London: Harrap, 1974.

———. "King John Barton." *Plays and Players* 21 (June 1974): 24–27.

Guy, Vincent. "Director in Interview: John Barton." *Plays and Players* 17 (November 1970): 48–49.

"Hal's Pals." *Stratford-upon-Avon Herald,* September 3, 1976.

Hayman, Ronald. "John Barton." *The Times* (London), September 9, 1972, 11.

Higgins, John. "The Realistic Economies of Doctoring Shakespeare." *The Times* (London), August 26, 1981, 9.

Hughes-Hallett, Lucy. "Putting Vigour Back into Sheridan." *The Times* (London), January 6, 1983, 8.

Kustow, Michael. "Synthesis." *Flourish* (1967): 14.

Lloyd Evans, Gareth. "Directing Problem Plays: John Barton Talks to Gareth Lloyd Evans." *Shakespeare Survey* 25 (1972): 63–71.

————. "How Far Can We Improve Shakespeare?" *The Guardian* (Manchester), November 26, 1964, 6–8.

"Personality of the Month." *Plays and Players* 7 (August 1960).

"The Romantic and the Sensualist." *Flourish* (1972): 1–5.

"Shakespeare: To Be Changed Or Not To Be Changed?" *The Guardian* (Manchester), September 26, 1966.

Watts, Janet. "Pillar of the RSC." *The Guardian Weekly* (Manchester), August 14, 1977.

————. "The Stratford Don." *Observer Colour Magazine,* November 15, 1981.

C. Books and Theses

Adams, Claire. "Alan Howard: The Environment of the '70's Actor." Master's thesis, University of Birmingham, 1979.

Addenbrooke, David. *The Royal Shakespeare Company: The Peter Hall Years.* London: William Kimber, 1974.

Alexander, Nigel. *Poison, Play, and Duel: A Study of Hamlet.* Lincoln: University of Nebraska Press, 1971.

Avern-Carr, Christine Ann. "*Twelfth Night* at Stratford-upon-Avon: 1958–1974." Master's thesis, University of Birmingham, 1975.

Barton, John. *The First Stage: A Chronicle of the Development of English Drama from Its Beginnings to the 1580's.* London: BBC Press, 1957.

————. "Playing Shakespeare." Unpublished manuscript of television script, 1982.

————, and Cavander, Kenneth. *The Greeks.* London: Heinemann, 1981.

————, and Hall, Peter. *The Wars of the Roses.* London: BBC Press, 1970.

Beauman, Sally, *The Royal Shakespeare Company: A History of Ten Decades.* Oxford: At the University Press, 1982.

Berry, Ralph. *On Directing Shakespeare: Interviews with Contemporary Directors.* London: Croom Helm, 1977.

Bradbury, Malcolm, and Palmer, David. *Shakespearean Comedy: Stratford-upon-Avon Studies 14.* New York: Crane, Russak and Co., 1972.

Brockett, Oscar. *History of the Theatre.* 3d ed. Boston: Allyn and Bacon, 1974.

————, and Findlay, Robert F. *Century of Innovation: A History of European and American Theatre and Drama Since 1870.* Englewood Cliffs, N.J.: Prentice-Hall, 1973.

Brook, Peter. *The Empty Space.* New York: Atheneum, 1968.

Brooke, Nicholas, ed. *Shakespeare: Richard II, A Casebook.* London: MacMillan & Co., 1973.

Brown, John Russell. *Shakespeare's Plays in Performance.* New York: St. Martin's Press, 1967.

————. *Theatre Language.* New York: Taplinger, 1972.

Burke, Kenneth. *Philosophy of Literary Form: Studies in Symbolic Action.* New York: Vintage Books, 1957.

Christy, James. "Five Twentieth-Century Productions of *Troilus and Cressida.*" Ph.D. diss., Stanford University, 1972.

Cole, Toby, and Chinoy, Helen Kirsch, eds. *Directors on Directing.* Rev. ed. Indianapolis, Ind.: Bobbs-Merrill, 1963.

Cook, Judith. *Directors' Theatre.* London: Harrap, 1974.

————. *Shakespeare's Players.* London: Harrap, 1983.

Croydon, Margaret. *Lunatics, Lovers, and Poets.* New York: McGraw-Hill, 1974.

David, Richard. *Shakespeare in the Theatre.* Cambridge: At the University Press, 1978.

Dukore, Bernard F., ed. *Dramatic Theory and Criticism: Greeks to Grotowski.* New York: Holt, Rinehart, and Winston, 1974.

Egan, Robert. *Drama Within Drama.* New York and London: Columbia University Press, 1975.

Elsom, John. *Post-war British Theatre.* London: Routledge and Kegan Paul, 1976.

Goodwin, John, ed., *Peter Hall's Diaries: The Story of a Dramatic Battle.* London: Hamish Hamilton, 1983.

Granville Barker, Harley. *Prefaces to Shakespeare.* 2 vols. Princeton, N.J.: Princeton University Press, 1946.

Hibbard, G. R., ed. *The Elizabethan Theatre VI.* Hamden, Conn: Archon, 1978.

Kantorowicz, Ernst H. *The King's Two Bodies: A Study in Medieval Political Theology.* Princeton, N.J.: Princeton University Press, 1957.

Kimberley, Michael E. "*Troilus and Cressida* on the English Stage." Master's thesis, University of Birmingham, 1968.

Knight, G. Wilson. *Shakespearean Production, With Especial Reference to the Tragedies.* Evanston, Ill.: Northwestern University Press, 1964.

Kott, Jan. *Shakespeare Our Contemporary.* Boleslaw Taborski, trans. Garden City, N.Y.: Doubleday, 1966.

Lambert, J. W. *Drama in Britain, 1964–1973.* London: Longman Group, 1974.

Lawrence, W. W. *Shakespeare's Problem Plays.* New York: Frederick Ungar Publishing Co., 1960.

Marowitz, Charles, and Trussler, Simon. *Theatre at Work.* London: Farrar, Strauss, and Giroux, 1967.

Martin, Priscilla, ed. *Shakespeare: Troilus and Cressida, A Casebook.* London: MacMillan & Co., 1976.

Mason, Pamela. "*Much Ado* at Stratford: 1949–1976." Master's thesis, University of Burmingham, 1976.

Nietzsche, Friedrich Wilhelm. *The Birth of Tragedy and The Geneology of Morals.* Francis Golfin, trans. Garden City, N.Y.: Doubleday, 1974.

Pistotnik, Vesnica. "Aspects of the 1968 and 1976 RSC Productions of *Troilus and Cressida.*" Master's thesis, University of Birmingham, 1980.

Price, Joseph G., ed. *The Triple Bond.* University Park, Penn.: Pennsylvania State University Press, 1975.

Righter, Anne. *Shakespeare and the Idea of the Play.* London: Chatto and Windus, 1962.

Roberts, Peter. *Theatre in Britain: A Playgoer's Guide.* London: Pitman Publishing Co., 1973.

Rossiter, A. P. *Angel with Horns.* Cambridge: At the Undiversity Press, 1962.

Royal Shakespeare Company: The Crucial Years. Stratford-upon-Avon: Max Reinhardt, 1963.

Rylands, George. *Words and Poetry.* New York: Payson and Clarke, 1928.

Saint-Denis, Michel. *Theatre: The Rediscovery of Style.* New York: Theatre Arts Books, 1960.

Shakespeare, William. *Hamlet.* T. J. B. Spencer, ed. [New Penguin edition] Hammondsworth: New Penguin, 1980.

———. *Richard II.* J. Dover Wilson, ed. [New Shakespeare edition] Cambridge: At the University Press, 1971.

———. *Troilus and Cressida.* Alice Walker, ed. [New Shakespeare edition] Cambridge: At the University Press, 1969.

Speaight, Robert. *Shakespeare on the Stage.* London: Collins, 1973.

———. *William Poel and the Elizabethan Revival.* Cambridge: At the University Press, 1954.

Sprague, Arthur Colby, and Trewin, J. C. *Shakespeare's Plays Today: Some Customs and Conventions of the Stage.* Columbia: University of South Carolina Press, 1970.

Stredder, James. "*Richard II* at Stratford, 1973." Master's thesis, University of Birmingham, 1973.

Styan, John L. *The Shakespeare Revolution: Criticism and Performance in the Twentieth Century."* Cambridge: At the University Press, 1977.

Taplin, Oliver. *Greek Tragedy in Action.* Berkeley: University of California Press, 1978.

Trewin, J. C. *Going to Shakespeare.* London: George Allen and Unwin, 1978.

———. *Shakespeare on the English Stage, 1900–1964.* London: Barrie and Rockliffe, 1964.

Wells, Stanley. *Royal Shakespeare.* Manchester: At the University Press, 1977.

Wills, J. Robert, ed. *The Director in a Changing Theatre: Essays on Theory and Practice with New Plays for Performance.* Palo Alto, Calif.: Mayfield Publishing Co., 1976.

Wilson, Edwin, ed. *Shaw on Shakespeare.* New York: E. P. Dutton and Co., 1961.

D. Essays and Articles

Almond, Paul. "Dramatic Adventure." *The Varsity* (Cambridge), November 1, 1952.

Amory, Mark. "John Barton Brings His Gift to the Greeks." *The Sunday Times Magazine,* February 3, 1980, 40–46.

Ansorge, Peter. "Director in Interview: Peter Hall." *Plays and Players* 17 (July 1970): 20–21.

————. "Director in Interview: Terry Hands." *Plays and Players* 15 (September 1968): 59–60.

————. "Director in Interview: Trevor Nunn." *Plays and Players* 17 (September 1970): 16–17.

Ashcroft, Dame Peggy. "Margaret of Anjou." *Deutsche Shakespeare-Gesellschaft West Jahrbuch 1974.* Heidelberg: Quelle and Meyer, 1974.

Attick, Richard D. "Symphonic Imagery in *Richard II.*" *PMLA* 62 (1947): 339–68.

Barber, John. "Curtain Up at Stratford." *Daily Telegraph* (London), April 1, 1970.

Barton, Anne. "*As You Like It* and *Twelfth Night:* Shakespeare's Sense of and Ending." In *Shakespearean Comedy,* edited by David Palmer and Malcolm Bradbury, 160–80. London: Stratford-upon-Avon Studies, 1972.

————. "He That Plays the King: Ford's *Perkin Warbeck* and the Stuart History Play." In *English Drama: Forms and Development,* edited by Marie Axton and Raymond Williams, 69–93. Cambridge: At the University Press, 1977.

————. Introduction to *Hamlet,* edited by T. J. B. Spencer. Hammondsworth: New Penguin, 1980.

————. "The King Disguised: Shakespeare's *Henry V* and the Comical History." In *The Triple Bond,* edited by Joseph G. Price, 92–117. University Park, Penn.: Pennsylvania State University Press, 1975.

————. "Shakespeare and the Limits of Language." *Shakespeare Survey* 24 (1971): 19–20.

Barton, John. "Elizabethan Tragedy and Artifice." *Flourish* 5 (Spring 1965): 10.

————. "Too Much Drama." *The Varsity* (Cambridge), February 9, 1952, 6.

Bell, Christopher. "Shakespeare at Cambridge." *Journal of the School of Languages* (Oxford), November 5, 1952.

Billington, Michael. "Our Theatre in the 60's." In *Theatre 71,* edited by Sheridan Morley, 208–33. London: Hutchinson, 1971.

Bradbrook, Muriel C. "Shakespeare and the Multiple Theatres of Jacobean London." In *The Elizabethan Theatre,* edited by G. R. Hibbard, 88–104. Hamden, Conn.: Archon, 1975.

————. "The Triple Bond: Audience, Actors, Author and the Elizabethan Playhouse." In *The Triple Bond,* edited by Joseph G. Price, 50–69. University Park, Penn.: Pennsylvania State University Press, 1975.

Brook, Peter. "*We Are All Menaced.*" *Flourish* II (1968): 7.

Brown, John Russell. "Free Shakespeare." *Shakespeare Survey* 24 (1971): 127–40.

————. "Originality in Shakespearean Production." *Theatre Notebook* 26 (1971–72): 107–15.

————. "The Royal Shakespeare Company 1965." *Shakespeare Survey* 19 (1966): 111–18.

————. "The Study and Practice of Shakespeare Production." *Shakespeare Survey* 18 (1965): 58–69.

————. "Three Kinds of Shakespeare: 1964 Productions at London, Stratford-upon-Avon, and Edinburgh." *Shakespeare Survey* 18 (1965): 147–55.

Bury, John. "Against Falsehood." *Flourish* 5 (Winter 1965): 6.

Byrne, Muriel St. Clare. "Fifty Years of Shakespeare Production: 1898–1948." *Shakespeare Survey* 2 (1949): 1–20.

"Can a Dramatist Dominate the Stage Today?" *The Times* (London), January 13, 1963, 6.

Cocks, Jay. "Class of a Very Classy Field." *Time* 117 (March 2, 1981): 94.

Coleman, Terry. "Elizabethan Manner." *The Guardian* (Manchester), September 4, 1972.

Cook, Judith. "Giving Voice to New Movements." *Plays and Players* 23 (October 1975): 17–19.

———. "King John Barton." *Plays and Players* 21 (June 1973): 24–27.

Cox, Frank. "Peter Brook." *Plays and Players* 15 (April 1968): 50–51.

Crutwell, Patrick. "Shakespeare Is Not Our Contemporary." *Yale Review* 59 (1969): 33–49.

David, Richard. "Actors and Scholars: A View of Shakespeare in the Modern Theatre." *Shakespeare Survey* 12 (1959): 76–87.

———. "Of An Age and For All Time: Shakespeare at Stratford." *Shakespeare Survey* 25 (1972): 161–70.

Edwards, Sidney. "The New Man at the National." In *Theatre 74,* edited by Sheridan Morley, 60–64. London: Hutchinson, 1974.

Ellis-Fermor, Una. "Discord in the Spheres." In *Discussions of Shakespeare's Problem Plays,* edited by Robert Ornstein, 17–24. Boston: D. C. Heath and Co., 1961.

Everitt, Anthony. "Why Stratford Faces Tough Times Ahead." *The Birmingham Post,* October 19, 1974.

Ewbank, Inga-Stina. "More Pregnantly Than Words: Some Uses and Limitations of Visual Symbolism." *Shakespeare Survey* 24 (1971): 13–18.

"Ex-Directory." *Times Literary Supplement,* March 1, 1974, 209.

Ferriman, Annabel. "Director's Four Facets of Success." *The Times* (London), August 28, 1976, 12.

Flannery, James W. "Portrait of a Theatre Community: The Royal Shakespeare Company of London." *Educational Theatre Journal* 19 (1967): 383–91.

"Four Speakers in Search of True Acting." *The Times* (London), February 25, 1963, 5.

Friedman, Donald. "The Day Is Yours." *The Varsity* (Cambridge), November 8, 1952.

Frith, Nigel. "Use All Gently—For God's Sake." In *Theatre 74,* edited by Sheridan Morley, 89–98. London: Hutchinson, 1974.

Gardner, Edmond. "Stratford 1960: A New Era." *Shire and Spire,* April 1960.

Gascoigne, Bamber. "Barton's Roses." *The Observer,* August 26, 1964.

Gielgud, John. "Directing the Classics." In *Effective Theatre,* edited by John Russell Brown, 225–33. London: Heineman, 1969.

Gilman, Richard. "Theatre: Kinky, Arrogant, and Frankly Magnificent." *Esquire* 66 (July 1966): 123–28.

Goodman, Ellen. "Interview with Michael Pennington." *RSC Newspaper,* Spring 1980, 5.

Gow, Gordon. "Energy, Freshness, and Exquisite Agony: Interview with Judi Dench." *Plays and Players* 26 (June 1979): 12–17.

———. "A State of Mind and Body: Interview with Michael Pennington." *Plays and Players* 26 (May 1979): 13–16.

———. "Through the Right Doorway: Ian Richardson in an Interview with Gordon Gow." *Plays and Players* 29 (September 1979): 10–13.

Guy, Vincent. "Director in Interview: John Barton." *Plays and Players* 17 (November 1970): 48–49.

Hale, Shiela. "Theatre Bus." *Weekend Telegraph* (London), June 22, 1966.

Hall, Peter. "Avoiding a Method." In *The Royal Shakespeare Company: The Crucial Years*, 1–15. Stratford-upon-Avon: Max Reinhardt, 1963.

———. "Is the Beginning the Word?" *Theatre Quarterly* 2 (1972): 5–11.

———. "Killing the Golden Goose" [letter to the editor]. *The Times* (London), August 28, 1964, 11.

"Hal's Pals." *Stratford-upon-Avon Herald*, September 3, 1976.

"Hands at the Helm." *The Times* (London), March 4, 1968, 8.

Hapgood, Robert. "The RSC's *Henry V* Treated in Depth." *Shakespeare Quarterly* 28 (1977): 264–66.

Hayman, Ronald. "John Barton." *The Times* (London), September 9, 1972, 11.

Hewes, Henry. "How to Use Shakespeare." *Saturday Review* 40 (July 13, 1957): 10–13.

"He Who Enters Next." *The Economist* (London), August 4, 1974.

Hiley, Jim. "A Company with Direction." *Plays and Players* 25 (October 1977): 14–21.

Hobson, Harold. "Directors Under Fire." *The Sunday Times* (London), January 28, 1973, 37.

Hodgdon, Barbara. "*The Wars of the Roses:* Scholarship Speaks on Stage." *Deutsche Shakespeare-Gesellschaft West Jahrbuch 1972.* Heidelberg: Quelle and Meyer, 1972.

"The Interpreter's Art." *The Times* (London), August 3, 1963, 7.

"John Barton Marries Cambridge Don." *Daily Telegraph* (London), August 10, 1980.

Jones, David. "What's with the Aldwych." *Flourish* 2 (Summer 1969): n.p.

Kustow, Michael. "Synthesis." *Flourish* (1967): 14.

Lahr, John. "Knowing What to Celebrate." *Plays and Players* 23 (March 1976): 24–25.

Lambert, J. W. "Requiem for the British Theatre." *The Sunday Times* (London), March 23, 1975, 35.

Leech, Clifford. "The 'Capability' of Shakespeare." *Shakespeare Survey* 11 (1960): 123–36.

Leggatt, Alexander. "The Extra Dimension: Shakespeare in Performance." *Mosaic* 10 (1977): 37–49.

Liehm, A. J. "Peter Brook Interview: Politics of Sclerosis, Stalin and *Lear.*" *Theatre Quarterly* 3 (1973): 13–18.

Littlewood, Joan. "Plays for People." In *The New British Drama*, edited by Henry Popkin, 557–60. New York: Grove Press, 1964.

Lloyd Evans, Gareth. "Directing Problem Plays: John Barton Talks to Gareth Lloyd Evans." *Shakespeare Survey* 25 (1972): 63–71.

———. "How Far Can We Improve Shakespeare?" *The Guardian* (Manchester), November 26, 1964, 8–10.

———. "Interpretation or Experience? Shakespeare at Stratford." *Shakespeare Survey* 23 (1970): 131–35.

———. "Judi Dench Talks to Gareth Lloyd Evans." *Shakespeare Survey* 27 (1974): 137–42.

———. "The Reason Why: The RSC Season 1968 Reviewed." *Shakespeare Survey* 22 (1969): 135–44.

———. "Shakespeare and the Actors: Notes Towards Interpretation." *Shakespeare Survey* 21 (1968): 115–25.

———. "Shakespeare, the Twentieth Century and Behaviorism." *Shakespeare Survey* 20 (1967): 33–42.

M., J. B. "Profile: John Barton, President of the A. D. C." *The Varsity* (Cambridge), May 12, 1951, 4.

MacOwen, Michael. "New Elizabethan Actors." *Radio Times*, May 15, 1953.

Marowitz, Charles. "Free Shakespeare! Jail Scholars!" *Plays and Players* 25 (February 1978): 12–15.

———. "Giving Them Hell." *Plays and Players* 24 (July 1977): 15–17.

Marris, Peter. "The Alchemist." *The Varsity* (Cambridge), December 2, 1950.

McKellen, Ian. "An Actor's Diary." In *Theatre 74*, edited by Sheridan Morley, 79–85. London: Hutchinson, 1974.

"Much Ado About Shakespeare." *The Times* (London), February 27, 1965.

Muir, Kenneth. "The Critic, the Director, and the Liberty of Interpreting." In *The Triple Bond*, edited by Joseph G. Price. University Park, Penn.: Pennsylvania State University Press, 1975.

———. "Fifty Years of Shakespearean Criticism: 1900–1950." *Shakespeare Survey* 4 (1951): 1–25.

Newlin, Jeanne T. "The Modernity of *Troilus and Cressida:* The Case for Theatrical Criticism." *Harvard Library Bulletin* 17 (October 1964): 353–74.

Nightingale, Benedict. "Royal Shakespeare Company." In *Theatre 74*, edited by Sheridan Morley, 74–88. London: Hutchinson, 1974.

———. "RSC Ascendant." In *Theatre 72*, edited by Sheridan Morley, 63–75. London: Hutchinson, 1972.

———. "Shakespeare Is as Shakespeare's Done." In *Theatre 71*, edited by Sheridan Morley, 154–68. London: Hutchinson, 1971.

Nunn, Trevor, and Jones, David. "Writing on Sand." In *Theatre 73*, edited by Sheridan Morley, 54–67. London: Hutchinson, 1973.

O'Brien, Timothy. "Designing a Shakespeare Play: *Richard II*." *Deutsche Shakespeare-Gesellschaft West Jahrbuch 1974*. Heidelberg: Quelle and Meyer, 1974.

Roberts, Peter. "The RSC: First Decade." In *Theatre 71*, edited by Sheridan Morley, 169–85. London: Hutchinson, 1971.

"The Romantic and the Sensualist." *Flourish* (1972): 1–5.

"Royal Shakespeare Company." *The Times* (London), September 1, 1964, 11.

"Royal Shakespeare Studio." *Flourish* 2 (Autumn–Winter 1964–65): 7–8.

Rylands, George. "The Poet and the Player." *Shakespeare Survey* 7 (1954): 25–34.

Salmon, Eric. "Shakespeare on the Modern Stage: The Need for New Approaches." *Modern Drama* 15 (1972–73): 305–19.

"A Shakespearean Marriage." *The Times* (London), August 13, 1968.

"Shakespeare's Play." *The Times* (London), August 29, 1970, 10.

"Shakespeare: To Be Changed Or Not To Be Changed?" *The Guardian* (Manchester), September 26, 1966.

Smallwood, Robert L. "Shakespeare Unbalanced: The Royal Shakespeare Company's *King John*." *Deutsche Shakespeare-Gesellschaft West Jahrbuch 1976*. Heidelberg: Quelle and Meyer, 1976.

Speaight, Robert. "No Nonsense about Shakespeare." *The Times* (London) January 8, 1965, 11.

———. "Shakespeare in Britain." *Shakespeare Quarterly* 15 (Autumn 1964): 377–89.

———. "Shakespeare in Britain." *Shakespeare Quarterly* 16 (Autumn 1965): 385–93.

———. "Shakespeare in Britain." *Shakespeare Quarterly* 17 (Autumn 1966): 389–98.

———. "Shakespeare in Britain." *Shakespeare Quarterly* 18 (Autumn 1967): 389–97.

———. "Shakespeare in Britain." *Shakespeare Quarterly* 19 (Autumn 1968): 367–76.

———. "Shakespeare in Britain." *Shakespeare Quarterly* 20 (Autumn 1969): 435–42.

———. "Shakespeare in Britain." *Shakespeare Quarterly* 21 (Autumn 1970): 439–50.

———. "Shakespeare in Britain." *Shakespeare Quarterly* 22 (Autumn 1971): 359–64.

———. "Shakespeare in Britain." *Shakespeare Quarterly* 23 (Autumn 1972): 383–87.

———. "Shakespeare in Britain." *Shakespeare Quarterly* 25 (Autumn 1974): 389–94.

———. "Shakespeare in Britain." *Shakespeare Quarterly* 27 (Winter 1976): 15–23.

———. "The Stratford-upon-Avon Season." *Shakespeare Quarterly* 24 (Autumn 1973): 400–404.

"Stratford Producer Marries." *The Birmingham Post,* August 10, 1968.

Stredder, James. "John Barton's Production of *Richard II* at Stratford-upon-Avon, 1973." *Deutsche Shakespeare-Gesellschaft West Jahrbuch 1976.* Heidelberg: Quelle and Meyer, 1976.

Swander, Homer D. "The Rediscovery of *Henry VI.*" *Shakespeare Quarterly* 29 (1978): 146–63.

Thomson, Peter. "A Necessary Theatre: The RSC Season 1970 Reviewed." *Shakespeare Survey* 24 (1971): 117–26.

———. "The RSC Season 1972 Reviewed." *Shakespeare Survey* 26 (1973): 139–52.

———. "Shakespeare Straight and Crooked: A Review of the 1973 Season at Stratford." *Shakespeare Survey:* 27 (1974): 143–55.

———. "The Smallest Season: The RSC at Stratford, 1974." *Shakespeare Survey* 28 (1975): 137–45.

Tillyard, E. M. "Shakespeare's History Plays." In *Shakespeare and His Critics,* ed. A. M. Eastman and G. G. Harrison, Ann Arbor: University of Michigan Press, 1964).

Totten, Eileen. "A Pair of Kings." *Plays and Players* 20 (June 1973): 26–28.

Trewin, J. C. "Stratford '70." *Flourish* 2 (Spring 1971), n.p.

———. "Talking About Shakespeareans." *Shakespeare Quarterly* 38 (1968): 133–43.

Tuck, Robin. "Julius Caesar in Retrospect." *The Varsity* (Cambridge), April 19, 1952, 9.

Tynan, Kathleen. "Directors' Curtain Call." *The Sunday Times* (London) February 6, 1977, 16–18.

Tynan, Kenneth. "Director as Misanthropist: On the Moral Integrity of Peter Brook." *Theatre Quarterly* 7 (1977): 20–28.

Usill, Hillary. "Our Revels Now Are Ended." *Records and Recordings,* April 1964.

Wardle, Irving. "Saint-Denis—Theatrical Lifeline with France." *The Times* (London), September 13, 1967, 6.

———. "The Theatre Sinks into Self-satisfaction." *The Times* (London), January 13, 1973, 8.

Warren, Roger. "Theory and Practice at Stratford, 1976." *Shakespeare Survey* 30 (1977): 169–79.

——. "A Year of Comedies at Stratford." *Shakespeare Survey* 32 (1979): 201–9.

Watts, Janet. "Pillar of the RSC." *The Guardian Weekly* (Manchester), August 14, 1977.

Waymark, Peter. "A Decade of Revolution: The Progress of the RSC." *The Times* (London), December 15, 1970, 12.

Weimann, Robert. "Shakespeare on the Modern Stage: Past Significance and Present Meaning." *Shakespeare Survey* 20 (1967): 113–24.

Wells, Stanley. "The Academic and the Theatre." In *The Triple Bond*, edited by Joseph G. Price, 3–19. University Park, Penn.: Pennsylvania State University Press, 1977.

——. "Directors' Shakespeare." *Deutsche Shakespeare-Gesellschaft West Jahrbuch 1976*. Heidelberg: Quelle and Meyer, 1976.

——. "Foul Paper Texts." *Review of English Studies* 31 (February 1980): 1–16.

——. "*The Revenger's Tragedy* Revived." In *The Elizabethan Theatre VI*, edited by G. R. Hibbard, 105–33. Hamden, Conn: Archon, 1978.

Wilders, John. "A Preview." *The Varsity* (Cambridge), April 18, 1953, 3.

Williamson, Jane. "The Duke and Isabella on the Modern Stage." In *The Triple Bond*, edited by Joseph G. Price, 149–69. University Park, Penn.: Pennsylvania State University Press, 1975.

"A Young Man Looks at The Shrew." *The Times* (London), April 1, 1967, 7.

E. Transcripts of Radio Programs

Barton, John. "Thought To Be Written by Shakespeare." BBC. November 25, 1963, and December 12, 1963.

——, and Rylands, George. "Midland Critics." BBC.
As You Like It. April 12, 1957.
Cymbeline. July 15, 1957.
Julius Caesar. June 9, 1957.
King John. May 9, 1957.

——, and Trewin, J. C. "Midland Critics." BBC.
The Tempest. August 15, 1957.

[N.B. The complete transcripts of each of these programs may be found in the Shakespeare Collection at the Birmingham Central Library.]

F. Reviews of John Barton Productions: 1949–1983

Reviews of productions directed by John Barton from 1949 through 1983 have been taken from the following sources. See the Notes for reviews of specific productions.

Newspapers
The Birmingham Mail
Birmingham Mercury
Birmingham Post
Bristol Evening Post
Cambridge Daily News

The Christian Science Monitor (Boston)
Coventry Evening Telegraph
Daily Express (London)
Daily Mail (London)
Daily Sketch (London)
Daily Telegraph (London)
Evening Echo (Watford)
Evening News (London)
Evening Standard (London)
Evesham Journal
Financial Times (London)
Glasgow Herald
Gloucester Citizen
The Guardian (Manchester)
The Guardian Weekly (Manchester)
The Illustrated London News
Ipswich Evening Star
Jewish Chronicle
Leamington Spa Courier
Leicester Mercury
Lincolnshire Echo
Liverpool Post
London Star
Mitcham News and Mercury
Morning Advertiser (London)
Morning Star (London)
News Chronicle (London)
Nottingham Evening News
Nottingham Post
Oxford Mail
Oxford Times
Petersborough Evening Telegraph
Reading Evening Post
Redditch Indicator
The Scotsman (Edinburgh)
Sheffield Telegraph
Shropshire Star
Solihull News
South London Press
South Wales Argus
The Star (London)
Stratford-upon-Avon Herald
Sun (London)
Sunday Mercury (Birmingham)
Sunday Telegraph (London)
The Sunday Times (London)
The Sunday Times Magazine (London)
The Times (London)
The Varsity (Cambridge)
Warwick Advertiser
Watford Evening News
Wednesbury Brothom News

Wolverhampton Express and Star
Worcester Evening News
Yorkshire Post

Journals and Magazines
John O'London
Lady
The Listener
London Magazine
The New Statesman
The Observer
Plays and Players
Punch
Queen
Radio Times
Shakespeare Quarterly
Shakespeare Survey
Spectator
Stage
Stage and Television Today
Tablet
Tatler and Bystander
Theatre Journal
Time and Tide
The Times Educational Supplement
The Times Literary Supplement
Today's Cinema

G. Program Notes

"All's Well That Ends Well." RSC Program for *All's Well That Ends Well.* RST, June 1967.

Barton, Anne. "Actions That a Man Might Play." [Excerpted from the Introduction to the New Penguin edition of *Hamlet.*] RSC Program for *Hamlet.* RST, July 1980.

——. *"Cymbeline."* RSC Program for *Cymbeline.* RST, June 1974.

——. "Marlowe Died . . ." RSC Program for *Doctor Faustus.* Aldwych Theatre, September 1974.

——. "Hell and Night." RSC Program for *Othello.* RST, September 1971.

——. *"King John."* RSC Program for *King John.* RST, March 1974.

——. "The King's Two Bodies." RSC Program for *Richard II.* RST, April 1973.

——. *"Love's Labour's Lost."* RSC Program for *Love's Labour's Lost.* RST, August 1978.

——. *"Much Ado About Nothing."* RSC Program for *Much Ado About Nothing.* RST, April 1976.

——. *"The Tempest."* RSC Program for *The Tempest.* RST, October 1970.

——. *"Twelfth Night."* RSC Program for *Twelfth Night.* RST, August 1969.

——. *"The Way of the World."* RSC Program for *The Way of the World.* Aldwych Theatre, January 1978.

————. "*The Winter's Tale.*" RSC Program for *The Winter's Tale.* RST, June 1976.

Barton, John. "From the Director's Notes at Rehearsal." RSC Program for *Troilus and Cressida.* RST, August, 1968.

————. "*The Greeks.*" RSC Program for *The Greeks.* Aldwych Theatre, January 1980.

————. "Marlowe's Text." RSC Program for *Doctor Faustus.* Aldwych Theatre. September 1974.

————. "The Owl and the Cuckoo." RSC Program for *Love's Labour's Lost.* RST, April 1965.

————. "Sources and Issues." RSC Program for *King John.* RST, March 1974.

————. "King of Vanity." [Excerpts from conversations among the directors.] RSC Program for *Richard II.* RST, June 1964.

————. "Polished Pertrubation! Golden Care." [Excerpts from conversations among the directors.] RSC Program for *Henry IV, Part 2.*

————; Hall, Peter; and Williams, Clifford. "The Morality Tradition and the Rejection of Vanity." [Excerpts from conversations among the directors.] RSC Program for *Henry IV, Part 1.* RST, June 1964.

————; Nunn, Trevor; and Williams, Clifford. "To the Play." [Excerpts from conversations among the directors.] RSC Program for *Henry IV, Part 1.* RST, April 1966.

Bryden, Ronald. "Divorce—Restoration Style." [Reprinted from *The Observer,* 1969.] RSC Program for *The Way of the World.* Aldwych Theatre. January 1968.

Brown, Ivor. "*The Taming of the Shrew.*" RSC Program for *The Taming of the Shrew.* RST, June 1960.

Cavander, Kenneth. "The Fifth Century." RSC Program for *The Greeks.* Aldwych Theatre, January 1980.

————. "Greek Verse." RSC Program for *The Greeks.* Aldwych Theatre, January 1980.

————. "The Myths." RSC Program for *The Greeks.* Aldwych Theatre, January 1980.

"Duke Misguided . . . Duke As Providence." RSC Program for *Measure for Measure.* RST, April 1970.

Ewbank, Inga-Stina. "Do You Know What We Are . . . We Pillars of the Community?" RSC Program for *The Pillars of the Community.* Aldwych Theatre, August 1977.

Hall, Peter. "Blood Will Have Blood." RSC Program Note for *The Wars of the Roses: Richard III.* RST, July 1963.

————. "The Empirical Empire." RSC Program for *Henry V.* RST, June 1964.

"*Julius Caesar.*" RSC Program for *Julius Caesar.* RST, April 1968.

"*A Midsummer Night's Dream.*" RSC Program for *A Midsummer Night's Dream.* RST, May 1977.

"Shakespearean Comedy." RSC Program for 1960 Season. RST, April 1960.

Tucker, Patrick. "*Faustus* as a Puppet Play." RSC Program for *Doctor Faustus.* Aldwych Theatre, September 1974.

"Tudor Opinions on War." RSC Program for *Henry V.* RST, June 1964.

Index

Abel, Lionel, 188

Achilles (The Greeks) (Barton, from Homer), 213, 218, 234

Actor's Company, the, 203

Adrian, Max, 25, 66, 75, 88, 266–67 n.54

Aeschylus, 135, 214, 215, 219

Agamemnon (The Greeks) (Aeschylus), 213, 214, 219

Albee, Edward, 64

Alchemist, The (Jonson), 25

Alcibiades, The (Sophocles), 210

Aldwych Theatre (London), 14, 63, 129, 134, 141, 142, 201, 204, 209, 211, 218, 227–28, 261–64, 280 n.162

Alexander, Nigel, 188

Almond, Paul, 30

Amateur Dramatic Club (ADC), 7, 23–24, 25, 249–50

Anderson, Miles, 225

Andrews, Harry, 25

Andromache (The Greeks) (Euripides), 212–13, 214, 221

Angel with Horns (Rossiter), 22, 282 n.38, 283 n.45

Annals, Michael, 202

Annis, Francesca, 79

Ansorge, Peter, 97, 176

Antigone (Anouilh), 26, 198, 270 n.11

Argo Records, 24, 25

Artaud, Antonin, 20

Ashcroft, Peggy, 24, 36–37, 51, 55, 232, 266–67 n.54, 294 n.13

Attick, Richard, 283 n.50

Avern-Carr, Christine, 87–88

Bacchae, The (Euripides), 210

Bainbridge, Martyn, 175

Bale, Bishop John, 128, 132, 284 n.75

Bannock, Sheila, 88, 89, 235–36

Barber, John, 88–89, 105, 108, 149, 170, 173, 201–2, 228, 279 n.121

Barbican Centre, 208, 224, 264

Barry, Cicely, 36

Barton, Anne (née Righter), 22, 85, 87–89, 94, 95, 103, 106, 107, 117, 120, 122, 140, 143, 145, 147, 172–73, 176, 186–97, 202, 203, 206, 279 n.122, 282–83 n.38, 289 n.5, 291 n.24, 292 n.57

Barton, Sir Harold Montague, 20, 23, 249

Barton, John: as acting teacher, 19, 31, 34–36; as actor, 19, 24–25, 26, 29, 30, 38, 249, 260, 264; and actors, relationship with, 36–37, 238–42; Brechtian influences on, 26–27, 53, 81, 122; at Cambridge, 7–8, 20–34, 39, 137, 198, 209, 249–51, 289 n.79; and Cambridge dramatic societies, 23–24, 249–50; and characterization in plays, 234–35; and Chekhovian elements in plays, 8, 26, 59, 87, 100, 105, 109, 112, 184, 208; chronology of his works, 260–64; "continuous copy," his theory of, 33, 40, 236; directing style of, 21, 90, 121, 146, 193, 228–48, 283 n.40, 294 n.18, 295 n.31; as director, 19, 25–26, 60, 62, 81, 87, 100–101, 198, 226; director's function, his views on, 227–28, 234, 236–37; at Eton, 19; as fight choreographer, 27, 52, 60, 63, 76, 268 n.42, 271 n.29, 272 n.44; and *The First Stage* (BBC Radio), 33, 199, 252–53, 266 n.49; and humanist philosophy, 34, 174, 234–35, 236; King's College (Cambridge), as Lay Dean of, 33; modern drama, his attitudes about, 32, 198–99; and music, use of, 9, 90–91, 216–17, 234; "My Story," 14, 32, 224; on narrative line, strength of, 234, 294 n.18; "Playing Shakespeare," 21, 35, 80, 82, 112–13, 143, 193, 212, 224, 229–33 (summary), 239, 242, 243, 246, 264, 294 n.13; as playwright, 29–30, 32, 209, 268 n.18; political beliefs of, 30, 34, 130, 204–5, 210, 293 n.6;

310